Basic Readings on the MMPI
A New Selection on Personality Measurement

Basic Readings on the MMPI

A New Selection on Personality Measurement

W. Grant Dahlstrom

and

Leona Dahlstrom

editors

UNIVERSITY OF MINNESOTA PRESS ☐ MINNEAPOLIS

0347263

112483

Published by the University of Minnesota Press,
2037 University Avenue Southeast,
Minneapolis, Minnesota 55455

Library of Congress Cataloging in Publication Data
Main entry under title:
Basic readings on the MMPI

   Bibliography: p.
   Includes index.
   1. Minnesota multiphasic personality inventory.
I. Dahlstrom, William Grant. II. Dahlstrom, Leona E.
[DNLM: 1. MMPI. WM145.3 D131b]
BF698.8.M5B35   155.2'83   79-25909
ISBN 0-8166-0903-9

To Starke and Jinny

Acknowledgments and Permissions

The editors wish to thank the organizations listed below for permission to use materials in this volume:

The *Journal of Psychology* for permission to reproduce the selections by S. R. Hathaway and J. C. McKinley appearing in Section I, articles 1, 2, and 3.

The *Journal of Educational Research* for permission to reproduce the selection by L. E. Drake and W. B. Thiede appearing in Section I, article 8.

The *Journal of Clinical Psychology* for permission to reproduce the selection by P. E. Meehl appearing in Section II, article 1; and the selection by C. E. Walker appearing in Section IV, article 4.

Psychometrika for permission to reproduce the selection by A. L. Edwards appearing in Section II, article 2.

S. Messick and J. Ross, editors of the volume published by John Wiley and Sons, from which the selection by D. N. Jackson and S. Messick was taken which appears in Section II, article 3.

Irvington Publishers for permission to reprint the selections by J. Block from the volume in the Appleton-Century-Crofts series appearing in Section II, articles 4 and 5.

The *Journal of Personality* for permission to reproduce the selection by D. Byrne appearing in Section III, article 3 (copyright 1961 by Duke University Press).

The American Psychological Association for permission to reproduce the following from:

The *Journal of Applied Psychology* the selections by J. C. McKinley and S. R. Hathaway appearing in Section I, articles 4 and 5; the selection by L. E. Drake appearing in Section I, article 7; and the selection by P. E. Meehl and S. R. Hathaway appearing in Section I, article 9.

The *Journal of Consulting Psychology* the selection by J. C. McKinley, S. R. Hathaway, and P. E. Meehl appearing in Section I, article 10; the selection by F. Barron appearing in Section III, article 2; and the selection by J. N. Butcher and A. Tellegen appearing in Section IV, article 3.

The *Journal of Consulting and Clinical Psychology* the selection by M. D. Gynther, B. R. Burkhart, and C. Hovanitz appearing in Section II, article 6 (with additional tabular material from W. L. Christian, B. R. Burkhart, and M. D. Gynther); and the selection by J. B. Taylor, M. Carithers, and L. Coyne appearing in Section II, article 7.

The *Journal of Abnormal and Social Psychology* the selection by Janet Taylor Spence appearing in Section III, article 1.

Psychological Monographs the selection by J. Wiggins appearing in Section III, article 4.

The *American Psychologist* the selection by S. R. Hathaway appearing in Section IV, article 1.

List of Contributors

Frank Barron, Ph.D. Professor of Psychology, University of California (Santa Cruz)

Jack Block, Ph.D. Professor of Psychology, University of Califormia (Berkeley)

Barry R. Burkhart, Ph.D. Associate Professor of Psychology, Auburn University

James N. Butcher, Ph.D. Professor of Psychology, University of Minnesota (Minneapolis)

Donn Byrne, Ph.D. Professor of Psychology, State University of New York (Albany)

Martha Carithers. Menninger Foundation

William L. Christian, Ph.D. Clinical Psychologist, Moccasin Bend Mental Health Institute, Chattanooga, Tennessee

Lolafaye Coyne. Menninger Foundation

W. Grant Dahlstrom, Ph.D. Professor of Psychology, University of North Carolina (Chapel Hill)

Lewis E. Drake, Ph.D. Director Emeritus of the Student Counseling Center, University of Wisconsin (Madison)

Allen L. Edwards, Ph.D. Professor of Psychology, University of Washington (Seattle)

Malcolm D. Gynther, Ph.D. Professor of Psychology, Auburn University

Starke R. Hathaway, Ph.D. Professor Emeritus of Psychology, University of Minnesota (Minneapolis)

Christine Hovanitz. Auburn University

Douglas N. Jackson, Ph.D. Senior Professor of Psychology, University of Western Ontario, London, Ontario

J. Charnley McKinley, M.D. (deceased) Formerly Head, Department of Neuropsychiatry, University of Minnesota (Minneapolis)

Paul E. Meehl, Ph.D. Regents Professor of Psychology, University of Minnesota (Minneapolis)

Samuel Messick, Ph.D. Vice-President for Research, Educational Testing Service, Princeton, New Jersey

Janet Taylor Spence, Ph.D. Professor of Psychology, University of Texas (Austin)

James B. Taylor, Ph.D. Professor of Social Welfare, University of Kansas (Lawrence)

Auke Tellegen, Ph.D. Professor of Psychology, University of Minnesota (Minneapolis)

Wilson B. Thiede, Ph.D. Professor of Continuing Education, University of Wisconsin (Madison)

C. Eugene Walker, Ph.D. Chief, Pediatric Psychology, University of Oklahoma Health Sciences Center, Oklahoma City

George S. Welsh, Ph.D. Professor of Psychology, University of North Carolina (Chapel Hill)

Jerome Wiggins, Ph.D. Professor of Psychology, University of British Columbia, Vancouver

Preface

Impetus for the present revision of the *Basic Readings* came from three general concerns. It was important to preserve for contemporary students and clinicians the papers published by the authors of the MMPI in which they described and reported the methods by which they constructed the basic scales of the test. The original volume published in 1956 made available for the first time the derivational work on three of these scales (5, 6, and 8) and assembled from the journal literature the research articles on the other scales making up the standard MMPI profile. Few psychological tests, before or since, have been so completely documented or so fully reported as has this inventory. All of these articles together with the construction work on Drake's Si (0) scale and the broad research basis on the K factor that led to the publication of the K scale comprise the first section of the present volume.

The second broad concern that dictated the selections to be included in this volume was the need to put into better perspective the several broad methodological and psychometric issues that have arisen in relation to the MMPI and similar inventories since the original collection was published nearly a quarter century ago. One of the major controversies centers upon the role and significance of response sets in controlling the way that a subject may fill out the answer sheet or sort the item cards in the test. The selections in section II take up this general issue as well as related ones concerning item subtlety, mediating self-perceptions, and the factor structure of the scales in the basic profile. In section III, additional measures that have been derived from the MMPI pool and that have been widely used in basic personality research and assessment are reported. These lines of research and the role that the MMPI has played in furthering these special applications have helped to dispel the perception of the inventory as a narrowly conceived psychiatric or psychopathological instrument.

The final concern has likewise emerged largely in the last two decades as the use of psychological tests has spread throughout the civilized world in ever-increasing volume and diversity: namely, the ethical use of test data and the safeguards needed for the protection of research subjects, clients, and patients. A number of these issues are addressed in the articles that make up section IV of this volume.

We are indebted to a number of people who have helped us in the selection, editing, and processing of this collection of articles. We wish to thank the authors of these papers for the time and effort they put into their reviews of our excerpts of their works. We regret the needed elisions dictated by space limitations and hope that we have been able to preserve the main thrust of each of these original publications. We are also grateful to Dr. George S. Welsh, one of the editors of the original *Basic Readings*, for his willingness to prepare an original article for this volume. Ms. Pamela Jenks helped in many ways to expedite the preparation of the manuscript, and Ms. Beverly Kaemmer of the University of Minnesota Press provided us with all the assistance and support we needed in assembling and processing these materials to final publication.

Chapel Hill, North Carolina   W. Grant Dahlstrom
June, 1979   Leona E. Dahlstrom

Table of Contents

Basic Readings on the MMPI

A New Selection on Personality Measurement

Section I
Original Scale Development

If one looks back nearly 40 years to the setting in which the Minnesota Multiphasic Personality Inventory (MMPI) was developed, it is possible to discern some of the reasons why the test has proved so enduring. As chairman of the Department of Neuropsychiatry at Minnesota, J. Charnley McKinley had assembled an unusual clinical staff just before World War II. Consistent with McKinley's Meyerian orientation, the department included psychiatrists, neurologists, medical psychologists, and psychiatric social workers. An unlikely collaboration had grown up between McKinley and Starke R. Hathaway, a young electrical engineer recently turned physiological psychologist [Hathaway, 1978]. McKinley's research involved close liaison with neurosurgery and neurophysiology as well. Hathaway's wide knowledge of neuroanatomy, statistical methodology, and psychotherapy, his versatility in the laboratory and in the clinic, and his innovations in psychophysiology and electrical transcription of psychotherapeutic interviews made him invaluable in the many research studies under way in this large and active department. In the course of these studies, both men became increasingly aware of the extreme limitations imposed upon further progress in clinical psychiatry and psychology by the lack of objective and reliable means of assessing personality patterns and measuring the clinical status of the patients seen in the neuropsychiatric outpatient clinics and inpatient wards. After trying out and rejecting many of the existing tests and scales in the areas of personality and psycho-

3

pathology [cf. Hathaway, 1939], they initiated a series of studies on a new personality "schedule" which culminated in the papers collected in this first section and ultimately in the publication of this schedule as the MMPI.

As can be seen in these articles, the authors of the MMPI modeled their scale development on the empirical approach that had proved so successful in the work of E. K. Strong on vocational interests. Criterion groups were collected which were made up of all individuals manifesting a common psychiatric syndrome in a relatively uncomplicated form. Each group was systematically contrasted with self-descriptions on the component items provided by normal volunteers who took the test while waiting in the corridors of the University of Minnesota Hospitals. Only those items showing stable differences between the particular criterion group and the normal adults were retained for inclusion in a tentative scale for that disorder. As the succeeding papers will make clear, these tentative scales were then subjected to various statistical checks and corrective weightings and to cross-validational analyses before final acceptance into the standard test profile. In all of these searching cross-checks, Hathaway and McKinley maintained a strongly pragmatic orientation: the separations between patients and normals provided by these clinical scales had to be meaningful and useful, not merely statistically stable at some arbitrary level of significance. The separations that were achieved initially were largely retained upon cross-validation, both at Minnesota and elsewhere, as the use of the test gradually spread (accelerated by the need for such instruments in various parts of the military during WW II). For the next decade and a half, however, the authors still considered some scales quite preliminary; it was not until the original *Basic Readings on the MMPI* was to be published in 1956 that Hathaway wrote a chapter describing the work on scales 5, 6, and 8 (see article I, 6 in the present volume). It should also be noted that sometime before McKinley's retirement from this project in the mid-40's, Paul E. Meehl, a former student of Starke Hathaway's, began his collaboration in this derivational work.

The general scale-development approach described above has been characterized by some as "dust-bowl empiricism," giving the strong impression that there was little wit or wisdom guiding the research. In the articles to follow, the discerning reader can see that the approach was in fact guided by a broad and unified view of emotional disorders as formulated by Adolph Meyer, by the results of a conscientious review of previous efforts to appraise psychiatric status by interview, observation, and objective testing, as well as by their own experience with existing tests and rating devices. As Meehl [1973; see particularly chapters 5 and 13] has noted, psychiatric diagnosis when done with care provides useful and meaningful criteria. The scales described in this section were for the most part developed using such professional judgments. What was not clear at the time of original publication, and what remained for later research to clarify, was how much of any of the syndromes used as the major classification of the cases in the criterion groups would be reflected in the characteristics of subjects scoring at given levels on the set of items identified by such contrasts. That is, do all of the features of the criterion syndrome correlate equally with the scale, or is the scale more sensitive to some common predispositional personality status than the more ephemeral symptoms of the acute upset? Is a high score on a given scale associated more with a level of probability of membership in a patient category or with a degree of severity of the criterion condition? Do scores on a given scale covary with remission or exacerbation of the syndrome? Are simultaneous elevations on two or more scales additive in their personological implications or interactive in configural patterns?

As research on the MMPI proceeded, it became clear that the basic clinical scales in the standard test profile had many implications for general personality measurement beyond the clinical syndromes on which they were constructed. That is, considerable variance in these scales apparently reflected predispositional features of the clients and patients antedating and often extending beyond the time of their psychiatric upset [Dahlstrom, 1972]. Similarly, data accumulated in many atlases and codebooks have served to document that major features of the criterion syndrome appear in the behavior of subjects identified solely on the basis of scale elevation, or elevations, on the MMPI but that the combinations are somewhat variable from one particular individual to another. This latter characteristic is true of the psychiatric manifestations themselves, too, a phenomenon that plagues and intrigues investigators in this field. Third, as some of the research of Endicott and his colleagues has served to document [Endicott and Endicott, 1963; Endicott and Jortner, 1966; Endicott, Jortner, and Abramoff, 1969], the level of elevation on a given scale has dependable ties with rated severity of disorder, and changes in elevation reflect alterations in clinical status of psychiatric patients.

These accomplishments are in no small part attributable to the care and consistency with which the original criterion cases were worked up and diagnosed at the University of Minnesota Hospitals, the insightful ways in which the component items were cast by Hathaway and McKinley, the laborious statistical analyses that were carried out on mechanical desk calculators by these co-authors and their research assistants, and the psychometric insights of the test authors. The following articles preserve many of these inspirations and insights.

The articles in this section came from the following sources: article 1 from S. R. Hathaway and J. C. McKinley. A multiphasic personality schedule (Minnesota): I. Construction of the schedule. *Journal of Psychology*, 1940, 10, 249-54; article 2 from J. C. McKinley and S. R. Hathaway. A multiphasic personality schedule (Minnesota): II. A differential study of hypochondriasis. *Journal of Psychology*, 1940, 10, 255-68; article 3 from S. R. Hathaway and J. C. McKinley. A multiphasic personality schedule (Minnesota): III. The measurement of symptomatic depression. *Journal of Psychology*, 1942, 14, 73-84; article 4 from J. C. McKinley and S. R. Hathaway. A multiphasic personality schedule (Minnesota): IV. Psychasthenia. *Journal of Applied Psychology*, 1942, 26, 614-24; article 5 from J. C. McKinley and S. R. Hathaway. The MMPI: V. Hysteria, hypomania, and psychopathic deviate. *Journal of Applied Psychology*, 1944, 28, 153-74; article 6 is an original manuscript prepared by S. R. Hathaway for the first edition of the *Basic Readings on the MMPI* (1956); article 7 from L. E. Drake. A social I. E. scale for the MMPI. *Journal of Applied Psychology*, 1946, 30, 51-54; article 8 from L. E. Drake and W. B. Thiede. Further validation of the social I. E. scale for the MMPI. *Journal of Educational Research*, 1948, 41, 551-56; article 9 from P. E. Meehl and S. R. Hathaway. The K factor as a suppressor variable in the MMPI. *Journal of Applied Psychology*, 1946, 30, 525-64; article 10 from J. C. McKinley, S. R. Hathaway, and P. E. Meehl. The MMPI: VI. The K scale. *Journal of Consulting Psychology*, 1948, 12, 20-31. We are indebted to the authors and to the publishers of the journals for permission to reproduce these articles in this form.

Construction of the Schedule

S. R. Hathaway and J. C. McKinley

For several reasons it has seemed that a multiphasic personality schedule might be constructed which would be of greater value in the medical or psychiatric clinic than is true of personality inventories already available. It is desirable that more varied subject matter be included to obtain a wider sampling of behavior of significance to the psychiatrist, rather than to utilize independent sets of items for special purposes such as one might use in studying any particular reaction type. Then, too, in dealing with clinic patients, there seemed to be a need for simpler wording and a simpler method of presentation than is usually the case, in order to stay within the comprehension of those individuals who are not of high intellectual or cultural level. Finally, it seemed desirable to create a rather large reservoir of items from which various scales might be constructed in the hope of evolving a greater variety of valid personality descriptions than are available at the present time.

The individual items were formulated partly on the basis of previous clinical experience. Mainly, however, the items were supplied from several psychiatric examination direction forms, from various textbooks of psychiatry, from certain of the directions for case taking in medicine and neurology, and from the earlier published scales of personal and social attitudes. The original list consisted of more than one thousand items. By deletion of duplicates and of those items which seemed to have relatively little significance for the purposes of this study, the inventory finally contracted to its present form of 504 items.

The separate items were formulated as declarative sentences in the first person singular. The majority were placed in the positive, the remainder in the negative. Interrogative sentences were not used. Simplified wording constituted the language of the items, the words used being selected as far as possible from those in most frequent use according to standard word frequency tables. Also, the statements were restricted to matters of "common knowledge." Idiomatic expressions were included when the idioms were common in the English language. Grammatical form was occasionally sacrificed in the interests of brevity, clarity, and simplicity. Each item was printed with its number in large type (16-point boldface) on a 3- x 5-inch card.

As a matter of convenience in handling and in avoiding duplication, the items were arbitrarily classified under 25 headings, though it was assumed that an item was not necessarily properly classified merely because it had been placed under a given subdivision. The arrangement was as follows: General Health (9 items); General Neurologic (19 items); Cranial Nerves (11 items); Motility and Coordination (6 items); Sensibility (5 items); Vasomotor, Trophic, Speech, Secretory (10 items); Cardiorespiratory (5 items); Gastrointestinal (11 items); Genitourinary (6 items); Habits (20 items); Family and Marital (29 items); Occupational (18 items); Educational (12 items); Sexual Attitudes (19 items); Religious Attitudes (20 items); Political Attitudes — Law and Order (46 items); Social Attitudes (72 items); Affect, Depressive (32 items); Affect, Manic (24 items); Obsessive, Compulsive (15 items); Delusions, Hallucinations, Illusions, Ideas of Reference (31 items); Phobias (29 items); Sadistic, Masochistic (7 items); Morale (33 items); and items modeled after suggestions of Hartshorne, May, and Shuttleworth [1930] to indicate whether the individual is trying to place himself in an improbably acceptable or unacceptable light (15 items).

For purposes of recording and subsequent interview with the patient, a separate mimeographed booklet of the items in classified form with their appropriate code was constructed.

Since a considerable number of the statements were in the negative, an answer by the subject of False would produce a double negative. Our subjects report that they experienced little difficulty in dealing with these double negatives.

The pack of 504 cards was split into two sections, each approximately one half of the total. Each section was placed in a separate box and marked respectively Section 1 and Section 2. Three guide cards were placed in each box marked True, False, and Cannot Say. The following directions were pasted into the inner side of the cover of the box and these directions were called to the patient's attention by reading them to him at the time of handing him the cards for sorting.

DIRECTIONS

Take the cards out from the front, one at a time and decide whether each is true or not.

If it is *mostly* true about you, put it *behind* the card that says *TRUE*.

If it is *not mostly* true about you, put it *behind* the card that says *FALSE*.

If a statement does not apply to you, or is something that you don't know about, put it *behind* the card that says *CANNOT SAY*.

There are no right or wrong answers.

Remember to give *your* opinion of *yourself*.

There are two boxes in this set.

In order that we may use your results, both boxes must be completed.

After the cards are sorted by the subject into the three categories, the responses are recorded on a tabulation sheet. The left-hand lower corner of each card bearing a statement which is significant if filed as False is clipped, whereas the right-hand lower corner is clipped in the case of cards with significance if filed as True. Thus, in each of the true or false categories it becomes possible by breaking the deck over these clipped corners to separate the psychiatrically significant from the nonsignificant responses. Only the significant and the Cannot Say responses need be recorded. Each section of cards is marked by a distinctively colored ink stripe along the top side of the pack from front to back. Thus, it becomes possible to locate at a glance a card which has crept into the wrong deck, been reversed, or turned upside down. After each administration of the inventory the sections are weighed to demonstrate whether or not all the cards for that section are still in the box. Before administration to another subject, each section is thoroughly shuffled so that the items come to the attention of the subject in random order. In this way no item has a constant effect on a subsequent item through any series of individual administrations. Theoretically, therefore, it should be possible either to delete old items or add new ones without producing any constant effect in the subsequent use of the inventory.

Subjects for standardization and development of scales are now being obtained from several sources:

1. A normal group from the University Hospitals and the outpa-

tient department (724 cases). These are individuals who themselves are not ill but are bringing relatives or friends to the clinic. They constitute the bulk of our so-called normal cases. The assumption is made, of course, that these people are in good health, which may not always be the case. To help establish them as real normals we ask them whether or not they are receiving treatment for any illness. Only those who say they are not under a physician's care are accepted in this group.

2. A normal group from the university Testing Bureau (265 cases). These are mainly precollege high school graduates who came to the Testing Bureau for precollege guidance, but there are a number of representatives from various college classes as well.

3. A group of normals whom we were able to contact through the courtesy of the local WPA (265 cases). These are all skilled workers from local projects.

4. Patients in the general wards of the University Hospitals (254 cases). These are individuals mainly on the medical service but also in lesser numbers from other services of the hospital whom we have contacted through the courtesy of various members of the staff of the University Hospitals. Of course, most of these patients are in the hospital for one or another physical disease. Some of these were suffering acute illnesses such as upper respiratory infections, jaundice, and the like; others were chronically ill with carcinoma, gastric ulcer, leukemia, and a variety of other conditions. All of these have been checked so that they do not include obvious psychiatric conditions.

5. Patients in the psychopathic unit of the University Hospitals and the outpatient neuropsychiatric clinic (221 cases). All the inpatients who are not too disturbed or otherwise unusable become subjects of the inventory regardless of the diagnosis.

On all normal groups the person's identity is withheld if the subject does not care to reveal his name, but information is obtained on age, sex, school level reached, occupational level, marital state, and children. The subjects report upon the presence of mental deficiency or of psychoses in the family. On the hospital patients one of two procedures is used. For those patients not seen and diagnosed by the neuropsychiatric staff, the hospital record is carefully read and an independent judgment is made as to the presence of mental disorder. If a disorder is present, a tentative diagnosis is made; if not present the case is classified "physical normal." This indicates a relatively normal mental state in a patient with a physical disease.

For those who have received full clinical work-up by the neuropsychiatric staff, the responsible clinician fills out a mimeographed

Table 1. Ages and Marital Status of Two Groups of Normals

	Male		Female	
Age	Single	Married	Single	Married
Group 1: Outpatient Department and Hospital				
16-25	62	45	70	28
26-43	39	194	26	123
44-54	8	61	5	38
55-65	2	14	0	9
Group 2: Testing Bureau				
16-25	152	0	113	0

symptomatic tabulation sheet of the patient's essential symptoms and problems and writes the diagnostic summary.

Separate items tabulations are being made on these subjects, divided into convenient subgroups. The groupings and the present state of records as they relate to Groups 1 and 2 are indicated in Table 1.

Some of these groups are still much too small to afford adequate norms or standards, but the general normals and hospital classes are being enlarged daily. The tabulations being made show the percentage frequencies of each of the three possible answers.

It is the authors' ultimate intention to publish the complete list of items with all the frequency statistics of the various normal groups when the number of cases becomes sufficiently large to provide adequate samples. We also plan to establish a series of scoring keys so that differential quantitiative scales can be made available as an aid in differential psychiatric diagnosis. The problem of reliability and validity of each scale to be developed will receive special attention so that the strengths and weaknesses of this multiphasic personality schedule will be disclosed. Continued research will then make possible continued refinements and the overcoming of weaknesses.

Scale 1 (Hypochondriasis)

J. C. McKinley and S. R. Hathaway

As the first group of clinical cases for study with the multiphasic schedule [Hathaway and McKinley, 1940 (see I, 1)], we have chosen our available cases of hypochondriasis. Since such individuals constitute a psychiatric and sociological problem of major interest and importance, it is fortunate for our purposes that they were the most numerous among our pathological groups. They were also favorable material for study in that they constituted one of the simpler and more definite nosological units from the clinical standpoint and thus represented a relatively stable clinical concept.

Hypochondriasis is defined for the purposes of this study as abnormal, psychoneurotic concern over bodily health. Our present usage is given authority in the American Psychiatric Association's *Statistical Manual* [1934] under the heading "Psychoneurosis, hypochondriasis." Thus we have arbitrarily limited statistical differentiation to the diagnostic group under the psychoneuroses and have excluded the symptomatic implications of the term as applied to the psychoses. This restriction to the narrower meaning added somewhat to our difficulties in the selection of cases by automatically eliminating many in which hypochondriasis as a symptom was prominent but was associated with other severe personality disturbances. Nevertheless, it was advantageous in that it provided us with a reasonably clear-cut concept.

Construction of the Scale for Hypochondriasis ($H - C_H$ Scale)

The group of pathological cases for scale construction was selected with meticulous care to exclude those with manifestations of the major psychoses; as far as it was possible for us to determine, only pure, uncomplicated hypochondriasis was included. All the cases had been studied intensively as inpatients in the psychopathic unit of the University of Minnesota Hospitals. Medical, neurological, psychiatric, and frequently psychometric surveys were followed through in detail. Diagnostic homogeneity was thus satisfactorily established. Though only 50 cases of this sort were available, the number was probably adequate, at least for our initial purposes, considering the care exercised in their selection. Fifty cases were inadequate, of course, for statistical analysis of the effect of such factors as social and marital status, sex, and intelligence. They were selected, however, to exlude the extremes of age or other obviously disturbing influences.

The series of "normal" or control cases from which the hypochondriacal cases were to be differentiated was as follows:

First, 109 males and 153 females between the ages of 26 and 43 inclusive. They were all married persons but seldom man and wife. These were from the group of individuals visiting patients in the hospital or bringing them to the various surgical and medical clinics of the outpatient department. They all asserted that they were not under a physician's care. In general, they represented a social stratum comparable with that of the patients in the hospital; both patients and this normal group belonged to the somewhat underprivileged classes. They came from all parts of Minnesota, both urban and rural.

Second, 265 college students from the University of Minnesota, mainly entering freshmen. These were not broken down into subcategories; they represented obviously an adolescent, unmarried group. They served as a control in the selection of scale items for the avoidance of inconsistent differentiations ascribable to differences in marital or parental status, age, socioeconomic level, intelligence, and education.

The procedure for identification of the differential items was set up in the usual manner. For each of the normal criterion groups, the percentage frequency of arbitrarily scored significant responses was recorded for each of the 504 separate items of the whole schedule. An item was selected tentatively for scale construction only if it showed a percentage frequency difference between the criterion group and the normal group which was at least twice its standard error; for most of the items selected, the differences were considerably more than twice the standard errors. The frequency of the significant response in nearly all the scale items was above 10 per cent for both groups; thus doubtful and rarely occurring responses were largely excluded. In a few of these items, the percentage of occurrence in the college group equaled or exceeded that of the hypochondriacal group, though both were significantly different from the adult normals. Such items were deleted on the basis of no differentiation between college students and hypochondriacal individuals. Where differences appeared to be obviously on such bases as marital status, or attitude toward one's children, the items were excluded on the ground that they did not apply generally in the population. Through similar reasoning a few more items were rejected on inspection of the list. Inter-item correlations were not calculated.

After experimenting with several tentative scales made up of items chosen in the manner described, the following items were finally settled upon as providing the best measure. The letter following each item indicates the answer (T = true; F = false) which is characteristic of the hypochondriacal response. Partly on the basis of the reliability of the percentage differences and partly on the basis of clinical judgment, evaluations were attempted with several weighted scales but they failed to show any superiority over unweighted items. Thus, each of the items is merely given a value of "one" in deriving this portion of the total score for an individual case.

1. During the past few years I have been well most of the time. (F) 2. I am in just as good physical health as most of my friends. (F) 3. I do not tire quickly. (F) 4. I seldom worry about my health. (F) 5. I believe I am no more nervous than most others. (F) 6. I have very few headaches. (F) 7. Much of the time my head seems to hurt all over. (T) 8. Often I feel as if there were a tight band about my head. (T) 9. There seems to be a fullness in my head or nose most of the time. (T) 10. The top of my head sometimes feels tender. (T) 11. I am troubled by attacks of nausea and vomiting. (T)

12. I seldom or never have dizzy spells. (F) 13. My judgment is better than it ever was. (F) 14. I cannot keep my mind on one thing. (T) 15. My eyesight is as good as it has been for years. (F) 16. I can read a long while without tiring my eyes. (F) 17. I do not often notice my ears ringing or buzzing. (F). 18. I feel weak all over much of the time. (T) 19. I have never been paralyzed or had any unusual weakness of any of my muscles. (F) 20. I have had no difficulty in keeping my balance in walking. (F) 21. I have little or no trouble with my muscles twitching or jumping. (F) 22. I frequently notice my hand shakes when I try to do something. (T)

23. I have few or no pains. (F) 24. Parts of my body often have feelings like burning, tingling, crawling, or like "going to sleep." (T) 25. I have numbness in one or more regions of my skin. (T) 26. I hardly ever feel pain in the back of the neck. (F) 27. My hands and feet are usually warm enough. (F) 28. Once a week or oftener I feel suddenly hot all over, without apparent cause. (T) 29. I cannot understand what I read as well as I used to. (T) 30. I sweat very easily even on cool days. (T) 31. I am almost never bothered by pains over the heart or in my chest. (F) 32. I hardly ever notice my heart pounding and I am seldom short of breath. (F) 33. There seems to be a lump in my throat much of the time. (T)

34. I have a good appetite. (F) 35. I have a great deal of stomach trouble. (T) 36. I am bothered by acid stomach several times a week. (T) 37. I am troubled by discomfort in the pit of my stomach every few days or oftener. (T) 38. I am very seldom troubled by constipation. (F) 39. I have had no difficulty in starting or holding my bowel movement. (F) 40. I have had no difficulty in starting or holding my urine. (F) 41. I wake up fresh and rested most mornings. (F) 42. My sleep is fitful and disturbed. (T) 43. Most nights I go to sleep without thoughts or ideas bothering me. (F) 44. I am about as able to work as I ever was. (F)

45. People generally demand more respect for their own rights than they are willing to allow for others. (F) 46. I enjoy social gatherings just to be with people. (F) 47. No one seems to understand me. (T) 48. I am usually calm and not easily upset. (F) 49. I cannot do anything well. (T) 50. I have had periods of days, weeks, or months when I couldn't take care of things because I couldn't "get going." (T) 51. It makes me nervous to wait. (T) 52. I have had periods of such great restlessness that I cannot sit long in a chair. (T) 53. Sometimes without any reason or even when things are going wrong I feel excitedly happy, "on top of the world." (F) 54. The sight of blood neither frightens nor makes me sick. (F) 55. I certainly feel useless at times. (T)

The preliminary score (H score) as above determined was then obtained on all the hospitalized psychiatric cases to whom the complete schedule had been administered. As one would expect on clinical grounds, many cases of frank psychosis (depression, for example) obtained high hypochondriacal scores. Contrary to expectation, however, a fair number of cases obtained high scores although the psychiatric staff had failed to elicit adequate evidence for the presence of hypochondriasis. On this basis, a correction scale seemed indicated and the following approach was undertaken for its construction.

Fifty cases with the highest H scores were selected from among the group of hospitalized psychiatric patients who clinically showed little or no hypochondriasis. The percentage frequency of the arbitrarily scored significant responses was recorded on each of the 504 separate items of the total schedule. The items showing significant percentage frequency difference between this group and the original group of 50 hypochondriacal individuals were then located. Those few items reappearing with differences in this comparison that had been included in the H scale were avoided; the remainder of the items with significant differences were collected into a separate grouping which we called the C_H scale (correction of the H scale). The C_H scale items are as follows with T or F chosen so that the item, answered as true or false, indicates differentiation between the groups in the direction of the nonhypochondriacal group:

1. I have had blank spells in which my activities were interrupted and I did not know what was going on around me. (T) 2. My hearing is apparently as good as that of most people. (F) 3. My speech is the same as always (not faster or slower, or slurring; no hoarseness). (F) 4. I drink an unusually large amount of water every day. (F) 5. The members of my family and my close relatives get along quite well. (F) 6. At times I have very much wanted to leave home. (T) 7. Once in a while I feel hate toward members of my family whom I usually love. (T) 8. I have been disappointed in love. (T) 9. I am apt to pass up something I want to do when others feel that it isn't worth doing. (T) 10. I have often lost out on things because I couldn't make up my mind soon enough. (T) 11. Religion gives me no worry. (F) 12. It is all right to get around the law if you don't actually break it. (F)

13. I am likely not to speak to people until they speak to me. (T) 14. I prefer to pass by school friends, or people I know but have not seen for a long time, unless they speak to me first. (T) 15. I should like to belong to several clubs or lodges. (F) 16. I am a good mixer. (F) 17. I seem to make friends about as quickly as others do. (F) 18. I do many things which I regret afterwards. (I regret things more or more often than others seem to.) (T) 19. What others think of me does not bother me. (F) 20. I have sometimes stayed away from another person because I feared doing or saying something that I might regret afterwards. (T) 21. I am so touchy on some subjects that I can't talk about them. (T) 22. I have at times had to be rough with people who were rude or annoying. (T) 23. Even when I am with

people I feel lonely much of the time. (T) 24. I have difficulty in starting to do things. (T)

25. I am apt to take disappointments so keenly that I can't put them out of my mind. (T) 26. I feel anxiety about something or someone almost all the time. (T) 27. I have met problems so full of possibilities that I have been unable to make up my mind about them. (T) 28. I am not easily angered. (F) 29. At times I feel like picking a fist fight with someone. (T) 30. I usually have to stop and think before I act even in trifling matters. (T) 31. I sometimes keep on at a thing until others lose their patience with me. (T) 32. I am sure I get a raw deal from life. (T) 33. I have often felt that strangers were looking at me critically. (T) 34. Someone has been trying to influence my mind. (T) 35. I believe I am being plotted against. (T) 36. I have had very peculiar and strange experiences. (T)

37. People say insulting and vulgar things about me. (T) 38. If given the chance I could do some things that would be of great benefit to the world. (T) 39. I have been afraid of things or people that I knew could not hurt me. (T) 40. I have no fear of water. (F) 41. I am afraid when I look down from a high place. (F) 42. I feel uneasy indoors. (T) 43. My plans have frequently seemed so full of difficulties that I have had to give them up. (T) 44. I often must sleep over a matter before I decide what to do. (T) 45. I have several times given up doing a thing because I thought too little of my ability. (T) 46. It makes me feel like a failure when I hear of the success of someone I know well. (T) 47. I have sometimes felt that difficulties were piling up so high that I could not overcome them. (T) 48. I am certainly lacking in self confidence. (T)

These items in an individual score were counted each as "one" and the total subtracted from the H score. The final, corrected score for hypochondriasis could thus be expressed as $H-C_H$. The superiority of the $H-C_H$ scale is demonstrable on the basis of empirical results. Comparison of the statistics of the H scale with those of $H-C_H$ shows that the latter provides differentiations from normals which are as good as the former for groups clinically characterized either by hypochondriasis as a clinical entity or by hypochondriasis as a symptom of other psychiatric conditions. On the other hand, $H-C_H$ permits exclusion of many cases from the hypochondriacal group which are not clinically hypochondriacal but which obtain high H scores. The pertinent data for comparing the two scores are shown in Table 1.

The principal points of interest in Table 1 have to do with the criti-

Table 1. Relative Differentiations of Various Psychiatric Groups from a
Normal Group by H and $H-C_H$ Scores

Group	N	H Score M	SD	Diff from Normals	$H-C_H$ Score M	SD	Diff from Normals	Diff/SE$_{diff}$ H Score	$H-C_H$ Score
A. Normal married males, ages 26-43 123		10.9	6.56		−3.9	5.64			
B. Hypochondriasis criterion group 50		29.1	7.88	18.2	14.3	7.80	18.2	15.4	14.9
C. C_H criterion group . . . 50		26.2	7.58	16.1	0.3	8.76	6.1	13.0	4.5
D. Hypochondriasis, new cases for test 25		29.1	6.36	18.2	14.0	6.30	17.9	13.0	13.1
E. Psychiatric cases with symptomatic hypochondriasis 28		20.9	10.20	10.0	3.6	7.24	7.5	5.0	5.1
F. Psychiatric cases with high H score but without symptomatic hypochondriasis 17		22.3	3.82	11.4	1.2	5.46	5.1	10.4	3.6

cal ratios in the last two columns. As might be expected, there is some decrease of the critical ratio of the $H-C_H$ score as compared with the H score of the criterion group of hypochondriacs (B in Table 1). The loss is evidently not appreciable, however, because a new group of hypochondriacs (D) shows slight improvement of the critical ratio of $H-C_H$ over the H score. The group of cases (C) by means of which C_H was derived tested high with the H score but were not clinically hypochondriacal though they were psychiatric cases; they were chosen as criterion cases for this reason. It is obvious that the $H-C_H$ score has pulled them away from the hypochondriacal group, as would necessarily be the case. A similar group of new psychiatric cases (F) behaves in like fashion when put to the test of the two scores. On the other hand, a group of psychiatric cases with symptomatic hypochondriasis occurring coincidentally in other psychiatric states (E) appears to be collectively as hypochondriacal with the $H-C_H$ score as with the H score alone. From these and other data, we conclude that some factor other than body concern is corrected out by the subtraction of C_H from H. Although we do not hold that two persons are alike whose final $H-C_H$ scores are both 20, the one with H = 20 and C_H = 0, the other with H = 40 and C_H = 20, we have been unable to disclose any difference between them related to hypochondriasis.

Application of the $H-C_H$ Score to Normal and Pathological Case Material

The $H-C_H$ score was now obtained on all other persons who had been subjects of the entire schedule. The normal individuals were divided into the groups as shown in Table 2. Since skewness was very slight in the frequency distributions, the numerical expressions of mean and standard deviation as given in the table represent very closely the true distributions. The range of the means of the various groups of normals is not large, though in a few cases the differences are statistically significant. We hesitate to draw conclusions on the basis of these differences in view of our relative clinical inexperience with the scale at the present time. Certain of the more consistent trends do seem to justify comment, however. For example, in com-

Table 2. $H-C_H$ Scores on Normal Cases

Group Designation	Marital Status	Sex	Age	Number	Raw Score Mean	SD
Normal clinic visitors . . . . . S	S	F	16-25	62	−3.5	6.34
Normal clinic visitors . . . . . M	M	F	16-25	45	−3.1	6.68
Normal clinic visitors . . . . . S	S	M	16-25	70	−4.3	4.82
Normal clinic visitors . . . . . M	M	M	16-25	28	−3.0	6.28
Normal clinic visitors . . . . . S	S	F	26-43	39	−3.9	5.12
Normal clinic visitors . . . . . M	M	F	26-43	194	−1.5	6.58
Normal clinic visitors . . . . . S	S	M	26-43	26	−5.2	5.10
Normal clinic visitors . . . . . M	M	M	26-43	123	−3.9	5.64
Normal clinic visitors . . . .M & S	M & S	F	44-54	69	+0.5	6.84
Normal clinic visitors . . . .M & S	M & S	M	44-54	43	−2.4	7.54
Normal college students . . . .M & S	M & S	F	16-25	113	−2.3	5.52
Normal college students . . . .M & S	M & S	M	16-25	152	−2.9	4.50

paring married and single individuals in each of the age groups where numbers permit their separation, the mean scores for married individuals were higher (more hypochondriacal) than for the corresponding unmarried persons. Likewise the scores for females are, without exception, higher than for the corresponding males. One might indulge in considerable speculation on these findings, but since the validity of the test within the normal group is at present in process of study, and the differences themselves are slight, we are not prepared to draw any conclusions as to the meaning of such differences.

Application of the Test to Clinical Cases

Since all the available hospitalized cases were used or culled over for the construction of the scale, we were limited in the selection of cases on which to put the scale to test to those patients who were admitted to our hospital wards after its construction and to the less desirable material from the outpatient department. The latter group was less satisfactory because of less complete clinical recording and the relative haste in clinical work-up demanded in the press of outpatient department practice. The test series consisted of 25 clinically diagnosed cases of hypochondriasis, 7 of which received intensive inpatient neuropsychiatric investigation, and the remaining 18 the routine outpatient work-up. The scores of the test cases are shown in Table 3 relative to the scores of two normal groups, the one without and the other with concomitant physical disease, and also to the scores of a group of miscellaneous psychiatric cases.

Table 3. Frequency Distributions of T Scores on the
H−C$_H$ Scale for Four Groups

T Scores	Normals (N = 699)	Hypochondriacs (N = 25)	Physical Disease Normals (N = 50)	Miscellaneous Psychiatric Patients (N = 45)
97-99		1		
94-96		0		
91-93		0		
88-90		0		
85-87		5		
82-84		2	2	
79-81	2	1	0	
76-78	5 (1%)	1	3	2
73-75	7	4	1	2
70-72	19 (5%)	5	2	2
67-69	18	0	3	4
64-66	37 (10%)	2	5	1
61-63	50	1	5	2
58-60	57	2	8	6
55-57	61	1	4	9
52-54	98 (50%)		2	2
49-51	95		4	4
46-48	63		3	2
43-45	77		4	6
40-42	46		3	0
37-39	24		0	1
34-36	20		1	0
31-33	9			2
28-30	5			
25-27	5			
22-24	0			
19-21	1			

The normal group without physical disease is the same as Group 1, as described in our first paper [Hathaway and McKinley, 1940], and that with physical disease the same as Group 4. The first group is made up of 699 cases; 50 cases make up the second. The 45 miscellaneous psychiatric cases were all inpatients who had been given detailed clinical study. The basic data for comparison with Table 3 are given in Table 4. It is obvious from simple inspection of the table that the scores of the hypochondriacal cases are distributed decidedly higher than any of the other groups. While overlap occurs, 8 of the 25 cases are beyond the highest score of any normal. Furthermore, the lowest score in the hypochondriacal group is above the mean of the normals. Since the selection of normals was really a random sample of functioning individuals who stated they were not under a physician's care, it is not surprising to note that a considerable number of them score within the distribution of the clinically hypochondriacal range. This coincides with and is at least a partial statistical verification of the frequently expressed opinion in medical and psychiatric circles that an appreciable proportion of the so-called normal population is suffering with hypochondriacal and other psychoneurotic disturbances.

The normals with physical illness constitute an especially important group. Since at the time of testing many of them were suffering physical pain, anxiety, and other reactions to organic diseases, one might expect a marked elevation of their scores. Only moderate elevation occurs; the group is much nearer the normals than it is the hypochondriacs. One concludes from this that physical symptoms alter the personality pattern only moderately in the direction of hypochondriasis.

The distribution of the 45 miscellaneous psychiatric cases also provides important data. These were individuals from the inpatient psychiatric service who had not been used in constructing or testing the scale. The only exclusion was the removal of psychoneurotic hypo-

Table 4. The Statistics of the Standard Score Equivalents
of the Three Test Groups[a]

Group Designation	Number	Standard Score Mean	Standard Score SD	Critical Ratio to Normal
Hypochondriacal cases 25		74.2	10.23	10.9
Normals with physical disease 50		58.1	11.34	4.0
Miscellaneous psychiatric cases 45		55.7	10.98	2.5

[a]Age and sex are corrected out. See also Table 3.

chondriacal cases and, of course, patients who could not cooperate. It is to be remembered that hypochondriasis as a symptomatic concomitant of other obvious psychiatric disorders was not excluded from this group. In our opinion, this group constitutes a most exacting test of the discriminatory power of the scale. Thus, depressive patients, as is well known, frequently exhibit hypochondriacal symptoms together with feelings of guilt, nihilistic delusions, and other self-depreciatory trends as the syndrome of the condition; similar comment is possible in relation to other included psychotic conditions. Yet the score distribution of these miscellaneous psychiatric cases is only slightly higher than that of the normal group and is definitely lower than that of the hypochondriacal cases. Thus, the group of clinically diagnosed hypochondriacs is differentiated by the schedule almost as well from the psychotic group as it is from the normal.

Conclusions

Differential study of groups of persons by a scale for hypochondriasis derived from our multiphasic personality schedule reveals that:

1. Significant separation of hypochondriacal cases from normals can be demonstrated.

2. A sizable proportion of the so-called normal population nevertheless overlaps the hypochondriacal group as is often stated in medical and psychiatric opinion.

3. The presence of physical disorder does not greatly raise the scores over the normal distribution in the direction of hypochondriasis.

4. The distribution of the hypochondriacal scores of psychotic patients is only slightly higher than that of the normals.

Addendum

In a personal communication S. R. Hathaway has outlined the subsequent modification of $H - C_H$.

It had been noted in the course of derivation of a scale for hysteria that the new scale 3 (Hy) differed from the hypochondriasis scale mainly in the items related to the correction C_H for H. Scale 1 (Hs) was therefore arbitrarily made into a somatic item scale by eliminating the C_H items and some of the old H items that did not stand up on further analysis. This decision was intended to make the diagnosed hysterics score high mainly on scale 3. When K was tried on scale 1, the results showed that the corrected scale improved the differentiation between hypochondriasis and hysteria. It appeared that too extreme a purification had been made when *all* the C_H items were taken out. The addition of .5K helped correct this error. As indicated in the K article [Meehl and Hathaway, 1946 (see I, 9)] the C_H items correlated well with K; the correlation was negative because the items were scored inversely. In short, modern Hs + .5K is a compromise between a pure somatic scale and the old H − C_H.

Scale 2 (Depression)

S. R. Hathaway and J. C. McKinley

The complete set of items in the MMPI has now been administered to about 3000 individuals of various normal and abnormal classifications. The chief normal group against which all hospitalized abnormal groups are considered is comprised of adults to whom the items were administered when they came as visitors to or brought patients to the University Hospitals. The only requirement for inclusion of these persons as normal was that they said they were not under a doctor's care at the time of testing. The word "normal" as used hereafter never implies more than this. The normal group so obtained represents a reasonably accurate cross section of the Minnesota population. The modal scholastic achievement is eighth grade, and socio-occupational ratings indicate that the modal occupational level is approximately that of the general adult population.

One scale has already been derived and published [McKinley and Hathaway, 1940 (see I, 2)]. This scale measures symptomatic hypochondriasis and yields a score indicating the degree to which the clinical picture of hypochondriasis is present in the individual. Hypochondriasis was chosen for the first scale because it was relatively clear-cut clinicially and because good clinical cases were relatively easy to obtain.

Derivation of the Depression Scale

The present paper deals with the development of a scale for measuring symptomatic depression. The term "symptomatic" is used

24

here because the authors wish to avoid the identification of the term "depression" with anything other than the presence at the time of testing of a clinically recognizable, general frame of mind characterized by poor morale, lack of hope in the future, and dissatisfaction with the patient's own status generally. In fact, such a clinical picture might result from economic or vocational frustration, from personal problems, from a depressive phase of a cycloid personality, or from any one of the other commonly known clinical backgrounds of depression. As seen in this way, the measured depression might represent a less stable trait in the individual than would the measured hypochondriacal tendency or, in fact, most other measured personality characteristics. It is well recognized that a few patients with a marked degree of depression on one day may change toward normal within twenty-four hours. The same tendency to shift is notable in a few individuals who may never develop a clinically important depth of depression. All these factors make rather difficult the problem of obtaining a group of patients clearly depressed at the time of testing.

The subjects for scale derivation consisted of (a) 139 normal married males between the ages of 26 and 43 and 200 normal married females between the ages of 26 and 43, (b) a group of 265 college students as a check for the effect of age on item frequency, (c) 40 normal persons having a high depression score on a preliminary depression scale, (d) a group of 50 patients without clinically observed depression but with a tendency to score high on the preliminary depression scale, and finally (e) a group of 50 carefully chosen depressed patients to serve as a criterion group.

The 50 patients of the criterion depression group (e), most of whom were in the depressed phase of a manic-depressive psychosis, had all been thoroughly investigated medically and psychiatrically and, as far as possible, represented relatively pure cases of depression. This group of depressed patients will hereafter be referred to as the criterion group. The group of male and female normals (a) against which comparisons were made will be referred to as the normal group. It should be noted that in the final presentation of the results of the scale, many more normals are included than are included in the normal group as described above. The college students (b) were mostly first- or second-year students and also included were a number of college applicants just out of high school. The 40 normal persons (c) who were depressed on the preliminary depression scale will be referred to hereafter as the depressed normal group. Some of these may have been true depression cases not in the hospital or under a doctor's care. The 50 University Hospitals patients (d) with high preliminary scores but with no clinically observed depression will be described later as the nondepressed group.

In deriving the significant items for depression, the preliminary statistical procedure consisted in listing the percentage occurrence among the normal group of each answer, True, False, and Cannot Say, for each item alongside the similar percentages for the criterion group. Analysis then included the checking of all items having a reliable difference between the percentages for normal and criterion groups. At this point in the derivation the requirement for reliability was that the difference be more than twice its standard error. After the items had been checked for the presence of a reliable difference, each was inspected and any item that had too great a sex difference, or that failed to differentiate between the criterion and college groups was eliminated. A few other items were eliminated because of some apparent inconsistency or because they seemed inappropriate. This left 70 items which were used as a preliminary depression scale.

All available psychiatric and normal cases were next scored on the preliminary scale. As was the case with hypochondriasis, it was found when all other clinic patients were scored on this preliminary depression scale and their scores were compared with the scores made by normals in general, a number of clinically studied cases scored high who had not been found by the psychiatric staff to present any important degree of depression. Since it was felt that, as had been true also of the hypochondriacal scale, extraneous factors were influencing the scores, a correction was necessary. This correction was derived by choosing from among carefully studied clinical cases 50 individuals to form the nondepressed group. The nondepressed group was selected as indicated above (d) on the basis of a high score on the preliminary depression scale, contrasting with an absence of depression as seen clinically. The percentage occurrence of all items for this group was now tabulated alongside the above tabulations for the criterion and normal groups. A depressed normal group of 40 persons (c) was next selected from among the large normal group. Those in this category were selected merely on the basis of having scored highest among the normals on the preliminary scale. All item tabulations of this group were also added to the above array, completing the data for the selection of the final scale items.

In choosing items for the final scale, the following requirements had to be met by the accepted item. First, each depressive item had to show a progressive increase in frequency from the normal groups through the depressed normal group to the criterion group since it was assumed that the depressed normals would be less depressed than the criterion cases but more than general normals. In all items primarily indicating depression, the difference in percentage between the normal and the criterion was 2.5 or more times its standard error. Second, the nondepressed group percentage for the item was required to approach that for normals. After careful analysis of all percentages for each of the 504 items, 60 items were chosen as the final depression scale.

The above procedure was devised to eliminate stray items that might occur beyond statistical limits if only two groups were used and to avoid items that would fail to differentiate in the desired direction under special conditions. Especially, the nondepressed group was used to assure the inclusion of correction items to hold the scores down on cases not belonging to the clinical category. In the present scale the correction is achieved without minus items, in contrast to the hypochondriasis scale although the same basic procedure is followed. In all, 11 of the 60 items of the present scale are primarily correction items and not especially indicative of depression. By this is meant that they showed little increase in percentage from normal to depressed but did clearly differentiate the nondepressed from the depressed group. Other items serve both purposes at the same time. By using the depressed normal group in the scale development, it was hoped that a more certain validity could be established for intermediate scale values between normal and clearly abnormal than would have been true for a scale contrasting the two extreme groups alone.

In the final scale all items are simply counted +1 when answered in the depressed direction. If any item is answered Cannot Say it is disregarded since there are few such responses. The following list contains all the final items with a T or an F after each to indicate the scored answer. Those items for which the chief function is correction rather than depression are starred.

1. During the past few years I have been well most of the time. (F) 2. I am in just as good physical health as most of my friends. (F) 3. I have never felt better in my life than I do now. (F) 4. I am neither gaining nor losing weight. (F) 5. I seldom worry about my health. (F) 6. I believe I am no more nervous than most others. (F) 7. I am troubled by attacks of nausea and vomiting. (T) *8. I have never had a fit or convulsion. (F) 9. I seem to be about as capable and smart as most others around me. (F) 10. My judgment is better than it ever was. (F)

11. My memory seems to be all right. (F) 12. I feel weak all over much of the time. (T) 13. I cannot understand what I read as well as I used to. (T) *14. I sweat very easily even on cool days. (F) *15. Sometimes, when embarrassed, I break out in a sweat which an-

noys me greatly. (F) *16. I do not have spells of hay fever or asthma. (T) *17. I have never vomited blood or coughed up blood. (T) 18. I have a good appetite. (F) 19. I am very seldom troubled by constipation. (F) 20. My sleep is fitful and disturbed. (T)

21. Most nights I go to sleep without thoughts or ideas bothering me. (F) 22. I am easily awakened by noise. (T) 23. I dream frequently about things that are best kept to myself. (F) 24. I am about as able to work as I ever was. (F) 25. I have at times stood in the way of people who were trying to do something, not because it amounted to much but because of the principle of the thing. (F) 26. It takes a lot of argument to convince most people of the truth. (F) 27. I like to flirt. (F) *28. I go to church almost every week. (F) *29. I believe in the second coming of Christ. (F) *30. Everything is turning out just like the prophets of the Bible said it would. (F)

31. I do not blame a person for taking advantage of someone who lays himself open to it. (F) 32. I prefer to pass by school friends, or people I know but have not seen for a long time, unless they speak to me first. (T) 33. I am a good mixer. (F) 34. I enjoy many different kinds of play and recreation. (F) 35. Criticism or scolding hurts me terribly. (T) 36. I wish I could be as happy as others seem to be. (T) 37. I usually feel that life is worthwhile. (F) 38. My daily life is full of things that keep me interested. (F) 39. I have difficulty in starting to do things. (T) 40. I have had periods of days, weeks, or months when I couldn't take care of things because I couldn't "get going." (T)

41. I brood a great deal. (T) 42. I cry easily. (T) 43. I don't seem to care what happens to me. (T) 44. I am happy most of the time. (F) 45. I have periods in which I feel unusually cheerful without any special reason. (F) 46. At times I am full of energy. (F) 47. Sometimes without any reason or even when things are going wrong I feel excitedly happy, "on top of the world." (F) 48. At times I feel like smashing things. (F) 49. At times I feel like picking a fist fight with someone. (F) *50. I sometimes keep on at a thing until others lose their patience with me. (F)

*51. When I leave home I do not worry about whether the door is locked and the windows closed. (F) 52. I do not worry about catching diseases. (F) 53. I am afraid of losing my mind. (T) *54. I sometimes tease animals. (F) 55. I find it hard to keep my mind on a task or job. (T) 56. I work under a great deal of tension. (T) 57. I certainly feel useless at times. (T) 58. I am certainly lacking in self-confidence. (T) 59. Once in a while I laugh at a dirty joke. (F) 60. At times I feel like swearing. (F)

For clinical use, the raw scores are transformed into standard scores in which the means of each of the whole normal groups of males and females between the ages of 16 and 45 are given the value 50; other raw scores are transformed so that the standard deviation will be 10. Larger scores than the mean, denoting more depression, are assigned to the range above 50 and those below the mean to the range below 50. In basing the standard scores on the age range of 16-45 inclusive, the whole population is well characterized even though there is a change with age. It is more acceptable clinically to permit a higher average score on depression with increasing age. The standard scores also eliminate the sex difference present in raw scores.

Evidences of Validity and Incidental Findings

In order to test the scale for validity, a group of 35 cases observed in the clinic subsequent to the scale derivation was selected. These are called test cases. The test cases were not all clear cases of depression but they were satisfactory to the extent that they should, as a group, be clearly different from normals although individuals might have recovered from their depression before testing. It was not possible to tell from the clinical record whether or not the rated depression was present at the precise time of administration of the inventory. As a further test of validity, a group of patients who had not actually received the diagnosis "depression" but who were marked by the staff as having or having had during their illness some degree of abnormal depression was selected from among the psychiatric records. This group, hereafter called the symptomatic depression group, probably includes some definitely depressed patients as well as some with little depression (especially at the time of testing). It also includes schizoid and neurotic patients in whom the depression was overshadowed by some other component. On the whole, the symptomatic group would be expected to score above all groups except the more definitely diagnosed depressed criterion and test groups.

Table 1 shows the results on 690 normals of ages 16-65. The scale is in the above standard score values and the 1, 5, 10, and 50 per cent points are marked as they were obtained with the origin at the depressed end of the distribution. Because of skewness, these are not at the standard values predicted from a normal curve. Distributed on the same standard scale are the scores of the 35 test depression cases. These provide the best available test of validity. The shape of the distribution for the normals is probably typical for personality traits

Table 1. Frequency Distributions of T Scores on Scale 2 (D) for Minnesota
Normals and the Depressed Test Cases

T Scores	Normals (N = 690)	Depressed Test Cases (N = 35)	T Scores	Normals (N = 690)	Depressed Test Cases (N = 35)
97-99. 0		3	61-63. 34		2
94-96. 1		2	58-60. 39		2
91-93. 1		3	55-57. 52		1
88-90. 0		2	52-54. 61		0
85-87. 2		2	49-51. . . . . 69 (50%)		0
82-84. . . . . 3 (1%)		5	46-48. 79		1
79-81. 7		1	43-45. 70		
76-78. 10		2	40-42. 65		
73-75. . . . . . . .11 (5%)		2	37-39. 53		
70-72. 13		2	34-36. 44		
67-69. 17		2	31-33. 21		
64-66. . . . . . . .26 (10%)		3	28-30. 10		
			25-27. 2		

where deviations in the normal direction are restricted relative to abnormal deviation.

Table 2 gives the raw score means and standard deviations for the groups described above, together with the probability values for several of the differences between the means. The groups are arranged according to the value of the mean raw score. As was indicated in Table 1, the test group shows a clear difference from normals. This difference is second in magnitude only to that of the criterion group. The statistics of the symptomatic depression group—which is a further test of validity since its members had depression as a symptom— are also given. In reality, this group is a very heterogeneous one, including many depressed patients who had other symptoms that were favored in their diagnosis as well as patients with little real evidence of depression. It is apparent that although there is some overlap the scale yields scores that differentiate at least 50 per cent of the test cases from normals and even from other psychiatric cases although the latter are, reasonably enough, more depressed than normal. Twenty-four of the 35 test cases made a standard score greater than 70.

Unfortunately, the nondepressed group also still shows a large and significant difference. Whether this is because they were really depressed and not observed by the clinicians to be so or whether they represent true errors of measurement cannot be determined. The former alternative is not unreasonable, however, since all of the score that could be corrected as being spurious was so corrected and since certain depressed patients are notably able to hide depression. The nondepressed were not frequent among all cases seen in the clinic and do not constitute a practical problem after partial correction.

Table 2. The Means and Standard Deviations of Various Groups

Group	N	M	SD	Diff[a]	Diff/SE$_{diff}$[a]
Criterion	50	36.68	4.7	18.54	26.9
Test depressed	35	32.49	7.4	14.35	11.0
Nondepressed	50	28.86	6.3	10.72	11.8
Symptomatically depressed . . .	223	28.20	7.3	10.06	19.0
Random psychiatric cases	413	24.44	7.2	6.30	15.8
Physically ill	229	21.70	5.2	3.56	8.9
Normals	690	18.14	4.9		

[a]The differences and their reliability values are in contrast with the statistics of the normal group.

The group in Table 2 called random psychiatric cases is made up of all clinic cases not diagnosed as any type of depression; but it does include the 223 symptomatic depression cases in whom some depression was observed. The random psychiatric cases as a group contrast with the physically ill cases of Table 2 which are from other wards of the hospital. To be on a psychiatric ward seems to increase the score. In reality, this difference is observable clinically among the psychiatric cases as is shown by the fact that it mostly disappears when the symptomatically depressed group is left out. The subjects in the physically ill group were patients on the open wards who were not special problems psychiatrically but who were in the hospital because of one or more physical complaints. These patients are often observably depressed as a reaction to their illness, which could be anything from a mild respiratory infection to very serious conditions. This group is reliably more depressed than the normal. Of special interest among this group is the relative standing of the men and the women. When the scores are transformed into standard scores, 18 per cent of the males but only 6 per cent of the females exceed the 5 per cent point of the normal group. The mean standard score of the males is 60 (+1 sigma) and that of the females is 55 (+.5 sigma). This finding shows the especial reaction of the males to disabling illness.

In consideration of Tables 1 and 2, another factor may play a part in the overlap of normal and test cases. The normal group included many persons who were visiting relatives or friends in the hospital for serious illnesses and consequently might themselves be reactively depressed. Although fluctuations of a more temporary sort would not be likely to greatly affect many traits, the depression scale is surely sensitive to them. There is no practical way to estimate from our available data the effect of the factor upon the overlap of the curves.

Table 3 gives some raw score means and standard deviations with the significance of the differences from the criterion group. As a group, the nondepressed are significantly different, showing that some correction has occurred, since there was no difference on the preliminary scale.

Although the primary approach has been through the establishment of what is best described as the clinical validity of the scales, some evidence of test-retest reliability is available. Although many retests have been recorded on our clinical material, these are not suitable for reliability correlations for obvious reasons. For 40 normal cases, the reliability coefficient is .77 ± .044. On the basis of this reliability the probable error of a score is 1.9 points.

For the previously published scale of hypochondriasis, H−C_H, the test-retest reliability coefficient is .80 ± .038 for the same group. The two tests on these normals were separated in time by never less than three days and up to more than a year. All of these 40 normals were employees and staff members but none knew that the test was to be repeated until they were asked to take it again. The range of the group was small on both scales.

Among a sample of 50 random normal cases in the age range 26 to 35, the intercorrelation with hypochondriasis as measured by H − C_H is .29 ± .087. On another sample of 50 from the normal group in the age range 16 to 25, the same procedure gives a correlation of .16 ± .093. This value rises to .62 ± .041 on a sample of 100

Table 3. Means and Standard Deviations of Several of the Groups in Contrast with the Statistics of the Criterion Group

Group	N	M	SD	Diff	Diff/ SE_{diff}
Criterion	50	36.68	4.7		
Test depressed	35	32.49	7.4	−4.19	3.0
Nondepressed	50	28.86	6.3	−7.82	7.0
Random psychiatric cases	413	24.44	7.2	−12.24	16.3
Normals	690	18.14	4.9	−18.54	26.9

random psychiatric cases. Part of the rather small degree of correlation for normals is no doubt due to overlap of the measuring instruments. In all, 22 items are common to both scales but five of these are counted oppositely. This leaves approximately 12 items working in a common direction if one corrects for the effect of the opposing items. That the two factors can be dynamically interrelated is shown when abnormal cases are used. One can hardly be deeply concerned over his health even on a delusional basis without being somewhat depressed as a result.

Among normal groups there are several differences that are of interest. Table 4 gives the raw score means and standard deviations for some of the subgroups. The college group appears here for the first time since it was not included in the general normal data presented above. These mixed college and precollege cases have the lowest score of any subdivision. Among the general normals there is an age difference with a clear tendency for a higher score at higher ages. The most constant difference, however, is that between sexes. At present the authors are not willing to interpret this difference but it may be due to some general bias in response that is not particularly related to depression.

Table 4. Age and Sex Differences in Mean Score

Group	Males			Females		
	N	M	SD	N	M	SD
College students	155	14.77	3.70	115	16.90	4.2
General population (by age)						
16-25	110	16.15	4.39	118	18.57	5.4
26-35	111	16.63	3.90	165	19.08	4.6
36-45	73	17.36	4.11	113	20.23	5.6
46-55	40	18.93	5.47	59	19.25	4.8
56-	13	21.46	6.43	19	21.58	6.0

Conclusions

Differential study of groups of persons by a scale for depression derived from our multiphasic personality schedule reveals that:

1. Significant separation of clinically depressed patients from normals can be demonstrated for a large percentage of cases.

2. Patients having only moderate degrees of depressive trend without specific abnormality can also be differentiated.

3. Depression scale scores are significantly higher for females than for males and they become higher with increasing age.

4. Unselected patients on a psychiatric ward test higher on depression than do patients on other wards and the latter are higher than the normal.

Scale 7 (Psychasthenia)

J. C. McKinley and S. R. Hathaway

The psychiatric classification of psychasthenia is applied to a group of individuals whose thinking is characterized by excessive doubt, by compulsions, obsessions, and unreasonable fears; these persons are often seen in psychiatric hospitals but are encountered much more frequently among normal groups by counselors and personnel workers. Certain phobias such as the fear of spiders, of snakes, or of windstorms are widespread among the population, but similar phobias become so strong and so numerous in some persons as to afford a source of considerable maladjustment vocationally, socially, or otherwise. Often a psychasthenic individual is characterized not so much by well-marked fears of individual things or acts as by great doubts as to the meaning of his reactions in what seems to be a hostile environment. In other cases the phobia becomes attached to certain acts or thoughts of the subject in such a way that he is forced through fear to compulsively perform needless, disturbing, or personally destructive acts or to dwell obsessively upon lines of thought which have no significance for his normal activities.

Compulsive acts are always characterized by the need felt by the subject to perform them without regard to rational considerations. For example, he may always be forced to count objects or to touch a certain spot on a wall or to avoid stepping on sidewalk cracks. If he fails to do these things he feels uncomfortable; if he does them he is forced to rationalize and justify his acts. Obsessive thinking is itself commonly accompanied by anxiety so that the patient may be tense and anxious over the content of his thoughts as when he thinks over and over again that he is useless. Similarly, he may find himself anxiously obsessed with such ideas as the impending likelihood that he will faint or that something terrible or threatening is about to happen. Again, he may be forced to think things which, while not in themselves producing anxiety, through his impatience and preoccupation with the fact that he cannot stop thinking them, do secondarily produce an anxious reaction; for example, compulsive counting itself has little attached anxiety since the patient is merely forced to count everything that he sees, but he may worry so much over his inability to stop counting as to have anxiety as a large component in his thinking. The general reaction type characterized by these compulsive and obsessive acts and thoughts is called psychasthenia. The word derives from the concept of a weakened will that cannot resist the behavior regardless of its maladaptive character.

The development of a scale for the measurement of the general symptomatic traits which are classed under the psychiatric designation of psychasthenia has demonstrated that there is an identifiable personality pattern underlying the varying symptomatic picture from case to case. Many of the items making up the psychasthenia scale are clearly much more general than the specific compulsions or phobias and apply to a more general personality make-up of which the subject is usually entirely unaware.

The methods of derivation for the present scale differ only in detail from the methods used in the scales reported earlier [McKinley and Hathaway, 1940 (see I, 2), Hathaway and McKinley, 1942 (I, 3)]. Unfortunately for the present study not many entirely satisfactory criterion cases of psychasthenia come into the closed wards of a psychiatric clinic. Many more are seen in the outpatient clinic or are advised by lay counselors and are never severely handicapped. Because we have felt unsure in the use of even carefully studied inpatients for purposes of scale derivation, we have avoided using criterion cases from the outpatient clinic. The criterion group is thus small and not entirely homogeneous. At least one of the cases appears to have been incorrectly diagnosed. Fortunately, the trait itself is the most homogeneous one so far described so that correlations of items with total score could be used as a guide. Otherwise, we would hesitate to publish the results with so few criterion cases.

The chief subjects for scale derivation consisted of (a) 139 normal married males between the ages of 26 and 43, and 200 normal married females between the ages of 26 and 43, (b) a group of 265 college students as a check of the effect of age on item frequency, and (c) a group of 20 psychiatric patients carefully selected as probable psychasthenia cases.

The criterion group included patients who had been intensively studied medically and psychiatrically and for whom the final diagnosis was psychasthenia in one or another form. Unfortunately, as mentioned above, it was necessary not only to use a rather small criterion group, but also to include in the group several persons who, as it subsequently developed, were probably not appropriate. For example, the two of this group who received the lowest final scores were young persons, one of 16 and the other of 17 years. One of these was not at all similar in item responses to the remainder of the criterion group. It is probable that this 16-year-old boy was wrongly diagnosed.

A preliminary step in deriving this scale was the tabulation of the item responses of the criterion group in contrast to the norm groups of men and women and the college students considered as a mixed normal group selected for age and for scholastic aptitude. All items that showed a differentiation of two or more times the standard error of the difference between the criterion and all of the nomal groups were chosen as a preliminary scale for psychasthenia. All available normal and psychiatric cases were then scored on this preliminary scale. It was possible at this point to check whether or not the scale seemed to be working in the right direction and to determine its apparent variability. Since the scale as derived in this preliminary fashion appeared to be unusually homogeneous and since there were other potentially useful items that had been doubtful in the statistics of the comparison of criterion and normal groups, item correlations were used to test all preliminary scale items as well as certain of the doubtful items not included in the preliminary scale.

Tetrachoric correlations were obtained for every preliminary item and all the doubtful items against total scores on the preliminary scale for a sample of 100 normal persons and for a sample of 100 randomly selected psychiatric patients. These data combined with the original comparison data of criterion and normal cases permitted us to select a final scale of 48 items. The following list contains all of these final scale items each followed by a T or an F to indicate the direction of the scored answer. After each item is given the tetrachoric correlation of the item with total score on the preliminary scale. The first figure is the correlation from normal cases and the second that from psychiatric cases. It was assumed that items were valid if they correlated with either group. In some cases only one correlation is given since the cell frequencies for a response might be too low to obtain a valid indication of the other correlation. A few of the items with low correlations were retained because the item had appeared very strong in the criterion group. The items are merely counted +1 when answered in the indicated direction.

Item		100 Normals	100 Psychiatric Patients
I seldom worry about my health	F	40	65
At times I have fits of laughing and crying that I cannot control	T	59	47
I seem to be about as capable and smart as most others around me	F	80	47
My memory seems to be all right	F		71
I feel weak all over much of the time	T	75	61
I cannot understand what I read as well as I used to	T	43	63
There seems to be a lump in my throat much of the time . . .	T	80	50
I wake up fresh and rested most mornings	F	65	80
Most nights I go to sleep without thoughts or ideas bothering me	F	32	77
I almost never dream	F	40	53
I like to study and read about things that I am working at . .	F		51
I do many things which I regret afterwards (I regret things more or more often than others seem to)	T	65	72
In school I found it very hard to talk before the class	T	57	44
I am easily embarrassed	T	56	70
I am more sensitive than most other people	T	77	53
I easily become impatient with people	T	52	
Even when I am with people I feel lonely much of the time .	T	55	81
I wish I could be as happy as others seem to be	T	60	67
My daily life is full of things that keep me interested	F	41	74
I have had periods of days, weeks, or months when I couldn't take care of things because I couldn't "get going"	T	66	66
I frequently find myself worrying about something	T	85	76
Most of the time I feel blue	T	80	82
Much of the time I feel as if I have done something wrong or evil	T	76	
I feel anxiety about something or someone almost all the time	T	52	
Once a week or oftener I become very excited	T	90	72
I have periods of such great restlessness that I cannot sit long in a chair	T	79	75
Sometimes I become so excited that I find it hard to get to sleep	T	63	50
I forget right away what people say to me	T	16	74
I usually have to stop and think before I act even in trifling matters	T	52	
I have a habit of counting things that are not important such as bulbs on electric signs, and so forth	T	45	67

Items		100 Normals	100 Psychiatric Patients
Sometimes some unimportant thought will run through my mind and bother me for days	T	82	62
Bad words, often terrible words, come into my mind and I cannot get rid of them	T	48	71
Often I cross the street in order not to meet someone I see . .	T	80	80
I have strange and peculiar thoughts	T	63	79
I get anxious and upset when I have to make a short trip away from home	T	58	55
Almost every day something happens to frighten me	T		82
I have been afraid of things or people that I knew could not hurt me	T	41	20
I have no dread of going into a room by myself where other people have already gathered and are talking	F	35	44
I am afraid of losing my mind	T		60
My hardest battles are with myself	T	45	50
I have more trouble concentrating than others seem to have . .	T	90	72
I have several times given up doing a thing because I thought too little of my ability	T	53	
I find it hard to keep my mind on a task or job	T	36	79
I am inclined to take things hard	T	56	53
Life is a strain for me much of the time	T	50	84
I certainly feel useless at times	T	70	74
I am certainly lacking in self confidence	T	52	
Once in a while I think of things too bad to talk about	T	46	70

The distributions of Table 1 show the scores of the normals, the criterion cases, and fifty symptomatic cases on the final scale. The scores used in Table 1 are standard score equivalents derived from the statistics for 293 normal males and 397 normal females between the ages of 16 and 45. Two standard score tables were used, one for the males and one for the females. This cancels the sex differences. (See Table 2.) The standard scores were fitted to a mean of 50 and a standard deviation of 10.

Validity and Incidental Findings

There was relatively little change in score with age. Table 2 shows the raw score statistics for ten-year intervals from 16 to 65. The college student group deviates markedly from the group of similar age chosen at random from the population. There is some difference between the sexes as observed with other scales but without further study no special significance should be attached to this difference.

It is, unfortunately, not possible to estimate the validity of the psychasthenia scale by testing it on a new group of psychiatric pa-

Table 1. Frequency Distributions of the T Scores on Scale
7 (Pt) for Minnesota Normals and Two Criterion Groups

T Scores	Normals (N = 690)	Criterion Psychasthenics (N = 20)	Symptomatic Cases (N = 50)
88-90		1	
85-87	1	1	3
82-84	1	1	1
79-81	5 (1%)	1	1
76-78	3	3	5
73-75	11	3	3
70-72	14 (5%)	2	4
67-69	21	3	4
64-66	34 (10%)	1	4
61-63	29		
58-60	39	2	4
55-57	66	1	7
52-54	58		4
49-51	63 (50%)		5
46-48	69		1
43-45	96		3
40-42	65		
37-39	72		1
34-36	39	1	
31-33	4		

Table 2. Changes in Score with Age and Sex

Group	Males			Females		
	N	M	SD	N	M	SD
College students	155	7.27	5.8	115	8.93	6.0
General population (by age)						
16-25	110	9.10	7.4	118	13.00	7.9
26-35	110	10.54	7.2	165	12.19	7.7
36-45	73	10.12	6.5	114	14.47	7.4
46-55	40	10.90	7.8	59	12.31	6.7
56-65	13	12.38	8.8	19	14.16	7.4

tients diagnosed psychasthenia only but not used in the derivation of the scale. A few new cases have been diagnosed by the clinic but another year will be required for the accumulation of a sufficiently large group to permit this type of statistical validation. Nevertheless additional individuals so far obtained by clinical diagnosis have been deviates on the scale.

The evidence of validity as given by the psychiatric cases with clinical symptoms of some degree of psychasthenia is relatively clear and positive. This has been shown by experience in the clinic but is more graphically shown in Table 1. The distribution marked symptomatic cases represents 50 psychiatric cases very heterogeneous in diagnosis but with the one common characteristic that they were marked by the staff as having some symptomatic evidence of obsessions or compulsions. Since none of these cases were finally diagnosed psychasthenia and since the clinician frequently overemphasizes symptoms as seen in a person otherwise abnormal, the cases should not be expected to be uniformly high in the scale. Nevertheless the trend toward high scores for the group is clearly significant. Only 10 per cent fall below the mean for the normal group.

Table 3 lists the means and standard deviations of several groups in comparison with the normal group. In contrast to previously derived scales, the physically ill individuals from other portions of the hospital test very little above normals not in the hospital. Psychiatric cases without recorded evidence of psychasthenia test above the normal average but the staff frequently fails to record the presence of some psychasthenic traits even though they are observed since the trends are not disabling.

Several measures of reliability are available. For a group of 47 normal cases retested at intervals of never less than three days and up to more than a year, the test-retest reliability coefficient is $.74 \pm .15$. Most of these cases were employees and staff but none knew that the test was to be repeated. The standard deviation of this group was 4.9 on the first test as compared with over 7 on general normals and undoubtedly the coefficient obtained represents a low limit rather than a true test-retest correlation value. The split-half coefficient obtained from a group of 200 random normal cases is $.84 \pm .07$. When a simi-

Table 3. Means and Standard Deviations for Several Groups

Group	N	M	SD	Diff	Diff/ SE$_{diff}$	Percentage Reaching or Exceeding Mean of Normals
Normals	690	11.70	7.7	. . .	. . .	. . .
Criterion psychiatric	20	27.05	9.4	15.35	7.2	95
Symptomatic psychiatric . .	50	21.02	9.1	9.32	7.1	90
Other psychiatric	576	16.15	10.1	4.45	8.6	63
Physically ill	266	12.12	7.9	0.42	0.7	48
College students	270	7.99	6.0	−3.71	7.9	28

lar sample of 100 psychiatric cases selected at random is used, the correlation is .89 ± .10. When these two correlations are statistically corrected to a full-length test, they are .91 ± .07 and .94 ± .10.

The test intercorrelation with hypochondriasis as measured by $H-C_H$ is .06 ± .10 as obtained from 100 normals. The intercorrelation with depression as measured by D on the same group was .44 ± .10. When 100 miscellaneous psychiatric cases are used, these two correlations are, with $H-C_H$, .28 ± .10 and, with D, .69 ± .10. The rise in the correlation with depression for psychiatric cases is probably to be expected since the complaint factors involved in psychasthenia are dynamically related to depression so that many persons tend to have the psychasthenic type of fears in greater degree as their morale becomes lower, and conversely to be reactively more depressed as they are troubled by psychasthenia.

Summary

The psychiatric designation psychasthenia as used in the present day refers to a group of individuals who are frequently troubled by compulsions, obsessions, and phobias and who are often disabled by vacillation, excessive worry, and lack of confidence. Through the differential study of persons having psychiatric evidences of psychasthenia, a scale was derived which is internally homogeneous and which differentiates clinic patients from normals in a large percentage of cases. Further evidence of validity is given by the fact that, on the average, persons exhibiting psychasthenic symptoms to only a minor degree score significantly higher than normals.

Scales 3 (Hysteria), 9 (Hypomania), and 4 (Psychopathic Deviate)

J. C. McKinley and S. R. Hathaway

The basic plan of approach in the development of the MMPI has been presented elsewhere [Hathaway and McKinley, 1940 (see I, 1)]. Three scales have been described as developed according to that plan [McKinley and Hathaway, 1940 (I, 2), Hathaway and McKinley, 1942 (I, 3), McKinley and Hathaway (I, 4)] and the present paper will present some salient points regarding three more scales for the detection respectively of hypomania, psychopathic deviation, and hysteria. These scales have been in preliminary use [Hathaway and McKinley, 1943].

The procedures for the derivation of the three scales are similar and can be presented generally for the three. It is essential to note that the details of scale development have involved many tentative trials with subsequent validating studies and finally the adoption of the best scale for inclusion in the inventory. A description of this process would be too detailed for profitable publication. It follows, though, that the establishment of validity of a scale becomes most important; consequently the scale descriptions rest more than is usual upon the establishment of clinical validity. Clinical criteria for validity present many potential pitfalls. There must be reasonable assurance that the clinical opinion and the scale derivation process are separated for each new validating case; the clinical diagnoses must be based upon valid and generally applicable concepts and one must be assured that the diagnostic judgments are not determined on a knowledge of the item content of the scale to be validated. When all the work of derivation and validation of a scale is centered in one laboratory the dangers in establishing validity are avoided only with difficulty. The following scales are presented with a full realization that their final validity and general usefulness will depend upon the experience of others, though we have endeavored to avoid obvious pitfalls.

The problems to be solved by the scales of the MMPI are frankly those of detecting and evaluating typical and commonly recognized forms of major psychological abnormality. The terminology and classification system are largely drawn from ordinary psychiatric practice. Where there are correlations between clinical syndromes, the scales tend to show correlation; where the clinically recognized diagnosis is impure the scales will tend to be impure. These are usually, therefore, not statistically pure scales. They often contain deliberately diverse types of items. One additional point should be especially stressed. Every item finally chosen differentiates between criterion and normal groups and that is the reason for acceptance or rejection of the items. They are not selected for their content or theoretical import. Frequently the authors can see no possible rationale to an item in a given scale; it is nevertheless accepted if it appears to differentiate. Some scales have been selected and put into experimental use in our clinic before the items were studied for content. Occasionally, items that differentiate have been rejected to eliminate some undesirable statistical trend. Thus items from the depression scale tend naturally to recur in most other scales and must be omitted in part at least if the intercorrelation is not to be undesirably high.

Specifically, the derivation of scales begins with the selection of a criterion group or groups. These persons have all been examined and diagnosed by the staff of the department of neuropsychiatry as patients in the inpatient service of the University Hospitals. The size of the criterion group varies usually between 25 and 50. For some scales it required several years to collect a sufficient number of cases to permit satisfactory scale derivation. These criterion cases are selected to be as representative as possible of the classical concept of the given syndrome. In practice, as any thoughtful clinician will agree, clear and uncomplicated cases of such common diagnostic classes as hysteria and mania are rare. There is most frequently an admixture of symptoms of other syndromes and commonly it is not at all certain that another skilled interviewer would agree as to the main diagnosis. To be psychologically abnormal in one recognized way seems to increase greatly the appearance of other psychologically abnormal states. This is easily understood in the case of depression but the connection is more obscure for other syndromes. It is to be emphatically understood that these scales are recognized to partake of the same defects that are found in the classification system now in general use. It would doubtless be more pleasing to the theoretically minded person if an approach were adopted involving a new nosology based on experimentally determined categories. All that can be said in our defense is that as a matter of practicality in the clinical setting of today the criterion groups correspond to the types that are now being generally recognized and the scales are deliberately prepared to aid in the kind of diagnostic judgments we now understand. It is to be hoped that the future will see much improvement in classification and when that time comes, new scales and possibly new techniques will need to be developed for better performance.

For each scale the responses of the criterion group or groups to each of the 550 items of the MMPI were tabulated to show the percentage frequency of occurrence of each possible answer—True, False, Cannot Say. These response frequencies were tabulated for comparison with expected frequencies as determined on normal groups.

The normal groups most commonly used for item by item contrast were composed of 339 persons selected from among general Minnesota normals and of 265 precollege cases from among high school graduates applying for admission to the university. The general sample was divided into 139 men and 200 women, tabulated separately to show sex differences. These persons were between the ages of 26 and 43 inclusive and were all married. They declared themselves to be not under a doctor's care at the time of taking the inventory and are considered normal on that single basis. The modal number of years of schooling was 8 and few had gone beyond high school. These particular persons were used because they were felt most likely to be stable and representative. The tabulation for the entering college students was based upon 151 men and 114 women. These latter tabulations were invaluable in controlling the strong tendency of responses to certain items to vary widely in accordance with age or intelligence, or both.

For all scales the percentages for the criterion groups were compared with each of the normal percentages and an initial reservoir of items was selected which included all those showing a consistent difference. Statistically no item was chosen that showed a difference less than twice its standard error and most items yielded differences greater than three times their standard errors. The steps in the selection of the final scale items were more variable and in part will be presented more completely with the descriptions of the separate scales.

To establish the validity of the various scales as they were derived, their power to differentiate test cases from normals was used as an indicator. "Test cases" is the term used in this paper to designate cases identified relatively or entirely independently of the criterion groups. For the most part, these cases were drawn from among hospitalized patients who were diagnosed routinely by the staff during the preliminary derivation of items and before any scale was made available. Where possible, test cases were taken from records and diagnoses made in an entirely different clinical setting. Naturally these latter cases are most desirable and where they were not available in suitable numbers for these scales, it is to be hoped that other workers will supply the necessary final validation. At least one such study has already been published [Leverenz, 1943].

It is important to note, nevertheless, that test cases were not so carefully selected as the criterion cases to represent either the pure syndromes or careful evaluation by the staff. This was necessary because of the small percentage of good clinical cases among all those seen. It was assumed that the best scale was the one which would most effectively separate test cases from normals and from other types of abnormals. The chief criterion for excellence of separation was the amount of overlap of the groups. It was recognized that even a perfect scale could not completely separate these test cases from normals since some of them were borderline and probably no worse than some of the "normal" group and some of them may have been incorrectly diagnosed clinically. Some also changed radically between the time of diagnostic summary and the time of testing. In considering the data presented showing the standard scores of test cases against the normal groups, it can usually be assumed that the data given represent a poorer picture than would be yielded if the cases could have been more carefully selected and the normals more adequately proved normal.

Scale 3 (Hysteria)

A scale for aid in the clinical diagnosis of hysteria was one of the earliest problems undertaken in the development of the MMPI. Almost at once, a promising preliminary scale was developed and many hours were then directed toward its improvement. Although the original scale was bettered somewhat, most of the series of experimental hysteria scales were differentially less effective than the original and it rapidly became apparent that our difficulty was due considerably to lack of definition in the clinical concept, to the concurrence of hysterical phenomena with other neurotic symptoms in the same individual, or to downright inability of the psychiatric staff to be sure of hysterical reactions in individuals who were under suspicion of developing organic disease.

The persons comprising the criterion groups were drawn mainly from the inpatient service of the psychiatric unit of the University of Minnesota Hospitals. They had each received the diagnosis psychoneurosis, hysteria, or had been especially noted as having characteristic hysterical components in the personality disturbance. In the assignment of these diagnostic terms the neuropsychiatric staff followed, as closely as possible, current clinical practice. Where cases showed a simple conversion symptom such as aphonia, an occupational cramp, or a neurologically irrational anesthetic area, the diagnosis was usually well agreed upon. In some cases there remained a doubt as to whether there was a true organic illness such as multiple sclerosis present or whether the syndrome reflected hypochondriasis or an early schizophrenic reaction.

Several tentative criterion groups were selected from these diagnosed cases. The final chief group was made up of 50 cases; the items finally selected were repeatedly identified, however, by the several criterion groups. The observed frequencies of True or False responses to all items were compared in percentages between criterion and normal groups; a basic pool of items was established.

The items could immediately be seen to belong to several categories. There was a strong group referring to somatic complaints and another negatively correlated consisting of statements tending to show that the patient considered himself unusually well socialized. Examples of the somatic items were complaints of headache, spells of dizziness, and tremor of the hands. The social items were well illustrated by his saying False to such items as "I frequently have to fight against showing that I am bashful," "I get mad easily and get over it soon," "Some people are so bossy that I feel like doing the opposite of what they request even thought I know they are right." In spite of their implication of a very socialized make-up the items include "unhappy" and "blue" admissions. These latter items are to be contrasted with those in which the patient says that he is not repressed or shy with others. Besides the foregoing item types there were certain others that persistently appeared in the statistical studies but for which we have no adequate interpretation. It was at once apparent that the correlation of any final scale adopted would be rather high with that previously developed for hypochondriasis (now Hs, formerly $H-C_H$ in the *Manual*). It seemed desirable to decrease this correlation by eliminating as many of the overlapping somatic items as possible.

In order to test the results of various changes in item content of the several trial scales, test cases were accumulated. These cases were obtained from several sources. A number of newly diagnosed and therefore independent cases were available from the neuropsychiatric clinic. In addition, two separate small groups of records were obtained through the cooperation of Dr. Burton P. Grimes and Major Carleton Leverenz. The latter cases had been received in an army station hospital and diagnosed psychoneurosis, hysteria.

Elimination of the somatic items resulted in a marked drop in the number of test cases identified and introduced another disturbing difficulty; if only the nonsomatic items were used, there was a strong relation with age and education. The mean score was more than a half sigma higher for the college group than for older persons. These results forced the inclusion of some somatic items in the final scale with consequent high correlation ($r = .52$ normals and $r = .71$ clinic cases) between Hs (hypochondriasis) and Hy (hysteria). Some relation still remains between age and intelligence and the Hy score. The relation seems valid clinically.

One of the reasons why the compromise intercorrelation was forced can be illustrated by the behavior of the two scales on two test groups. The first test group was composed of 75 cases diagnosed hypochondriasis. Of these, 13 per cent received a T score of 70 or above on Hs *alone*. (T scores are standard scores with the mean of normals adjusted to 50 and the standard deviation adjusted to 10; 70 represents plus two sigma.) In all, 76 per cent received a score of 70 or above on Hs alone or on *both* Hs and Hy. Finally, only 12 per cent had such a score on Hy *alone*. Contrast these data with the results on a test group of 60 cases diagnosed hysteria. Of these, 32 per cent received a T score of 70 or above on Hy *alone*. In all, 72 per cent received a T score of 70 or above on Hy alone or on *both* Hy and Hs. Finally only 7 per cent had such a score on Hs *alone*. Study of these figures shows among other things that if Hy were discarded because of correlation with Hs in favor of using only the latter, 32 percent of the test group of hysteria cases would have been missed. Part of these data are illustrated in Table 1. This shows the standing of the two test groups against the scores of normals for Hy. Table 1

Table 1. Frequency Distributions of T Scores on Scale 3 (Hy) for Minnesota Normals and for Hy and Hs Test Cases (T Scores on Scale 1 (Hs) Are Also Shown for Comparison)

T Scores	Normals on Scale 3 (N = 690)	Hy on Scale 3 (N = 60)	Hs on Scale 3 (N = 75)	Hy on Scale 1 (N = 60)	Hs on Scale 1 (N = 75)
103-105			2		
100-102			2		
97-99		1	4		1
94-96		1	1	1	2
91-93		1	2		5
88-90		0	7	2	1
85-87	2	4	3		9
82-84	1	8	10	1	10
79-81	2	7	4	5	7
76-78	2 (1%)	9	7	4	6
73-75	3	8	6	4	10
70-72	11	4	5	6	4
67-69	14 (5%)	2	7	11	9
64-66	34 (10%)	2	1	5	4
61-63	48	2	5	2	2
58-60	63	1	3	5	1
55-57	76	2	3	3	3
52-54	89 (50%)	5	1	2	
49-51	95	3	1	3	
46-48	73			4	1
43-45	61			2	
40-42	42				
37-39	33		1		
34-36	18				
31-33	11				
28-30	4				
25-27	7				
22-24	1				

also shows the standing of the two test groups on Hs. It will be seen that Hy discriminates the hypochondriac as an abnormal as well as does Hs itself. It is possible from these results to omit scoring cases on Hs in situations where no clinical follow-up is intended.

Although the above and other statistical points contributed to the continued use of both Hy and Hs, the most important determiner was clinical experience. All clinicians who used both scales were emphatic that there was indubitably a valid clinical difference between two persons having high scores on Hs and Hy but differing in that one score was higher. There was a different prognosis and treatment indicated for the two. Where Hs was higher the physical complaints were diffuse and frequently required much less study to establish the presence of an important psychological factor in the disability. On the other hand, when Hy was dominant, the person frequently appeared normal psychologically and his physical complaints were likely to mimic closely or be accompanied by some common physical syndrome of the type now called psychosomatic. The final decision will lie with other clinics. The scale is presented with the expectation that others will check these clinical and admittedly subjective impressions.

The 60 items selected for the final Hy scale are as follows; each is followed by a T or an F to indicate the direction of the hysterical response.

1. During the past few years I have been well most of the time. (F) 2. I am in just as good physical health as most of my friends. (F) 3. I have never felt better in my life than I do now. (F) 4. I do not tire quickly. (F) 5. I have very few headaches. (F) 6. Much of the time my head seems to hurt all over. (T) 7. Often I feel as if there were a tight band about my head. (T) 8. I am troubled by attacks of nausea and vomiting. (T) 9. I seldom or never have dizzy spells. (F) 10. I have never had a fainting spell. (F) 11. My eyesight is as good as it has been for years. (F) 12. I can read a long while without tiring my eyes. (F) 13. I feel weak all over much of the time. (T) 14. I have had no difficulty in keeping my balance in walking. (F) 15. I have little or no trouble with my muscles twitching or jumping. (F)

16. I frequently notice my hand shakes when I try to do something. (T) 17. I have few or no pains. (F) 18. My hands and feet are usually warm enough. (F) 19. Once a week or oftener I feel suddenly hot all over, without apparent cause. (T) 20. I am almost never bothered by pains over the heart or in my chest. (F) 21. I hardly ever notice my heart pounding and I am seldom short of breath. (F) 22. There seems to be a lump in my throat much of the time. (T) 23. I have a good appetite. (F) 24. I wake up fresh and rested most mornings. (F) 25. My sleep is fitful and disturbed. (T) 26. I drink an unusually large amount of water every day. (F) 27. I believe that my home life is as pleasant as that of most people I know. (F) 28. I am about as able to work as I ever was. (F) 29. I have often lost out on things because I couldn't make up my mind soon enough. (F) 30. It takes a lot of argument to convince most people of the truth. (F)

31. I like to read newspaper articles on crime. (F) 32. I enjoy detective or mystery stories. (F) 33. I am worried about sex matters. (T) 34. My conduct is largely controlled by the customs of those

about me. (F) 35. I am always disgusted with the law when a criminal is freed through the arguments of a smart lawyer. (F) 36. I think a great many people exaggerate their misfortunes in order to gain the sympathy and help of others. (F) 37. I think most people would lie to get ahead. (F) 38. Most people will use somewhat unfair means to gain profit or an advantage rather than to lose it. (F) 39. I feel that it is certainly best to keep my mouth shut when I'm in trouble. (F) 40. I am likely not to speak to people until they speak to me. (F) 41. When in a group of people I have trouble thinking of the right things to talk about. (F) 42. I find it hard to make talk when I meet new people. (F) 43. It is safer to trust nobody. (F) 44. I can be friendly with people who do things which I consider wrong. (T) 45. I wish I were not so shy. (F)

46. What others think of me does not bother me. (F) 47. I frequently have to fight against showing that I am bashful. (F) 48. I resent having anyone take me in so cleverly that I have had to admit that it was one on me. (F) 49. Often I can't understand why I have been so cross and grouchy. (F) 50. My daily life is full of things that keep me interested. (F). 51. Most of the time I feel blue. (T) 52. I am happy most of the time. (F) 53. I have periods of such great restlessness that I cannot sit long in a chair. (T) 54. I get mad easily and then get over it soon. (F) 55. In walking I am very careful to step over sidewalk cracks. (F) 56. Some people are so bossy that I feel like doing the opposite of what they request, even though I know they are right. (F) 57. I commonly wonder what hidden reason another person may have for doing something nice for me. (F) 58. The sight of blood neither frightens me nor makes me sick. (F) 59. I find it hard to keep my mind on a task or job. (T) 60. At times I feel like swearing. (F)

The raw score mean and standard deviation for 475 normal females were M = 18.80, SD = 5.67, and for 345 males they were M = 16.50, SD = 5.50.

Test-retest data from 47 cases with an interval of three days to more than a year gave an r of only .57. On a group of 98 high school girls retested after about one year the value was only r = .47. (Data were provided by courtesy of Dora Capwell and the Minnesota State Bureau for Psychological Services.) These low values also need explanation. Test-retest values for other scales of a comparable number of items are above .70. Again the above clinical arguments must be resorted to. It has not been proved so by other objective tests but clinically observed exacerbations and recessions of the symptomatic picture of hysteria in a given case are marked. An apparently normal person placed under sufficient strain will surprise everyone by developing symptoms. A case with a clear paralysis may get well momentarily and be undetectable except on the basis of the history.

Assuming the validity of the scale, the implications in routine testing of the foregoing discussion are interesting. If at the time of testing, the subject is under strain and experiencing symptomatic evidence of hysterical conversions, the scale identifies him. If he is always on the borderline he is probably identified but if he is not under strain at the time he may not show the potentiality. It may be that similar thinking could explain the observed clinical fact that some cases of uncomplicated and obvious hysterical conversion are not identified by this scale or by any that could be derived in the present studies.

It is pertinent to introject that the statistical thinking derived from aptitude and achievement testing should be amended when personality tests are considered. Many traits of personality are highly variable. Otherwise there would be little meaning to psychotherapy or preventive mental hygiene. Test-retest data on MMPI scales are more a measure of trait variance than of reliability of scales. In some cases scales correlate consistently much higher with other scales than with themselves. This will need future expanded interpretation but it at once indicates that several factors of personality commonly vary together. Again common observation recognizes these variations as they are seen in those about us.

Table 2 gives the intercorrelations of Hy with all other scales as obtained from random normal and clinic records. The higher correlations with Hs and D are apparent. The rise of these for the abnormal group indicates the dynamic factor alluded to above. In clinical practice the three scales constitute a kind of "neurotic trio" that characterizes the greater number of the cases observed.

In summary, a scale called Hy for aid in identification of hysterical tendency has been derived. This scale appears to measure a rather variable trait which is closely allied to and likely includes the earlier scale of hypochondriasis. The person who is especially characterized by Hy tends to be less obviously neurotic and to have, during disabled periods, a more specific set of physical symptoms.

Table 2. Correlations of Hy with Other Scales

Group	Hs	D	Pd (rev.)	Pa	Pt	Sc	Ma
100 normal cases	.52	.55	.37	.44	.13	.28	.05
100 psychopathic hospital cases	.71	.68	.18	.40	.33	.23	−.13

Scale 9 (Hypomania)

Hypomania refers to the milder degrees of manic excitement occurring typically in the manic-depressive psychoses. The cardinal symptoms of maniacal conditions are generally stated to be an elated but unstable mood, psychomotor excitement, and flight of ideas. Hypomanic trends follow the same pattern in general, but in lesser degrees that may be at times so unobtrusive as not to impress even an expert. Thus, among normal individuals one may recall acquaintances who tend at times to be overtalkative, distractible, restless. Such a person may feel and appear to be extraordinarily well, enthusiastic, and energetic, but the use of his energy is likely to be inefficient because he tries to do too many things at a time. He is usually full of ideas which may be basically sound but they are not adequately worked out and if put into execution are seldom carried through to a satisfactory conclusion. Emotionally he may be a bit elated and too happy, he may be impatient and irascible or he may express ideas of feeling gloomy and somewhat frustrated; commonly the mood swings rapidly within minutes or hours from one to another of these attitudes, often without any corresponding environmental explanation for the shifts. Viewed over a longer period of time it is often discernible that these persons tend to have periods of definite depression rather than elation or euphoria. Along with these characteristics, there is often egocentricity, lack of appreciation of the ineptitude of his behavior in given settings, and a certain obvious disregard for others. In many respects these patients, during their episodes, are reminiscent of the asocial type of psychopathic personality. In some of the cases their abnormal characteristics disappear completely between attacks.

A group of 24 such cases was selected for scale construction. These criterion cases had all been studied intensively as inpatients in the psychopathic unit of the University Hospitals. Only manic patients of moderate or light degree were usable, since the more severe cases could not cooperate adequately in sorting the inventory items. The clinical diagnoses were either hypomania or mild acute mania, depending on the severity of the case. Care was exercised to exclude individuals with delirium, confusional states, or with excitements associated with other psychoses such as schizophrenia; the agitated depressions were likewise excluded. Naturally, routine but searching medical, neurologic, psychiatric, and psychological studies were performed on these patients as indicated. The number of cases is obviously too small to permit an analysis of the effects of factors like sex, age, marital status, and economic level, but as a criterion group they are satisfactorily uniform for scale construction purposes.

The selection of the differential items was done by essentially the same methods as for previously reported scales. The percentage frequency of significant responses was obtained on the normal and criterion groups of persons for each of the 550 separate items of the inventory. Several scales were tentatively constructed and the following 46 items were finally selected as representing the best scale for hypomania. The hypomanic response is indicated for each item according to the answer being True (T) or False (F). As in all scales each item has been assigned a value of "one" in obtaining the raw score.

1. I have had periods in which I carried on activities without knowing later what I had been doing. (T) 2. I have had attacks in which I could not control my movements or speech but in which I knew what was going on around me. (T) 3. I have had blank spells in which my activities were interrupted and I did not know what was going on around me. (T) 4. At times I have fits of laughing and crying that I cannot control. (T) 5. My speech is the same as always (not faster or slower, or slurring; no hoarseness). (F) 6. I sweat very easily even on cool days. (T) 7. A person should try to understand his dreams and be guided by or take warning from them. (T) 8. I drink an unusually large amount of water every day. (T) 9. My people treat me more like a child than a grown-up. (T) 10. Some of my family have habits that bother and annoy me very much. (T) 11. At times I have very much wanted to leave home. (T) 12. I have often had to take orders from someone who did not know as much as I did. (T) 13. It makes me impatient to have people ask my advice or otherwise interrupt me when I am working on something important. (F) 14. I have at times stood in the way of people who were trying to do something, not because it amounted to much but because of the principle of the thing. (T) 15. I believe women ought to have as much sexual freedom as men. (F)

16. I have been inspired to a program of life based on duty which I have since carefully followed. (T) 17. I feel that I have often been punished without cause. (T) 18. When I was a child I belonged to a crowd or gang that tried to stick together through thick and thin. (T) 19. I have never done anything dangerous for the thrill of it. (F) 20. I am always disgusted with the law when a criminal is freed through the arguments of a smart lawyer. (F) 21. I do not blame a person for taking advantage of someone who lays himself open to

it. (T) 22. If several people find themselves in trouble, the best thing for them to do is to agree upon a story and stick to it. (T) 23. I don't blame anyone for trying to grab everything he can get in this world. (T) 24. At times I have been so entertained by the cleverness of a crook that I have hoped he would get by with it. (T) 25. It wouldn't make me nervous if any members of my family got into trouble with the law. (T) 26. When I get bored I like to stir up some excitement. (T) 27. When in a group of people I have trouble thinking of the right things to talk about. (F) 28. I find it hard to make talk when I meet new people. (F) 29. I never worry about my looks. (T) 30. It makes me uncomfortable to put on a stunt at a party even when others are doing the same sort of things. (F)

31. It is not hard for me to ask help from my friends even though I cannot return the favor. (T) 32. Something exciting will almost always pull me out of it when I am feeling low. (T) 33. I have met problems so full of possibilities that I have been unable to make up my mind about them. (T) 34. Once a week or oftener I become very excited. (T) 35. I have periods of such great restlessness that I cannot sit long in a chair. (T) 36. At times I feel that I can make up my mind with unusually great ease. (T) 37. At times my thoughts have raced ahead faster than I could speak them. (T) 38. I sometimes keep on at a thing until others lose their patience with me. (T) 39. At times I have a strong urge to do something harmful or shocking. (T) 40. Some people are so bossy that I feel like doing the opposite of what they request, even though I know they are right. (T) 41. I am an important person. (T) 42. I know who is responsible for most of my troubles. (T) 43. I am afraid when I look down from a high place. (F) 44. I work under a great deal of tension. (T) 45. Sometimes when I am not feeling well I am cross. (F) 46. My table manners are not quite as good at home as when I am out in company. (F)

Some of these items are obviously enough applicable to the usual concept of hypomania, but others are not explicable at present. The raw score mean and standard deviation from 379 females were $M = 13.65$, $SD = 4.50$, and the values from 294 normal males were $M = 14.51$, $SD = 4.42$.

Elated, overactive, or clearly hypomanic cases rarely occur among the neuropsychiatric clinic cases available to test the Ma scale. From among nearly a thousand clinic cases only 38 valid records are available on persons marked by the staff as having some overactivity or elation. These exclude of course the criterion cases. Of the 38 only 5 were diagnosed manic-depressive psychosis. They received scores of

77, 75, 79, 66, and 61; the latter two were marked "mild hypomanic." The remainder of the whole group received various diagnoses, chiefly some form of schizophrenia. There was evidence that hypomanic cases are more difficult for the staff to diagnose than are others. As might be expected from clinical experience, there were a number of cases called psychopathic personality.

Among more than 900 available clinic cases 30 received scores of 70 or more without any clinical note especially indicating hypomania. These cases also illustrate the tendency for psychopathic personality to be indicated by the hypomanic scale since 10 of them received this diagnosis or were chronic alcoholic cases. There also appeared to be a tendency for cases with organic deterioration of the brain to receive high scores.

Table 3 shows the distributions of the scores of the patients with overactivity or elation (the criterion cases), 300 randomly selected psychiatric clinic cases, and the whole normal group. In several of the criterion patients with low scores there is a high probability that the manic state has been superseded by a normal or depressed phase at the time of testing. The summary of symptoms made by the staff was not correlated in time with the administration of the inventory so that if a patient alternated between manic and depressive or normal phases, his state at the particular time of testing cannot now be determined. The evidence for the validity of Ma is certainly not conclusive. There is, however, a tendency for persons with hypomanic symptoms to secure high scores. It is to be hoped that the scale would appear distinctly better if the criterion cases were better. This is one of several scales that will need to be checked further before final acceptance. Table 4 gives the correlations of Ma with other scales as observed on normal and clinic cases.

The correlation with D is slightly negative as might be expected. In clinical practice it is common to find both depression and manic overactivity in the same patient at the same time as is the case with some of the agitated depression patients. This was seen frequently on the test profiles; it probably explains the low correlation. As was indicated in the validity study above there is a degree of positive relationship between Ma and Pd.

The test-retest correlation for Ma is .83. This indicates that the trait has a surprising degree of stability in normal persons. No test-retest is available on clinic cases. There is probably an important constant personality factor represented together with a variable factor. The constant factor is likely to be something akin to what is commonly called optimism. Among our acquaintances, those whom we think of as optimists are rather consistently so, as are the pessimists. Apart from optimism there is also a variable tendency related to the usually episodic excitement of mania or hypomania which is seen in abnormal degree. The abnormal factor comes and goes and seems not to be strong among normal persons. Further analysis is needed to develop these theories.

Table 3. Frequency Distributions of T Scores on Scale 9 (Ma)
for Minnesota Normals and Three Psychiatric Groups

T Scores	Normals (N = 690)	General Psychiatric Cases (N = 300)	Ma Criterion Cases (N = 24)	Ma Test Cases (N = 38)
94-96	1	1		
91-93		2	1	
88-90		2		
85-87	2	1	2	1
82-84	1	1	1	
79-81	1	4	2	4
76-78	2 (1%)	1	2	1
73-75	6	4	2	4
70-72	10	5	1	3
67-69	18 (5%)	21	5	3
64-66	28 (10%)	13		3
61-63	56	19	3	10
58-60	51	14	1	2
55-57	72	29		1
52-54	97 (50%)	25	1	1
49-51	96	23	1	1
46-48	80	39		1
43-45	69	44	2	
40-42	41	25		
37-39	26	13		3
34-36	17	8		
31-33	8	3		
28-30	5	1		
25-27	2	2		
22-24	1			

Table 4. Correlations of Ma with Other Scales

Group	Hs	D	Hy	Pd	Pa	Pt	Sc
100 normal cases	.28	−.02	.05	.49	.30	.39	.56
100 psychiatric hospital cases	.08	−.21	−.13	.43	.31	.14	.36

The Ma scale has proved to be quite useful in the clinic. The juvenile delinquent, the overactive adult, and the agitated depression with ambivalent affect are not frequent but nevertheless important to recognize. The delinquent with a high Ma score and lower Pd has seemed more likely to benefit by counseling and being given another chance. The rather good prognostic indications in the adult case with an isolated Ma score are apparently in accord with general psychiatric opinion.

In spite of the small number of criterion and test cases available, a scale for hypomania is presented. It is the best that we could derive from the patients seen over a five-year period. The scale is certainly valid as to trend and it has proved distinctly useful in the clinic. The correlations with other scales are low.

At least two factors are apparently measured. These are dominant constant factors allied to ebullient optimism and a more variable factor that accounts for abnormal periods.

Scale 4 (Psychopathic Deviate) ·

It is not our intention in this paper to add to the already long list of definitions of the general clinical group "psychopathic personality." Our study has accepted, as a basic group, those persons seen by us who fit approximately into the asocial type of psychopathic personality as described by Henderson [1939], Cleckley [1941], and others.

Among these psychopathic personalities it was early recognized that there was an important subgroup, composed of individuals who were probably identifiable by a questionnaire. A preliminary study [Hathaway, 1939] indicated that these persons were partly characterized by a tendency to answer in ultra-perfect ways, as shown by such general scales as the B_1N component on the Bernreuter Personality Inventory. Subsequent to this earlier work five trial scales for the identification of these persons have been developed. The best of these is now referred to as Pd (revised).

The chief criterion group consisted of patients diagnosed psychopathic personality, asocial and amoral type, after study by the staff of the department of neuropsychiatry. They were from both sexes and were mostly within the approximate age range 17 to 22 years. None was psychotic or neurotic, and most of the hysterical and schizophrenic cases were eliminated.

The symptomatic backgrounds of the criterion cases were highly varied but can be characterized in several ways. Most often the complaint was stealing, lying, truancy, sexual promiscuity, alcoholic over-indulgence, forgery, and similar delinquencies. There were no major criminal types. Most of the behavior was poorly motivated and poorly concealed. All the criterion cases had long histories of minor delinquency. Although many of them came from broken homes or otherwise disturbed social backgrounds, there were many in whom such factors could not be seen as particularly present. Among the criterion cases there was a somewhat larger proportion of girls than of boys; this may have been due to the social selection that results from differential treatment by courts of boy and girl delinquents. This factor, if it operated, could account for the larger number of girls since many of the cases came for study on request of the courts.

Response frequencies to items as observed on the criterion group were compared with similar response frequencies observed on a sample of the married Minnesota population and the sample of college applicants. A number of items were then selected. This tentative list included many items later discarded. These items were studied further as individual items and more extensively as they fell into subgroups. Examples of such subgroups are items related to home difficulty, such as "My parents and family find more fault with me than they should," and social trouble items, such as "I played hookey from school quite often as a youngster." From numerous minor studies a preliminary scale was derived. The scale was immediately valuable in the clinic. The clinical demand was dependent in part upon the uncertainty of the average clinician when he attempts to examine a case of suspected psychopathic personality.

Two groups of test cases were available. One group was composed of patients in the psychopathic unit of the University of Minnesota Hospitals who had been studied subsequent to the selection of the criterion cases. These were not so carefully checked to eliminate doubtful cases since it was assumed that the group as a whole should show the desired tendency. For the other test group, we were fortunate in obtaining records from 100 men prisoners at a federal reformatory. These cases were collected by H. D. Remple, psychologist, with the cooperation of the medical staff and released to us for study through the courtesy of Dr. John W. Cronin and the United States Public Health Service. All the reformatory cases had received a psychiatric diagnosis of psychopathic personality. It is important to note, however, that they were not differentiated as to type and could not be expected to be uniformly of the asocial type although their presence in a reformatory would indicate that the majority might be so.

The test groups were used to try the excellence of various combinations of items (but these groups were not used to select individual items), and 50 items were eventually chosen as the final scale. These items make up the Pd (revised) scale. The following list gives the final items together with a T or an F to indicate the abnormal answer.

1. I am neither gaining nor losing weight. (F) 2. I have used alcohol excessively. (T) 3. My family does not like the work I have chosen (or the work I intend to choose for my life work). (T) 4. I believe that my home life is as pleasant as that of most people I know. (F) 5. There is very little love and companionship in my family as compared to other homes. (T) 6. I have been quite independent and free from family rule. (F) 7. My parents have often objected to the kind of people I went around with. (T) 8. My parents and family find more fault with me than they should. (T) 9. I have very few quarrels with members of my family. (F) 10. At times I have very much wanted to leave home. (T) 11. My relatives are nearly all in sympathy with me. (F) 12. I have been disappointed in love. (T) 13. I liked school. (F) 14. My sex life is satisfactory. (F) 15. I like to talk about sex. (F) 16. In school I was sometimes sent to the principal for cutting up. (T) 17. During one period when I was a youngster I engaged in petty thievery. (T)

18. My conduct is largely controlled by the customs of those about me. (F) 19. I am always disgusted with the law when a criminal is freed through the arguments of a smart lawyer. (F) 20. I am against giving money to beggars. (F) 21. I have never been in trouble with the law. (F) 22. I have never been in trouble because of my sex behavior. (F) 23. No one seems to understand me. (T) 24. When in a group of people I have trouble thinking of the right things to talk about. (F) 25. I find it hard to make talk when I meet new people. (F) 26. I do not mind being made fun of. (F) 27. I do many things which I regret afterwards (I regret things more or more often than others seem to). (T) 28. I wish I were not so shy. (F) 29. What others think of me does not bother me. (F) 30. It makes me uncomfortable to put on a stunt at a party even when others are doing the same sort of things. (F) 31. I wish I could be as happy as others seem to be. (T) 32. My daily life is full of things that keep me interested. (F) 33. Much of the time I feel as if I have done something wrong or evil. (T) 34. I have not lived the right kind of life. (T)

35. I am happy most of the time. (F) 36. I have periods in which I feel unusually cheerful without any special reason. (F) 37. Sometimes without any reason or even when things are going wrong I feel excitedly happy, "on top of the world." (F) 38. At times my thoughts

have raced ahead faster than I could speak them. (F) 39. If people had not had it in for me I would have been much more successful. (T) 40. Someone has it in for me. (T) 41. I am sure I get a raw deal from life. (T) 42. I am sure I am being talked about. (T) 43. I have had very peculiar and strange experiences. (T) 44. I know who is responsible for most of my troubles. (T) 45. I have very few fears compared to my friends. (F) 46. These days I find it hard not to give up hope of amounting to something. (T) 47. My hardest battles are with myself. (T) 48. I am easily downed in an argument. (F) 49. I find it hard to keep my mind on a task or job. (T) 50. My way of doing things is apt to be misunderstood by others. (T)

Inspection of the final scale items will show them to fall naturally into several general groupings. For one, social maladjustment items are prominent. Another group is made up of items related to depression and the absence of strongly pleasant experiences. There are also a number of items suggesting paranoid trends. All these subgroupings were found to contribute to validity. The composite scale weights of the groups as expressed in the number and occurrence frequencies of their items are apparently nearly optimal in the final scale. It was difficult to account for or predict variations in validity that were observed among the earlier scales; this indicates that the diagnosis is based upon a complex of factors rather than upon any one. Also, unlike the scale for psychasthenia, the items do not show a strong tendency to be highly intercorrelated. The final scale is, therefore, certainly not pure but deliberately mixed in factor content to yield greater clinical usefulness.

Table 5 shows the standing on the final scale of 294 males and 397 females of the general norm group. As is common with frequency curves from personality traits having one end recognized as abnormal, there is a slight negative skewness of the curve. About 4.6 per cent of these normal cases fall above 70 (two sigma above the mean). In these normative data there is no significant mean score change with increasing age, but it is probably significant that 56 per cent of the cases with standard scores above 70 are from the 16 to 25 age range; these young people make up only 33 per cent of the total norm group. The raw score sex difference amounts to 0.45 of a point between means and 0.23 between standard deviations. These differences are probably insignificant but a correction in standard score is made for sex since the observed values are still the most likely correct. The means and standard deviations for raw scores are M = 13.44, SD = 4.23, for 397 females and M = 12.99, SD = 4.00, for 294 males.

Table 5 also shows the standard score standings of the two groups of test cases. There are 78 cases diagnosed psychopathic personality from the psychopathic unit and 100 prisoners from the reformatory. Again it must be emphasized that the scale was expected to identify only the asocial fraction of these miscellaneous cases. The separation of the prison group is better than that of the clinic group, chiefly because of the selective factor determining a greater frequency of the asocial type among the prisoners. Among the prisoners 59 per cent obtained scores at or above 70 and among the clinic cases 45 per cent of the scores were above that level. The mean raw scores and the standard deviations are M = 22.61, SD = 4.43, for prisoners and M = 21.44, SD = 6.23, for clinic cases.

Table 5. Frequency Distributions of T Scores on Scale 4 (Pd) for Minnesota Normals, Federal Reformatory Inmates, and Pd Clinic Test Cases

T Scores	Normals (N = 690)	Federal Reformatory Cases (N = 100)	Pd Clinic Test Cases (N = 78)
103-105			1
101-102			1
97-99			
94-96			4
91-93		7	5
88-90			1
85-87	1	5	2
82-84	1	6	2
79-81	2	4	4
76-78	3 (1%)	13	3
73-75	13	15	8
70-72	15 (5%)	9	4
67-69	16	7	4
64-66	18 (10%)	7	8
61-63	35	8	8
58-60	47	11	7
55-57	58	1	1
52-54	64	6	3
49-51	72 (50%)		5
46-48	87	1	3
43-45	81		
40-42	65		3
37-39	49		
34-36	34		1
31-33	18		
28-30	8		
25-27	2		
22-24	1		

The validity of the scale appears still better if the whole profile of each test case is inspected. The profile is made up of all scores at present obtained from the MMPI. When the other personality components are graphically presented in the same standard scores, a number of the test cases scoring below 70 on the present scale show up as plainly outstanding. Thus, it is common for scores on other scales to be uniformly from one-quarter to one-half standard deviation distance below the mean, leaving the Pd score clearly dominant. It is possible that this effect, which appears to be a general reduction in the measured abnormality, is produced by overly scrupulous, conscious avoidance of any betrayal by abnormal answers on the part of the subject. More likely these persons simply feel themselves to be overly perfect. Evidence for the latter suggestion lies in the fact that they seem clinically to be characterized by great self-esteem and self-interest.

Inspection of the items in the scale shows that there is a group of items on which the significant answer shows this over-perfect tendency. Consider, for example, the item "I find it hard to talk when I meet new people." Most of the normal group admit such failings but the psychopath has no such reaction. It is interesting that these persons who might be most likely to attempt consciously to hide their character are partly identifiable by the attempt itself. It is, however, unlikely that such reactions are conscious; they are more likely submerged from the conscious level by the insightless egocentricity.

The test-retest correlation obtained for the scale is 0.71; this was obtained on a normal sample of 47 cases repeated with an interval of a few days to more than a year. The correlations with other scales commonly used on the MMPI are given in Table 6. It is interesting that, contrary to what is true with other MMPI scales, the correlations are smaller as obtained from the psychopathic unit cases.

The random cases from the psychopathic unit included a few psychopathic personality diagnoses; they were predominantly neurotic and schizophrenic. Although the increase is slight, the correlations with paranoia and mania are somewhat higher than with other scales. This is in accord with clinical experience. The hypomanic patient of-

Table 6. Correlations of Pd (revised) with Other Scales

Group	Hs	D	Hy	Pa	Pt	Sc	Ma
100 normal cases	.42	.29	.37	.38	.48	.60	.49
100 psychopathic unit cases	.37	.14	.18	.40	.23	.31	.43

ten gets into trouble during one of his attacks in ways that are confusingly similar to the behavior of the psychopathic personality. Similarly, the case with a psychopathic personality is frequently somewhat paranoid. Being basically confident of his abilities, he naturally often feels persecuted by society when he is punished for behavior he thinks he will be able to control in the future.

The introductory sentence to the present section of this paper stated that we did not wish to add to the list of definitive statements about psychopathic personality. Yet it seems apparent from the foregoing facts that an appreciable percentage of clinically recognized cases are identified on the Pd (revised) scale. Generally speaking, these persons are those diagnostically classified in most clinics as psychopathic personality, asocial type. Nevertheless, to avoid confusion we have named the scale psychopathic deviate (Pd). The term implies a variation in the direction of psychopathy. The scale itself is a definitive device and the following descriptive material is merely an attempt to state some general facts about cases selected by the scale.

Most prominently the typical case has a shallow emotional life. The clinician may work very hard and become intensely interested in the patient but fail to receive in return more than a transitory and superficial loyalty. Sexual and other appetitive drives are not deeply effective in the patient's life. For example, although there may be promiscuity or actual prostitution, the female is frequently frigid and engages in sexual acts primarily as a means to social entertainment. Females are often masculine in interests. The psychopathic deviate seems to the observer to seek more and more dangerous or embarrassing experiences in the attempt to feel emotion like that of the normal. They sometimes commit suicide or more often nearly do so. This is again from shallow emotional sources rather than deep depression or normal recognition of failure.

As they become older it is common for many of these cases to avoid more successfully real conflict with society. The lying, alcoholism, sexual promiscuity, or other behavior may persist; but it is somewhat more restrained and also society seems to feel less outraged. While these persons can usually verbalize as to the consequences of their behavior, there is often a failure to appreciate its significance for them in terms of their long-time social adjustment. Depression, when present, is usually expressed as fear of immediate punishment and loss of liberty rather than any reaction in guilt, regret, or the like. The tendency to blame others or to excuse themselves for their predicament is common. They claim in self-extenuation that they were misled by others who took advantage of their innocence, that the family discipline had been too severe so they rebelled, or some similar explanation.

In clinical practice, the Pd scale has been most valuable. So many of the cases with high scores are recidivists in delinquency that it is helpful to be put on guard. If the person is 16 to 19 years of age and has a score twenty T points above most other scores on the profile, there is little likelihood that the person can stay out of trouble if not under rigid discipline. Older persons, however, more often avoid open breaks. In therapy, young persons with a high Pd should not be pushed toward maximal scholastic or vocational levels even when they have the capacities for training.

One special advantage in the prediction afforded by the scale is that the type identified is so often characterized by a relatively appealing personality together with good intelligence and background. These factors are misleading to clinicians so that a halo effect operates toward a too lenient view of the clinical problem. The overly optimistic treatment is not only wasteful of social resources but also permits the fixation of undesirable habits in the patient; furthermore, the patient is permitted to continue until a more serious offense requires penal action.

In summary, a final scale has been developed which will identify half or somewhat more of the cases routinely classed psychopathic personality clinically. The cases best identified are those with strong asocial trends. The scale is called psychopathic deviate to indicate that it is not expected to differentiate all the cases of psychopathic personality. The scale appears to have fair reliability and intercorrelations with other scales are low.

It is in the clinic, however, that the value of the scale is best illustrated. The clinician usually finds himself at a loss in the diagnostic evaluation of the psychopathic personality, and the scale has been found to be particularly useful in this regard.

Scales 5 (Masculinity-Femininity), 6 (Paranoia), and 8 (Schizophrenia)

S. R. Hathaway

Material relative to the derivation and validity of three MMPI scales, Mf, Pa, and Sc, has not hitherto been published. These three scales were characterized as preliminary in the earlier *Manual* [Hathaway and McKinley, 1943]. The intent was to indicate that revised scales together with the appropriate derivational and validity data would later be prepared and published in final form.

Some principles of derivation of MMPI scales have also not been published. It is impossible to describe fully the steps in selection of the MMPI scale items. As emphasized in earlier publications, all the items were empirically selected by contrast of criterion groups with other clinical groups and with various normal groups. All scales were tested by one or more cross-validation samples. Frequency distributions of the cross-validation samples were constructed to show the separation of the criterion abnormal type from normals, from patients who were physically ill (but not obviously with mental symptoms), and finally from miscellaneous psychiatric cases having diagnoses other than the one being studied. This multiple checking of items and scales is probably the most characteristic general procedure relative to the derivation. Beyond this, specific steps in scale development were so varied that they cannot be completely described.

As a first step, the criterion group item frequencies were compared with frequencies on normals and miscellaneous psychiatric patients. In this initial comparison, items that showed consistent and statistically reliable response differentiation of the criterion were chosen as

65

a basic pool from which the scale would later be selected. These items were then followed in successive tabulations showing the frequencies of significant answers as observed in other samplings by diagnosis. The items were also checked to make certain that college students did not behave in some way that might detract from the validity of the item.

An important point is that a great many good basic pool items were eliminated from a final scale because they showed overlap in validity with some other clinical syndrome. Clinical depression samples, for example, show significant answers for numerous items that discriminate schizophrenia. In order to hold down the intercorrelation of scales, groups of items that seemed to be contributing equally to two scales were eliminated from both scales or used in only one. In some cases, as with scales Pt and Sc, an arbitrary decision had to be made about the proper amount of overlap. These scales correlate and the syndromes as observed in clinical cases also overlap. It would be undesirable to eliminate this correlation in measurement of the syndromes. The correlation was deliberately built in by leaving in each scale certain items that had been observed to be valid for the other syndrome. No statistical or theoretical preciseness was available to determine the optimal size of the intercorrelations.

These intercorrelations are the basis for the pattern effects that are thought to be so characteristic of MMPI profiles. Certain scales are expected to vary together; when they do not, unfamiliar configurations occur that indicate less routine interpretation than usual. Fortunately, these intercorrelations decrease the number of different profiles one is likely to encounter; they increase the frequency of some profiles. If the ten regular MMPI scales were more independent, experience with profiles would be so limited that one could not expect to become proficient on the basis of having seen a number of a given kind. Ten variables with low intercorrelations would so rarely provide two similar profiles that no practical number of cases would provide experience with populous classes of profile.

If the ten variables of the MMPI were independent, there would be 90 different but equally probable variations of the two highest coded points on profiles. If each variable showed a 5 per cent frequency greater than 70 T score, the rate of occurrence of each of these moderately deviant profile types would be one in 18,000. It could be that deviant personality is recognizably divisible into 18,000 different classes, but if so the use of a statistical method of analysis or prediction would require electronic memory systems. Of course if one had as few as six independent variables, then the number of different patterns of the two highest points would be only 30. It would not be hard to remember these, but deviant ones would still be infrequent. In passing, it seems unlikely that every profile type would be about equally probable as is implied in the zero covariance condition.

The above argument is based upon the assumption that clinically significant variables are really patterned [Meehl, 1954], that they cannot be combined in a simple manner to arrive at useful evaluation of the personality. Among other things, this assumption means that one could not go across the profile and add appropriate positive adjectives for the position of each scale to end up with a meaningful description. On the contrary, it is assumed that a person with greatest deviation on variable one is definitely different even in the expression of the implied correlates of variable one by the fact that no other variable is so deviant. The proper descriptive adjectives [Black, 1953] are peculiar to the profile, not to the unique deviant value of variable one.

Another procedure that contributed an arbitrary element to the derivation of scales concerned the treatment of highly intercorrelated item groups. When several items were intercorrelated so that the answer to one of them was determinative of answers to the others, part or all of the group were accepted or rejected according to the same principles that governed the acceptance or rejection of one item; the group would be considered as an unusually valid item and much thought often went into decisions about it because of the extra scale variance involved. If it should happen that four items were perfectly correlated, then their contribution to scale variance would be four times that of a single item with comparable individual variance. If such multiple-item clusters are clearly and broadly valid, they are very important to a scale. Often, however, they are valid for only a single symptom that, though itself valid, would not be broad enough. For example, several items might relate to having delusions of reference. Such delusions are highly valid as evidence of paranoid mentation but such ideas are not present in the majority of paranoid patients. Construction of a scale would require consideration of the effect of four such items on both the mean and the variance since they might overemphasize this one symptom. In this one way manifest item content did enter at times into decisions about item choice for scales.

Perhaps it should again be stated that except for items with high covariance, derivation of the items for a scale did not appreciably depend upon the manifest content of the item. The break from the face validity approach to item selection for a scale was the result of a conscious decision. No item was ever eliminated from a scale because its manifest content seemed to have no relation to the syndrome in question; conversely no item was arbitrarily accepted if the validating evidence for the item was not strong.

This method of scale derivation is not possible unless one has a considerable supply of clinical cases and adequate staff study of them to assure that the validity criterion will represent a broadly based opinion. It is unlikely that all the syndromes of the MMPI scales will survive the next comparable study. Several are probably basic; of these, a likely example is Pd. But within the relatively large clinical staff where considerable democracy prevailed in the assessment of the people who made up the criterion groups, there may have been a greater than usual degree of coherence in the classifications. MMPI scales were *ad hoc*. Clinical practice as it occurred in the psychiatric unit indicated the variables that were needed for routine work and for statistical accounting. The patients were short-time residents who stayed an average of twenty days, and they differed through the whole range of severity and diagnosis. Mostly the ones used for scale derivations were not psychotic and many of them were not even very ill. More often than not they were in a mental hospital for the first time. Few were private cases and the majority had less than a high school education. A few were sent in by courts for study as an aid in evaluation of the significance of their unlawful acts.

Growing recognition of the complexity of the validity issue in personality scale derivation has made it hard to say when a scale is satisfactory. We do not yet know causes of mental disorders and prognosis or specific treatments do not provide a convincing basis for classification. No real evidence has established the usefulness of the theory that factor purity is either characteristic of personality or the choice basis for a classificatory system. We are handicapped by indecision. It has not been established whether criteria should be based upon overt social behavior, upon the self-evaluation, or upon subtle and intrinsic aspects of mentation. Every clinician knows that social and self-evaluations are not perfectly correlated. Where a person considers himself to be maladjusted and inferior and his associates consider him to be reasonably like others, one scale value cannot properly represent the two aspects.

It could be that an MMPI scale like Sc is more valid than we have yet discovered. Consider an analogous illustration from physical medicine. When a test specific to a disorder is discovered, it is often found that there are many persons who are positive on the test but negative on clinical symptomatology. The typhoid bacillus is closely related to the severe clinical syndrome of typhoid fever. Suppose that the bacillus had been discovered long before the typhoid fever patient could be differentially separated from patients with similar sicknesses. A criterion group of sick persons (some of whom actually had another disease) would have shown a higher than average percentage with the bacillus but not all would have had it. In our test terminology these would be called false negatives. Also, since many persons carry the bacillus without developing symptoms, the well group of controls would show false positives.

Except for patients who try for high scores with an ulterior purpose, patients who obtain a high T score on a scale are *ipso facto* validly like the group from which the scale was derived. This indisputable statistical validity should be more widely recognized and studied by clinicians. A case record is called a false positive if it is deviant on a scale that derived its validity from persons to whom the given case does not seem sufficiently similar. False positives on a scale are false only in the first instance. They initially appear so from the observation that certain expected correlates of the scale score are not clearly present in the observed behavior. There is a possibility that we do not recognize the pertinent core of the syndrome.

The symptoms of many deviant persons do not happen to get them into trouble. There is no necessity for assuming a high correlation between mental aberration and behavior judged to be socially undesirable. Some clinicians seem to be unaware of this fact and without qualification they classify a person as normal or average in pattern of personality simply because he is undistinguished in his social behavior. But it would be equally fallacious to assume that all high-scoring persons on some MMPI scale are usefully categorized by the fact.

Since criteria are not closely intercorrelated, the validity problem depends upon the use to which a scale is to be put. For some purposes scale deviation alone may be useful; such a situation is simplest but is rare. The variables represented by MMPI scales or by any other substitute for the validating behavior always fall below perfect relationship. This is clearly illustrated in the more mature context of the measurement of intelligence. No intelligence test shows a perfect correlation with any behavior that it is expected to predict. With some applications a close correlation is expected; with others only a loose relationship. Too high a validity for one use may prejudice the validity for another. MMPI scales can be related in varying degree to various criteria. Probably the most common criterion in clinical work relates them to social adjustment as seen by the clinician or the family. But it may be just as common and useful to relate them to the patient's self-evaluation. It is a little surprising that they are at all valid when one considers the dissimilarity between answering test items and the complexity of social and personal adjustment. What apparently preserves the relationship is the power of the self-concept expressed in the "I am" statements of the items that determines a degree of identity between the manifest or latent content of these and social behavior.

Sooner or later psychometric devices must be perfected either against criteria such as specific cause, specific treatment, or specific course of disease, or, less desirably, they must be perfected by the boot-straps [Cronbach and Meehl, 1955] effect. Intelligence scales began by reference to inferior criteria but, by the boot-straps effect, lifted themselves into the criterion position. The original criteria are now evaluated against the scales. The boot-straps effect depends upon the discovery of a number of correlates of a personality scale so that it comes to have a broad construct validity. A possible example may be found in the Pd scale. This is related to success in practice teaching [Gough and Pemberton, 1952], to social responsibility [Gough, McClosky, and Meehl, 1952], to fear of mental patients [Hovey, 1953], and to delinquency [Hathaway and Monachesi, 1953] among already known correlates discovered from various approaches.

The foregoing discussion is intended as a rationale for the continued use of scales that do not show high validity against the clinical diagnosis criterion. If a scale accounts for some useful variance in a number of criterion situations, one may excuse its failure to account for more variance of any particular criterion. It is recognized that this is a dangerous doctrine. Obviously the validities for critical applications must be reasonably better than those available by other scales. In addition, the useful validity must be evaluated against the economic use of clinician man-hours.

Scale 8 (Sc)

No scale received more attention in the attempt to identify a useful variable than was the case with the Sc scale. The folders of data on the derivation of this scale contain at least two basic stocks of items from which at least four basic scales were derived and from which more than twelve differential scales were attempted. The basic scales and the stock items were all derived from two partly overlapping groups of 50 patients who had been diagnosed schizophrenic. These cases were of assorted diagnostic subtypes and included about 60 per cent females and 40 per cent males. The final Sc scale was derived from a stock group of 152 items all of which showed statistically reliable differences for the schizophrenia criterion cases but many of which also differentiated depression cases, hypochondria cases, and other special groups.

From the very first it was found that differential cuts on cross-validation groups could not be pushed above a positive 50 to 60 per cent of the diagnosed cases identifiable with an apparently false positive rate of 10 or 15 per cent out of general normal cases. Because the early Sc scales did not work as well as had been the case for other MMPI scales, efforts were made to improve them by breaking down the criterion into component parts. These parts were at first the subclassifications of schizophrenia: catatonic, paranoid, simple, and hebephrenic. Separate scales were derived for each of these groups. These more limited scales were tested both as basic scales and as secondary scales to modify the score on general Sc scales. None of these systems was successful in raising the cross-validation ratio of true to false positive cases. More than twelve of these subscales were tried out in the various combinations.

Another seemingly fruitful line was the attempt to derive a subscale from patient records that were false negatives among the original criterion groups. These test misses were used as a criterion to develop "miss" scales. Several of these miss scales were checked both as independent scales and in combination with basic scales. Again no manipulation could effect much change in the basic percentage of cross-validation cases that were identified.

As a result of all these efforts, which consumed hundreds of hours of clerical work, the published scale was the best among the basic Sc scales. This final scale was originally Sc 4, the fourth basic scale derived, and it was only slightly better than were the ones that were rejected. As time passed, no appreciable change in the published scale seemed justified and the matter was at a standstill until the work on the K scale was undertaken.

The K scale, an outgrowth of Meehl's work on the derivation of a scale for a normal control component in behavior, finally provided a device by which the discrimination of the Sc scale could be sharpened. Data given in the K article [McKinley, Hathaway, and Meehl, 1948 (see I, 10)] illustrate the status before and after development of the K correction. The 91 cross-validation cases that were used for these tables were assorted psychiatric cases diagnosed schizophrenic but many of these would not have been suitable for criterion cases because of one or another doubtful aspect of the clinical syndrome. They should not therefore be expected to be as highly differentiated by any scale as would more carefully selected examples of the diagnostic category. Only 31 per cent of these cases obtained a T score on Sc of 70 or greater. On the original norm distribution this score was reached or exceeded by 4.5 per cent of the normals. The K correction raised the percentage of cross-validation cases reaching or exceeding T score 70 to 59 and the corresponding percentage of normals dropped to 2 per cent. With these cases the K correction effected a marked improvement in the discriminative ability of the original scale. Even with the correction, a considerable number of the cross-validation cases managed to stay below the T score 61.

Various investigators have found the clinical diagnosis of schizophrenia to be reproduced independently on the same patients by different clinicians in only 30 to 60 per cent of the cases. These figures are certainly not too low if less psychotic patients are used for the experiment. The MMPI Sc scale suggests, as do similar scales on other inventories, about the same degree of reproduction of the diagnosis in such clinical groups. There is no accepted way to assert that either the scale or the diagnosis is wrong. In the long run the decision should rest upon the useful correlates of test and diagnosis. The better diagnostic device will provide the more useful correlates with such items as therapeutic response and prognosis.

Scale 8 correlates highly with scale 7. This correlation has been variously given from .68 [Hathaway and Monachesi, 1953] to .84 [Cottle, 1949, 1953]. The two syndromes are clinically similar but as the *Atlas* diagnostic tables illustrate, a definite discrimination is possible [Hathaway and Meehl, 1951]. *Atlas* cases with a diagnosis of psychasthenia show a rate of 57 per cent for scale 7 occurring highest or second highest in code position; for scale 8 the corresponding rate is only 32 per cent. By contrast, the cases diagnosed schizophrenic have scale 7 high or second high 17 per cent of the time and scale 8 in those positions 48 per cent of the time.

Relative to the same point, follow-up data from ninth-grade public school MMPI records indicate reliable differences in behavior between boys with high 7 and those with high 8 codes. The high 8 boys have a larger delinquency rate and their delinquent acts tend to be more severe. In particular, truancy, running away from home, and violation of probation show the relatively largest differences. High 8 boys also get into trouble at an earlier age than is true of the high 7 boys.

Scale 6 (Pa)

Scale 6 was derived from patient samples judged to have paranoid symptoms. Diagnostically these were rarely called paranoia. The most common diagnoses were paranoid state, paranoid condition, and paranoid schizophrenia. Symptomatically they tended to have ideas of reference, to feel that they were persecuted by individuals or groups, and to have grandiose self-concepts. Milder symptoms included suspiciousness, an excess of interpersonal sensitivity, and an underlying rigidity of opinions and attitudes.

As with other scales, several different scales were derived and tested by cross-validation. This cross-validation was always disappointing and the published scale was considered weak although it was the best that could be developed. One factor that seemed to justify at least temporary use of the scale was that there were few false positives. When a person had a high score, he tended to be diagnosed as paranoid or at least he was felt to be sensitive and rigid in personal relationships.

As was at first true with scale 8, the hope that the temporary scale 6 would be bettered was not rewarded. Even the K variable failed to sharpen the differentiation. It was felt that the K correction did not help because more than 20 per cent of the scale 6 items were already subtle in character [McKinley, Hathaway, and Meehl, 1948 (see I, 10)].

Scales 6 and 8 were in progress of derivation at the same time and attempts were made to derive a special scale for the patients diagnosed paranoid schizophrenic. No single scale operated as well to distinguish these patients as did the combination of 8 and 6.

Scale 5 (Mf)

The difficulty in deriving a better Mf scale centered in the problem of a criterion by which the validity could be established. The published scale was derived by contrasting item frequencies from a small group of 13 homosexual invert males with those of average males and also by contrasting a group of more feminine males as determined from the Terman and Miles I Scale [1936] with average males. A final less important criterion was the comparison of male and female frequencies. At first it seemed reasonable to collect relatively large samples of homosexual invert males and of homosexual females for more complete criterion evidence. The plan went awry because it became apparent that the homosexual samples were too heterogeneous. As we worked with the homosexual males and females, we came to feel that the groups were much more obviously divisible into several subtypes than was true for other clinical categories. For example, there is a pseudo-homosexual type where neurotic features related to inferiority seem to be dominant; there is a psychopathic variety with a strong tendency to high scores on Pd; and there is an invert group in which a constitutional factor seems probable. These and possibly other subgroups seem definite enough so that clinical study could separate them and much better and purer Mf scales might be derived. Because the task was dependent upon having a comparatively large number of cases of each type and also because of the press of other research, this project was never finished. In the meantime, the Mf scale has become widely used and although it was omitted from much of our experimental work, it contributes considerably to routine clinical interpretations.

One attempt was made to improve the Mf scale. A number of records from women whose personal problems included homosexuality as one issue were used as a criterion group. A scale designated Fm was derived by a process similar to that used for Mf. The new scale correlated .78 to .95 with Mf on a number of samples. This correlation and the fact that cross-validation did not particularly favor the new scale, even for identification of homosexual females, indicated its abandoment.

Discussion

By this time a number of papers on the validity of these scales have been published by others. Evidence is varied, some positive and some negative. It is not helpful merely to list the relative frequency of positive and negative findings. Some of the designs and hypotheses were so ill-conceived as to be inappropriate for evidence. The *Atlas* [Hathaway and Meehl, 1951] was intended as a primary source on the validity of scales 6 and 8 as well as the other clinical scales. Some evidence can also be found relative to scale 5. Those who must interpret profiles that show a high 6 or 8 should read the *Atlas* cases with these codes. If the reader finds coherence among such case records, then this is the best clinical preparation and evidence of validity.

In addition to the *Atlas*, Cottle's review [1953] suggests other sources. The bibliography and reviews in the present volume are useful as source material on the application of all MMPI scales for various purposes. The above brief discussion of the problem of validity should make it clear that no one validity has wide meaning. Every different application invokes a different validity concept.

The reliability of the three scales has been best estimated by Rosen [1953]. He obtained test-retest data on 40 male VA hospital cases tested within a short interval. These reliabilities were scale 5 (Mf) .64; scale 6 (Pa) .75; and scale 8 (Sc) .86. Cottle [1950], using a group with smaller scale 6 and scale 8 variance (68 male and 32 female college students), got these values: scale 5, .91; scale 6, .56; and scale 8, .86. Holzberg and Alessi [1949] got correlations of .76 for scale 5, .78 for scale 6, and .89 for scale 8 on psychotic state hospital patients. It is always difficult to evaluate any of the usual reliability data on personality measures that are likely to show valid time-related variance in the individual subjects. All the MMPI scales are sensitive to therapeutic and other effects. Since both the motivation and the life situation of the subjects are likely to change almost momentarily, it is always possible that an observed change in score is valid variance instead of error variance.

Scale 0 (Social Introversion)

L. E. Drake

The Minnesota T-S-E Inventory [Evans and McConnell, 1941] has been used as a part of the standard battery of tests administered to students in the guidance program at the University of Wisconsin for over a year. The inventory has yielded data that have been useful in counseling students. Since, however, the Minnesota Multiphasic Personality Inventory [Hathaway and McKinley, 1940 (see I, 1)] is also a part of the standard battery and since many items of the latter resemble items in the former, it was thought desirable to try to devise keys to score the MMPI to yield data now obtained by means of the T-S-E Inventory. This report is limited to results obtained for a social I. E. scale. Scales for thinking and emotional introversion-extroversion are not yet ready for publication.

Procedure

An item analysis of the MMPI was made by contrasting the percentage responses of two groups of students to the items. One group consisted of 50 students who obtained centile ranks of 65 and above on the T-S-E Inventory when scored for social introversion-extroversion. The second group consisted of 50 students who obtained centile ranks below 35 on the T-S-E Inventory. The students were all females because of the small male population in the university, but the scale

76

was validated with a male population as will be shown later. There was no other factor used in the selection of cases except that three cases were not included because the L scores on the MMPI were quite high.

Items were selected for the key which showed a difference between the percentage responses of the upper and lower groups of at least twice the standard error of the difference. Some significant items, however, were eliminated because there was an extremely high or extremely low frequency of response for both upper and lower groups.

After the item selection had been completed a new group of MMPI record sheets were scored with the obtained key for purposes of validation. These record sheets contained the responses of a group of female students who cleared through the testing office after the group of students who provided the data for the item analyses. The scores obtained with the new key were next correlated with the social I. E. scores obtained on the T-S-E Inventory. The key was then used for scoring all available record sheets for male students, providing there were T-S-E scores also available, and these scores were correlated with the T-S-E scores.

Finally, norms were established by scoring all available MMPI record sheets. The norms are reported in terms of T scores obtained in the customary way, namely:

$$T = 50 + \frac{10 \ (X_i - M)}{SD}$$

where X_i is the raw score, M the mean, and SD the standard deviation of the raw scores for the normative group.

Results

The items for this key are listed in Table 1 according to the way they are designated on the MMPI record sheets. The raw score is obtained by counting one point for every cell on the record sheet having an X corresponding to the key and one point for every cell which is blank corresponding to a 0 on the key. The cells containing question marks are not counted [McKinley and Hathaway, 1940 (see I, 2)].

Twenty-eight of the items on this key have not been used on any keys reported by Hathaway and McKinley.

Record sheets for 87 female students were then scored with this key and the scores were correlated with the social I. E. scores on the T-S-E. The resulting coefficient of correlation was —.72. The coefficient was negative because the key for the MMPI was constructed so that a high score would indicate introversion whereas on the T-S-E a low score indicates introversion.

Record sheets for 81 men students were likewise scored and the scores correlated with social I. E. scores on the T-S-E. The resulting

Table 1. Scoring Key for Social I. E.

Item No.	Scoring Direction	Item No.	Scoring Direction	Item No.	Scoring Direction	Item No.	Scoring Direction	Item No.	Scoring Direction
A36. . . .X		D50. . . .X		E36. . . .X		F8. X		H18. . . .0	
A37. . . .X		D53. . . .X		E38. . . .X		F9. X		H51. . . .X	
A38. . . .X		D54. . . .X		E43. . . .X		F30. 0		H52. . . .X	
B6. X		E18. . . .X		E44. . . .X		F31. . . .X		I21. . . .0	
B22. . . .X		E23. . . .X		E46. . . .X		F34. . . .X		I25 X	
C20. . . .X		E26. . . .X		E47. . . .X		F36. . . .X		I26 X	
C25 X		E27. . . .X		E49. . . .X		F41. . . .X		I27 X	
C48. 0		E28. . . .X		E52. . . .X		F45. . . .X		I28 X	
C55 X		E29. . . .X		E55 X		G18. . . .X		I29 X	
D2 0		E30. . . .X		F2. X		G24. 0		I38 X	
D34. 0		E32. . . .X		F3. X		G35. . . .X		I41 X	
D35. 0		E33. . . .X		F4. X		G42. 0		J24 0	
D37. 0		E34. . . .X		F5. X		H2 X		J32 0	
D45. 0		E35. . . .X		F6. X		H12. 0		J33 X	

Table 2. The T Scores for the Social I. E. Scale

Raw Score	T Score	Raw Score	T Score	Raw Score	T Score	Raw Score	T Score
70. . . . 97		52. 79		34. 61		16. 41	
69. . . . 96		51. 78		33. 60		15. 40	
68. . . . 95		50. 77		32. 58		14. 39	
67. . . . 94		49. 76		31. 56		13. 38	
66. . . . 93		48. 75		30. 55		12. 37	
65. . . . 92		47. 74		29. 54		11. 36	
64. . . . 91		46. 73		28. 53		10. 35	
63. . . . 90		45. 72		27. 52		9. 34	
62. . . . 89		44. 71		26. 51		8. 33	
61. . . . 88		43. 70		25. 50		7. 32	
60. . . . 87		42. 69		24. 49		6. 30	
59. . . . 86		41. 68		23. 48		5. 29	
58. . . . 85		40. 67		22. 47		4. 28	
57. . . . 84		39. 66		21. 46		3. 27	
56. . . . 83		38. 65		20. 45		2. 26	
55. . . . 82		37. 64		19. 44		1. 25	
54. . . . 81		36. 63		18. 43			
53. . . . 80		35. 62		17. 42			

coefficient was −.71. Hence the key was used for both male and female students in obtaining norms.

Table 2 gives the T scores for this scale based upon records for 350 female students and 193 male students. Separate norms were computed for males and females, but they were so similar, differing by only 2 from raw score 0 to 6 and being identical for most of the range, that the tables were combined for both sexes.

Summary

1. Using the social I. E. scores on the Minnesota T-S-E Inventory for a group of female students as a criterion, an item analysis of the MMPI was made.

2. The derived key appears to have equally good validity for both male and female students.

3. An attempt is being made to derive thinking and emotional I.E. scales in a similar way.

Further Validation of Scale 0 (Si)

L. E. Drake and W. B. Thiede

A group of 594 female students who came to the University of Wisconsin Student Counseling Center for assistance and for whom the information was complete provided the data for this study. Only females were included because the data were collected from students who were in the university during the period of 1944 and 1945 and it was thought that the male students in residence at that time might be atypical due to the war. Foreign students, veterans, and married students were excluded because they were also assumed to be atypical.

Each student filled out a detailed information blank which included items regarding high school and college extracurricular activities. The activities were grouped into six categories as follows: Literary, Dramatics, Debating, Music and Art, Athletics, and Student Government. A score of one was assigned to each area in which the student indicated she participated regardless of the amount of participation in that area. An error may be involved in this since it is not known whether the categories are equivalent in relation to I. E. However, it is apparent that the error would be increased if the total number of activities participated in was used as a score rather than the number of types of activities since this would increase the effect of these inequalities if they exist. The ratings, then, for activity participation ranged from zero to six. All the students took the MMPI (card-sorting form) as a part of the testing for counseling purposes.

Results

Since the size of the community in which a person has lived most of his life might have some relationship to social I. E., it was thought desirable to study this factor first. Hence the students were classified according to the following population groups: farm to 2499; 2500 to 9999; 10,000 to 99,999; 100,000 and up.

The chi square test was applied to a contingency table to determine whether the students participating in 0 or 1, 2, 3, 4, and 5 or 6 types of high school activities are proportionately distributed in each population group. The resulting chi square with 12 degrees of freedom gives $p(\chi^2 > 30.5) = 0.001$ indicating highly significant differences between population groups with respect to activity participation. Hence it was deemed necessary to make separate analyses for the four population groups even though the χ^2 for a contingency table made up of population groups with respect to Si scores with 24 degrees of freedom gives $p(\chi^2 > 27.2) = 0.30$.

However, if a separate analysis is made for each of the population groups in terms of the five quantities of activity participation listed above, the numbers in some categories as distributed are rather small. Hence the cases were combined in each population group to make two categories as follows: (1) those who participated in 0, 1, or 2 types of high school activities; and (2) those who participated in 4, 5, or 6 types of activities. Those who listed three types of activities were omitted since the means of the population groups ranged from 2.6 to 3.4.

Table 1 shows the Si scores for the four population groups as divided into the two categories and the t-test results for the significance of the difference between means.

In every case the differences are highly significant—at less than the 0.05 of 1 per cent level of confidence. The mean score on the Si scale

Table 1. Comparison of Si Scores for High School Activity Groups

Group	Students Reporting 0, 1, or 2 Types of Activity			Students Reporting 4, 5, and 6 Types of Activity			Differences			
	Mean	SD	N	Mean	SD	N	M_{diff}	t	df	p
Farm-2499	57.850	10.800	40	49.711	11.101	52	8.139	11.558	90	<.0005
2500-9999.	54.730	10.690	26	48.533	10.363	45	6.197	7.659	69	<.0005
10,000-99,999 . .	55.943	11.337	70	45.724	8.383	58	10.219	18.058	126	<.0005
100,000-over . . .	52.093	9.165	86	47.667	9.313	45	4.426	7.863	129	<.0005

of the students who participated in 4, 5, or 6 activities is in the direction of extroversion (low scores indicate extroversion) and the mean for those participating in 0, 1, or 2 activities is in the direction of introversion. The percentage of students participating in 4, 5, or 6 types of activities who reach or exceed the mean for students who participate in 0, 1, or 2 types of activities for each population group is as follows: Group I, 23 per cent; Group II, 28 per cent; Group III, 15 per cent; and Group IV, 22 per cent.

Since freshman women are not permitted to participate in major activities it was necessary to omit all students so classified in the study of the relationship of Si and college activity participation. This left 283 cases for study. The chi square test was applied as before to a contingency table made up of the number of types of activity participation with respect to the size of the town in which the student said she had spent most of her life. The resulting chi square with 6 degrees of freedom gives $p(\chi^2 > 8.8) = 0.19$. Applying the same test to a table made up of size of town with respect to Si scores with 12 degrees of freedom gives $p(\chi^2 > 14.25) = 0.29$. Since the differences cannot be assumed to be significant, the group of 283 students was studied without regard to the size of the home community.

The mean number of types of activities participated in by these students while in the university was 0.94. The comparison was made, then, between those students who participated in no activities and those who participated in two or more types of activities. Table 2 shows the result of the comparison.

Table 2. Comparison of Si Scores for University Activity Groups

Group	Mean	SD	N
Students reporting no activities	53.153	11.025	124
Students reporting two or more types of activities	48.171	8.920	70

The difference in means is 4.981, yielding a t of 10.349 which with 192 degrees of freedom gives $p < 0.0005$. The difference is highly significant with the activity-participation group deviating toward the extrovert end of the scale. Only 28 per cent of this group reach or exceed the mean Si score for the nonparticipating group in the introverted direction.

The K Factor as a Suppressor Variable in the MMPI

P. E. Meehl and S. R. Hathaway

History and Problem

Among the very large number of structured personality inventories which have been published, it is by now quite generally admitted that there are relatively few which are of practical value in the clinical situation. There are a number of reasons, both obvious and subtle, for this fact, some of which will be developed by implication in the present paper. One of the most important failings of almost all structured personality tests is their susceptibility to "faking" or "lying" in one way or another, as well as their even greater susceptibility to unconscious self-deception and role-playing on the part of individuals who may be consciously quite honest and sincere in their responses. The possibility of such factors having an invalidating effect upon the scores obtained has been mentioned by many writers, including Adams [1941], Allport [1928, 1937, 1942], Bernreuter [1933a, 1933b, 1940], Bills [1941], Bordin [1943], Eisenberg and Wesman [1941], Guilford and Guilford [1936], Humm and Humm [1944], Humm and Wadsworth [1935], Kelly, Miles, and Terman [1936], Laird [1925], Landis and Katz [1934], Maller [1930], Olson [1936], Rosenzweig [1934, 1938], Ruch [1942], Strong [1943], Symonds [1932], Vernon [1934], Washburne [1946], Willoughby and Morse [1936], and others. One of the assumed advantages of the projective methods is that they are relatively less influenced by such distorting factors, although this assumption should be critically evaluated.

The existence of a distorting influence in test-taking attitude is so obvious that it has been thought hardly necessary to establish it experimentally, although a number of investigations have demonstrated the effect. Frenkel-Brunswik [1939] investigated tendencies to self-deception in rating oneself, finding in some cases marked negative relations between self-judgments and the evaluation of others. Hendrickson [1932], cited by Olson [1936], reported that a group of teachers earned significantly more stable, dominant, extroverted, and self-sufficient scores on the Bernreuter scales when instructed to take the test as though they were applying for a position than when under more neutral instructions. Ruch [1942] showed that college students could fake extroversion on the Bernreuter to the extent of achieving a median at the 98th percentile of Bernreuter's norms, as contrasted with a "naive" median at the 50th percentile. Bernreuter [1933b] found that college students could produce marked shifts in their Bernreuter scores in the "socially approved" direction although he interpreted this finding as indicating the comparative unimportance of the faking tendency. His reasoning was that had the need for giving socially approved responses operated in the first administration to any appreciable extent, the effect of special instructions to take this attitude should not have been great. This reasoning seems rather tenuous, inasmuch as the occurrence of a shift merely shows that conscious and permitted faking can produce greater effects than those which may have been operating in the "naive" original testing. The insignificant correlations between naive and faked scores were also used by Bernreuter to support his view, an argument which is not comprehensible to the present writers, especially in view of the probably gross skewness of the faked scores. What is clear from his investigation is that people are able to influence their scores to a considerable extent if they choose to, and that the average student's stereotype of what is "socially desirable" seems to be an individual who is dominant, self-sufficient, and stable. Maller [1930], Metfessel [1935], Olson [1936], and Spencer [1938] have studied the effects of anonymity on responses to self-rating situations and shown that the requirement of signing one's name has a definite effect on the scores. Kelly, Miles, and Terman [1936] demonstrated the great ease with which scores on the Terman-Miles Masculinity-Femininity Test could be "faked" in either direction once the subjects had been let in on the secret of what the test measured. Strong [1943], Bills [1941], Steinmetz [1932], and Bordin [1943] have presented evidence on the ability of subjects to distort their interest patterns when taking the Strong Vocational Interest Blank.

It is a significant sociological fact about psychologists that in spite of the strong reasons, both a priori and experimental, for accepting the reality of this phenomenon in objective personality testing, very few systematic efforts have been made to correct for it or to overcome it. In published articles one continually finds brief and inadequate references to the "assumption of frankness" and the necessity for arousing a "sincere desire to know oneself better," but the treatment is usually extremely sketchy and no very concrete suggestions are given for producing such test-taking attitudes or, what is almost as important in practice, for determining the extent to which they have been present. It almost seems as though we inventory-makers were afraid to say too much about the problem because we had no effective solution for it, but it was too obvious a fact to be ignored so it was met by a polite nod. Meanwhile the scores obtained are subjected to varied and "precise" statistical manipulations which impel the student of behavior to wonder whether it is not the aim of the personality testers to get as far away from any unsanitary contact with the organism as possible. Part of this trend no doubt reflects the lack of clinical experience of some psychologists who concern themselves with personality testing, and the very strong contemporary trend which stresses the statistical interrelationships of item responses much more than the relation of the latter to external nontest criteria. The establishment of "validity" (*sic!*) in terms of various criteria of internal consistency naturally leads to an unconscious neglect of the problem of nontest behavior correlates.

Among the many authors who recognize the problem there are a few who have made specific suggestions for its solution. The inclusion of special exhortations to frankness and objectivity in the test directions themselves is common, but we have no evidence as to its effectiveness. Obviously, if a subject is consciously determined to fake, he will do so; whereas if his motivation to distortion is of a more subtle, nonverbalized nature, such exhortations can hardly be expected to be efficacious. Another method is to attempt disguise of the items, so that the "significance" of a given response is less obvious. Traditional approaches to the measurement of personality render this technique practically impossible, inasmuch as the items are selected to begin with for their *obvious* psychological significance and hence, unless changed so greatly as to no longer elicit the desired information, almost inevitably continue to betray their origin. An effective use of a set of "subtle" items is only possible when the initial item pool is very large and the *initial selection* (not only the final validation) of items is ruthlessly empirical. Those items whose significance would not have been guessed by the test-maker will then be equally mysterious to the testee. When the projective and role-playing components of test-taking behavior are clearly seen to be present in objective personality inventories [Meehl, 1945a (see II, 1)], this approach to the problem is very fruitful. A simple stratagem along the item-disguise line is to state about half of the items negatively, so that an affirmative response is not consistently a "bad" or maladjusted one. However, such techniques cannot eliminate the problem entirely.

A spurious anonymity using secret coding for identifying the testee is a possibility suggested by the studies cited above, but is clinically impractical for obvious reasons. The deception involved is not desirable, and in any case the clinical patient, unlike the sophomore student, knows perfectly well that the examiner is interested in *his* score individually. Instead of anonymity, it has been suggested by Olson [1936] that the name be signed at the conclusion of the administration instead of at the top of the page. This suggestion was carried into practice by Maller [1932] in his Character Sketches. This investigator also stated the questions in the "indirect" (third person) form, requiring the subject to indicate whether he was the *same* or *different* from the person described. Maller presents evidence that this procedure aroused considerably less annoyance in his subjects, although direct proof that this decrease in annoyance led to increased validity is lacking. For reasons which have been given in more detail elsewhere [Meehl, 1945a], it is doubtful whether the removal of personal reference is wholly desirable, since there is reason for believing that the same role-playings and self-deceptions which operate to invalidate *some* of our measurements are an important factor in making *other* measurements possible.

Another technique for reducing the effect of signing one's name is to have the items printed on cards which are then sorted by the subject, making all writing unnecessary and possibly lessening the feeling that one is making a permanent record of his personal failings. This has been done by Maller in a revised test (Personality Sketches) and by Hathaway and McKinley in the MMPI [1943].

Although all these stratagems may have a considerable value, especially in the aggregate, the fact still remains that they do not by any means remove the possibility of "faking." What is much more important, they are mainly directed at the sort of *conscious* falsehood which most writers have stressed, while ignoring the more subtle tendencies to self-deception which are probably of even greater importance in affecting scores. In the third place, they neglect to stress the existence of trends in the opposite direction—namely, those trends which exaggerate the apparent abnormality or maladjustment of the individual rather than soft-pedaling it. It is only natural that the tendency of a testee to put himself in a favorable light should have received more attention than the contrary tendency, which makes much less "sense" psychologically at least from a superficial point of view. There is evidence that this latter tendency does exist, however, and that it is a much more important factor in determining scores on personality inventories than has generally been supposed. Some of this evidence will be presented in the present paper, while other indications have been given elsewhere [Meehl, 1945b]. It is also probable that certain systematic differences in item interpretation, not necessarily a function of personality dynamics of the defensive or self-critical sort but relatively "neutral" psychologically (e.g., semantic variation), lead to score deviations that are misleading. Such problems have been investigated by Benton [1935], Eisenberg [1941], and Eisenberg and Wesman [1941].

A more fruitful attitude was taken by Rosenzweig [1934] in which he reiterated that self-ratings are untrustworthy and indicated that instead of trying to eliminate completely these sources of error we should recognize them and attempt to "correct" for them in interpreting the results. He says:

> Astute phraseology in the instructions and questions of the test have sometimes been resorted to, but such expedients are rarely very effective. Might it not be more effective to recognize at the outset that such tests have certain limitations that can never be completely circumvented and then go on to the measurement of these limiting factors themselves, thus obtaining information by which a correction may be applied to the subject's answers? [1934]

Rosenzweig's specific proposal for achieving this end was to include among the usual self-rating items a set of items of the form "I should like to be the sort of man who . . ." on the theory that if we knew something of the strength of certain "ideal-self" trends in the person, we could make appropriate correction for these trends in interpreting responses to the traditional items. Rosenzweig never carried this idea into practice and there is no way of telling whether or not it would have worked. It seems to the writers that it would be relatively ineffective, since what is desired is not a statement of the strength or number of ideals for the self, but a measure of the extent to which they are allowed to distort responses. In other words, a subject might easily have quite lofty ideals verbally expressed, but might be too honest, insightful, objective, or self-critical to distort his responses into agreement with these ideals. It is, for example, rather characteristic of psychasthenic persons to express high and often unattainable ideals of perfection and achievement; whereas at the same time they are prone to be excessively self-critical, a fact which is psychometrically reflected in the negative correlation of the Pt (psychasthenia) scale of the MMPI with some of the subtle "lie" scales which will be discussed below.

Maller [1932] attempted to solve this problem in another way in his Character Sketches, by including a small set of items which were supposed to measure the subject's "readiness to confide." The occurrence of very normal, well-adjusted scores in combination with a low measured "readiness to confide" would lead one to be skeptical of the validity of the measurement. This was a material advance in principle, except that the "readiness to confide" items were themselves self-ratings on that very readiness. In the later form called Personality Sketches Maller does not make use of this procedure so we may assume that it was unsuccessful or at least did not materially improve validity.

To carry Rosenzweig's thinking to its logical conclusion, the obvious procedure is to give the subject a good *chance* to distort his answers in accordance with some self-picture or conscious façade, and observe the extent to which he does so. The difficulty here is that such a procedure requires a knowledge of the objective facts (and the subjective facts!), which are usually inaccessible to us. Here there are three possibilities open to the test-builder. First, he may sidestep the problem of getting directly at the objective truth, and attempt to establish falsehood by obtaining internal contradictions. This was another technique employed by Maller in his earlier test. Cady [1923], in his application of a modified form of the Woodworth Psychoneurotic Inventory to the measurement of juvenile incorrigibility, had earlier made use of repeated items to increase reliability of the scores, although the aim of detecting inconsistency of the "fake" sort was not explicit in his rationale. Each question appeared twice, once in each section of the test, except that in the second appearance the question was phrased in the negative. Theoretically the subject's response should also be reversed; and the number of failures to reverse is an indication of some inconsistency and hence, Maller assumes, of noncooperation or dishonesty. The "inconsistency score" obtained in this way was to be subtracted from the adjustment score to get a sort of corrected score as proposed by Rosenzweig. It is by no means obvious that the shift to a negative form of item will leave the projective properties of the stimulus simply reversed in meaning, so that the fact of an "inconsistency" in the strict logical sense would not necessarily imply lack of cooperation or dishonesty. However, it would seem reasonable that a very large number of such inconsistent pairs would cast grave suspicion upon the scores, either for dishonesty or for some other equally serious reason. This technique also was abandoned by Maller in his revised instrument.

The second method of using distortion is to present opportunities for answering in a very favorable way but in a way which could almost certainly not be true. This idea was employed by Hartshorne and May in the Character Education Inquiry [1928]. Since there are very few aspects of behavior for which one could have complete confidence that no subject would be "ideal" in them, it is necessary to present a considerable number of such opportunities and progressively reduce the probability that any flesh-and-blood individual would be as described. Everyone has at least a few highly desirable traits, and no one has all of them. Without knowing anything whatsoever about a particular person, we can write down on common-sense grounds a list of extremely good and rare human qualities which it is statistically absurd to suppose will all or in large part be his. If he says, however, that he has all (or a very great many) of them, we decide that he is not telling the truth. To practically clinch this argument it is only necessary to choose desirable attributes which will very rarely belong, even singly, to anyone, and which furthermore relatively few normal persons claim for themselves when given the chance. In the mass the answers to these items may yield very strong evidence of deception. "I sometimes put off until tomorrow what I ought to do today" can be answered False by *very* few honest people. If a subject gives such responses with some considerable frequency, the inference is obvious. A more detailed discussion of this approach will be given below in the section on the L scale.

The Humm-Wadsworth Temperament Scales and the MMPI have both made use of this method, the latter more explicitly. Humm and Wadsworth [1935] deserve credit for having been among the first investigators of structured personality measurement to lay great stress upon the problem of detecting noncooperation and distortion of response when evaluating a particular profile of scores. They were also among the first to adopt an explicit and uncompromising empiricism in selecting items from a large initial pool. The two scales which serve as "checks" or "correctors" for the remainder of the profile on the

Humm-Wadsworth are the "Normal" component and the "no-count." The Normal component is rather difficult to evaluate from the theoretical point of view, for reasons which have been given elsewhere by one of the present writers [Meehl, 1945b]. It is sufficient here to indicate merely its function as described by Humm and Wadsworth, which is to assess the strength of a general inhibiting, controlling, or normalizing factor in personality which serves to act as a "brake" upon strong abnormal tendencies on the other variables. This means that in interpreting a given profile, the significance of any deviation on one of the abnormal components must be established with the size of the Normal score in mind. To the extent that the Normal component measures what the authors claim for it, it is not especially relevant to the present problem; but if it actually operates by detecting something other than the personality component they describe, it would perhaps be of significance here. For a more detailed discussion of this question the reader is referred to the study cited above.

The "no-count" is based upon the number of items to which the subject responds in the negative. Inasmuch as approximately 76 per cent of the scored items (87 per cent of the total pool) of the Humm-Wadsworth are "obviously" suggestive of abnormality when replied to affirmatively, the no-count is to some extent a measure of the testee's tendency to avoid, consciously or otherwise, saying "bad" things about himself when taking the test. That this relationship obtains is further supported by the tendency for the no-count to correlate positively (.77) with the Normal component and negatively (−.39 to −.72) with the various abnormal components [1935]. If the no-count is excessively great, the inference is that the subject has responded in a very defensive or possibly (as in some psychotics) stereotyped fashion; and therefore the particular testing is of doubtful validity. In another article, Humm and Wadsworth state that as high as 25 or 30 per cent of normals seem to invalidate their scores in this way, a proportion which would seem to be impractically high for clinical purposes. In a later article Humm, Storment, and Iorns, 1939, attempt to reduce the proportion of useless tests by a "correction" for the no-count based upon multiple regression procedures. Humm and Wadsworth state that in a subsequent group of cases "well known" to them, the improved validity of profiles thus corrected was demonstrated. An unpublished study of hospitalized psychiatric cases by Arnold [1942] indicated that even the exclusion of cases with "invalid" no-count did not result in any greater validity clinically than was obtained using all cases. Humm (in a personal communication) states that improved multiple regression techniques have resulted in a very marked reduction in the proportion of test misses and of uninterpretable profiles. These more recent data on the Humm-Wadsworth have not been published. On present evidence it is difficult to say to what extent the use of the multiple regression technique was successful in improving validity.

Washburne, in revising his "Test of Social Adjustment" (OSPA), included a set of 21 items modeled after the "lie" items of Hartshorne and May and referred to the total score on this set of *objectivity*. This score was included to detect both lying and unintentional inaccuracy, and the author reports that interviews with people having very low objectivity scores showed that "it was useless to question them." A very low objectivity score was said to invalidate the test as a whole, and a weighted objectivity score was included in the total score on the entire test [1935].

Another application of the second method for detecting invalidity by identifying the presence of distortion was the "lie" scale (and its complement, F) of the MMPI, which will be discussed in detail in the section below on the L scale.

The third technique available is the empirical derivation of a "fake" scale by making use of the item shifts obtained when persons take a test under normal "naive" conditions and then are retested with instructions to fake. This method has been used by Ruch to construct an "honesty" key for the Bernreuter. It is interesting that a procedure so logical and straightforward, invented to solve a problem so obvious and insistent, should have been employed for the first time over twenty years after the appearance of the first personality inventory. Ruch says:

> The argument is rather simple. If answers to items on a test like the Bernreuter can be faked at all, the chances are that some are easier to fake than others. Therefore, it should be possible to give each item a weight to represent the extent to which it can be faked by the average college student. This was done by tabulating the frequency of each answer to each question for the standard condition and for the influenced condition. These frequencies were converted into percentages, and an "honesty" weight was assigned to each reply according to the magnitude of the critical ratio of the difference between the frequency of the reply in the honest and in the influenced condition.[1942]

In applying this honesty scale to a new group he was able to show that all cases of "real" introverts would be detected in an attempt to make themselves appear extroverted on the test. There are a number of interesting problems presented by this method, such as the extent to which the key would work if the subjects were not under actual instructions to fake extrovert but were being more subtle and actually trying to deceive an examiner in a real-life situation. Presumably the deviation toward dishonesty would not be as great under such circumstances. The use of the critical ratio as a basis for weighting items might also be open to some question. In any event, Ruch seems to have been the first investigator to attempt empirical derivation of a fake key for a question-answer personality inventory. The results of applying this procedure to work on the MMPI will follow in the present article.

As was mentioned earlier, there is some evidence of a tendency in the opposite direction in taking personality tests. It is difficult to characterize such a tendency, especially since it may occur on several different bases. A patient in the hospital may, for instance, engage in a sort of psychiatric malingering for strictly conscious reasons, presenting a profile on a test such as the MMPI which shows abnormalities out of all reasonable proportion to what is apparent from other considerations. Again, there may be somewhat general traits of verbal pessimism or self-deprecation which, while of some relevance personologically, act so as to distort systematically the results of personality measurement. We shall dichotomize the test-attitude continuum by the two opposed terms "defensiveness" and "plus-getting," not implying anything as to the degree of conscious, deliberate deception involved in either. The corresponding *extremes*, where such deliberate deception seems likely, we shall refer to as "faking good" and "faking bad" respectively. It is recognized that, like the defensive tendency, the plus-getting tendency may exist in all degrees from a mild self-criticality or merely objectivity to a deliberate, conscious attempt to make oneself look psychiatrically abnormal. Whether this represents simply the extreme of a continuum with faking good at the opposite end, or an entirely new and different factor, we shall for the moment leave aside. At any rate it would be desirable to develop a scale for detecting these tendencies to put oneself in a bad light when answering a personality inventory, so that allowance might be made in such cases in the light of a deviant score obtained on such a scale. The F scale of the MMPI was not originally developed with this in mind, but subsequent evidence showed that it could be used in this way (see below). Presumably the two "correction" scales C_H [McKinley and Hathaway, 1940 (see I, 2)] and C_D [Hathaway and McKinley, 1942 (I, 3)] which were found necessary in the early attempts to detect hypochondriasis and symptomatic depression were at least partially dependent upon the operation of such a plus-getting tendency.

A systematic investigation of the plus-getting tendency was attempted by one of the present writers, which resulted in the development of a somewhat more generalized correction scale which was called N. The details of derivation and interpretation of this scale are reported elsewhere [Meehl, 1945b] and will not be repeated here. Suffice it to say that from a study of the item responses made by a group of presumably normal persons who showed abnormal MMPI profiles as contrasted with a group of clinically abnormal persons with matched profiles, a group of items was isolated which could be used to quantify in a rough fashion the plus-getting tendency. It was found that normal persons who show distinctly abnormal (maladjusted) profiles on the personality scales proper tended to answer this selected set of N items in the "obviously" maladjusted direction, which was with few exceptions also the direction of response given by a minority of the unselected normal population. In other words, a person who is clinically normal in spite of having an abnormal profile shows a tendency to give statistically uncommon answers which are also "maladjusted" answers in the sense that by inspection they would be considered evidence of psychiatric involvement. For example, about 48 per cent of the unselected general population normals answer True to the item "A windstorm terrifies me." Yet we find that among those normals selected specifically for showing apparently *abnormal* profiles on the personality scales proper, about 62 per cent give an affirmative answer to this question. Persons having MMPI profiles no more deviant than these plus-getting normals, but who are actually abnormal clinically, give an affirmative answer about 26 per cent of the time. Thus if a person shows an otherwise deviant profile but states that he is terrified by windstorms he stands a better chance of being clinically normal than one who gives the a priori more "normal" or "adjusted" response. Similar items on the N scale include such things as "I am afraid of fire," "I have a fear of water," "People often disappoint me," "I did not like school," and so on. Inspection of these items and an examination of the correlations between N and the other MMPI scales led to a conviction that the N scale was actually detecting a diffuse plus-getting tendency of the sort described. It was further shown that either the inspectional or the mechanical use of the N scale in order to under-interpret profiles having the plus-getting tendency led to a reduction in the number of false positives in identification of psychiatric cases. However, the

N scale was rather long, and was also apparently loaded with genuine psychiatric factors which led to an undesirable under-interpretation of profiles belonging to grossly abnormal persons. It is therefore to be seen merely as a beginning attempt which was supplanted by K, as will be described below.

MMPI Scale F

The MMPI variables F and L were not formally validated originally, but were presented on face validity, that is, we assumed their validity on a priori grounds. The F variable was composed of 64 items that were selected primarily because they were answered with a relatively low frequency in either the true or false direction by the main normal group; the scored direction of response is the one which is rarely made by unselected normals. Additionally, the items were chosen to include a variety of content so that it was unlikely that any particular pattern would cause an individual to answer many of the items in the unusual direction. A few examples are these: "Everything tastes the same." (True) "I believe in law enforcement." (False) "I see things, animals, or people around me that others do not see." (True) The relative success of this selection of items, with the deliberate intent of forcing the average number of items answered in an unusual direction downward, is illustrated in the fact that the mean score on the 64 items runs between two and four points for all normal groups. The distribution curve is, of course, very skewed positively; and the higher scores approach half the number of items. In distributions of ordinary persons the frequency of scores drops very rapidly at about seven and is at the 2 or 3 per cent level by score twelve. Because of this quick cutting off of the curve the scores seven and twelve were arbitrarily assigned T-scored values of 60 and 70 in the original F table.

From the first it was recognized that F represented several things. Most simply, since the subject would need to sort almost all the items according to expectation in order for these low scores to result, any error in recording, such as mistaking true items for false items and the like, would raise the F score appreciably. Similarly, if a subject could not understand what he was reading adequately enough to make conventional answers to these items, the F score would obviously be higher. It was felt to be axiomatic that this method would eliminate as invalid records of subjects who could not read and comprehend or who refused to cooperate sufficiently to make expected placements.

In addition, however, it was early discovered that schizoid subjects and subjects who apparently wished to put themselves in a bad light also obtained high scores. The schizoid group obtained high scores because, owing to delusional or other aberrant mental states, they said very unusual things in responding to the items and thus obtained high F scores. This is referred to as distortion since we feel that an impartial study would not justify the patient's placements. Among more normal persons some high scores were also observed where the individual had rather unusual ways of responding to conventional stimuli such as are represented by the items involved. For example, to the item "I have had periods in which I carried on activities without knowing later what I had been doing," most persons answered False. Some persons, however, included periods of sleep in the implication of the item. One might argue that such ways of thinking are often allied to schizoid mentation generally and that the answers in this case indicate a true abnormality. At the very least, however, the person is responding to some items in a way that differs from that of most individuals. Such persons might, therefore, not be appropriately approached through this method of personality measurement. It seems a reasonable enough possibility that there are individuals whose habitual ways of reacting to items are so different from their fellows that measurement of their personalities through the use of verbal items of this type would reflect the unusualness of their reactions to the items more than any clinical abnormality. This semantic factor has been treated more completely elsewhere [Benton, 1935; Eisenberg, 1941; Meehl, 1945b]. Insofar as such a possibility may exist we have not yet separated it from the clinically more important abnormality expressed in the Sc scale. Parenthetically, one of the most persistent difficulties with developing the Sc scale was this very fact, that an appreciable number of individuals obtained high scores on Sc without being marked by a clinically important degree of abnormality. They nevertheless, as indicated above, were responding differently from other people about them as represented by the original data from the general population. It appears that the essential difference clinically is concerned with the particular manifestation of unusual mentation in the individual. If this is not too clearly counter to society's mores, the person may not be thought of as schizoid by those about him though he is often recognized as queer.

Clinical experience suggests that the usual critical score of $T = 70$ is too low in the case of F. We have found that scores ranging up to $T = 80$ (raw score 16) are more often a reflection of "validly" unusual symptoms and attitudes than an indication of invalidity in the rest of the profile due to misunderstanding, etc. Raw scores much above this, however, strongly suggest an invalid record.

With the problems of measurement that developed in the armed forces where a subject might be expected frequently to attempt to put himself in a bad light in answering the MMPI, the F score became especially interesting. It was, of course, immediately possible to consider the F score as an evidence of this attempt to malinger and obtain fallaciously bad scores on other scales. As a check on this interpretation, a group of 54 ASTP men who had completed a considerable portion of their training in psychology were asked to take the MMPI twice. The group took it in the usual way and also took it under instructions to assume that they wished to avoid being accepted in the draft and in order to be rejected they were to obtain adverse scores without giving themselves away. Half the group took it with "fake" instructions first, half second. Through this plan we had a "faked bad" record and a "normal" record. The data showed that 96 per cent of the "faked bad" records had a raw score F of 15 or more (T $\geqslant$ 78), indicating that even these men who were somewhat cognizant of psychological measurements betrayed themselves when they attempted to fake a bad record. The resulting profiles were nearly all unusually abnormal in character, and to one who has seen a large number of abnormal profiles, most of them would have appeared invalid from their pattern alone.

From this experiment it appeared that F was a very good device for identifying the intentional faking that could be set up in an experimental situation. It still seemed desirable, however, to attempt to separate among the individuals obtaining relatively high F scores those who were of the above-described schizoid type or who were simply overpessimistic in their view of themselves, from those who for one reason or another faked a bad score or did not understand the items.

The L Scale

The original 15 L items making up the L scale were selected under the inspiration of the work of Hartshorne and May. Each of the items presents a situation desirable socially, but rarely true of the individual. For example in the item "I read all the editorials in the newspaper every day," we have a type of behavior that might be generally considered desirable but which is true of only a small percentage of the population. It was recognized that very conscientious persons would frequently have more than the average number of these L items truly positive but for a person to have six or eight of them seemed almost impossibly good. The 15 items of this type scattered among the main body of the items constituted a fairly subtle trap for anyone who wanted to give an unusually good impression of himself.

Among the various normal groups the mean score on the L items lies between three and five. As in the case of F the frequency curves are all skewed sharply in the positive direction. Very few individuals obtain raw scores of seven or more, and the 2 or 3 per cent level is at about ten. These values were arbitrarily called the 60 and 70 T-score points, respectively. As the L score was used in the clinical setting and as some data began to accumulate from personnel workers in industrial situations, it became apparent that the assumptions regarding the meaning of L were in the main correct, but that there were also other valid interpretations of L, at least in the range from T score 56 to 70. In fact we found ourselves placing considerable emphasis on T scores of 56 to 60, which indicated that the original arbitrary assignment of T scores had been too conservative. On the other hand while the positive presence of the rise in the L score seemed quite valid as an indicator that the individual taking the test was being dishonest and might be somewhat unreliable, if no rise in L was observed, the finding could not be so positively and clearly interpreted. The L score was a trap for the naive subject but more sophisticated subjects easily avoided it.

To check the assumption that L would not identify the more sophisticated subject an experiment was performed with ASTP psychology students. As in the study cited above, 53 men were given the MMPI twice. The "faked good" data were obtained by instructing the men to make certain in taking the test that they would be acceptable to army induction. These records showed no appreciable rise in L. It is also true, however, that the majority of the profiles were only slightly, if any, better than the corresponding non-fake profiles. This experiment would have been improved if persons whose true profiles were abnormal had been used. Some data have been collected from such cases but the number is small. At least, one may conclude that the intent to deceive is not often detectable by L when the subjects are relatively normal and sophisticated.

The K Scale

In summary there were two basic lines of experimental approach to the problem of identifying the attitude a subject takes toward the items that he is faced with in the personality inventory [Wiener,

1948]. Each of these two approaches permits a subdivision into several methods. First, we may have the subject deliberately assume a generally defined attitude, as in the study by Ruch. For example, we may ask him to attempt deliberately to obtain adverse scores while not betraying his intention, and secondly, we may choose records in which there is presumptive likelihood that a special attitude has been assumed. The first approach may be subdivided into those experiments in which the "faking" is directed toward obtaining adverse scores and the approach in which the intention is to obtain desirable scores. In both latter cases an additional set of responses must be obtained relatively simultaneously with the "faked" responses in which the individual assumes his ordinary attitude. The "faked" and "normal" records can then be contrasted for study. One may make an item analysis to discover the items that are most frequently changed from the "normal" records as contrasted to the "fake" records. By use of these "fake" approaches, several scales were derived.

It was found that the items indicating an attempt to obtain a bad record are not necessarily those derived by analysis of records where the subjects attempted to obtain a good record. Our first finding in this regard was that either of these procedures provided a scale that would be about as good for the other type of faking as it was for the one from which it was derived when such scales were applied to test cases not used in the original derivations. It was further found that using two such scales separately did not materially increase the predictive value. As has already been pointed out, it was also found that the original F scale was as effective as was needed to identify those persons who intentionally attempted to obtain a bad score, at least within the range of the experiments that we conducted. Conversely, the L scale was not effective nor were any of the specially derived scales especially effective in identifying sophisticated persons who deliberately attempted to obtain better scores. In all these experiments the findings were so complex and the time devoted to many subprojects was so great that we shall only present data for the final scale K (see below).

In the second line of experimental approach there are also several subdivisions. One may find among presumably functional and normal records those records which are so abnormal as to indicate that the individual should have been in a hospital and attempt to discover the items among these records that will differentiate them from the records of actually abnormal persons. For the counterpart to this approach one chooses cases who were in the hospital but whose records show a normal profile. These may likewise be compared by item analysis to the records of hospital patients with suitably abnormal profiles who would be assumed to have had no interfering test-taking attitude. Using this approach we also derived several scales and made many experimental tests of them. Again the details of all of these are not worthy of the complex presentation they would require and these preliminary results will merely be summarized.

The first and most important finding was that whichever of these methods was used, as was the case with the "faked" approach above, the resultant scales were about equally effective and about equally unsatisfactory regardless of the approach and of the particular item content. These scales were also rather effective in differentiating the "fake" group and in some cases were just as valid for that purpose as were the scales derived by that approach. After some two years of this experimentation all the scales that had shown any promise were reconsidered by applying them to various available groups that had not been used in their derivation and from among them all a single scale which was originally called L_6 was chosen as the best. It should be recognized that L_6 was not entirely satisfactory but its action in several of the sample situations resulted in its tentative adoption. Although as indicated in the above summary the particular derivation does not seem to play an important part since we could not easily distinguish a scale as having been derived by a special process when we examined its action, nevertheless it may be desirable to tell how L_6 was derived. It must not be forgotten that several other scales resulting from the other methods were very nearly as good as was L_6, especially the plus-getting scale N. However, when the N scale and L_6 were compared and even applied to the test situation set up for the N scale, L_6 was a close competitor to N and in several instances was actually better.

In brief, L_6 was derived by an item analysis of the responses of 25 males and 25 females in a psychopathic hospital whose profiles showed an L score of T = 60 or more and who, with the exception of six normal cases, had diagnoses indicating the probability that they should have had abnormal profiles but whose profiles were in reality within the normal range. The diagnoses given to these cases by the psychiatric staff were mostly psychopathic personality, alcoholism, and allied descriptive terms indicating behavior disorders rather than neuroses. In general one would expect persons with such diagnoses to be rather more likely to be defensive in taking a personality test than cases of psychoneurosis. There are a few exceptions, however, in the case of hysteria where as has been pointed out in previous papers [McKinley and Hathaway, 1944 (see I, 5); Meehl (1945a, 1945b)] there is a tendency for the hysteria to be based upon something closely allied to the assuming of an overly perfect attitude in answering personality items. A particular listing of the diagnoses among these cases is not given here because the diagnostic categories are not clear enough to be of additional value. In summary, two criteria were employed in the selection of the criterion group. Practically all of them were individuals known to be characterized by deviant behavior but they obtained relatively normal profiles and were thus what we have called misses for the MMPI; and all of these criterion cases were also characterized by having a tendency to obtain elevated scores on the original L scale.

The item responses of these fifty cases handled separately for males and females were compared to the male and female item frequencies from the general group of males and females that has been used in past scale derivations. In all, 22 items were chosen as a result of this comparison. All these items showed a percentage difference of 30 or more between the criterion cases and the control group.

These 22 items are given below with a T or an F to indicate the direction of the answer that would agree with the tendency of the criterion group. Since the criterion group is assumed to be a group with intent to obtain good scores the larger raw scores on these items are in the same direction as the larger raw scores on the original L scale. The content of these items would seem to suggest an attitude of denying worries, inferiority feelings, and psychiatrically unhealthy symptoms, together with a disposition to see only good in others as well as oneself. The over-all impression is one of "impunitiveness" if we may apply Rosenzweig's term in a situation where no particular frustration is involved.

B-55. I have very few quarrels with members of my family. (T) C-18. I worry over money and business. (F) C-27. It makes me impatient to have people ask my advice or otherwise interrupt me when I am working on something important. (F) C-33. It takes a lot of argument to convince most people of the truth. (F) D-53. I think nearly anyone would tell a lie to keep out of trouble. (F) D-54. Most people will use somewhat unfair means to gain profit or an advantage rather than to lose it. (F)

E-43. When in a group of people I have trouble thinking of the right things to talk about. (F) E-44. I find it hard to make talk when I meet new people. (F) E-52. People often disappoint me. (F) F-8. It makes me uncomfortable to put on a stunt at a party even when others are doing the same sort of things. (F) F-33. Often I can't understand why I have been so cross and grouchy. (F) F-34. Criticism or scolding hurts me terribly. (F) F-43. At periods my mind seems to work more slowly than usual. (F) F-46. I frequently find myself worrying about something. (F)

G-18. I have periods in whch I feel unusually cheerful without any special reason. (F) G-29. I get mad easily and then get over it soon. (F) G-30. At times my thoughts have raced ahead faster than I could speak them. (F) G-31. At times I feel like smashing things. (F) I-22. I have often met people who were supposed to be experts who were no better than I. (F) I-31. I have sometimes felt that difficulties were piling up so high that I could not overcome them. (F) I-37. I certainly feel useless at times. (F) I-38. I often think "I wish I were a child again." (F)

Following the final choice of L_6 as the best of the scales available, we subjected it to more careful study and went back through hospital and normal records to find out if it seemed to be of any help in interpreting individual profiles. There were relatively few data on normal cases but on hospital cases a fairly extensive symptomatic summary was available that would permit us to judge whether or not a patient should have had a normal profile. We could then look up the profile and if it was normal we could check to see if the L_6 deviated in an upward direction indicating that the patient had attempted to place himself in a good light. As a result of this study L_6 appeared effective but left much to be desired.

Since in the summary of scales when L_6 was chosen for intensive study it had seemed about as adequate for the detection of plus-getting as was N or any of the other experimental scales, the records of a new series of presumably normal persons showing deviant profiles were examined and it was again true that L_6 appeared to work at the plus-getting end of the test-attitude continuum. That is to say, a relatively low score on L_6 could be used to under-interpret an otherwise deviant profile and so avoid some of the presumably false positives in the normal population sample. Thus L_6 seemed useful at "both ends" of the test-attitude continuum, defensiveness and plus-getting.

The most outstanding difficulty in such a procedure was that L_6 tended to be low on severe depressive or schizophrenic patient records and thus led to an under-interpretation in spite of the fact that the patients were very grossly abnormal. To partly correct for this tendency, items were added that would work in the opposite direction. To choose these we studied the item tabulations for the group of ASTP men who had attempted to fake good and bad scores. In this study there were many items which showed no tendency to change with an alteration in the test-taking attitude. That is, the percentage of true or false, as the case might be, remained constant whether the attitude was the normal one or the faked one. From among these items, a subgroup was chosen which showed differences between schizophrenic and depressive criterion groups and general population normals. The procedure rested upon the admittedly somewhat shaky assumption that any item that did not appear to be much affected by the test-taking attitude as approached by a normal person attempting consciously to "fake" good or bad but which did occur as a frequent item to differentiate depressed or schizophrenic patients would be useful in correcting the tendency of our L_6 scale to go too low for schizophrenic and depressed patients. Of course such an item was scored in a way that would make it work against the tendency of the L_6 scale. Eight items were selected by this method. The effect of adding these 8 items to the 22 on L_6 was to elevate slightly the mean score of normals and make it more nearly approach the mean score of abnormal cases on the complex of all 30 items. The 8 items chosen by this procedure are given below. The letter F indicates the response scored in the "lie" direction, and in the direction characteristic of schizophrenic and depressed cases.

A-3. I have never felt better in my life than I do now. (F) C-28. I find it hard to set aside a task that I have undertaken, even for a short time. (F) D-48. I think a great many people exaggerate their misfortunes in order to gain the sympathy and help of others. (F) D-51. I am against giving money to beggars. (F) F-7. What others think of me does not bother me. (F) F-20. I like to let people know where I stand on things. (F) G-23. At times I am all full of energy. (F) J-51. At times I feel like swearing. (F)

As a final step these 8 items were combined with the 22 L_6 items into a single scale which we have called K. The K scale represents the final outcome of many experiments in the general field of measuring test attitude. The K scale is far from perfect for its purpose as measured by the various available data. Generally speaking it is about as good as any other single scale derived for any one of the single purposes that have been described. In individual applications it is inferior now to one scale and now to another but the differences are never great enough to be very significant practically and the small number of items in this scale gives it a distinct advantage over one or two of the longer scales such as N. Finally, as was stated above it is not expedient to present more than a single scale although a slight advantage could have been gained if two scales analogous to the original L and F scales had been separately presented.

The construction of K being what it was, odd-even or Kuder-Richardson reliabilities were not computed. Test-retest coefficients were .72 and .74 computed on two groups, one of which was retested at intervals varying from one day to over a year, the other after a lapse of 4-15 months.

Since the K scale was derived as a correction scale or suppressor variable [Horst, 1941; Meehl, 1945c] for improving the discrimination yielded on the already existent personality scales, it was not assumed to be measuring anything which in itself is of psychiatric significance. Actually, its relationship with such clinical variables as the subtle Hy items (see below) might suggest an interpretation of K alone; further, it is presumably a significant fact about a person that, in answering a personality inventory, he tends to behave as a "liar" or a "plus-getter." However, the real function of K is intended to be the correction of the other scores, and validity will be discussed with reference to this function only.

It is first necessary to choose criterion cases of the sort on which K can conceivably be of value. It is clear that such cases will be characterized by the presence of what may be called *borderline* profiles, i.e., those showing T scores, say, between 65 and 80. The reason for this is that in studying hundreds of deviant profiles after the addition of K, almost no individuals were found with T scores above 80 in the normal sample, and it was not statistically profitable to correct elevations of such magnitude to the point of calling them normal. On the other hand, when a curve shows no elevations at all above 65, even the presence of a high K score does not enable the clinician to form any adequate notion of what the peak, if any, would have been had the K factor not been operating to distort the results. In other words, there are upper and lower limits beyond which deviations on K cannot effectively operate. Profiles showing scores above 80 are to be interpreted as probably "abnormal" no matter how low K falls; while if a profile shows no scores above 65 we cannot tell whether a high K means the profile should be adjusted toward more severe scores or is merely that of an actually normal person who for some reason or other took a defensive attitude when being tested. The kind of curve which gives interpretative difficulty and which could conceivably be improved by knowledge of the influence of K would be a curve in the doubtful, borderline region. Accordingly, a group of cases from the normal and hospital groups was chosen on the basis of having achieved such borderline curves. We selected for this study all cases in the files showing at least one personality component (excluding

Mf) elevated as high as T = 65, but no component elevated to T > 80. Among the normals, there were 174 having such borderline curves, of which 71 were males and 103 were females. Corresponding to these cases, 129 males and 208 females with similar borderline profiles were located among our clinically abnormal cases. The data for the two sexes were treated separately.

The analysis of these data was in terms of the ability of the K scale, used mechanically as will be described, to separate the curves of the actual normals from those of the actual abnormals. For each sex group, the procedure was to arrange the whole set (normals and abnormals combined) in order of the magnitude of their K scores. The distribution of K was cut on the basis of the proportion of normals and abnormals in the sample, with all cases above the cut called "abnormal" and all those below "normal." A fourfold table was set up on this basis, and chi squares of 20.436 for the males and 29.540 for the females were obtained. Both of these are highly significant (p < .001) with 1 df. If, instead of locating an optimal cutting score, the K distribution is cut at the mean of the general population K distribution (i.e., at T = 50 regardless of the present samples) the cutting point of the males is unchanged, whereas that for the females shifts enough to lower their chi square to 17.750, which is still highly significant. In other words, if one considers miscellaneous profiles which lie in the borderline range between 65 and 80, regardless of the kind of elevation and irrespective of the clinical diagnosis of those who are clinically abnormal, he can separate them into "actual" normals and abnormals significantly better than chance by using a cutting score on K. It must be emphasized again that K in this instance is operating chiefly as a suppressor of certain test-taking tendencies, since K by itself does not practically differentiate unselected normal and abnormal cases (difference of 1 to 2½ raw score points between means for various samples). In terms of percentages, it was found that for the males 72 per cent of the abnormals and 61 per cent of the actual normals were correctly identified. For the females, 66 per cent of the abnormals were identified as such and 59 per cent of the normals were so classified. These percentages are based upon the separations at a K = 50, and take, therefore, no account of the actual normal-abnormal proportions among the present cases.

Evidence from examination of the test misses spotted by K in the above data, combined with our knowledge of the correlation between K and other MMPI scales, indicated that the K correction was more important in the case of some scales than of others. Therefore, it was decided to analyze the borderline groups in terms of the peak elevation of their profiles, in the attempt to identify those particular curves on which K could be used with profit.

The entire group of 511 borderline curves (males and females, normals and abnormals pooled) was divided into eight subgroups, each subgroup being composed of cases having the peak score on the same one of the eight personality components. Thus, there were 60 curves having the peak on Hs, 91 on D, 119 on Hy, 66 on Pd, 38 on Pa, 25 on Pt, 28 on Sc, and 52 on Ma. (The difference between this total of 479 cases and the 511 used in getting the over-all chi square is due to the exclusion of 32 profiles on which no "peak" could be fairly assigned, since two or more of the components showed identical T scores and these were the highest on the given curve.)

The normals and abnormals having borderline curves with the same peak score were then separated mechanically by the use of a cutting score on K, the proportion of cases above the cutting score being determined on the basis of the proportion of actual abnormals versus normals in each subgroup. This was unavoidable in the present analysis because the relative proportions of actual normals and abnormals varied widely from scale to scale and the use of the mean of K would have been grossly misleading since in some instances the proportions were extremely asymmetrical [Zubin, 1934]. For the eight groups studied in this manner, only three showed a significant chi square ($p < .01$), namely those having peaks on Hs, Pd, and Sc. The Ma group yielded a chi square between the .10 and .20 level of significance. On D, Hy, Pa, and Pt the chi squares were all below the .20 level of significance; and the pooled chi square for these five scales (5 df) gave a $p > .22$. It would seem, therefore, that the K factor may be used with profit in interpreting some kinds of profiles but not others. Of course, the failure to discriminate with K when grouping profiles by peak score does not establish that a K correction might not be profitably added to the single scores themselves. This problem will be treated at length in a sequel to the present paper [McKinley, Hathaway, and Meehl, 1948 (see I, 10)].

One other validating study was done on K. In this instance, we made use of a group of 22 normals and 22 abnormals employed in a previous study [Meehl, 1945b]. The normals in this set consisted of a random selection from a large group of profiles showing any elevation of 70 or over (excluding Mf). The abnormals consisted of a heterogeneous group also having at least one score over 70, and included seven psychoneurotics, seven schizophrenics, three psychopaths, two alcoholics, two manic-depressives (depressed), and one paranoid state, chosen randomly from recent hospital cases. These groups had been selected for a different purpose and had not entered into the derivation of K in any way. They can also be considered, therefore, a fair test group for validation purposes. Without regard for any other information concerning the profiles, all cases showing $K > 50$ were arbitrarily guessed as abnormals, whereas those with $K < 50$ were called normals. The cutting score was therefore also independent of the statistics of the present group. Here the K scale worked phenomenally well, being much better than the N scale (which was derived on cases some of which were included in this blind diagnosis study). Of the entire group of 44 cases, 37 were correctly classified when K was used in this way, a total of 85 per cent hits. It will be recalled that we are here trying to separate normals and abnormals all of whom have deviant profiles, so that this percentage is quite impressive considering the task set for K. Of the seven errors in classifying, six are "false positives," i.e., cases of normals showing elevated profiles and $K > 50$, called therefore abnormal. The chi square for the fourfold table of these data is 21.569 which with 1 df is highly significant ($p < .001$). This corresponds to a contingency coefficient of .57. Here we have striking evidence of the validity of K when used to differentiate between deviant curves of actual normals and abnormals. We are not prepared to explain the superiority of this result to that given by the analysis previously discussed, except to say that the range of abnormal scores in the present analysis was from 70 to 90 whereas in the previous analysis we used "borderline" scores defined as lying between 65 and 80. In what way this could make K appear to function more effectively in the one case than the other is not clear. Also the present study involved only males, on whom K in general seems to work a little better than on females.

The fact that K is less effective as applied to some scales than others would suggest separate interpretations or cutting scores depending upon the kind of profile with which one is confronted. Furthermore, the rough classification into "normal" and "abnormal" on the basis of a single arbitrary cutting score obviously sacrifices some quantitative information about the actual magnitude of the personality scale elevations with respect to the magnitude of the K score. We do not intend to propose such a rough cutting method as the most efficient manner of application for K, but are using that form here simply to indicate that K has differentiating power for what it was hoped to differentiate. The optimal mathematical procedure in using K as a suppressor involves complex issues which we shall have to reserve for a later publication.

Relation of K to Other Test Variables

The correlation of the K scale with other MMPI variables should throw some light upon the question of its differential efficiency on these scales, as well as give us some insight into its psychological nature. Table 1 below shows the intercorrelations of K with the other personality components measured by the MMPI. These correlations are based upon 100 cases, chronological ages 26-45, in each of the four groups indicated, excluding records having "?" > 70 or F > 80.

Of interest in this table are the following facts. With the exception of Hy and one of the four coefficients of D, the correlations are consistently negative. This is of course to be expected if K represents the defensive, lying, or self-deceptive test-taking attitude it was derived to measure. The negative correlations with Hs combined with the positive correlations with Hy indicate that there must be a fairly high positive correlation between K and those nonsomatic items on Hy which have been previously referred to—the "zero" items on Hy or what Wiener and Harmon, [1946] have called "Hy-subtle" (henceforth designated Hy-S). Since this latter set of items, although derived by its empirical separation of clinical hysterias from normals, seems to reflect the self-deceptive and impunitive attitude of the hysterical temperament, it is consonant with our interpretation of K that it should be markedly correlated with Hy-S. The direct evidence on this point will be reported below. The only correlations of very impressive magnitude which appear in this table are those with Pt and Sc. Here they are high negative—the person who makes responses characteristic of compulsive and schizoid persons has the opposite of the self-deceptive and defensive attitude. In other words, he tends to be a plus-getter and in this way is distinctly unlike the hysteric. These correlations are also in harmony with our clinical knowledge of the components in question, especially in the case of the psychasthenia. The Pt scale has never been considered very satisfactory, and it has been shown in unpublished studies that Pt can actually be used as a correction scale in the way in which N was used. It is perhaps signifi-

Table 1. Intercorrelations of K with Other MMPI Variables

Group	Hs	D	Hy	Pd	Pa	Pt	Sc	Ma	Mf
Normal males	−.30	.15	.48	−.17	−.07	−.67	−.59	−.36	
Normal females . . .	−.35	−.03	.30	−.06	−.02	−.64	−.58	−.28	
Abnormal males. . .	−.42	−.29	.11	−.26	−.19	−.60	−.60	−.37	−.08
Abnormal females. .	−.17	−.16	.17	−.21	−.13	−.63	−.58	−.38	.04

cant that of all the MMPI scales, Pt is the only one for which, since there was not a sufficiently large criterion group, methods of internal consistency were employed in the item selection. Here again we would expect to get a greater operation of nonclinical test-taking factors of the K variety.

It might be thought that such low correlations as occur in the table above would preclude any possibility of the use of K as a suppressor. There is a tendency for the scales on which K seems "valid" by the chi square test to show the higher correlations, with the exception of Pt. It will be shown in a subsequent paper that, for the use to which K is put, correlations as low as .20 can be utilized to yield very significant and useful improvements in discrimination [McKinley, Hathaway, and Meehl, 1948 (see I, 10)].

At this point we may briefly review some of the previously developed scales which are now known to be saturated with what we may call the K factor, since their diverse sources and methods of derivation furnish additional strong evidence for our theoretical interpretation of K. Two of these scales have never been published, so that their derivation and properties must be briefly summarized here. About three years before research on the test-taking attitude was begun, Hathaway and W. K. Estes, using a variant of the method of internal consistency, developed a scale called G. This scale is the only MMPI scale which was derived without the use of any kind of criterion external to the test; like those personality tests being developed by factor analytic methods at the present time, the selection and scoring of items were based wholly upon the intercorrelations among the items themselves. Essentially, the procedure consisted in locating among a group of 101 unselected normals those individuals who, when their answer sheets were used as scoring keys, produced the maximum variance of the other 100 scores. The assumption was that these persons were the most extreme deviates on whatever factor or factors contributed most heavily to the variance and covariance of the total pool of MMPI items. From the evidence adduced by Mosier [1936], it is of course clear that the "purity" or factorial unity of this hypothetical underlying continuum is by no means guaranteed by such a procedure. Another way of looking at this procedure is to consider the fact that one maximizes the variance of a set of items by scoring them in such a direction as to maximize their mean covariance—since the item variances are unaffected by the direction of scoring. Instead of actually calculating the variances for the 2^{550} ways of scoring the test, we select *individuals* who approximate the optimal scoring key. It was found that the scoring keys for some 10 individuals selected by this method tended to form two distinct clusters, each of which consisted of keys (individuals) showing high correlations with one another and high negative correlations with the members of the other cluster. An item analysis was then carried out on these two small groups, and the items resulting were combined into a scale called G (general factor).

The G scale had a number of interesting properties which were not interpretable at the time of its derivation. It showed a very large variability, both in absolute terms and as indicated by a coefficient of variation. The scores *among normals* ranged from those who answered none of the items in the scored direction, to those who answered all but 8 of the 62 items in the scored direction—a phenomenon unheard of in the other MMPI scales. The odd-even reliability of G was about .93, which is considerably higher than the coefficients we typically find in the MMPI scales. The item content was that of the typical "neurotic" or "maladjustment" sort which predominates on a priori scales such as the Thurstone or Bernreuter B_1N. Examples of items are these: "When in a group of people I have trouble thinking of the right things to talk about" (T); "I cry easily" (T); "I am certainly lacking in self confidence" (T). It is perhaps significant that the most powerful single item in the internal consistency sense— which happens in the sample studies to have a correlation of 1.00 with the entire G scale—is almost a distilled essence or prototype of so-called neurotic schedule items: "I am easily embarrassed" (T). The G scale, although derived without recourse to any clinical group whatever, nevertheless showed a correlation of .91 with Pt. The mean MMPI curves for unselected normals with high G (the "neurotic" end) showed elevations on F, Hs, D, Pd, Pa, Pt, Sc, and Ma, especially on Pt and Sc, whereas L (raw score) and Hy tended to fall below the mean. The mean profile for normals with low G was almost an exact mirror image of this curve. However, G was not found to be very effective in the detection of any clinical group or to be particularly useful for any purpose; and since at that time no theoretical basis was available for interpreting it, the scale was abandoned. Another scale, called + ("plus"), was derived in a similar but not identical manner.

In the derivation of the original hypochondriasis key, there was developed a correction scale called C_H, the function of which was to separate actual clinical hypochondriacs from a group of nonhypochondriacal abnormals (mostly schizophrenic and depressed) who attained spuriously elevated scores on H. The item content of this C_H key was quite puzzling, because although the correction was successful, the items did not seem to refer to anything either hypochondriacal or anti-hypochondriacal. In fact it was difficult to see what psychological homogeneity, if any, they possessed. For a more detailed description of this scale (now no longer in use since the appearance of the modified Hs key) the reader is referred to the original article [McKinley and Hathaway, 1940 (see I, 2)]. For present purposes it is merely necessary to state that the great majority of the items on C_H were scored if answered in the statistically rare and obviously "maladjusted" direction and that they apparently measured some nonsomatic component of test responses which resulted in spuriously elevated H scores in persons who were not actually hypochondriacal.

Still another scale of the same general sort was derived by Meehl and called N. To repeat briefly what has been said above, this scale differentiated normals showing elevated profiles from clinical abnormals showing no greater profile elevations, and was interpreted as detecting a plus-getting test attitude for which scores on the personality components proper should be corrected. The type of item occurring on the scale N has been discussed above.

Lastly, we recall to mind the Hy-S items which have been described above as reflecting this kind of component, although scored in the opposite direction from N, C_H, and G.

It is of considerable interest to examine the correlations between K and these other variables, derived in their diverse ways. Table 2 presents the correlations between K and the various scales thought to be loaded with the factor in question; the correlations are based upon scores of 100 individuals ages 26-45 in each of the groups indicated.

Table 2. Correlations of the K Scale with Other Variables
Thought to Be Loaded with the "K Factor"

Group	+	G	N	C_H	Hy-S
Normal males	−.64	−.76	−.70	−.67	.81
Normal females	−.62	−.73	−.64	−.63	.78
Abnormal males.	−.70	−.75	−.69	−.64	.74
Abnormal females.	−.70	−.81	−.72	−.71	.74

Considering the relative unreliability of some of these variables, the above is a very impressive group of intercorrelations. We have two scales (G and +) which were derived wholly by internal item relationships and without regard to criteria of any nontest behavior; a scale (N) which corrects for the self-criticality of certain plus-getters who show deviant profiles; a scale (C_H) which differentiates hypochondriacs from nonhypochondriacal abnormals who have elevated H scores; and a subset of items (Hy-S) which were chosen because they differentiate a clinical group—hysterics. There is, however, a considerable item overlap among these scales, tending to raise these correlations. On the other hand, it will be recalled that the scale K is not actually "pure" for the hypothetical test-taking attitude because it is a composite of the test-taking scale L_6 plus the eight "psychotic" items. This would presumably tend to lower the correlations. Accordingly, we have substituted L_6 for K, removed the item overlap among the scales G, N, C_H, L_6, and Hy-S, and calculated correlations among these reduced keys. Table 3 shows the interrelations among these five nonoverlapping keys, based upon the responses of 150 unselected normal males between the ages of 26 and 45; records with $? > 70$ or $F > 80$ were rejected. All scales were scored so as to render the correlations positive.

This correlational matrix has been subjected to a factor analysis, repeated three times in successively approximating the communalities because of the small number of tests. The first factor extracted leaves no residuals larger than .049, and the SD of the residuals is .032, which is less than the SE of .041 attached to the mean r in the matrix. When the significance of the residuals was tested by the formula chi square $= \Sigma(z_0 - z)^2 (n - 3)$ the chi square on the deviation of observed r's from those predicted with the first factor loading was not significant (chi square $= 5.101$, 5 df, $p > .30$). It appears that one common factor is quite sufficient to account for the intercorrelations of these scales. The factor loadings of the scales G, C_H, L_6, N, and Hy-S are .927, .868, .847, .818, and .770 respectively. It is interesting to find such a powerful factor running through scales derived by such diverse methods. It is also worth noticing that the largest loading of the K factor is in the one scale constructed wholly by "internal consistency" methods, whereas the smallest loading is that

Table 3. Intercorrelations of Five Scales Thought to Be Loaded
with the Test-Taking Attitude, No Item Overlap
(N = 150 Normal Males)

Scale	G	C_H	L_6	N
C_H · · · · · · · · · · · ·	.82			
L_6· · · · · · · · · · · · ·	.76	.71		
N · · · · · · · · · · · · · ·	.78	.73	.66	
Hy-S · · · · · · · · · · ·	.70	.63	.70	.59

of the clinical variable Hy-S. If we extract a second factor just to see what it looks like, none of the loadings is over .20 and the meaning of the second factor would be quite uninterpretable on our data. Although we have been thinking in terms of a "K factor" on the basis of the apparent community of practical function shown by these various scales, it is reassuring to find that the term "factor" may be used here without doing violence to the more technical meaning of that term as used by factor analysts.

Considering the nature of the items which are involved in scales such as L_6, N, and G, this finding perhaps sheds some light on the relative inadequacy of "neurotic" inventories such as the B_1N when applied to clinically diagnosed neurotics. Here we have a kind of item which, while it does not (in its own right) appear to discriminate normal from abnormal individuals very successfully, does reflect some kind of a test-attitude or self-critical component. Those "neurotic" persons who happen to be characterized by this particular manifestation of self-criticism, such as certain compulsives, will probably be differentiated by such a set of items. On the other hand, other equally "neurotic" persons such as hysterics, who are characterized by the opposite attitude, will not be successfully spotted by the scale. If anything, they should be discriminated backward! Furthermore, the central tendency of abnormals in general is the same as that of normals, and it is quite possible that in developing personality questionnaires set up in the traditional, a priori fashion and "refined" by statistical manipulation we are merely setting up groups of items to differentiate among people with respect to various test-attitude continua of little or no psychiatric relevance. It will be recalled that the scale G consisted of items having the heaviest loading with whatever factor (or factors) contribute most to the variance and covariance of the entire 550 items in the MMPI pool. Yet this scale turns out to have little or no clinical value (*except* as a suppressor) and to be the scale most saturated with respect to the test-taking attitude. We feel that psychologists have tended to forget the fact that when one constructs a personality inventory by studying the item associations, whether by old-fashioned methods of internal consistency or by factor analysis of item correlations, he is merely locating certain covariations in verbal behavior. When a final scale based upon that kind of derivation is presented to the clinician, all that the clinician can be assured of is that *persons who say certain things about themselves also have a tendency to say certain other things about themselves.*

Willoughby's argument [1935] that the non-chance covariation of item responses establishes "validity" with respect to *some* underlying, common trait which gives rise to the covariation may be admitted without contradicting what we have just said. That items should exhibit consistency in this covariant sense in spite of not being valid for the traits sought, or in fact even being negatively valid, has been shown by many studies, most particularly those of Landis and his associates [Landis and Katz, 1934; Landis, Zubin, and Katz, 1935; Page, Landis, and Katz, 1934]. The "underlying disposition" which leads a subject to respond in a certain way to such questions may or may not be identical with the dispositions we recognize as clinical variables, or with those that might be suggested by the item content. It is quite clear on present evidence that this identification cannot be established by an assumed equivalence between nontest behavior and the verbal report. Hence, as has been repeatedly stressed by the present writers, both a priori selection of items and the psychological naming of a statistically homogenous scale from its item content are fraught with possibilities of error.

An obvious line of investigation which is suggested by these considerations is the systematic study of the relationships which exist among variables such as K, G, and N, which are fairly definitely known to be chiefly test-taking variables, and other personality scales which have been developed by variants of the method of internal consistency. Because of the influence of socioeconomic or educational level upon the K factor (see the section below) such studies should ideally be carried out upon subjects from the general population. At present, we can only report a few preliminary studies which seem to have some bearing upon this question. All these studies happen to be concerned with the batteries developed by Guilford and Martin (GAMIN, STDCR, and the Personnel Inventory). We wish to emphasize that the presentation of these scattered data on our part is intended simply to raise some questions concerning the construction of scales by internal consistency methods where factors such as K are probably in operation; the validity of the Guilford-Martin scales must of course be assessed upon other grounds. We wish further to stress that in comparing these tests with the MMPI we do not intend to set the latter up as a "criterion," although it does of course have the advantage that each item is known to differentiate certain defined criterion groups which literally define the scales on which the item occurs. It should also be made clear that Guilford, as one of the foremost contributors to the factor analytic approach to personality test construction, has explicitly called attention to the importance of the problem of test-taking attitudes as "factors," when he says:

We must constantly remember that the response of a subject may not represent exactly what the question implies in its most obvious meaning. Subjects respond to a question as at the moment they think they are, with perhaps a lack of insight in many cases as to their real position on the question. They also respond as they would like themselves to be and as they would like others to think them to be and as they wish the examiner to think them to be. They also respond with some regard to self-consistency among their own answers. Whether these determining factors are sufficiently constant to set up individual differences which are uniform in character and so constitute common factors in themselves is difficult to say. Should any one of them be so pervasive it should introduce an additional vector in the factor analysis. [Guilford and Guilford, 1936, p. 118]

It is our opinion that the data we have presented indicate that the answer to Guilford's question is in the affirmative, and that the inclusion of a few K-type scales in a factor analysis would probably result in a somewhat different interpretation of the other tests and factors than would otherwise be the case.

Elaine Wesley [1945] has studied the relationships existing between the Guilford-Martin Personnel Inventory of traits O-Ag-Co and the MMPI scales, using the test records of 110 presumably normal college women. The three traits measured by the Personnel Inventory are called *objectivity, agreeableness,* and *cooperativeness* by their authors. High scores are in the direction of the traits named, and low scores indicate the presence of what is called in composite the "paranoid" personality. Wesley found that the composite Personnel Inventory score correlated only .11 with the MMPI Pa scale which, while still in a preliminary stage, does consist of items which are empirically known to distinguish clearly paranoid groups of persons from people in general. Together with this rather disconcerting finding, she also discovered that the "paranoid" score on the Personnel Inventory correlated .50 and .57 with the MMPI scales Pt and Sc— both of which are relatively weak scales from the standpoint of clinical differentiation but are known to be heavily loaded with the K factor. The correlations of "objectivity" with Pt and Sc were both —.62, which led her to correlate trait O with the correction scale N, leading to the same figure. None of the other correlations of the Guilford scales with MMPI scales exceeded .45, and the majority of them were under .20. The mean MMPI profile of subjects selected on the basis of having low raw scores on N (the "defensive" end) showed a pattern hardly distinguishable from that of subjects selected for having high scores on factor O. It is interesting to note in passing that of the seven items of very similar wording which occur on both the Guilford-Martin Inventory and the MMPI Pa scale, five are scored as "paranoid" in the opposite direction on the two scales. For example, to say that most people inwardly dislike putting themselves out to help others, that most people would tell a lie to get ahead, that some people are so bossy and domineering that one feels like doing the opposite of what they tell him to do, are responses scored as paranoid on the Guilford-Martin; whereas it is found empirically that these verbal reactions are actually significantly *less* common among clinically paranoid persons than they are among people generally. This kind of finding suggests that paranoid deviates are characterized by a tendency to give two sorts of responses, one of which is obviously paranoid, the other "obviously" not. But these two sorts of responses are negatively correlated among people generally, and hence appear scored oppositely on scales developed by internal consistency methods.

It is of course possible to begin the development of scales by internal consistency or item-intercorrelation procedures, and having built a scale by these methods, to apply it to various criterion groups for validation. But it would seem that if the aim is to find items which will optimally perform such a discriminating function, the most direct route to that goal is immediate empirical item selection from the start. It may be agreed that scales developed through item-correlation techniques have more statistical "purity" and hence are in a certain special sense better for what they *do* measure. One's attitude toward this problem is likely to reflect his more fundamental views as to the nature of a so-called measurement in personality testing, complete discussion of which would take us beyond the present paper. It seems clear that the results of factor analysis to date have not, whatever their theoretical validity, made possible the construction of single personality items which can be called even approximately "pure." For example, in Guilford's factor analysis of 89 personality items originally chosen (on the basis of suggestions from a previous factor analysis) to sample seclusiveness, thinking introversion, and rhathymia, after the extraction of nine different factors the majority of the items still showed communalities less than .50. Torrens [1944], Wesley [1945], and Loth [1945] all found that the typical scale intercorrelation among the variables of the Guilford-Martin batteries STDCR, GAMIN, and the Personnel Inventory is actually higher than the typical intercorrelations of scales on the MMPI which were developed with almost no consideration for questions of scale purity or freedom from item overlap.

Louis Wesley (in a personal communication) has suggested that the contrast between the two methods of scale derivation is between *maximal measurement* and *meaningful measurement*. By this is meant that internal consistency methods lead to scales which measure whatever they measure with high consistency, large variance, great discrimination. This is "maximal" measurement. It is suggested that the most important nontest behaviors, which it is the aim of the test to predict, may not be associated with the same variables that lead to the kind of consistency involved. We may, as in the case of the Pa scale, have to sacrifice the desire to have high item intercorrelations in order to score items so as to achieve the more fundamental aim of criterion discrimination. Since scales are so very "impure" at best, there does not seem to be any very cogent reason for sacrificing anything in pursuit of the rather illusory purity involved.

There are multiple determiners which enter into a subject's decision when he answers a personality item. One might say that all but a very few personality items have an inherently "multiphasic" character, exceptions being such items as "I am a male." Obviously, if there existed or could be invented verbal items which were even approximately pure, the "scales" of such items could be extremely short and in fact the practical value of substituting an inventory for a few brief oral questions would be much in doubt. But the items are not uniquely determined. This simple behavioral fact imposes certain limitations upon the progress of personality measurement, as has been pointed out by many critics. From the common-sense point of view, the situation is not very different from what occurs in medical diagnosis or in the psychiatric interview. Almost all the symptoms or responses which are in evidence are known to arise upon diverse bases.

During a psychological interview, a woman may miscall her husband by the name of a former suitor, a phenomenon which is in itself ambiguous; perhaps she has recently seen the man in question, perhaps she has been reading a novel in which that name appears, and perhaps—the psychiatrically significant possibility—she feels somewhat regretful for not having married him instead. Later, we find that she developed a headache on her wedding anniversary, also an ambiguous datum if it stands alone. Again, she is excessively effusive about how happy her married life is, and so on. It is through the hypothesis of marital dissatisfaction that these different behaviors find a common explanation. When we accumulate such single items about her behavior, we are merely piling up the probabilities. It seems a little foolish to locate these behavior particles or their "sum" on a continuum of measurement, except in the most crude ordinal and probability sense. It is further quite likely that important configurational properties are also involved here, so that the significance to be assigned to one of these single facts should be a function of the other facts we know.

The traditional scoring procedure of simply counting *how many* responses belonging to a certain class have been made seems to be very crude; fortunately it has been repeatedly found that the various weightings, compositions, and nonlinear refinements which the behavioristic logic might suggest do not usually make sufficient practical difference in the ordering and sorting of people to be worth doing. The fact that we find it convenient to treat these behaviors in certain mathematical ways (independent scoring, unit weights, summation, linear transformations, etc.) should not mislead us into supposing that we are doing anything very close to what the physicist does when he cumulates centimeters. From this point of view, methods aimed at either "purity" or "internal consistency" are not easy to justify. At the very best, we have a rather heterogeneous collection of verbal responses which have a rough tendency to covary in strength. It may or may not be true that the most important (powerful) determiners of this tendency to covary are clinically relevant or personologically significant. For example, disliking one's husband is not the most powerful "factor" in determining the frequency of headaches among people generally. Nor is it the most potent factor in determining whether one calls him by the wrong name. Furthermore, the tendency to do these two things may not be covariant at all among people in general. None of these reasons, however, would lead us to reject the two facts in trying to evaluate the hypothesis of marital unhappiness.

From both the logical and statistical points of view, the best set of behavior data from which to predict a criterion is the set of data which are among themselves not correlated. This is well known and made use of in the combination of scales into batteries; but for some reason psychologists are uncomfortable if the same reasoning is applied within scales. The statistical considerations are of course quite general, applying as well to items as to scales. It is likely that the insistence upon high internal consistency and "item validity" in the item-test correlation sense springs in part from a feeling that all the items ought to be "doing the same thing." This certainly sounds like a reasonable demand as it stands, but it requires clarification. As is clear from the factor analysis studies, one simply cannot find any appreciable number of nonidentical verbal items which all "do the same thing." Every one of them depends upon many things, and the item as a unit is like the old-fashioned atom—uncuttable and hence permanently impure. Items "do the same thing" when they are so combined in pools that it is very unlikely that the subject will answer many of them in the scored direction unless he is characterized by a certain strength or range of nontest behaviors which in turn depend upon the one (or few) "variables" that are common to the items. It may still (unfortunately) be the case that the heaviest contribution to each item consists of variables other than the ones we are interested in. That this is in fact true is indicated by the typical values of item communalities.

It is this state of affairs which we believe imposes limitations upon the efficiency of such suppressor scales as K. Since we cannot find items which depend upon only clinical abnormality, we try to find items which depend upon abnormality to an appreciable extent even though they unavoidably depend upon other things as well. The suppressor consists of items which unavoidably depend to some slight degree upon clinical abnormality, but to a greater extent upon the objectionable factors in the first set. By cumulating responses to the second set of items, we hope to get an indication of the strength of these other factors, which information is then used to correct for their undesired contribution to a score attained on the first. The impurity of the suppressor itself, however, sets limits to the efficiency of such a process. Thus, a subject may obtain a high depression score because he is a plus-getter. The strength of his plus-getting tendency is assessed by items such as those of K. However, a sufficiently great degree of depression will yield considerable deviations on K, since the K items themselves are not pure for the plus-getting tendency but are also slightly loaded with clinical abnormality. In such cases K operates against us. It is interesting to note that the K scale, itself a suppressor, also *contains* a suppressor in the form of the eight "psychotic" items—but here also the effort to suppress the unwanted components of the suppressor can only be imperfectly carried out. No refinements of statistical technique enable us to escape the basic psychological fact that our smallest behavior units, the responses made to single items, are inherently of this multiphasic character.

Relation of K to Age, Intelligence, and Socioeconomic Status

In the study of the correction scale N it had been observed that college students (actually, high school graduates tested at the university Counseling Bureau prior to actual matriculation) showed a distinct elevation in the "lie" direction, averaging about one sigma above the general population mean. It was also found that the younger age group (16-25) showed a similar although smaller deviation, which was accounted for by the presence of a considerable number of medical students in that group. Furthermore, college graduates who had been some ten years out of college showed a mean T score of about 60 on the N scale. A similar trend is discernible in the case of K. The mean T score of a group of 84 medical students is at 62, a deviation which is significant at the .01 level. Both male and female precollege cases average a T of 57 on K. This tendency falls in line with the fact that the mean MMPI curve for several college and precollege groups, including some obtained elsewhere than at Minnesota, is a curve with a slight but consistent elevation on Hy, in spite of having an Hs below the mean. This indicates, as usual, a tendency to respond in the hysteroid fashion which elevates Hy-subtle enough to more than counteract the tendency to answer the somatic items on Hy in a non-hypochondriacal fashion. We are not prepared on present evidence to give an interpretation of this phenomenon. That it is not primarily a reflection of intelligence differences is suggested by a correlation of only .04 between K and ACE score among the precollege cases, which, even taking their relative homogeneity into account, should be higher if intellect as such is the reason for the difference. If the factor at work here is not intelligence, or the mere fact of being in college when tested, two other possibilities are socioeconomic status and chronological age. A group of WPA workers in the young age group 16-25 showed no elevation on K whatsoever, which would favor the socioeconomic interpretation. The mean K of a group of 50 normals aged 16-25, excluding college graduates and persons in college, was 13.5 (T = 52). These figures would seem to eliminate mere chronological age as the chief basis of differentiation. We are left with socioeconomic status as the most plausible remaining variable. What is needed is a study of a group of persons in the upper socioeconomic group who are not college students and have never been college educated. Unfortunately, we do not have a large enough sample of such persons to enable us to draw conclusions with certainty. The mean raw score on K for a group of 18 normal subjects classified in Groups I and II in the Goodenough classification, who were not, however, college graduates or attending college, was 18.50, which corresponds to a T score of 61. In spite of the small N, this difference is great enough so that a t ratio comparing their mean with that of 156 unselected normals from the other economic classes was highly significant (t = 6.055, p < .01). It seems plausible that the college, precollege, and college-educated elevation is reflecting chiefly a difference in socioeconomic status, although further evidence on this topic should be collected. If this is confirmed by subsequent investigation, it will be interesting to speculate upon the possible ways in which membership in the upper classes generates the particular kind of defensiveness involved.

Summary and Conclusions

The general problem of test-taking attitudes in their effect upon scores obtained on structured personality inventories is discussed. The literature on the subject is briefly surveyed, and a discussion given of the various approaches which have been taken in an effort to solve this problem. The final result of many efforts to derive special scales for measuring various attitudes in the taking of the MMPI is presented, with some indication of its validity. The relationship of this scale, called K, to other variables is used as a basis for discussing certain general problems in the theory of personality measurement. Conclusions are as follows:

1. The conscious or unconscious tendency of subjects to present a certain picture of themselves in taking a personality inventory has a considerable influence upon their scores.

2. We may distinguish two directions in this test-taking attitude: the tendency to be defensive or to put oneself in a too favorable light, and the opposed tendency to be overly honest and self-critical (plus-getting). The extremes of these tendencies are deliberate, conscious efforts to fake bad or lie good.

3. The defensive tendency appears to be related to the clinical picture of hysteria, whereas plus-getting is related to the picture of psychasthenia.

4. The MMPI scales L and F, while relatively effective in detecting extreme distortion, do not seem to be sufficiently subtle to detect the more common and often unconscious varieties of defensiveness or plus-getting. It has been found convenient to begin interpretation of L in the range of T scores 55 or 60, whereas F does not clearly establish invalidity even up to T score 80 (raw score about 16).

5. By contrasting item frequencies of abnormal persons showing normal MMPI profiles and elevated L scores with the records of unselected normals, an empirical key called K has been derived which is relatively successful in detecting the influence of disturbing test-taking attitudes and can be used to improve the discrimination between normals and abnormals.

6. In studying the intercorrelations among a group of scales derived by various means but all functioning with some effectiveness to detect such attitudes, it was found that one common factor is sufficient to account for all the intercorrelations. The scale (G) which has the largest factor loading was derived by a method of internal consistency and without recourse to any external criterion. Since K is the scale being used to measure this factor, the factor in question has been called the K factor.

7. On the basis of these findings and study of the relationship of the MMPI to certain of the Guilford-Martin scales, it is suggested that perhaps the construction of personality inventories by means of item-correlation and factor analytic methods leads to the development of tests which are excessively loaded with such test-taking attitudes. The procedure of internal consistency in its various forms is called into question as a profitable method for the construction of personality inventories.

The K Scale

J. C. McKinley, S. R. Hathaway, and P. E. Meehl

The K scale of the MMPI was developed in an attempt to correct the scores obtained on the personality variables proper for the influence of attitudes toward the test situation. The rationale of the approach as well as the empirical procedure employed in deriving K has been presented in a previous publication [Meehl and Hathaway, 1946 (see I, 9)] and will not be dealt with here except very summarily. The present paper is to be read as a sequel to the original and aims chiefly to present norm data on K for various groups, an improved technique for applying K statistically, and certain miscellaneous observations such as its effects on the validity and intercorrelations of the other scales of the MMPI.

The K scale was derived by studying the item response frequencies of certain diagnosed abnormals who had *normal* profiles. It was here assumed that the occurrence of a normal profile was suggestive of a defensive attitude in the patient's responses. The response frequencies were contrasted with those from an unselected sample of people in general ("normals"). The differentiating items were then scored so that a high K score would be found among abnormals with normal curves, whereas a low score would be found in clinical normals having deviant curves. In this operational sense, it can be said that a high K score is indicative of a defensive attitude, and a low K score suggests unusual frankness or self-criticism ("plus-getting"). The extremes of defensiveness and plus-getting may be called "faking good" and "faking bad" respectively.

The earlier procedure for applying K was one of subjectively correcting profiles on the basis of the K score. Thus, a given borderline curve would be "under-interpreted" if K was considerably below the mean, since the examinee would be presumed to have achieved a bad curve because of his plus-getting tendency. If the same profile occurred in the presence of an elevated K, the clinician would assume that the curve ought to be "over-interpreted," since the examinee showed evidence in his high K of having been defensive.

In the following presentation we will first give the more practical data referent to the routine use of K. Following the description of the determination of K-correction factors and specific data on validity we will return to the more general facts bearing on clinical interpretation integrated with the whole profile.

The original method of using K was admittedly vague and inspectional, and would require considerable experience on the part of the individual clinician. It was clear that the influence of the K factor upon scores was not the same for all MMPI variables, so that the optimal interpretation of the personality scales proper on the basis of a given K deviation varied. It is obvious that the amount of experience required to make a satisfactory use of K in profile interpretation would be very great, even assuming that the clinician would be able subjectively to record, retain, and analyze the welter of impressions with reference to the nine personality components. For this reason, it seemed that a more rigorous and objective procedure for taking account of the K score would be desirable.

Since high K scores represent the defensive or "fake good" end of the test attitude continuum, the most obvious approach to the problem is to add K (or some function of K) to the raw score on each personality variable, i.e., increase the score in the direction of abnormality. Thus, a psychopath who is very defensive in taking the test is presumed to have attained a lower raw score on the Pd scale than he "should" have, i.e., than he would have had he been less defensive. This defensiveness will also tend to reflect itself as a high K score. The obtained score on Pd should accordingly be corrected by adding some amount, the amount added being dependent upon the degree of defensiveness present as indicated by K. The problem is simply one of determining the optimal weight for the K factor with respect to any given scale, taking a linear function as an adequate approximation for practical purposes.

Our first attempt was crude in that it treated K as what may be called a "pure" suppressor, whose only contribution lay in its correlation with the noncriterion components of the personality variable [McNemar, 1945; Meehl, 1945c]. In a preliminary study of the Hs scale, using an unusually carefully selected group of diagnosed hypochondriacs, the Hs score was increased by a fraction of K proportional to the regression weight of Hs on K among the normals. In other words, in place of Hs alone we now were using the *residual* of Hs regressing on K, i.e., that part of Hs which is K independent. This procedure is inexact since it assumes that K itself is uncorrelated with the dichotomous criterion, and also because it neglects the correlation of Hs with K among the abnormals. In spite of this crudeness, it was encouraging to find that the corrected Hs score now enabled us to detect 89 per cent of the hypochondriacs as contrasted with about 70 per cent of the same sample when Hs was used alone. This separation was achieved on a test group which had not entered into the derivation of either Hs or the K weight, and involved no increase in the number of false positives among normals (about 5 per cent in both cases).

The desirability of taking account of the correlation of K with the personality scales among both normals and abnormals, as well as any differentiating power of its own which K might have on certain sorts of cases, suggests the use of the discriminant function for determining the optimal weight. In the present problem, the variances among normals and abnormals were not always alike, nor was it convenient to restrict our analysis to the usual case of equi-numerous groups. We experimented with a modification of the discriminant function which added variances rather than sums of squares, but decided to reject this also for the following reason: The region in which differentiation is clinically most important is around 60 to 80 T score. There is little or no basis at present for interpreting the personality scores which are below the mean. All methods which are based upon maximizing the ratio of the variance of criterion group means to some type of pooled variance *within* groups will be taking account of the entire distribution. This results in a K weight based upon information which there seems to be no reason to include. The skewness of MMPI variables and the obvious doubts one might have as to the influence of K at different points of the distribution led us to determine the optimal weight by a study of a more restricted region, within which refinement was of greatest consequence. It is unfortunate that this decision entails procedures which are mathematically inelegant and in sore need of analytic justification but we have not been able as yet to devise acceptable alternatives. It is hoped that the procedure now to be described will seem reasonable, and that others will attempt a formally simple solution and will study the sampling distribution of the test employed. In the present case, there is reason to suspect that a general maximizing solution is impossible without making assumptions regarding distribution form which are empirically inadmissible.

Consider a given personality variable, represented in deviate score form by x, where the deviation is from the mean of normals. Let the K deviate score be represented by z. Let λ be an arbitrary weight, whose optimal value is to be determined. *Optimal value* refers here to the λ which achieves the best differentiation between a criterion group of abnormals diagnosed as having the abnormality in question (e.g., hypochondriasis) and a sample of unselected normals. In other words, we are here considering the personality variables singly, by specific diagnosis, rather than "abnormals" as a whole. Then the deviate *corrected* score on the given abnormal component is

$$y = x + \lambda z$$

Let us now restrict our attention to the cases scoring above the mean of *normals* on y, i.e., consider only cases such that $x + \lambda z > 0$. We now define a sum of squares for those abnormals whose corrected score is above the *normal* mean. That is, for cases such that $x + \lambda z > 0$, we define a sort of "half sum of squares,"

$$SS_a = \Sigma_a(y)^2 = \Sigma_a(x + \lambda z)^2$$

The same quantity is computed for the normals,

$$SS_n = \Sigma_n(y)^2 = \Sigma_n(x + \lambda z)^2$$

The ratio of these two sums of squares, which we shall call the *differential ratio,*

$$\frac{SS_a}{SS_n} = \frac{\Sigma_a(x + \lambda z)^2}{\Sigma_n(x + \lambda z)^2}$$

is then taken as an index of the degree of differentiation achieved by a given value of λ.

It can almost be seen by inspection that a straightforward analytic solution for the optimal λ cannot be carried through by maximizing this ratio, since the number of cases involved in numerator and denominator will occur in the resulting derivative and will itself fluctuate with the choice of a λ in a manner that cannot be known without special specifications of the joint distribution of x and z. Even if special assumptions are made, such as normal bivariate surface and equal correlation for normals and abnormals (neither being true in this sort of material), the solution of the problem presents serious mathematical complications. We hope to be able to make further progress in this direction and invite more mathematically competent readers to attack the general case. We fell back upon a straight trial-and-error method. We assigned arbitrary values of λ ($= .1, .2, .3, .4,$ etc.) and for each of these values we distributed y for normals and criterion cases separately. The ratio SS_a/SS_n was then calculated for each of these λ values, and these ratios were plotted as a function of λ. A smooth curve was drawn by inspection through the plotted points, and a rough maximum was estimated therefrom. Where several different samples of abnormals were available, such curves were drawn separately for each, in the hope of having more confidence in the estimated maximum on the basis of agreement in curve "trend."

One further qualification needs to be mentioned. Since squares emphasize extreme deviations, and in view of what has been said above concerning "clinically important range," it was felt desirable to limit the influence of extreme deviations upon the ratio. Therefore, after the distribution of y for a given λ had been obtained, all scores of the normal and abnormal groups lying above three standard deviations on the basis of a given $x + \lambda z$ normal distribution (corrected T score of 80) were arbitrarily reduced to that value. A change in λ which produced further elevations of abnormals already at three sigma would therefore not result in further improvement in the differential ratio. It is possible that four sigma should have been chosen instead, since recent work on pattern analysis in differential diagnosis among abnormals suggests that elevations above three sigma may be important. In fact, we would not be prepared to defend vigorously the use of this restriction at all.

The graphical method used gave opportunity to observe the behavior of the differential ratio as λ was varied, and to check the degree of disparity with other indicators of separation. In general, it was found that the λ which maximized the ratio tended to agree fairly well with that selected by such measures as percentage of abnormals above the top decile of normals. Research on a different problem suggests that the differential ratio gives results similar to but not identical with the critical ratio. In the present study, the λ's finally chosen were sometimes based upon compromises between the curve maxima of the differential ratio for various criterion groups, as well as counting measures of overlap.

Table 1 shows typical data on the differential ratio as applied to Sc + λK. Groups I and II are composed of 25 and 28 males diagnosed schizophrenia and Groups III and IV of 24 and 14 female cases respectively. There were some minor differences in the clinical constitution of the four groups but since the curves were similar in maximum points these differences can be disregarded. From these data we chose the λ weight for Sc to be 1K.

The K weights which were finally adopted by these procedures are given below:

$$Hs + .5K \qquad Sc + 1.0K$$
$$Pd + .4K \qquad Ma + .2K$$
$$Pt + 1.0K$$

It must be emphasized that these weights are optimal, within our sample, for the differentiation of largely inpatient psychiatric cases of full-blown psychoneurosis and psychosis from a general Minnesota "normal" group. For other clinical purposes it is possible that other λ values would be more appropriate. Thus, it seems likely that for the best separation of "maladjusted normals," such as those which abound in a college counseling bureau and would be formally diagnosed in a psychiatric clinic as *simple adult maladjustment,* other weights might be better.

Table 1. Values of the Differential Ratio as a Function
of the K Weight (λ) for the Sc Scale

λ	Schizophrenic Group			
	I	II	III	IV
0.0	.08	.07	.04	.04
0.1	.23	.19	.15	.08
0.2	.39	.35	.27	.14
0.3	.54	.49	.37	.19
0.4	.69	.63	.46	.25
0.5	.86	.79	.59	.34
0.6	.98	.76	.69	.39
0.7	1.13	.95	.81	.45
0.8	1.18	1.18	.91	.52
0.9	1.28	1.33	1.03	.61
1.0	1.23	1.35	1.06	.63
1.1	1.18	1.36	1.07	.62
1.2	1.13	1.32	1.05	.68
1.3		1.22	.97	.53
1.4			.88	.57
1.5			.81	.60

The mode of applying these weights has been described already in the supplementary manual for the MMPI published by the Psychological Corporation [Hathaway, 1946]. This manual contains a set of tables to be used in making the K correction, and new test blanks are also available to be used with K. Briefly one determines the weighted K value by referring to the table, which is based directly upon the proportions just cited. Thus, in correcting Hs for K, one begins by determining .5K either mentally or from the table (K here is the *raw* score). This quantity is then added to the original *raw* score on Hs, to yield Hs + .5K. This sum is called the *corrected raw score* on Hs. This corrected raw score is then entered in a second table of Tc (corrected T scores). This T table is of course based upon the mean and standard deviation (on general normals) of the quantity Hs + .5K. Similar processes are involved in the case of the other scales.

It will be noted that only five scales receive a K correction. The scales D, Hy, and Pa are uncorrected. (Mf was not studied in this respect.) It may seem paradoxical that in the original article on K, we found only three scales on which K would "work." This finding was based on a crude test using a single cutting score and a chi-square analysis. In the case of Pt, the sample studied originally was very small and significance hard to attain. The present K weights are to be accepted as the best indication of the "improvement" achieved by K, rather than the chi squares cited previously.

We see then that Pt and Sc are most affected by K, Hs and Pd mediumly, Ma least, and D, Hy, and Pa not at all. It is interesting to speculate upon this hierarchy. It will be recalled that the scale D already contains a correction scale, called C_D [Hathaway and McKinley 1942 (see I, 3)]. Hy already contains the K factor in the Hy-subtle items [Meehl and Hathaway, 1946 (I, 9); McKinley and Hathaway, 1944 (I, 5)]. While Pa has no explicit correction scale, almost one fourth of the Pa items are of the Hy-subtle type (eight being actually "0" items on the scoring key). These items, with the indicated response scored for Pa, are as follows:

B-54. My mother or father often made me obey even when I thought that it was unreasonable. (F) D-46. Most people inwardly dislike putting themselves out to help other people. (F) D-50. Most people are honest chiefly through fear of being caught. (F) D-52. I think most people would lie to get ahead. (F) D-53. I think nearly anyone would tell a lie to keep out of trouble. (F) D-54. Most people will use somewhat unfair means to gain profit or an advantage rather than to lose it. (F) D-55. The man who provides temptation by leaving valuable property unprotected is about as much to blame for its theft as the one who steals it. (F) G-50. Some people are so bossy that I feel like doing the opposite of what they request, even though I know they are right. (F) H-9. I tend to be on my guard with people who are somewhat more friendly than I had expected. (F)

If one calculates the percentage of "0" items for each of the eight personality scales (excluding Mf), the proportion of such items per scale is Hs = 0%, Sc = 3%, Pt = 4%, Ma = 15%, Pd = 16%, Pa = 20%, D = 27%, Hy = 33%.

These figures at least suggest that the proportion of zero items per scale tends to be negatively associated with the K weight found to be optimal. One way of looking at this finding is to say that scales which are more *subtle* are less subject to distortion by such test attitudes as K, and hence cannot be improved much by application of a K correction. It cannot be decided on present evidence whether this is the correct view rather than the view that the subtle items, although not derived as suppressors, already contain "suppressor" components for the obvious items.

The Effect of the K Correction on Validity as Related to Diagnosis

Table 2 gives an idea of the diagnostic effect achieved by the K correction. The cases designated "test cases" were not always clear cases of the given diagnostic category but represented patients who were noted by the psychiatric staff as being at least in part characterized by traits belonging to the category. Hence it is probably fair to assume that the percentages of these cases lying above the three given T values are smaller than would be true of more carefully selected patients. The 200 standard sample normal records used as reference were made up of 100 males and 100 females from the general normative files who were specially selected to be representative of the whole population.

For Hs and Hs + .5K, the data are given on both Hs and Hy test groups. The figures for these groups as distributed by Hy are also included. (See also Table 3.) One may compare not only the Hs with Hs + .5K but also Hs + .5K with Hy. It is apparent from Table 2 and from correlational data that the addition of K to Hs makes it act more like Hy. This could be predicted from the communality of K and Hy-subtle [Meehl and Hathaway, 1946 (see I, 9)]. In terms of the group data of Tables 2 and 3, one is justified in using both scales. As was argued in an earlier publication [McKinley and Hathaway, 1944 (see I, 5)], clinical evidence is at present in favor of the con-

Table 2. The Effect of the Final K Corrections on Test Case Groups Contrasted to a Standard Sample of 200 Normal Cases (The Values Given Are the Percentages of Cases at or above the Given T-Score Points)

T Score	Hs 200 Normals	Hs 101 Hs Test Cases	T Score	Hs + .5K 200 Normals	Hs + .5K 101 Hs Test Cases
70.0	3	59	70.0	5.5	74
69.8	5	62	70.3	5	72
65.0	10	69	62.9	10	89

T Score	Hy 200 Normals	Hy 101 Hs Test Cases	T Score	Hs 200 Normals	Hs 74 Hy Test Cases
70.0	4	64	70.0	3	38
67.5	5	74	69.2	5	42
63.3	10	79	65.0	10	55

T Score	Hs + .5K 200 Normals	Hs + .5K 74 Hy Test Cases	T Score	Hy 200 Normals	Hy 74 Hy Test Cases
70.0	5.5	54	70.0	4	53
70.3	5	51	67.5	5	62
62.9	10	69	63.3	10	66

T Score	Pd 200 Normals	Pd 89 Pd Test Cases	T Score	Pd + .4K 200 Normals	Pd + .4K 89 Pd Test Cases
70.0	5	52	70.0	3.5	55
70.0	5	52	67.5	5	65
65.0	10	65	62.7	10	76

T Score	Pt 200 Normals	Pt 36 Pt Test Cases	T Score	Pt + 1K 200 Normals	Pt + 1K 36 Pt Test Cases
70.0	6.5	42	70.0	4	61
71.5	5	40	68.5	5	67
67.2	10	47	64.0	10	67

T Score	Sc 200 Normals	Sc 91 Sc Test Cases	T Score	Sc + 1K 200 Normals	Sc + 1K 91 Sc Test Cases
70.0	4.5	31	70.0	2	59
69.0	5	31	64.0	5	69
62.5	10	43	61.2	10	75

T Score	Ma 200 Normals	Ma 89 Ma Test Cases	T Score	Ma + .2K 200 Normals	Ma + .2K 89 Ma Test Cases
70.0	8	62	70.0	2.5	65
66.3	5	72	65.7	5	74
61.8	10	79	63.1	10	84

tinued use of both scales because they are complementary when operating in the individual case. For example, Table 3 indicates that the joint use of both scales results in the identification of more hypochondriacs and hysterics than would the use of either separately. We hope soon to publish further data relative to the clinical significance of the two scales used together.

Table 3. Comparison of the Action of Hs + .5K and Hy on Test Cases
Diagnosed Psychoneurosis, Hypochondriasis, and Psychoneurosis, Hysteria

	Percentage of Hs Test Cases with T Score 70 and above	Percentage of Hy Test Cases with T Score 70 and above
On Hs + .5K alone	16	9
On Hy alone	6	12
On both scales	58	41

The gains for Pd + .4K over Pd are most marked at the 5th and 10th percentiles. This results from a flattening of the frequency curve for the normals in the range of 60 to 70 T score. We have already tended to interpret Pd as having clinical significance at around T = 65 when it appears as a clear "spike" or when certain other values (especially the neurotic triad) are below 50. The above data probably add justification to this interpretation.

The increased validity of Pt + 1K is a function of both increased normality in the frequency curve for normals and relatively higher scores for the test cases. The Pt + 1K is likely to be more clearly a "clinical" scale than was the Pt. We have pointed out [Meehl and Hathaway, 1946 (I, 9)] that Pt is a rather good measure of the K factor and one would expect partial removal of this variance to result in a remainder "purer" for the real clinical component. Good clinical data on psychasthenia relatively independent of schizophrenia are difficult to obtain and we can give no further evidence at this time.

Sc was never a very satisfactory scale [Hathaway, 1956 (see I, 6)] in terms of the number of schizophrenic patients identified, although when it is elevated Sc is quite valid. When Sc + 1K is used, a very gratifying improvement is apparent. These gains with a K correction are from all standpoints the best of the five scales.

The improvement of Ma + .2K over Ma is not great but if the effect upon the frequency curve for normals is combined with that on the test group, it is definitely worth while to use the correction. Ma is the most common single deviate score in both high and low directions. Among the profiles of unselected normals, Ma occurs as a "peak" score more often than does any other scale, and it also occurs as a lowest score more often than any other. This is presumably a statistical consequence of the fact that Ma correlates with the other scales less than they tend to correlate among themselves. Ma probably has more independent clinical significance than any other single scale. These facts add to the importance of any gains in validity.

The General Interrelationship of K and K-Corrected Scales

Table 4 shows the means and standard deviations for various groups. We attribute no certain significance to the variations that can be observed in these statistics. The normals designated in this table are the general normals that have been described elsewhere in publications on the MMPI as a reasonably satisfactory cross section of Minnesota residents. While there are several possible sex difference trends as seen in the separate age groups, a grand compilation of all these normal males contrasted with all the females shows no appreciable differentiation.

The two groups referred to as "mixed psychiatric" included all diagnoses observed in the psychiatric unit and are not necessarily typ-

Table 4. The K Means and Standard Deviations of Various Groups

Group	N	Sex	M	SD
Normals age 16-25 inc.	115	F	12.61	4.96
Normals age 16-25 inc.	73	M	13.79	5.27
Normals age 26-35 inc.	153	F	12.82	5.21
Normals age 26-35 inc.	105	M	12.41	5.85
Normals age 36-45 inc.	105	F	10.41	4.60
Normals age 36-45 inc.	69	M	12.49	5.14
Normals age 16-45 inc.	373	F	12.08	5.07
Normals age 16-45 inc.	247	M	12.84	5.64
Mixed psychiatric	372	M	14.57	5.85
Mixed psychiatric	596	F	14.34	5.21
University	50	M	16.10	5.15
University	50	F	15.66	5.01
University (Drake, Wisconsin)	379	F	15.58	4.20
High School (Capwell)	73	F	14.96	5.46
Reform school (adolescent) (Capwell)	88	F	12.77	4.99
Reformatory (adult) (Capwell)	34	F	14.18	4.86
Graduate electrical engineers (Minneapolis-Honeywell)	100	M	16.72	4.19
Miscellaneous employed (American Airlines)	100	F	15.38	6.05

ical of a psychiatric hospital of the usual type. Many of the patients presented behavior problems of types that would not be committed to an institution for the insane and in general the group would be a borderline group between the obviously psychotic and the normal. The moderate rise in the means for these groups is chiefly contributed by the psychopathic personality and criminal individuals who would make up about 20 per cent of the whole number. University students have a relatively higher mean as contrasted with general normals of their age range. An interesting point is evident in the means for the Capwell [1945b] girls. Here the reform school cases obtain a lower mean than otherwise similar adolescents in high school. This low mean is contradictory to the tendency that we observed in adult offenders which is illustrated by the reformatory women whose mean score is somewhat higher than the general norm. It is of interest in this connection that a K correction slightly decreased the differentiation of the Capwell cases from their matched partners when the Pd scale was used as a discriminator. We have no explanation at present for this finding.

The largest mean that we have observed was obtained from the graduate electrical engineers. These men were studied during the war and were mostly around 30 years of age. They were exempted from military duty in order to carry on aviation research and at the time of testing were applying for special airplane control testing at high altitude. The final group of miscellaneous employed was obtained from a sample of airline employees most of whom were college graduates or had several years of college work. These were in skilled clerical or minor administrative type positions.

We have described elsewhere [Meehl and Hathaway, 1946 (see I, 9)] experiments in which ASTP men and several other groups were asked to fake good and bad profiles on the MMPI. In these experiments half the class faked a good or bad profile and the other half took the inventory in a supposedly honest way. At a subsequent session of the class, the roles of these two groups were reversed. All the subjects were naive in regard to personality inventories and in regard to the MMPI in particular.

This procedure afforded a check upon the action of F and L as well as K. In brief, it was found that F was very efficient in distinguishing faked bad records but L was not at all effective in detecting a faked good record among the men and was only moderately effective with women. We at first presumed that the failure of L for men was in part due to the relatively obvious items of which L is composed.

Among 48 student nurses asked to fake a good record, 16, or 33 per cent, obtained a raw score L greater than or equal to 7 (T score greater than or equal to 60) in contrast to only one out of 48 when the same girls took the test with a supposedly honest attitude. If a raw score L greater than or equal to 6 (T score greater than or equal to 56) is used, these figures become 54 per cent identified as faked for the faked records, as contrasted with 10 per cent "false positive" among the honest records. This finding accords with our clinical experience that it is profitable to begin interpretation of L at T = 60 or even lower [Meehl and Hathaway, 1946 (see I, 9)].

When we turn to the K distributions for these two groups, the most interesting findings are that the mean K score for the 48 nursing students taking the MMPI "honestly" is 18.3, standard deviation 3.80, and the corresponding statistics for 107 ASTP men are 19.8 and standard deviation 4.10. These two means correspond to general normal T values of about 61 and 63 respectively. These means are definitely larger even than the means of college students in general as given in Table 2. Some factor seems to have operated on these two experimental groups to produce an unusually high average value of K when they were supposedly taking the test with an honest attitude.

As might be expected, when data were obtained from the 54 of the ASTP men faking a bad profile, the mean K values shifted markedly downward. The statistics for this group of faked bad data are a mean of 8.1 and standard deviation 4.04. The mean corresponds to a normal T value of 41. We have no corresponding statistics for women. K is in this case equally sensitive with F in differentiating the faked bad profiles. By contrast, the average K score for the 53 ASTP men who attempted to fake a good score was very little different from their normal mean as given above. The mean of this group's faked good records was 20.2 and the standard deviation 3.66. The mean would correspond to a normal T of 64. This result was similar to the finding among the student nurses who obtained a mean K score of 19.7 and a standard deviation of 3.90 on faked good records. The normal T score for this mean is about 64. It should be kept in mind that when the ASTP men attempted to fake a bad profile the resulting profiles were very severe, differed to a remarkable extent from the individual's "honest" profile, and could be recognized as invalid from the profile form alone. In contrast again to this, neither the men's nor the women's faked good profiles could readily be distinguished in any consistent way from their honest profiles, or from the ordinary profiles of normal persons in general. The obvious experiment in which one would take a group who had deviant profiles and ask them to attempt to fake good was not performed. Further evidence on the behavior of K and F in the "fake bad" situation can be found in a recent article by Gough [1947].

In consideration of these data, it seems justifiable to postulate that in these experiments the differentiation of the faked good profiles by the use of K is impossible because the "honest" was already in some sense faked good. The evidence that the "honest" represented something already related to faking can be derived from the fact that the "honest" means of both these groups were more than a standard deviation elevated in terms of the general normal mean statistics for K and at least half a standard deviation in T score above the means obtained from other college data. This elevation over the three other means given in Table 2 would be even greater in standard scores on the basis of the college data considered as norms. Some unidentified factor related to K must have operated in the experimental situation where the faking data were obtained. This latter assumption would be more certain if the rise in the means had not been observed from such different groups as student nurses and ASTP men. It is possible, however, to link these two groups provisionally in one significant element. Both the nurses and the men were under impulsion not to jeopardize in any possible way their continuance in the war-related programs that they were following. This pressure would contrast with the situation of the miscellaneous college students who were tested either before or after the war and probably in even greater degree with the attitudes of the general MMPI norm groups that provided the normative statistics for the T table of K.

The nearest approach to data on faked good scores as obtained from persons with *initially* deviant profiles is embodied in some incidental data obtained from our records where psychiatric hospital patients repeated the MMPI for one reason or another. By searching the duplicate records, we were able to find a few cases where patients had taken the inventory twice and where the K raw score for the second test was four or more points higher than that for the first test. Most of these patients had originally deviant profiles. The obtained differences are not worthy of statistical analysis but all scales show a tendency to decrease in T score under these conditions. The most marked changes occurred on Hs, D, Pt, and Sc. Naturally, since these patients were not asked to fake a good score, the finding yields only presumptive evidence.

Correlational Data

The test-retest correlation of K is available on two groups. For a group of 85 high school girls (Capwell data) retested at an interval of 110 to 410 days the correlation was .72. For a group of miscellaneous normals retested after four days to one year the correlation was .74. It is of course impossible to say to what extent these coefficients are to be viewed as indicators of "reliability."

A second question that may be raised regards the effect of the K correction upon the intercorrelations of the other MMPI scales. Table 5 gives the correlation coefficients for the same group with and without the K correction having been made before correlating. The intercorrelations for the original scores are indicated in ordinary type, while the corresponding coefficient upon the same sample after making the K correction is indicated immediately to the right of the originals in italic. These coefficients are based upon a sample of 100 normal males, all college graduates, employed as engineers in an industrial concern (Honeywell cases of Table 4). We see that some of the correlations are raised by the K correction, that others are lowered, and that this is true whether they are considered in the absolute or algebraic sense. The increases preponderate over the decreases. Inspection suggests that the greatest shifts occur in the case of pairs of scales one of which suffers a considerable K correction and the other none (e.g., Hy and Pt). We are not prepared to give any special interpretation of this table and include it here only for the sake of completeness.

Summary and Conclusions

Specific arguments and data are presented establishing the rationale of using the K factor as a suppressor on certain MMPI clinical scales. Five scales seem to be improved by the correction, as indicated by increased correspondence between scores and clinical status. The scales Pt, Sc, Hs, Pd, and Ma receive K corrections of varying amounts. The scales Hy, D, Mf, and Pa are not so treated nor is it established that the K score should be taken into account subjectively in evaluating them. A new statistic was used to determine the K-correction factors. This statistic, called the differential ratio, is described as appropriate to establishing maximal differentiation between two distributions with emphasis upon the region of their overlap.

Normative statistics on the distributions of K for various groups are presented.

Table 5. Correlations among Scales before and after K Correction, with the Latter in Italic.
(N = 100 Employed Male College Graduates)

	Hs	D	Hy	Pd	Mf	Pa	Pt	Sc	Ma
Hs									
D . .,. . .	33 *33*								
Hy	33 *65*	31							
Pd . . .	28 *37*	36 *37*	25 *47*						
Mf	27 *17*	26	21	28 *22*					
Pa	08 *22*	17	37	15 *24*	33				
Pt.	47 *47*	28 *45*	-17 *38*	33 *43*	41 *44*	16 *45*			
Sc	51 *59*	20 *26*	-03 *51*	31 *44*	45 *32*	19 *39*	72 *66*		
Ma	25 *04*	-07 *-05*	-13 *00*	32 *01*	30 *34*	06 *12*	50 *26*	53 *21*	
K	-25	08	53	09	-08	22	-65	-46	-42

The chief finding of interest here is a tendency for college and college-educated persons to deviate in the upward direction between one-half and one standard deviation. It was suggested in the original article on K that this difference is chiefly a function of socioeconomic status.

Some evidence was presented to show that K behaves in the expected manner when persons attempt to fake a "bad" profile, although the corresponding effect in faking "good" was not demonstrated on any experimental group. Some clinical support for this latter effect had been found.

The addition of K had a variable effect on the intercorrelations of clinical scales. There seems to be some indication that the optimal amount of K correction for a given clinical scale is inversely related to the proportion of "subtle" items the scale already contains.

It is suggested that the K correction should be made routinely by users of the MMPI and that old records should be scored and redrawn if any research or validation study is to be carried on.

Section II
Psychometric Characteristics

The primary focus of the articles in this section is the sample of behavior provided by answers to the MMPI items. What do these item endorsements reveal about a test subject? Some inferences may be quite direct, but often the test interpreter may conclude something about a respondent that has little resemblance to the content of the items that were endorsed in the course of testing. A sizable portion of the MMPI research literature has been devoted to how various aspects of the psychodynamics of taking the test may affect the dependability of the behavioral sample and the accuracy of the inferences to be drawn from scores on component scales. Professor Meehl's paper leading off this section is by now a classic in this area. In it he sounded the call for an intensive and sophisticated analysis of the dynamic interaction of test features, subject characteristics, and examination setting as they interact in determining test answers and scores.

As was indicated in the article on the K factor (I, 9), numerous experimental studies have documented the susceptibility of inventory scale scores to distortions arising from instructions to slant one's answers in various ways. The findings from these faking studies fitted in well with the accumulating experience of psychologists with the MMPI in various clinical settings in which test subjects entered into the examination with a number of different orientations and kinds of motivation. The validity scales L and F had proved to be quite useful in identifying those protocols that had been generated under such instructional sets. It was natural therefore to assume that clients and patients could differ one from another in *self-administered* sets guiding their completions of the test blanks that were not unlike the explicit sets employed in the laboratory situations. The K factor and its role as a suppressor of non-criterion variance was but one example of such test-oriented sets and the ways that they could enter into the self-descriptions that test subjects were providing via the MMPI.

Basic research on another such orientation, variously termed "social favorability" set [Heineman, 1952] or "social desirability" set [Edwards, 1953, 1957a], got an additional impetus with the publication of basic itemmetric data on the MMPI item pool in the appendix material of the Dahlstrom and Welsh *Handbook* in 1960. (See also Appendixes A through F in Dahlstrom, Welsh, and Dahlstrom, 1975.) The basic position of this line of research is summarized in the second selection. It is an excerpt from Allen Edwards's article published in 1964. Here Edwards makes a very persuasive argument for the interpretation of the primary source of variance in virtually all of the scales in the MMPI as manifestations in varying degrees of a set to create a favorable or desirable impression on the test examiner. It takes a discerning reader to avoid being lulled into believing along with Edwards that all the common variance is attributable to this one source, the manipulation of impressions, rather than to any intention to describe oneself as accurately as possible on the various items presented in the test. From this report and many similar publications from Edwards, it is easy to understand why many other investigators came to join him in deriding the MMPI and other similar instruments as too vulnerable to the influence of one pervasive response set.

Paradoxically, in a parallel series of studies, Douglas Jackson and Samuel Messick, collaborating at that time at the Educational Testing Service, came to a similar conclusion about personality inventories like the MMPI. They viewed them as seriously limited instruments because of their susceptibility to a massive response set conceived not as social desirability, but as "response acquiescence." That is, test subjects are seen as not giving a very accurate picture of the way they really see themselves in their answers to these items but instead are strongly subjected to the influence of the examiner and what he/she seems to want them to say. The main thrust of their argument and the kinds of data on which they based their conclusions are illustrated in the third selection which was originally part of a presentation at a conference on personality measurement at ETS in late 1960. The acquiescence-set formulation also generated a very large research literature.

As can be seen in the two selections, both lines of research, social-desirability set and acquiescence-response set, flow from the two major dimensions of common variance in the MMPI clinical profile. Numerous debates arose about the respective portions of variance to be accounted for by each response set. It remained for Jack Block to bring about a resolution of these controversies in a prize-winning monograph appearing in the Appleton-Century-Crofts series in 1965. Large portions of this study are reproduced in selections 4 and 5. The interested reader is urged to consult the full monograph, but it is hoped that sufficient material from this careful analysis has been presented here to enable the reader to follow the argument. Professor Block carefully analyzes the statistical and methodological complexities that have led prior investigators to conclude that there were massive response sets operating which were independent of personality characteristics of the test subjects and which were elicited by all tests that have this basic format, to the detriment of any psychometric or personological use to which they might be applied. Focusing upon each general view in turn, Block is able to put these formulations back into proper perspective and bring forth evidence showing that instead of artifactual response sets, there are two important personality dimensions, ego resilience and ego control, that can be validly measured in special scales described in his two articles. From Block's work it is clear that the lack of external evidence of the nature of these sources of variance (true-score or error variance) had hampered the attempts of previous investigators to evaluate the roles of social desirability and response acquiescence in MMPI test patterns. Unfortunately, many psychologists in positions of influence (in review committees, editorships, dissertation committees, etc.) have obtained only a hasty impression from the research published on response sets in the MMPI, believing mistakenly that these sets impose a serious limit to the usefulness of all such test instruments. Careful reading of the work of Block should be instrumental in offsetting this particular stereotype.

The last two studies in this section serve to clarify additional aspects of the MMPI item content and the general self-presentation efforts that subjects go through in completing the test. Gynther and his colleagues have undertaken a systematic study of the role of subtlety of content in the items making up the basic MMPI scales. The present selection is one of a series of investigations on the component scales based on the ratings of item subtlety obtained from college undergraduates. The study presented here focuses upon the various components of scale 4 (Pd). Data from the basic item rating study [reported by Christian, Burkhart, and Gynther, 1978] have been included as Tables 2 and 3 in this selection with the kind permission of those authors. Although item subtlety probably covaries in important ways with the level of sophistication of the test respondents, the ratings provided by these college-level judges are undoubtedly more useful than the categorical judgments employed in earlier research on this topic [e.g., Wiener and Harmon, 1946; Seeman, 1952, 1953]. The general issue of item content will be taken up again in the next section in Wiggins's work on content scales (see III, 4).

In the final article in this section, Taylor and his colleagues report research carried out while the senior investigator was at the Menninger Research Foundation. The results of this replicated analysis shed light on the complexities of the self-perceptions that test subjects have and apparently use to determine appropriate endorsements to items like those in the scales of the MMPI. The work of these researchers opens up many intriguing lines of investigation about the subjects' frame of reference in personal experience, self-evaluation, and interpersonal attribution which may be mediating the intraindividual processes between item presentation and item answering and may be providing the stable sources of variance tapped by various clinical and research scales of the MMPI.

The articles in this section came from the following sources: article 1 from P. E. Meehl. The dynamics of "structured" personality tests. *Journal of Clinical Psychology*, 1945, 1, 296-303; article 2 excerpted from A. L. Edwards. Social desirability and performance on the MMPI. *Psychometrika*, 1964, 29, 295-308; article 3 excerpted from D. N. Jackson and S. Messick. Response styles and the assessment of psychopathology. In S. Messick and J. Ross (Eds.). *Measurement in personality and cognition*. New York: John Wiley and Sons, Inc., 1962; articles 4 and 5 excerpted from J. Block. *The challenge of response sets*. New York: Appleton-Century-Crofts, 1965; article 6 from M. D. Gynther, B. R. Burkhart, and C. Hovanitz. Do face-valid items have more predictive validity than subtle items? : the case of the MMPI Pd scale. *Journal of Consulting and Clinical Psychology*, 1979, 47, 295-300 (additional tabular material excerpted from W. L. Christian, B. R. Burkhart, and M. D. Gynther. Subtle-obvious ratings of MMPI items: new interest in an old concept. *Journal of Consulting and Clinical Psychology*, 1978, 46, 1178-86); article 7 from J. B. Taylor, M. Carithers, and L. Coyne. MMPI performance, response set, and the "self-concept hypothesis". *Journal of Consulting and Clinical Psychology*, 1976, 44, 351-62 (additional tabular material added from ASIS/NAPS archives). We are indebted to the authors and to the publishers of the journals and books for permission to reproduce these articles in this form.

The Dynamics of "Structured" Personality Tests

P. E. Meehl

In a recent article [1945] Lt. Max L. Hutt of the Adjutant General's School has given an interesting discussion of the use of projective methods in the army medical installations. This article was part of a series describing the work of clinical psychologists in the military services, with which the present writer is familiar only indirectly. The utility of any instrument in the military situation can, of course, be most competently assessed by those in contact with clinical material in that situation, and the present paper is in no sense to be construed as an "answer" to or an attempted refutation of Hutt's remarks. Nevertheless, there are some incidental observations contained in his article which warrant further critical consideration, particularly those having to do with the theory and dynamics of "structured" personality tests. It is with these latter observations rather than the main burden of Hutt's article that this paper is concerned.

Hutt defines "structured personality tests" as those in which the test material consists of conventional, culturally crystallized questions to which the subject must respond in one of a very few fixed ways. With this definition the present writer has no quarrel, and it has the advantage of not applying the unfortunate phrase "self-rating questionnaire" to the whole class of question-answer devices. But immediately following this definition, Hutt goes on to say that "it is assumed that each of the test questions will have the same meaning to all subjects who take the examination. The subject has no opportunity of organizing in his own unique manner his response to the questions."

143

These statements will bear further examination. The statement that personality tests assume that each question has the same meaning to all subjects is continually appearing in most sources of late, and such an impression is conveyed by many discussions even when they do not explicitly make this assertion. It should be emphasized very strongly, therefore, that while this perhaps has been the case with the majority of question-answer personality tests, it is not by any means part of their essential nature. The traditional approach to verbal question-answer personality tests has been, to be sure, to view them as self-ratings; and it is in a sense always a self-rating that you obtain when you ask a subject about himself, whether you inquire about his feelings, his health, his attitudes, or his relations to others.

However, once a "self-rating" has been obtained, it can be looked upon in two rather different ways. The first, and by far the commonest approach, is to accept a self-rating as a second best source of information when the direct observation of a segment of behavior is inaccessible for practical or other reasons. This view in effect forces a self-rating or self-description to act as surrogate for a behavior sample. Thus we want to know whether a man is shy, and one criterion is his readiness to blush. We cannot conveniently drop him into a social situation to observe whether he blushes, so we do the next best (and often much worse) thing and simply ask him, "Do you blush easily?" We assume that if he does in fact blush easily, he will realize that fact about himself, which is often a gratuitous assumption; and secondly, we hope that having recognized it, he will be willing to tell us so.

Associated with this approach to structured personality tests is the construction of items and their assembly into scales upon an a priori basis, requiring the assumption that the psychologist building the test has sufficient insight into the dynamics of verbal behavior and its relation to the inner core of personality that he is able to predict beforehand what certain sorts of people will say about themselves when asked certain sorts of questions. The fallacious character of this procedure has been sufficiently shown by the empirical results of the MMPI alone, and will be discussed at greater length below. It is suggested tentatively that the relative uselessness of most structured personality tests is due more to a priori item construction than to the fact of their being structured.

The second approach to verbal self-ratings is rarer among testmakers. It consists simply in the explicit denial that we accept a self-rating as a feeble surrogate for a behavior sample, and substitutes the assertion that a "self-rating" constitutes an intrinsically interesting and significant bit of verbal behavior, the nontest correlates of which must be discovered by empirical means. Not only is this approach free from the restriction that the subject must be able to describe his own behavior accurately, but a careful study of structured personality tests built on this basis shows that such a restriction would falsify the actual relationships that hold between what a man says and what he *is*.

Since this view of question-answer items is the rarer one at the present time, it is desirable at this point to elucidate by a number of examples. For this purpose one might consider the Strong Vocational Interest Blank, the Humm-Wadsworth Temperament Scales, the MMPI, or any other structured personality measuring device in which the selection of items was done on a thoroughly empirical basis using carefully selected criterion groups. In the extensive and confident use of the Strong Vocational Interest Blank, this more sophisticated view of the significance of responses to structured personality test items has been taken as a matter of course for years. The possibility of conscious as well as unconscious "fudging" has been considered and experimentally investigated by Strong and others, but the differences in possible interpretation or *meaning* of items have been more or less ignored—as well they should be. One is asked to indicate, for example, whether he likes, dislikes, or is indifferent to "conservative people." The possibilities for differential interpretation of a word like "conservative" are of course tremendous, but nobody has worried about that problem in the case of the Strong. Almost certainly the strength of verbs such as "like" and "dislike" is variably interpreted throughout the whole blank. For the present purpose the MMPI will be employed because the present writer is most familiar with it.

One of the items on the MMPI scale for detecting psychopathic personality (Pd) is "My parents and family find more fault with me than they should." If we look upon this as a rating in which the *fact* indicated by an affirmative response is crucial, we immediately begin to wonder whether the testee can objectively evaluate how much other people's parents find fault with them, whether his own parents are warranted in finding as much fault with him as they do, whether this particular subject will interpret the phrase "finding fault" in the way we intend or in the way most normal persons interpret it, and so on. The present view is that this is simply an unprofitable way to examine a question-answer personality test item. To begin with, the empirical finding is that individuals whose past history and momentary clinical picture is that of a typical psychopathic personality tend to say "Yes" to this much more often than people in general do. Now in point of fact, they probably should say "No" because the parents of psychopaths are sorely tried and probably do not find fault with their incorrigible offspring any more than the latter deserve. An allied item is "I have been quite independent and free from family rule," which psychopaths tend to answer False—almost certainly opposite to what is actually the case for the great majority of them. Again, "Much of the time I feel I have done something wrong or evil." Anyone who deals clinically with psychopaths comes to doubt seriously whether they could possibly interpret this item in the way the rest of us do (cf. Cleckley's [1941] "semantic dementia"), but they *say* that about themselves nonetheless. Numerous other examples such as "Someone has it in for me" and "I am sure I get a raw deal from life" appear on the same scale and are significant because psychopaths tend to *say* certain things about themselves, rather than because we take these statements at face value.

Consider the MMPI scale for detecting tendencies to hypochondriasis. A hypochondriac says that he has headaches often, that he is not in as good health as his friends are, and that he cannot understand what he reads as well as he used to. Suppose that he has a headache on an average of once every month, as does a certain "normal" person. The hypochondriac says he often has headaches, the other person says he does not. They both have headaches once a month, and hence they must either interpret the word "often" differently in that question, or else have unequal recall of their headaches. According to the traditional view, this ambiguity in the word "often" and the inaccuracy of human memory constitute sources of error; for the authors of the MMPI they may actually constitute sources of discrimination.

We might mention as beautiful illustrations of this kind of relation the nonsomatic items in the hysteria scale of the MMPI [McKinley and Hathaway, 1944 (see I, 5)]. These items have a statistical homogeneity and the common property by face inspection that they indicate the person to be possessed of unusually good social and psychiatric adjustment. They are among the most potent items for the detection of hysterics and hysteroid temperaments, but they reflect the systematic distortion of the hysteric's conception of himself, and would have to be considered invalid if taken as surrogates for the direct observation of behavior.

As a last example might be mentioned some findings of the writer [1945b] in which "normal" persons having rather abnormal MMPI profiles are differentiated from clearly "abnormal" persons with equally deviant profiles by a tendency to give statistically rare as well as psychiatrically "maladjusted" responses to certain other items. Thus a person who says that he is afraid of fire, that windstorms terrify him, that people often disappoint him, stands a better chance of being normal in his nontest behavior than a person who does not admit to these things. The discrimination of this set of items for various criterion groups, the intercorrelations with other scales, and the content of the items indicate strongly that they detect some verbal-semantic distortion in the interpretation and response to the other MMPI items which enters into the spurious elevation of scores achieved by certain "normals." Recent unpublished research on more subtle "lie" scales of the MMPI indicates that unconscious self-deception is inversely related to the kind of verbal distortion just indicated.

In summary, a serious and detailed study of the MMPI items and their interrelations both with one another and with nontest behavior cannot fail to convince one of the necessity for this second kind of approach to question-answer personality tests. That the majority of the questions seem by inspection to require self-ratings has been a source of theoretical misunderstanding, since the stimulus situation seems to request a self-rating, whereas *the scoring does not assume a valid self-rating to have been given.* It is difficult to give any psychologically meaningful interpretation of some of the empirical findings on the MMPI unless the more sophisticated view is maintained.

It is for this reason that the possible differences in interpretation do not cause us any a priori concern in the use of this instrument. Whether any structured personality test turns out to be valid and useful must be decided on pragmatic grounds, but the possibility of diverse interpretations of a single item is not a good *theoretical* reason for predicting failure of the scales. There is a "projective" element involved in interpreting and responding to these verbal stimuli which must be recognized, in spite of the fact that the test situation is very rigidly structured as regards the ultimate response possibilities permitted. The objection that all persons do not interpret structured test items in the same way is not fatal, just as it would not be fatal to point out that "ink blots do not look the same to everyone."

It has not been sufficiently recognized by critics of structured personality tests that what a man says about himself may be a highly significant fact about him even though we do not entertain with any confidence the hypothesis that what he says would agree with what complete knowledge of him would lead others to say of him. It is rather strange that this point is so often completely passed by, when clinical psychologists quickly learn to take just that attitude in a diagnostic or therapeutic interview. The complex defense mechanisms of projection, rationalization, reaction formation, etc., appear dynamically to the interviewer as soon as he begins to take what the client *says* as itself motivated by other needs than those of giving an accurate verbal report. There is no good a priori reason for denying the possibility of similar processes in the highly structured "interview" which is the question-answer personality test. The summarized experience of the clinician results (one hopes, at least) in his being able to discriminate verbal responses admissible as accurate self-descriptions from those which reflect other psychodynamisms but are not on that account any the less significant. The test analogue to this experience consists of the summarized statistics on response frequencies, at least among those personality tests which have been constructed empirically (MMPI, Strong, Rorschach, etc.).

Once this has been taken for granted we are prepared to admit powerful items to personality scales regardless of whether the rationale of their appearance can be made clear at present. We do not have the confidence of the traditional personality-test maker that the relation between the behavior dynamics of a subject and the tendency to respond verbally in a certain way must be psychologically obvious. Thus it puzzles us but does not disconcert us when this relation cannot be elucidated, the science of behavior being in the stage that it is. That "I sometimes tease animals" (answered False) should occur in a scale measuring symptomatic depression is theoretically mysterious, just as the tendency of certain schizophrenic patients to accept "position" as a determinant in responding to the Rorschach may be theoretically mysterious. Whether such a relation obtains can be very readily discovered empirically, and the wherefore of it may be left aside for the moment as a theoretical question. Verbal responses which do not apparently have any *self*-reference at all, but in their form seem to request an objective judgment about social phenomena or ethical values, may be equally diagnostic. So, again, one is not disturbed to find items such as "I think most people would lie to get ahead" (answered False) and "It takes a lot of argument to convince most people of the truth" (answered False) appearing on the hysteria scale of the MMPI.

The frequently alleged "superficiality" of structured personality tests becomes less evident on such a basis also. Some of these items can be rationalized in terms of fairly deep-seated trends of the personality, although it is admittedly difficult to establish that any given depth interpretation is the correct one. To take one example, the items on the MMPI scale for hysteria which were referred to above as indicating extraordinarily good social and emotional adjustment can hardly be seen as valid self-descriptions. However, if the core trend of such items is summarily characterized as "I am psychiatrically and socially well adjusted," it is not hard to fit such a trend into what we know of the basic personality structure of the hysteric. The well-known *belle indifférence* of these patients, the great lack of insight, the facility of repression and dissociation, the "impunitiveness" of their reactions to frustration, the tendency of such patients to show an elevated "lie" score on the MMPI, may all be seen as facets of this underlying structure. It would be interesting to see experimentally whether to the three elements of Rosenzweig's "triadic hypothesis" (impunitiveness, repression, hypnotizability) one might add a fourth correlate—the chief nonsomatic component of the MMPI hysteria scale.

Whether "depth" is plumbed by a structured personality test to a lesser extent than by one which is unstructured is difficult to determine, once the present view of the nature of structured tests is understood. That the "deepest" layers of personality are not verbal might be admitted without any implication that they cannot therefore make themselves known to us via verbal behavior. Psychoanalysis, usually considered the "deepest" kind of psychotherapy, makes use of the dependency of verbal behavior upon underlying variables which are not themselves verbalized.

The most important area of behavior considered in the making of psychiatric diagnosis is still the form and content of the *speech* of the individual. I do not mean to advance these considerations as validations of any structured personality tests, but merely as reasons for not accepting the theoretical objection sometimes offered in criticizing them. Of course, structured personality tests may be employed in a purely diagnostic, categorizing fashion, without the use of any dynamic interpretations of the relationship among scales or the patterning of a profile. For certain practical purposes this is quite permissible, just as one may devote himself to the statistical validation of various "signs" on the Rorschach test, with no attempt to make qualitative or really dynamic personological inferences from the findings. The tradition in the case of structured personality tests is probably weighted on the side of nondynamic thinking; and in the case of some structured tests, a considerable amount of experience and clinical subtlety is required to extract the maximum of information. The present writer has heard discussions in case conferences at the University of Minnesota Hospitals which make as "dynamic" use of MMPI patterns as one could reasonably make of any kind of test data without an excessive amount of illegitimate reification. The clinical use of the Strong Vocational Interest Blank is another example.

In discussing the "depth" of interpretation possible with tests of various kinds, it should at least be pointed out that the problem of validating personality tests, whether structured or unstructured, becomes more difficult in proportion as the interpretations increase in "depth." For example, the validation of the "sign" differentials on the Rorschach is relatively easier to carry out than that of the deeper interpretations concerning the basic personality structure. This does not imply that there is necessarily less validity in the latter class of inferences, but simply stresses the difficulty of designing experiments to test validity. A very major part of this difficulty hinges upon the lack of satisfactory external criteria, a situation which exists also in the case of more dynamic interpretations of structured personality tests. One is willing to accept a staff diagnosis of psychasthenia in selecting cases against which to validate the Pt scale of the MMPI or the F% as a compulsive-obsessive sign on the Rorschach. But when the test results indicate repressed homosexuality or latent anxiety or lack of deep insight into the self, we may have strong suspicions that the instrument is fully as competent as the psychiatric staff. Unfortunately this latter assumption is very difficult to justify without appearing to be inordinately biased in favor of our test. Until this problem is better solved than at present, many of the "depth" interpretations of both structured and unstructured tests will be little more than an expression of personal opinion.

There is one advantage of unstructured personality tests which cannot easily be claimed for the structured variety, namely, the fact that falsehood is difficult. While it is true for many of the MMPI items, for example, that even a psychologist cannot predict on which scales they will appear or in what direction certain sorts of abnormals will tend to answer them, still the relative accessibility of defensive answering would seem to be greater than is possible in responding to a set of inkblots. Research is still in progress on more subtle "lie" scales of the MMPI and we have every reason to feel encouraged on the present findings. Nevertheless the very existence of a definite problem in this case and not in the case of the Rorschach gives the latter an advantage in this respect. When we pass to a more structured method, such as the TAT, the problem reappears. The writer has found, for example, a number of patients who simply were not fooled by the "intelligence-test" set given in the directions for the TAT, as was indicated quite clearly by self-references and defensive remarks, especially on the second day. Of course such a patient is still under pressure to produce material and therefore his willingness to reveal himself is limited in its power over the projections finally given.

In conclusion, the writer is in hearty agreement with Lieutenant Hutt that unstructured personality tests are of great value, and that the final test of the adequacy of any technique is its utility in clinical work. Published evidence of the validity of both structured and unstructured personality tests as they had to be modified for convenient military use does not enable one to draw any very definite conclusions or comparisons at the present time. There is assuredly no reason for us to place structured and unstructured types of instruments in battle order against one another, although it is admitted that when time is limited they come inevitably into a very real clinical "competition" for use. The present article has been aimed simply at the clarification of certain rather prevalent misconceptions as to the nature and the theory of at least one important structured personality test, in order that erroneous theoretical considerations may not be thrown into the balance in deciding the outcome of such clinical competition.

Social Desirability and Performance on the MMPI

A. L. Edwards

Given a set of statements of the kind ordinarily found in personality scales and inventories, it is possible to have judges rate each statement in terms of how socially desirable or undesirable they consider the content of the statement to be. The distributions of ratings assigned to the statements can then be used to find the social desirability scale values of the statements. Once the social desirability scale values of the statements have been obtained, we have a basis for ordering the statements on a psychological continuum of social desirability ranging from highly socially undesirable, through neutral, to highly socially desirable.

There is now considerable evidence to show that when a representative or random set of personality statements is rated for social desirability by different groups of judges, the relative ordering of the statements on the social desirability continuum is much the same from group to group. The product-moment correlations between scale values derived from the judgments of two different but comparable groups of judges are typically .90 or greater [Edwards, 1957a; Edwards and Diers, 1963; Edwards and Walsh, 1963; Messick and Jackson, 1961a]. Even when social desirability scale values are derived from the judgments of such diverse groups within our own culture as high-school students [Klett, 1957b], Nisei [Fujita, 1957], psychotic patients [Cowen, Staiman, and Wolitzky, 1961; Klett, 1957a; Taylor, 1959], sex offenders [Cowen and Stricker, 1963], alcoholics [Zax, Cowen, Budin, and Biggs, 1962], novice nuns [Zax,

Cowen, and Peter, 1963], and a geriatric sample [Cowen, Davol, Reimanis, and Stiller, 1962], the correlations between the scale values are generally found to be .85 or higher.

* * *

If a set of personality statements is administered to a group of subjects with instructions to describe themselves by answering each statement True or False, we can find for this sample the percentage answering each statement True. I refer to this percentage as the probability that an item will be endorsed in self-description under the *standard* instructions ordinarily used in administering personality scales and inventories. If the social desirability scale values of the statements are also known, then it is possible to determine the relationship between probability of endorsement and social desirability scale value.

For a set of 140 personality statements, I found that probability of endorsement was a linear increasing function of social desirability scale value, the product-moment correlation between the two variables being .87 [Edwards, 1953]. A correlation of this magnitude might be considered an artifact, either of the particular set of statements investigated or of the particular group of subjects tested, but subsequent research has shown that the relationship holds for all of the sets of statements which have been investigated provided the statements do not have a restricted range of social desirability scale values [Cowen and Tongas, 1959; Cruse, 1963; Edwards, 1957a, 1957b, 1959a; Hanley, 1956; Kenny, 1956; Taylor, 1959]. The largest population we have studied consists of 2,824 descriptive statements of personality. For a serial sample of 176 statements drawn from this larger population of 2,824 statements, James Walsh and I found a correlation of .92 between probability of endorsement and social desirability scale value [Edwards and Walsh, 1963].

There is evidence to show that the relationship observed between probability of endorsement and social desirability scale value is not uniquely characteristic of American college students, but that it holds true for other diverse groups within our own culture as well [Cruse, 1963; Taylor, 1959]. In fact, there is reason to believe that probability of endorsement should be substantially correlated with social desirability scale value in cultures other than our own [Edwards, 1964].

If we know the social desirability scale value of a statement, then it is possible to define the concept of a *socially desirable response* to the statement. I originally defined a socially desirable response as a

True response to a statement with a socially desirable scale value or as a False response to a statement with a socially undesirable scale value, leaving the concept undefined for statements with precisely neutral scale values of 5.0 on a 9-point social desirability rating scale [Edwards, 1957a]. I regard the tendency to respond True to statements with socially desirable scale values and False to statements with socially undesirable scale values as a general personality trait.

A scale designed to measure the tendency to give socially desirable responses in self-description under the standard instructions ordinarily employed with personality scales and inventories is called a Social Desirability (SD) scale [Edwards, 1957a]. In an SD scale all of the items are keyed for socially desirable responses. Since the concept of a socially desirable response is, of necessity, undefined for items with precisely neutral scale values, items of this kind would not be included in an SD scale. In fact, we have found that responses to items falling within the neutral interval, 4.5 to 5.5 on a 9-point scale, are, in general, less consistent than and not highly correlated with responses to items falling outside the neutral interval. The various SD scales we have developed have thus consisted of items with scale values falling to the left of 4.5 or to the right of 5.5 on the 9-point rating scale.

* * *

Consider now one of the existing personality scales designed to measure some personality trait such as, for example, hostility, cooperativeness, dominance, rigidity, introversion, neuroticism, or the like. For each of these scales there is a scoring key which indicates whether the trait response to an item is keyed True or False. Presumably, individual responses to the items in these scales are content or trait oriented so that individuals who have a high degree of the trait are assumed to have a higher probability of giving the trait response to each item than individuals who have a low degree of the trait. Thus, if an individual obtains a high score on one of these scales he has given many trait keyed responses and, in this case, it is assumed that he did so because he has a high degree of the trait which the scale was designed to measure. If he obtains a low score he has given few trait keyed responses, and it is assumed, in this instance, that he did so because he has a low degree of the trait which the scale was designed to measure.

If we obtain social desirability scale values for the items in each of these trait scales, then it is also possible to determine whether the trait response to an item is a socially desirable or a socially undesirable response. If all of the items in a given trait scale are keyed for both trait and socially desirable responses, then, obviously, the trait keying and the social desirability keying of the items in the scale are completely confounded. It may be argued that individuals who obtain high scores on the trait scale are responding to the items in terms of the trait which the scale was designed to measure, but it is equally plausible that they are responding to the items in terms of a trait which the scale was *not* designed to measure, namely, the tendency to give socially desirable responses. If the latter is the case, then scores on the trait scale should be positively correlated with an independently constructed measure of the tendency to give socially desirable responses such as the SD scale.

Similar considerations apply to trait scales in which the trait keying is identical with the social undesirability keying. If all of the items in a scale are keyed for both trait and socially undesirable responses, then low scores may be obtained by individuals who have little of the trait which the scale was designed to measure. But, if the tendency to give socially desirable responses is also operating, then low scores on the trait scale should also be characteristic of individuals who have strong tendencies to give socially desirable responses. In this case, scores on the trait scale should be negatively correlated with scores on the SD scale.

Consider three examples from the MMPI. First, let us take a scale in which the trait keying is confounded with the social undesirability keying. The Psychasthenia (Pt) scale of the MMPI is a good example because it contains 48 items of which 47 are keyed for socially undesirable responses. Thus, individuals with strong tendencies to give socially desirable responses, as indicated by high scores on the SD scale, would be expected to obtain low scores on the Pt scale and the correlation between the two scales should be negative. It is. For a sample of 150 college males, the correlation between the Pt and SD scales was found to be -.84.

Second, let us take a scale in which the trait keying is confounded with the social desirability keying. An example is the Leadership (Lp) scale of the MMPI. This scale contains 50 items with 44 of the 50 items keyed for socially desirable responses. In this instance, we would expect high scores on the Lp scale to be associated with high scores on the SD scale and the correlation between the two scales should be positive. It is. The obtained correlation between the two scales for the same sample of college males was found to be .77.

As a third example, let us take a scale in which the number of items keyed for socially desirable responses is approximately the same as the number of items keyed for socially undesirable responses. The

Masculinity (Mf) scale of the MMPI contains 60 items of which approximately half or 28 are keyed for socially desirable responses, and approximately half or 32 are keyed for socially undesirable responses. Since the trait keying of the items in this scale is fairly well balanced for socially desirable and for socially undesirable responses, the scale should have a fairly low correlation with the SD scale. It does. For the sample of college males the correlation was -.16.

The three examples I have cited are not isolated cases. For a set of 43 MMPI scales, I found that the correlation between the MMPI scales and the SD scale was directly related to the proportion of items in the MMPI scales keyed for socially desirable responses. The product-moment correlation between the proportion of items keyed for socially desirable responses and the observed correlation of the scale with the SD scale was .92 [Edwards, 1961].

* * *

I believe that scores on various trait scales are correlated with scores on the SD scale to the degree to which the trait scales are measuring the same common factor or personality dimension as that which I believe the SD scale to be measuring, namely, the tendency to give socially desirable responses in self-description. A standard technique for determining the degree to which different scales are measuring a common factor is to intercorrelate the scores on the scales and to factor analyze the resulting correlation matrix. To do this, of course, it is necessary to have available scores on a number of personality scales. Furthermore, if we wish to demonstrate that scores on all of these scales are measuring in varying degrees the common or general trait which I describe as the tendency to give socially desirable responses, it would be of value if each scale included in the analysis had been developed to measure some trait which the other scales were not designed to measure.

One source for a variety of personality scales is the MMPI. When the MMPI was first published the authors [Hathaway and McKinley, 1951] provided scoring keys for only a limited number of clinical and validity scales. But, over the years, many investigators must have felt that the original scales did not tap the full potentialities of the MMPI item pool. I say this because they proceeded to develop additional MMPI scales which, presumably, they believed would measure some personality trait not already being measured by one of the existing MMPI scales. By 1960 there were, according to Dahlstrom and Welsh [1960], scoring keys for a minimum of 212 MMPI scales, and there is no reason to believe that the end is yet in sight.

Factor analyses have been carried out with as few as 11 and with as many as 58 of these MMPI scales. Since there are only 566 items in the MMPI, there is item overlap in the different MMPI scales, even when only the clinical and validity scales are factor analyzed. This is a confounding variable and one to which I shall return later. However, regardless of the number of MMPI scales included in the factor analysis, there is general agreement that there is one dominant bipolar factor which accounts for the major proportion of the total and common variance. This factor, depending on which pole of the factor the investigator has chosen to emphasize, has been variously labeled as anxiety [Welsh, 1956], psychoticism [Wheeler, Little, and Lehner, 1951], general maladjustment [Tyler, 1951], ego-strength [Kassebaum, Couch, and Slater, 1959], acquiescence [Messick and Jackson, 1961a], deviance [Barnes, 1956], ego-resiliency [Block, II, 4], and last, but not least, social desirability [Edwards and Diers, 1962; Edwards, Diers, and Walker, 1962; Edwards and Heathers, 1962; Fordyce, 1956].

What basis do we have for choosing among these various interpretations of the first MMPI factor? The choice cannot be made solely on the basis of the names of the scales which have high loadings on the factor. For example, consistent with the social desirability interpretation of the first factor is the fact that the SD scale has a high loading on the factor. But, then so also does a scale designed to measure anxiety and so also do a number of other scales which were, presumably, designed to measure still other personality traits. Thus, if I suggest to you that the first MMPI factor is a social desirability factor, I must have more compelling evidence than the mere fact that the SD scale has a high loading on the factor. I do. Let me cite to you the results of a study which Carol Diers and I did [Edwards and Diers, 1962].

We obtained MMPI records from subjects under three sets of instructions: standard instructions, instructions to give socially desirable responses, and instructions to give socially undesirable responses. We intercorrelated and factor analyzed 58 MMPI scales for each set of instructions. The first-factor loadings for all three sets of instructions were highly correlated, the lowest correlation being .97. We also obtained the proportion of items keyed for socially desirable responses in each of the 58 MMPI scales. We then correlated the first factor loadings under standard, socially desirable, and socially undesirable instructions with the proportion of items keyed for socially desirable responses in the scales. These correlations were .89, .92, and .94, respectively.

It is obvious that with correlations of this magnitude the first-factor loadings can be predicted quite accurately from knowledge of the proportion of items in the scales keyed for socially desirable responses. Scales with high loadings at one pole of the factor tend to have a large proportion of items keyed for socially desirable responses and scales with loadings at the opposite pole of the factor tend to have a large proportion of items keyed for socially undesirable responses. Since the loadings of the scales on the first factor vary directly in terms of the proportion of items keyed for socially desirable responses, and since this is precisely what the social desirability interpretation of the first factor would predict, I see no need to resort to such concepts as anxiety, ego-strength, and the like, in describing or interpreting the first factor. In fact, I see no way in which these concepts could be used to predict the loadings of MMPI scales on the first factor.

* * *

Is it possible to develop True-False scales which will measure psychologically significant traits and such that scores on these scales will be relatively independent of scores on the SD scale? I believe that it is possible and elsewhere I [Edwards, 1964] have described some techniques which may prove useful in the process. We know, for example, that if a scale has a balance in its social desirability keying and/or if the items are not too extreme in their social desirability scale values, then either of these two conditions tends to be characteristic of MMPI scales which have low correlations with the SD scale.

We are currently applying these and other principles in an attempt to develop rational scales which are trait and content oriented, which have a high degree of internal consistency, and which are also relatively independent of one another and of the SD scale. Our objective, in other words, is to try to maximize what Philip DuBois [1962], in his presidential address to the Psychometric Society, described as redundancy within each scale and, at the same time, to minimize redundancy across or between scales.

Whether our efforts will be successful or not remains to be seen. But I hope that we are going to be able to develop scales which will measure traits other than the tendency to give socially desirable responses in self-description. As I have tried to show we already have, within the MMPI, an ample abundance of scales which are excellent measures of this trait.

Response Styles and the Assessment of Psychopathology

D. N. Jackson and S. Messick

Wiggins [1962b], in a careful analysis of response consistencies in personality inventories like the MMPI, has suggested a further distinction between components of response variance—a distinction between *strategic, method,* and *stylistic* variance. By *strategic* variance, Wiggins refers to response variation which reflects a subject's similarity to a normative group in contrast with some criterion group. The nature of such variance depends upon the strategy of constructing scales to discriminate between criterion and normative populations and upon the nature of the criterion groups. By *method* variance, Wiggins refers to response consistencies attributable to constraints imposed by the available response options and to the idiosyncratic nature of particular item pools with respect to such characteristics as the proportion of true and false items and the variation in item popularity. By *stylistic* variance, Wiggins refers to expressive response consistencies, independent of specific item content, having relevance not only to the particular test format but to more general modes of commerce with the environment. Wiggins' analysis cuts across previous separations of response variance into content and stylistic components, and in the interest of clarity we should like to explicate further our distinction between content and style, with particular reference to personality questionnaire data.

* * *

The separation of *response style* from content can be made more

159

clearly at the conceptual level than at the level of data for two important reasons: (a) a given response can be considered a function of each, in some proportion, but in any case confounded to a degree difficult to determine; (b) stylistic consistencies, such as the tendency to acquiesce, may reflect or be related in some degree to personality characteristics and need states. Thus, while the response style to endorse desirable personality items may not in itself be classifiable simply as conformity, the fact that a relation exists between some aspects of conformity and a desirability response style [Marlowe and Crowne, 1961] serves to illustrate that these styles may be related to, and sometimes moderate, content effects. Other examples of interactions between content and style may be found in the measurement of authoritarian attitudes, where it has been suggested that an all "true" item format [Gage and Chatterjee, 1960] or an extremely-worded item style [Jackson and Messick, 1958; Couch and Keniston, 1960; Clayton and Jackson, 1961] may have greater empirical validity for appraising authoritarian behavior.

There is a further problem in defining response style, namely, that of differentiating trivial response biases, or method variance, from valid variance reflecting important behavioral predispositions. Wiggins [1962b] has approached this by defining method variance in distinction to stylistic variance. There is a serious difficulty in clearly separating these at the level of data, however, despite the importance of this distinction conceptually. If one confines an analysis to the internal structure of a single test, there is little basis for distinguishing response style from method variance. In any event, the interpretation of stylistic consistencies as method variance or bias on the one hand, or as valid indicators of personality traits on the other, depends as much upon the aims of the investigator and his preferred strategy of assessment as upon the potential validity coefficients obtained with diverse criteria for the particular response style in question. Whether interpreted as bias or as valid variance, accumulating evidence supports the view that where response style variance is pervasive and intimately associated in varying degrees with content, as it is in the MMPI, only the most careful analysis and separation of these components will allow inferences to be drawn regarding responses to items, particularly inferences regarding response content.

Subject to the above qualifications, variance associated with *response style* has reference to expressive consistencies in the behavior of respondents which are relatively enduring over time, with some degree of generality beyond a particular test performance to responses both in other tests and in non-test behavior, and usually reflected in

assessment situations by consistencies in response to item characteristics other than specific content. These characteristics may include
the following:

(a) Some aspect of the form or tone of item structure, such as difficulty level [Gage, Leavitt, and Stone, 1957], positive or negative
phrasing [cf. Bass, 1955; Jackson and Messick, 1957; Chapman
and Bock, 1958; Elliott, 1961], style of wording [Jackson and
Messick, 1958; Hanley, 1959; Buss, 1959], ambiguity or specific-
ity of meaning [Bass, 1955; Nunnally and Husek, 1958; Stricker,
1962], and extreme generality vs. cautious qualification [Clayton
and Jackson, 1961]; and

(b) Some general aspect of the connotations of the items, such as desirability [Edwards, 1957a], deviance [Berg, 1955; Sechrest and
Jackson, 1961], controversiality [Fricke, 1956; Hanley, 1957],
communality [Wiggins, 1962a, 1962b], subtlety [Edwards, 1957a;
Hanley, 1957], or some perceived difference between communality and desirability, as revealed in the MMPI Lie scale or in scales
derived empirically to detect malingering [Cofer, Chance, and
Judson, 1949] or defensiveness [Hanley, 1957].

Consistencies in response to formal item properties that are restricted in time to a single test session and recurrent consistencies observed
only on a specific test form are referred to as *response sets* [Cron-
bach, 1946, 1950]. In an attempt to evaluate on the MMPI the respective contributions of consistent responses to item content on the
one hand and of stylistic determinants on the other, three factor analytic studies were undertaken, but this version of the paper presents
the results only for a sample of prison inmates (see Jackson and Messick [1962a] for a discussion of studies using samples of hospitalized
neuropsychiatric patients and college students). In these studies the
two response styles of acquiescence and desirability were highlighted,
and in order to appraise their relative effects new measures of both
styles were constructed. Five desirability (Dy) scales, with all of their
items keyed true, were developed to obtain scores reflecting acquiescence at systematically varying levels of item desirability [Jackson
and Messick, 1958, 1961]. Construction of the Dy scales was accomplished by dividing all MMPI items into five levels of judged desirability in terms of Heineman's [1952] scale values and using a table of
random numbers to select items within each level to comprise a
"scale." Item overlap between keys for Dy and MMPI clinical scales
was systematically limited by substituting additional randomly selected items for those initial Dy items found to be keyed also for
clinical scales. The five scales developed in this manner were labeled

Dy1 for the scale having the highest judged item desirability through Dy5 for the scale with the lowest judged item desirability; Dy3 was composed of items judged neutral in desirability. Each desirability scale contained 60 items except Dy1, which, because of the relative scarcity of extremely desirable items on the MMPI, contained only 50 [Jackson and Messick, 1961].

By obtaining Dy scale reliabilities, intercorrelations, and relationships with MMPI clinical scales, it is possible to estimate the degree of response consistency due to the generalized stylistic components of acquiescence and desirability, as contrasted with variance attributable to responses to specific item content.

* * *

The booklet form of the MMPI was administered under standard instructions to 201 male inmates of a state correctional institution [Jackson and Messick, 1961]. Clinical and validity scales were scored in the usual way with one important exception: In order to appraise acquiescence variance systematically, separate scores were obtained for items keyed true and for items keyed false, thus producing two scores for each scale, the sum of which would generate the usual total scale score. This permitted an evaluation of the possibly differential influence of acquiescence on "true" and "false" items. In addition, Welsh's [1956] "pure factor" scales, A and R, believed to reflect different combinations of desirability and acquiescence variance [Jackson and Messick, 1958; Wiggins and Rumrill, 1959], were also scored.

Intercorrelations were obtained among 30 MMPI variables (true and false parts of 11 clinical and validity scales, five Dy scales, and the K, A, and R scales), and the resulting matrix was factor analyzed by the method of principal components. Communalities were estimated by the highest correlation in each column. An examination of the relative sizes of the 30 latent roots led to the retention of eight factors, which together accounted for 69.7 percent of the total variance. These factors were rotated analytically to a modified quartimax criterion of orthogonal simple structure [Saunders, 1960].

The rotated factor loadings, together with the percentages of variance accounted for by each factor, are presented in Table 1. Two very large factors emerged, accounting for 45 and 31.3 percent of the common variance, respectively. The next six factors were extremely small in magnitude, together accounting for a portion of common variance less than one-fourth that explained by the first two factors.

This finding is consistent with other factor analytic studies of MMPI scales, which have also usually yielded only two or three large common factors [French, 1953; Messick and Jackson, 1961a].

The interpretation of these first two large dimensions is facilitated

Table 1. Factor Loadings for the Prison Sample* (N = 201)

Variable	I	II	III	IV	V	VI	VII	VIII	h^2
					Factors				
1. F_t	31	57	-02	11	*48*	01	-01	04	.67
2. F_f	-37	40	10	-07	00	19	-23	*33*	.51
3. Hs_t	23	50	*-46*	-06	-10	-23	12	-02	.59
4. Hs_f	-06	66	-08	07	-06	*-44*	08	06	.66
5. D_t	50	51	*-37*	-12	02	09	*-28*	-12	.75
6. D_f	-61	35	04	-03	-13	*-31*	-25	06	.68
7. Hy_t	34	48	*-55*	00	02	-10	-02	-04	.66
8. Hy_f	-60	14	-13	-17	03	*-51*	01	14	.71
9. Pd_t	60	42	-22	-11	11	12	-13	20	.68
10. Pd_f	-51	03	08	-07	-06	-06	-10	*45*	.49
11. Mf_t	69	09	-07	-17	08	*-26*	-22	-10	.64
12. Mf_f	-46	17	-04	*-50*	-04	-12	01	12	.53
13. Pa_t	45	54	07	-07	*42*	-03	00	-01	.68
14. Pa_f	-61	-10	-11	*-30*	09	*-30*	-12	-03	.60
15. Pt_t	64	57	*-25*	*-30*	-05	-07	-05	-05	.91
16. Pt_f	04	59	-14	04	*-29*	-23	-14	11	.55
17. Sc_t	57	66	-11	-13	24	02	-05	01	.85
18. Sc_f	-10	52	07	01	-11	-03	-12	*45*	.52
19. Ma_t	79	21	-04	01	05	05	20	08	.73
20. Ma_f	-23	-22	-01	-02	06	-09	12	*59*	.47
21. Si_t	60	60	-01	-06	-16	14	-18	*-27*	.87
22. Si_f	-70	40	04	-11	-09	14	-07	-12	.71
23. K	-78	-37	00	05	17	-19	05	20	.85
24. Dy1	36	-79	-01	-01	08	03	00	01	.76
25. Dy2	55	-62	-08	-02	08	02	-04	-05	.71
26. Dy3	88	00	00	05	-04	-07	00	-03	.78
27. Dy4	78	49	06	-05	-03	09	03	08	.86
28. Dy5	53	71	-09	-01	18	03	-04	-05	.82
29. A	71	56	-08	*-28*	-04	-05	-05	-09	.91
30. R	-82	21	04	-15	11	04	02	-02	.76
% Tot. Var.	31.4	21.8	3.0	2.3	2.5	3.4	1.5	3.8	69.7
% Com. Var.	45.0	31.3	4.3	3.3	3.6	4.9	2.1	5.4	

*Loadings above .25 are italicized for factors III-VIII.

by examining a plot of their test vectors (Figure 1). Since the Dy3 scale was composed entirely of "true" items of moderate desirability and heterogeneous content, it was considered to be a possible criterion measure of acquiescence. Hence the first axis was placed directly through the Dy3 vector by means of Saunders' [1960] pattern quartimax procedure, the second axis being oriented orthogonal to the first in the plane of the two major dimensions. The first factor seemed clearly identifiable as acquiescence, since not only did Dy3 receive the highest loading on it, but all of the "true" scales had positive loadings and all but one of the "false" scales had negative loadings; the one exception, Pt_f, received an essentially zero coefficient. Thus, by differentiating true and false keys for MMPI scales, a complete separation of their loadings was obtained on the first factor. There were also marked tendencies for scales moderate in desirability, rather than those extremely desirable or undesirable, to show the highest positive and negative loadings on this factor.

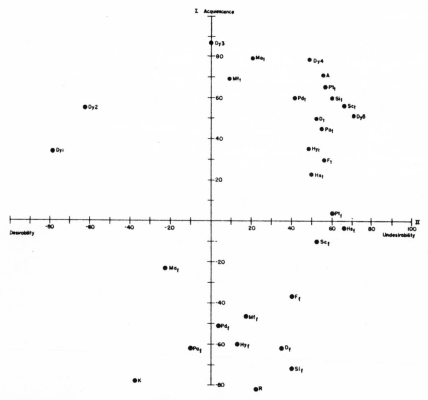

Figure 1. Prison Sample.

The second factor displayed a marked separation in loadings for scales with high and low desirability values. This dimension was interpreted as a clear reflection at one extreme of the tendency to respond desirably and at the other extreme of the tendency to respond undesirably, as evidenced by a correlation between loadings on this second factor and the mean judged item desirability of each scale (with "false" items appropriately reflected) of .95.

Although the obtained pattern of test vectors on the first two factors is easily interpreted, it does not meet criteria for simple structure, nor was this to be expected. Rather, with scales varying on a continuum of average judged desirability and with an inseparable dependence in the same set of items of various levels of acquiescence-eliciting potential, we would expect the scale vectors to form a circle [Schaefer, 1959]. Such a circular array is evident in Figure 1, indicating a kind of reciprocity between acquiescence and desirability for a given scale—as desirability or undesirability of content increases from neutrality, the acquiescence component becomes smaller. The relative lack of vectors in the two left quadrants of Figure 1 is attributable in this battery to the poor representation of both "true" and "false" scales of highly desirable content. Inclusion of such scales would be expected to fill out the circle, with quadrants consisting of items keyed (a) desirable "true," (b) undesirable "true," (c) undesirable "false," and (d) desirable "false."

The remaining six factors taken together accounted for only 16.5 percent of the total variance and 23.6 percent of the common variance. Since they were individually quite small, explaining from 2.1 to 5.4 percent of the common variance each, interpretation was sometimes difficult. Interpretation was made particularly complicated by the fact that considerable item overlap exists between many of the scales with high loadings on these small factors. By eliminating from consideration factors probably attributable to item overlap, three dimensions (IV, VII, and VIII) remained which seemed to warrant psychological interpretations (see Jackson and Messick [1961] for a discussion of item overlap factors and their appraisal).

Factor IV received moderate loadings for Mf_f, Pa_f, Pt_t, and A. From an examination of relevant item content of these scales, it would appear that high scorers would reject content suggestive of hyper-masculine "toughness" and cynicism, in denying, for example, that "most people are honest chiefly through fear of being caught" (common to Mf_f and Pa_f). They would also tend to admit more freely to diverse symptoms of anxiety. One might speculate that such persons would be deviant in a prison. It is notable that while Mf_f is highly loaded on this factor, Mf_t is not, which is consistent with their −.15 correlation but inconsistent with the MMPI practice of adding the two scales together. It also argues against a simple identification of Factor IV as femininity.

Factor VII, although quite small, provides a rare instance in which the true and false keys of a given scale, in this case D, appear on the same factor. Thus, there indeed appears to be some consistent responses to content in items characteristic of depressed persons when the major stylistic determinants are first partialled out by factor analysis. It is necessary, however, to take these stylistic determinants into consideration, since the original correlation between D_t and D_f was only −.11.

Factor VIII appeared to be a combination of correlated independent responses and item overlap. Although Ma_f and Pd_f on the one hand and Sc_f and F_f on the other have common items, there is little item dependence between these two sets of scales. All loadings, however, are in the false direction, and the item content associated with these scales would suggest that subjects scoring high on them might be reflecting tendencies to deny certain classes of deviant material. Clinically, high scores on the above (complete or total) scales are commonly associated with alcoholism [Meehl, 1956], impulsivity, chronic trouble with the law, an amoral outlook, rebellion against established authority, a degree of social brashness, and employment instability—characteristics which might be represented in the aggregate with greater than average frequency within a prison inmate population, but which were also found to be of more general relevance in the hospital and college samples studied.

* * *

The results of this study, along with the similar investigations of hospitalized mental patients and college students cited earlier, reveal a strikingly consistent pattern. Approximately three-fourths of the common variance and about one-half of the total variance was interpretable in terms of the response styles of acquiescence and desirability. Of the remaining very small factors, roughly half their variance was attributable to item overlap, and hence is of little or no psychological significance. While consistencies interpretable in terms of reliable responses to item content did indeed appear in all three samples, with moderate replication in the diverse groups, their aggregate contribution to the total response variance was not great in comparison with other sources of variance. To interpret scale scores presumably reflecting such content factors without taking into account the rather massive response style effects would be quite hazardous. Because of the marked influence of acquiescence and desirability on virtually all of these empirically derived scales from the MMPI, there is a decided tendency for the scales to share substantial common variance, particularly when "true" and "false" items are considered separately, causing considerable redundancy and further reducing any unique contribution of a given scale to the assessment of psychopathological behavior.

The Challenge of Response Sets: Acquiescence

J. Block

I

A number of recent articles have conjectured and finally concluded that the widely used Minnesota Multiphasic Personality Inventory (MMPI) is most profitably to be interpreted in terms of response sets rather than in terms of content. Two response "styles," acquiescence and desirability, are championed as necessary and perhaps sufficient dimensions for understanding the MMPI. The response "style" of acquiescence, as defined by Couch and Keniston [1960] and as employed here and conventionally, refers to the tendency of an individual to agree or say "yes" to personality inventory statements, regardless of the content of the items. The response set of social desirability is to be understood as the tendency of an individual "to give socially desirable responses to items in personality inventories, regardless of whether the socially desirable response is True or False" [Edwards, 1959b, p. 108].

Demonstrations in support of these reinterpretations have appeared frequently and have not, in the main, been countered. If only because of reiteration, there seems to be a growing consensus in the literature that the more recent viewpoints represent an advance in understanding of what is being measured by personality inventories. Because inventories have been, are, and may be expected to be employed as fundamental measurement tools in the realm of personality psychology, the radical revaluation of such devices as the MMPI is a highly significant development warranting, in its turn, most careful examination.

The advent of these newer interpretations, however, has not brought comfortable clarity and insight to the MMPI. Rather, controversy has shifted its locus with arguments now about the comparative primacy of these two response sets and the ability of the one response style to encompass the relationshps claimed for the other. Thus, in commenting on the content-interpreted factor analysis reported by Kassebaum, Couch, and Slater [1959], Edwards and Heathers [1962] reinterpret the first MMPI factor as reflecting social desirability while Messick and Jackson [1961a] view the identical factor as signifying acquiescence. A measure Couch and Keniston [1960] put forward as an index of agreement-response set can be construed with equal plausibility as a measure of social undesirability, suggest Edwards and Walker [1961]. Whereupon Couch and Keniston [1961] call attention to the possible presence within Edwards' Social Desirability (SD) scale of a strong acquiescence component.

These notes of discord have not caused any retreat from the essential response-set position that the MMPI is best conceived in these newer terms. Although there continues to be disagreement about the relative importance and priority of social desirability and acquiescence, there is unanimity among the primary protagonists of these response sets that both emerge as significant factors within the MMPI [Edwards, Diers, and Walker, 1962; Couch and Keniston, 1961; Messick and Jackson, 1961a]. For Edwards, the few relationships within the MMPI that are not due to the operation of the social desirability variable arise because items with neutral social desirability values are involved. With such items, he suggests that acquiescent tendencies may be operating [Edwards, 1961]. For Messick and Jackson [1961a], the instance where an acquiescence interpretation encounters anomalous findings can be understood readily by invoking the additional response style of social desirability.

It is the purpose of the present monograph to contest the interpretation that "acquiescence, as moderated by social desirability, plays a dominant role in personality inventories like the MMPI" [Messick and Jackson, 1961a, p. 303]. It will be argued that the beleaguered MMPI, though by modern standards a less than optimal personality inventory, is by no means as innocent of psychological meaning as response-set adherents have suggested. As corollaries of this assertion, which it is believed follows from the several analyses to be reported, it will be further contended that (1) acquiescent-response set is *not* a significant component underlying the MMPI and (2) the social desirability interpretation, although seemingly applicable in many MMPI contexts, has achieved its support for fortuitous and epiphenomenal reasons.

Our argument is involved and prolonged and it has seemed best to adopt the dialectical strategy of focusing in detail upon acquiescence before considering social desirability.

Two lines of evidence have been invoked in support of acquiescence-response style as an important determiner of the scores an individual achieves on MMPI scales. The first of these, now to be evaluated, takes an indirect route, seeking to show by various derivative analyses that some recurrent patterns of MMPI results are strikingly assimilable to an acquiescence interpretation or that MMPI relationships exist which are discrepant from a content-oriented point of view but concordant with the acquiescence hypothesis. Recent and already important instances of this approach are the reinterpretation of the factor structure of the MMPI based upon observation of a curious correlate of the factor loadings of MMPI scales [Messick and Jackson, 1961a] and the impressive separation of "true" and "false" MMPI subscales as revealed by factor analysis [Jackson and Messick, 1961; 1962b].

The second, direct method of studying the ramifications of acquiescence we consider in the next section. This form of the empirical argument relies upon "pure" acquiescence scales and the consequent MMPI correlates of these content-free measures. One recent such measure is the Dy-3 MMPI scale, used as a "marker variable" or criterion for acquiescence in one study [Jackson and Messick, 1961] and found to have the highest acquiescence representation in another [Jackson and Messick, 1962b]. The study by Couch and Keniston [1960], which has been particularly influential in advancing the cause of acquiescence, also hinges on a "pure" acquiescence measure albeit one derived outside the MMPI and only later related to it.

The typical result of the dozen or so factor analyses of MMPI-scale intercorrelations available in the literature (and the many more not published) is the finding of two main factors and a variety of smaller, presumably less important factors. (It is important to note that when the intercorrelations of MMPI *items* are factored [e.g., Comrey, 1957a, 1957b, 1957c, 1958a, 1958b, 1958c, 1958d, 1958e] or when MMPI *subscales* are analyzed [Lingoes, 1960], a radically different factor structure emerges.) The first two factor dimensions are highly reproducible from sample to sample and explain a very large percentage of the communal variance; the factors beyond the first two tend to explain small portions of the variance and to be more ephemeral, probably being functions of the particular subject sample studied.

Messick and Jackson [1961a], in a recent look at factorial studies of the MMPI, noted a further consistency in the results reported. For each of eleven factor-analytic studies of MMPI scales, they correlated the factor loadings of the scales on the first factor with an index of the extent to which a scale had the poential for reflecting acquiescence. The index of acquiescence which they employed "was the proportion of items keyed true on each scale, which, assuming that the acquiescence-evoking properties of items are uniform over all MMPI scales, can be considered to reflect the extent to which total scores on a scale are influenced by consistent tendencies to respond 'true'" [Messick and Jackson, 1961a, p. 300]. The correlations between factor loadings and the proportion of items keyed true were, in the Messick and Jackson study, significant in 8 of the 11 separate tests of their hypothesis that "the largest factor is interpretable in terms of acquiescence." The coefficients were often astonishingly high (4 above .85), and even in the few instances where their hypothesis was not supported, the factor structures involved could in all likelihood have been rotated to produce a much better fit to the acquiescence measure.

Such consistent support for the Messick and Jackson hypothesis, however, does not carry the necessary implication that one of the primary factors in the MMPI is *better* conceptualized as an acquiescence dimension. Certainly, an explanation must be forthcoming for the pattern of the Messick and Jackson results, but their evidence for an acquiescence-response style is no more than circumstantial. Strictly, their findings demonstrate only that *a confounding of acquiescence and of content exists in the MMPI scales,* that *acquiescence is as tenable an interpretation of one primary MMPI factor as is a content interpretation.* What is required next—and before affirming a preference— is an unconfounding of acquiescence and content in MMPI scales so that these competing interpretations can run their race. Until acquiescence and content are separated and their respective contributions to MMPI-response consistency assessed, no positive claims can be made for either interpretation. Traditional MMPI users cannot ignore the possibility that acquiescence may be importantly, even decisively, involved in the test. Nor can propounders of the acquiescence viewpoint assert that content is unimportant. In the body of their paper, Messick and Jackson implicitly recognize the confounding problem by carefully and qualifiedly phrasing their argument for acquiescence as a suggested and possible alternative to an interpretation in terms of meaning. It is unfortunate that in their final, summary remarks, they advance their preferred interpretation more conclusively than the logic of their analysis warrants.

Editors' Note:

At this point in his original presentation, Professor Block introduced a straightforward demonstration that the factor structure which Jackson and Messick had found among the MMPI subscales formed by dividing each scale on the basis of true-keyed and false-keyed items and which they had attributed to the operation of a powerful acquiescence response set could be generated by merely factoring the item-overlap matrix. That is, the extent of common items among the various short subscales would generate coefficients of correlation among these scales, and the factor structure of this matrix of correlations essentially reproduced the factors that Jackson and Messick had interpreted as supporting their response set views.

It would appear then, that the factor structures obtained by Jackson and Messick in their analyses of "true" and "false" MMPI subscales are susceptible to an alternative interpretation and do not speak compellingly for the acquiescence interpretation so long as the potent and permeating influence of item overlap resides in their design.

Another simpler and more direct finding of Jackson and Messick presents, if not positive evidence for acquiescence, perhaps inferential support of their view. This is their observation that the correlations between the "true" and "false" portions of MMPI scales are disappointingly low and even reversed in certain instances. Clearly, the notion of acquiescence *could* provide a sufficient explanation of these data. However, again, closer analysis blurs the conclusiveness of any interpretation.

To begin, it must be noted that the situation is not quite so bad as their analysis suggests. Quite properly, they recognized the attenuating effects of unreliability upon their correlations and adjusted for this effect. Unfortunately, their correction was in partial error.

In order to correct for the limiting effects of unreliability, estimates of the reliabilities of the subscales are required. Jackson and Messick employed as their estimates either the Kuder-Richardson Formula 21 reliability of a subscale or its communality within their factor analysis, *whichever was higher.* Almost invariably, they used the communality estimate. Their reasoning was that Kuder-Richardson reliabilities underestimate somewhat the stability of measures while communality in factor theory is always less than but may approach the true reliability of a measure. Accordingly, the calculated communalities should, if higher than the understating Kuder-Richardson figures, be employed as the better reliability estimate because they are higher lower bounds.

However, this rationale fails to recognize the effect of item overlap in their factor analysis which, as we have shown, inappropriately raises calculated communalities. Since the correction for unreliability is small when the reliability estimates used are high, the usage by Jackson and Messick of overstatements of the reliability does not fully adjust for this perturbation. When due allowance is made, by subtraction from their communality figures, for the communal variance unfairly introduced by item overlap, the picture changes.

Restricting recomputation again to the eight clinical scales of the MMPI, we find that the "true" and "false" portions of the Hs, Pt, and Sc scales correlate to the limit set by their reliabilities and thus may be said to be content-representing. The "true" and "false" components of the remaining five scales are not conceptually equivalent judging from the three Jackson and Messick samples. It is only with respect to these latter scales that the question may be asked: Are these discrepancies ascribable to the canceling influence of acquiescence? Or, may these nominally equivalent but differently functioning subscales be viewed instead as measuring psychologically different dimensions?

The question is a large one, calling for complicated analyses beyond the interests of this monograph. It may even be an unfair statement of the problem since the failure of equivalence between "true" and "false" portions of certain MMPI scales when applied to psychologically heterogeneous (or differently homogeneous) subject samples does not mean that when these scales are employed with samples comparable to the original standardization samples, the subscales will again prove noncomparable. The empirical method of scale construction used in evolving the clinical scales of the MMPI required that all keyed items be criterion-relevant. The relationships among the items defining a scale can well change when noncomparable samples are studied, as has been the case subsequently. As a rule, psychologists have been slow to recognize that the pattern of correlations among personality variables (items) is often a reliable function of the specific subject population being sampled.

For the moment, our line of argument is to show that the failure of full equivalence between the "true" and "false" portions of certain MMPI scales can as well be construed in contentual terms as via the notion of acquiescence. In so doing, we rely heavily on earlier demonstrations that various of the clinical scales of the MMPI have, when applied to clinically heterogeneous samples, poor internal consistency properties and that when psychologically homogeneous subscales are developed, an imbalance of keying may exist in the newly partitioned scales. The reader interested in details may consult the work of Harris and Lingoes [1955], Little and Fisher [1958], and the series of papers by Comrey [1957a; 1957b; 1957c; 1958a; 1958b; 1958c; 1958d; 1958e].

II

For many of the MMPI scales, the scale-defining items are keyed predominantly "true" or predominantly "false." It has been argued that an extreme score on a scale keyed one-sidedly could as well arise from a blanket tendency to acquiesce to (or to deny) all items as from a reaction to the content of the items involved. Reciprocally, we have maintained that no MMPI index of "pure" acquiescence yet proposed has been shown to be free of the confounding influence of content. As noted earlier, the requirement of reliability for an acquiescence measure inevitably develops the possibility of a content-based alternative explanation of the index. Is it possible, however, to construct content-oriented MMPI scales which indisputably or sufficiently eliminate the presence of an acquiescence component, thus permitting the scores an individual attains to be unambiguously interpretable? We suggest there is a quick and easy technique, not new, but infrequently employed, which can be applied — even retroactively — to the MMPI to exclude the influence of acquiescence.

This simple way of preventing acquiescence-response set from affecting the scores an individual earns on a scale is to insure that half of the scale-defining items are scored for the answer "true" and half for the answer "false." "Balanced scales should serve to cancel out any contamination due to agreeing response set" [Couch and Keniston, 1960, p. 156], and therefore the individual differences, correlates, and factor structure of such balanced scales can be interpreted without recourse to an acquiescence component. It is likely, as one beneficial consequence of the concern raised about acquiescence, that future inventory scales will be developed so that they are balanced.

Messick and Jackson [1961a], by their use of degree of imbalance of "yesses" and "noes" as a proper index of acquiescence, of course, imply that a balanced scale provides a proper control on this response style. In another, conjointly appearing paper, however, although largely agreeing with the effectiveness of the control on acquiescence achieved by a balanced scoring key, these authors open the door to quite another logic for operationalizing the concept of acquiescence. Jackson and Messick [1961] note the possibility that the "true" and "false" components of a scale, although balanced with respect to number of items, may yet "pull" differential amounts of variance. They suggest it is equalization of "true" and "false" variance in a scale that should be sought if the effect of acquiescence is to be considered eliminated because, in principle, a scale balanced with respect to the number of "trues" and "falses" it contains could be deriving all of its variance from only the "true" or only the "false" items.

However, this door to a new and presumably ultimate way of controlling acquiescence, although ajar, permits no reliable passage as was noted almost immediately: the "nuance (of equating the amount of variance contributed by true-keyed and false-keyed items to a scale) could be achieved only with considerable labor, if at all" [Messick, 1962, p. 42]. Yet, despite its unachievability and despite the significant control acknowledged as provided by balancing "yesses" and "noes", Messick has been reluctant to abandon this advocacy of hypothetical variance balancing: "A simple balancing of the number of true and false items . . . appears to provide important, but not always sufficient, insurance against the spurious influence of acquiescence response set upon total scores . . ." [Messick, 1962, p. 43]. Astonishingly, Messick provides no operational rule by which the researcher may know when a balancing of the number of true- and false-keyed items excludes the adulterating effects of acquiescence and when it does not. It would appear that a "double-bind" has been created: the control we can achieve (of balancing the number of "yesses" and "noes") may always be threatened by a denial of sufficiency and by a demand for a control that cannot be achieved (the equation of variance contributions by the true- and false-keyed portions of a scale). This state of controlled ambiguity is, of course, insupportable. *Ad hoc* invocations cannot take the place of *a priori* criteria; a concept which cannot be stabilized by a set of operations can hardly prove useful.

In the primary analyses of MMPI scales to be reported later, we have used scales balanced with respect to the number of "true" and "false" items. In one supplementary analysis, out of curiosity rather than conviction, the previously untried approach of balancing variance contributions was explored and found wanting. In choosing to ignore the significance of such differences as may arise between the "true" and "false" variance components of MMPI scales in favor of balancing item-keying, we have chosen for what we consider a superior logic, one that is established, incisive, and empirically testable. Much of what follows depends on balancing the number of "trues" and "falses" in MMPI scales as an adequate control for acquiescence; and the reader must at this juncture, or perhaps a bit later after reviewing some results derived within the variance-equalization approach, formulate his own judgment of the sufficiency of the control that has been employed.

With the approach of balancing responses thus argued for as both parsimonious and capable, how may we use it to unconfound *existing*, response-unbalanced scales? The way we have chosen to revise current MMPI scales so that acquiescence no longer may be said to contribute to the total score is to balance these scales as well, after the fact of their development. By dropping out, at random, enough items from the subset of "true" or "false" items predominating in a scale, a balanced scale may be derived. For example, the Pt scale of the MMPI contains 48 items, 39 of which are keyed in the "true" direction. Using a table of random numbers, 30 of the 39 "true"-keyed Pt items may be deleted leaving a shorter, 18 item Pt scale now balanced with 9 items keyed "true" and 9 items keyed "false."

It is important that the psychometric properties of MMPI scales balanced in this fashion be understood. Such scales will be shorter and therefore tend to be less reliable. The characteristics of these shorter scales depend on the conceptual model presumed to underlie the MMPI.

III

A first decision involved fixing upon the set of MMPI scales to be analyzed in unbalanced and balanced forms. The eight usual "clinical" scales of the MMPI were included, together with the F and Si scales. The L scale which has 15 items, all keyed "false," and the K scale, whose 30 items include only one keyed "true", were both excluded. Obviously, neither of these scales can be balanced for they would be shortened to nothingness. Additional scales employed were: the Social Desirability (SD) scale [Edwards, 1957a]; the Ego-Strength (Es) scale [Barron, 1953]; the Intellectual Efficiency (Ie) scale [Gough, 1953]; the Leadership (Lp) scale [Oettel, 1953]; the Social Participation (Sp) scale [Gough, 1952]; the Social Status (St) scale [Gough, 1948]; the Dominance (Do) scale [Gough, McClosky, and Meehl, 1951]; the Social Introversion (Si) scale [Drake, 1946]; and the Neurotic Under-Control (NUC) scale [Block, unpublished work presented in Dahlstrom and Welsh, 1960]. Neither Welsh's A scale nor his R scale could be used in these analyses because, as earlier noted, they are not amenable to balancing. Instead, two scales developed some time ago by this writer to measure the first two factor dimensions of the MMPI in nonpathological populations were substituted. These scales, labeled Psychoneurosis (Pn) and Ego-Control, Form 4 (EC-4), do permit balancing. Their functional equivalence with the A and R scales is attested by correlations at about the limits set by the unreliabilities of the scales involved and so the interchange is warranted. Thus, a total of 21 scales was selected as representative of extant MMPI measures with respect to number, content, and kind of origin.

A balanced version of each of these 21 scales was derived in the manner just described. The number of items in each MMPI scale and its balanced version may be read from Table 1.

For each of five different samples, the following sequence of data analysis was applied:

1. The MMPI protocols were scored on the 21 unbalanced MMPI scales and on the 21 corresponding balanced versions of these scales.

2. The reliabilities (Kuder-Richardson Formula 20) of all scales were determined.

3. The correlation between each scale and its balanced version was calculated.

4. The 21 unbalanced MMPI scales and, *separately,* the 21 balanced MMPI scales were factor-analyzed by the principal-components method.

5. The comparability of the unrotated factor structures derived from analysis of the unbalanced and the balanced MMPI scales was assessed. Only the first two factors from each analysis were contrasted because, as noted earlier, the first two dimensions within the MMPI extract the great proportion of the communal variance. The factors were compared prior to rotation to eliminate all possibility of preferential positioning of the factor axes. It so happens that in four of the five samples studied, the unrotated factor dimensions are directly and even compellingly interpretable, as will be seen. But the reader should recall that any rigid translation of the factor axes will maintain invariant the relations among the variables being studied and, therefore, any conclusion derived from comparing unrotated factor structures will apply as well to these factor structures when they are comparably rotated. Although the equivalence of factors may often be judged sufficiently well simply by inspection, to objectify this comparison in the present study rank-order correlations were computed between the corresponding elements of the contrasted factors. In ad-

Table 1. Descriptive Characteristics of the 21 MMPI Scales Studied

Scale	Number of Items in Unbalanced Scale	Reliabilities of Unbalanced Scales	Number of Items in Balanced Scale	Reliabilities of Balanced Scales	Correlations of Unbalanced and Balanced Scales
F	64	.45, .58, .50, .66, .64	40	.40, .53, .49, .40, .67	.83, .91, .87, .93, .96
Hs	33	.69, .66, .75, .82, .85	22	.64, .55, .68, .78, .82	.93, .89, .94, .95, .97
D	60	.42, .42, .50, .62, .74	40	.24, .31, .53, .62, .74	.84, .82, .88, .91, .93
Hy	60	.32, .60, .71, .41, .70	26	.08, .42, .52, .37, .64	.68, .73, .86, .77, .88
Pd	50	.36, .48, .50, .51, .61	48	.38, .47, .49, .50, .62	.99, .99, .99, .99, .99
Mf	60	.37, .62, .61, .48, .44	56	.40, .58, .62, .50, .53	.98, .99, .98, .96, .95
Pa	40	.20, .26, .25, .26, .35	30	.08, .30, .22, .23, .09	.90, .91, .91, .90, .90
Pt	48	.81, .80, .83, .88, .91	18	.61, .54, .54, .75, .75	.90, .85, .86, .93, .91
Sc	78	.73, .78, .69, .87, .90	38	.37, .58, .24, .68, .75	.78, .83, .60, .91, .95
Ma	46	.59, .55, .51, .49, .57	22	.21, .37, .20, -.05, .37	.78, .76, .80, .69, .82
Pn	33	.86, .69, .74, .80, .80	20	.80, .57, .65, .68, .70	.94, .89, .89, .92, .91
SD	39	.70, .76, .79, .83, .86	18	.58, .61, .64, .69, .74	.86, .89, .90, .92, .94
Es	68	.53, .61, .54, .68, .78	50	.38, .36, .43, .50, .69	.89, .87, .89, .93, .96
Ie	39	.62, .67, .58, .68, .76	30	.61, .61, .50, .64, .73	.96, .96, .97, .97, .97
Lp	50	.72, .72, .83, .82, .84	28	.57, .51, .61, .67, .70	.84, .86, .92, .91, .93
Sp	25	.56, .66, .56, .69, .65	16	.45, .58, .50, .59, .60	.91, .90, .93, .93, .93
St	34	.48, .59, .50, .65, .56	30	.48, .55, .48, .60, .48	.99, .97, .98, .98, .97
Do	28	.33, .62, .37, .59, .58	14	.19, .30, .07, .20, .28	.79, .82, .81, .80, .82
Si	70	.76, .77, .87, .85, .88	68	.76, .77, .87, .85, .88	1.00, 1.00, 1.00, 1.00, 1.00
EC-4	33	.70, .64, .62, .46, .58	26	.55, .49, .44, .16, .50	.96, .95, .94, .91, .95
NUC	33	.82, .76, .56, .76, .69	17[a]	.69, .49, .33, .56, .43	.92, .89, .80, .87, .88

[a] It was discovered, after the present analyses were well under way, that the balanced version of the NUC scale was in slight error, containing one too many statements keyed "true." This mistake does not affect the sense or substance of the present findings in any significant way.

dition, the Wrigley-Neuhaus [1955] *coefficient of factorial similarity*—
an index analogous to the product-moment correlation developed to
express the congruence between the factors in the two studies—
was calculated for each pair of corresponding factors.

The five samples studied may be briefly characterized:

1. 100 Air Force captains, with a mean age of 34.6.

2. 95 men, with a mean age of 38.9, who had participated in a
study conducted at the Children's Hospital of the East Bay of familial
factors in childhood diseases.

3. 46 men, with a modal age of 37, who had participated in the
longitudinal study being carried out at the Institute of Human
Development, Berkeley, California.

4. 110 women, with a mean age of 35.2, who had participated in
the above mentioned study of familial factors in childhood diseases.

5. 49 women, with a modal age of 37, who had participated in the
IHD longitudinal study.

Five different samples were employed so that the consistency of
the results obtained could be evaluated. These particular samples
were selected because of certain additional data available for them.

In Table 1 are presented the reliabilities of the MMPI scales being
evaluated, for each of the five samples. The table displays the trends
to be expected solely from psychometric considerations—the balanced
scales tend to be somewhat less reliable than the original, unbalanced
scales, the extent of drop in reliability being an approximate function of the extent of shortening of the scale. The reliabilities of the
acquiescence-removed balanced scale, however, although lower because of scale shortening, are not fundamentally changed.

Table 1 also contains the correlations, for each sample, between
each unbalanced scale and its corresponding balanced version. These
are part-whole correlations since all the items in the balanced scale
are contained also in the unbalanced scale. But this is as it should be,
given the logic of balancing. The resulting high correlations reflect no
artifact but rather are proper indicators of the extent to which the
balanced scales have the same psychological meaning—but with
acquiescence removed— as the scales from which they derive. These
high correlations between corresponding unbalanced and balanced
scales also foretell (indeed, entail) the results obtained through factor
analysis.

We note that the results in Table 1 do not appear to be due to any
special characteristics of the set of balanced MMPI scoring templates
used. It will be recalled that a random basis was employed to delete

the necessary number of items scored in the predominant direction. Although methodologically our design would have been improved somewhat if for each subject in each sample a unique set of randomly balanced templates had been used, this formidable nicety was disregarded after preliminary checks showed impressive consistency of scores over different versions of equivalently-constituted balanced scales.

Separate factor analyses were carried out for each sample. In Table 2 one representative set of factor loadings is presented. The results on the remaining four samples were essentially the same. That is, the first two factors derived from the unbalanced MMPI scales and the first two factors derived from the balanced versions of these scales correspond remarkably well. By inspection, *it is indisputably clear that the factor structure of the MMPI does not change when the possibility of interference from an acquiescence response set is removed.*

The independent psychological significance of these repetitively found MMPI dimensions is explored elsewhere (see II, 5), but at this juncture a brief assay of the factors found in the acquiescence-removed analyses is useful. For those knowledgeable of earlier factor

Table 2. The First Two Unrotated Dimensions Derived from Separate Factor Analyses of Unbalanced and Balanced MMPI Scales, Sample A

Scale	Unbalanced MMPI		Balanced MMPI	
	Factor 1	Factor 2	Factor 1	Factor 2
F	−.59	−.20	−.37	−.26
Hs	−.79	.13	−.77	.04
D	−.24	.44	−.51	.14
Hy	.19	.26	.00	.16
Pd	−.35	−.35	−.32	−.39
Mf	−.31	−.31	−.28	−.44
Pa	−.10	−.02	.10	.11
Pt	−.89	−.10	−.82	−.21
Sc	−.85	−.23	−.68	−.10
Ma	−.46	−.65	−.04	−.71
Pn	−.90	.01	−.83	−.12
SD	.89	−.06	.82	−.07
Es	.59	−.19	.43	−.25
Ie	.61	−.18	.57	−.08
Lp	.80	−.22	.77	−.04
Sp	.42	−.58	.48	−.51
St	.17	−.63	.19	−.67
Do	.48	−.22	.19	−.30
Si	−.56	.56	−.67	.39
EC-4	.21	.81	.04	.80
NUC	−.72	−.43	−.56	−.49

analyses of the MMPI, no great surprises will be occasioned by our results. The first factor underlying the balanced scales, to which we give for the present the noncommital name of Alpha, is defined at its negative end by a cluster of scales purporting to reflect a neurotic and maladaptive character structure (e.g., Pt, Sc, Pn) and at the other end by scales, led by Edwards's SD measure, which relate to a more self-satisfied and culturally valued adjustive mode (e.g., Lp, Sp, St, Ie). Alpha is very well—perhaps too well—measured by MMPI scales and much economy would be introduced by settling on but one or two of these scales to represent this dimension.

For Edwards, Alpha is the Social Desirability dimension; for Welsh, the preferred label for this dimension (reversed) is Anxiety; for earlier MMPI workers, this component—usually indexed by twin peaks on the Pt and Sc scales—has been interpreted as relating to an agitated despair imbedded within a neurotic character structure.

The second factor emerging from the analyses of the balanced scales, temporarily labeled Beta, is the dimension that formerly— when confounding existed—was often construed as strongly reflecting acquiescence-response set [Jackson and Messick, 1961; Jackson and Messick, 1962b; Edwards, Diers, and Walker, 1962]. Now, with the exclusion of interference from an acquiescence component and from knowledge of the external criteria used to establish its defining measures, Beta can be identified as relating to the way individuals characteristically monitor their impulses. At one end of the dimension is a scale specifically measuring over-control (EC-4), and at the other end a few scales related to impulse expression and social expansiveness (e.g., Ma, Sp, St, Pd). Beta is not so redundantly measured within the MMPI as is the first factor largely because, as will be seen, the MMPI-item pool contains comparatively few items pertinent to this dimension. Welsh's second factor, from which he derived his R (repression) scale, clearly is akin to this dimension; the writer earlier has preferred to conceptualize the Beta continuum as *ego-control*. A larger effort to understand and interpret this MMPI factor is best deferred until after an examination of its behavioral correlates.

To summarize matters at this point in our analytical progression, we may clearly affirm the inconsequentiality of acquiescence-response set insofar as the factorial structure of the MMPI is concerned. Comparison of the factor structure of the MMPI when acquiescence conceivably could be operating with the factor structure existing when acquiescence is denied effect reveals an astonishing parallelism. If the present five samples may be taken as a basis for generalization, it follows that the impact of acquiescence is so minute as to often not warrant the complications attendant upon excluding its effect. Previous work employing unbalanced MMPI scales appears not to have been vitiated by failure to consider the possible contribution of acquiescence; subsequent researchers employing the MMPI will have to decide for themselves whether the gains of using balanced scales outweigh the possible costs of thereby excluding from usage numerous valid items which cannot be balanced within the existing item pool.

IV

Having shown that when acquiescence is prevented from intruding, the internal structure of the MMPI remains the same, we are left with the insistent question: Why did the MMPI scales, when they were initially constructed, prove to be so unbalanced and in ways admitting of an interpretation in terms of acquiescence-response set?

To help unravel this woolly matter, a number of additional analyses were executed. Within each of the five samples, a group of Alpha Highs and a group of Alpha Lows were designated based upon the factor scores which were available for each individual. Factor scores were computed using the Holzinger-Harman short-form method which weights the factor-score contribution of each scale according to its factor loading. Then, for each sample, the MMPI-response protocols of the Alpha Highs were contrasted with the MMPI-response protocols of the Alpha Lows in order to identify, by means of a differential frequency of response, the items which distinguish the two groups. Additionally, the Alpha Highs from the five samples were combined and their MMPI answers compared with those of the combined groups of Alpha Lows.

Now, the Alpha dimension was derived from analysis of *balanced* MMPI scales and therefore, high and low scorers on this dimension have earned their placement uninfluenced by an acquiescence-response set. Accordingly, the simple hypothesis might follow that when only the items differentiating Alpha Highs from Alpha Lows are examined, there should be about as many items responded to more affirmatively (i.e., with greater frequency) by the Alpha Highs as there are items responded to more affirmatively by Alpha Lows. In other words, a scale to measure the Alpha dimension based upon contrasting, via item-analytic procedures, groups of Alpha Highs and of Alpha Lows would be expected, by the null hypothesis, to have as many responses keyed "true" as are keyed "false."

For the item-analyses, Fisher's exact method for testing the significance of 2 x 2 contingency tables was used, the criterion for considering an item as discriminating being set at the .05 level. It should be noted that, as reported elsewhere [Block, 1960], only about 1.7 or 2% of the MMPI items should reach the .05 level of significance by chance when a nonpsychiatric sample is being studied. Table 3 presents the summary results of these analyses.

Equivalent item-analyses of the Beta dimension were carried out after groups of Beta Highs and Beta Lows were formed. The five groups of Beta Highs, combined, were also contrasted with the combined groups of Beta Lows. The summary results of these analyses may be read from Table 4. Again, the expectation would be that, because acquiescence had no influence upon the Beta dimension, Beta Highs should be as "yea-saying" as Beta Lows.

Before considering the implications of each table separately, it is illuminating to compare the analyses of Alpha with the analyses of Beta. It may be seen that the Alpha dimension is profusely represented within the MMPI-item pool and that the Beta dimension, although not "pulling" nearly so many items, also constellates a nonchance set of items.

If the informal criterion of the number of items reaching the .05 level of significance is taken to indicate the extent of representation of a dimension within the item pool, then the Alpha dimension carries about three times the influence of the Beta dimension within the MMPI. Indeed, the number of items strongly associated with the Alpha dimension is astonishing—about 63% significant at the .05 level when sizable groups are compared. This redundancy far exceeds the requirements of good measurement and, coupled with the item-overlap problem previously mentioned, clarifies why the first factor underlying MMPI scales is so dominant, leaving little MMPI-scale variance remaining.

It should be noted that, although earlier evidence and the results we shall report later testify to the behavioral significance of the Alpha dimension within the MMPI, it does not follow that this redundantly-indexed MMPI component is *behaviorally* more important than other MMPI factors which are less distinctly specified within the MMPI-item pool. Indeed, our results will show that in nonpsychiatric samples, the Beta dimension relates to behavior as pervasively as does the Alpha dimension.

Yet, in fairness to the MMPI and the rationale underlying its construction, it must be recognized that in psychiatric samples (for which the inventory was developed), the apparent redundancy of the measurement of the Alpha dimension may be warranted if subfactors or groupings of symptoms related to psychiatric entities are found to exist within the sprawling domain of Alpha. These subfactors are not so readily discernible when non-psychiatric samples are being studied

Table 3. Summary Results of Item Analyses of Alpha Highs versus Alpha Lows

Sample	Number of Alpha Highs	Number of Alpha Lows	Number Significant at .05 Level	Percent Significant at .05 Level	Number Answered More Affirmatively by Alpha Highs	Number Answered More Affirmatively by Alpha Lows
A	20	20	130	22.97	32	98
B	19	20	112	19.79	25	87
C	17	17	32	5.65	5	27
D	20	20	208	36.75	58	150
E	18	13	76	13.43	25	51
Combined Samples	95	97	355	62.72	100	255

Note: The slight inconsistency between the N's reported for the combined samples (95 and 97) as compared to the N's calculated by summing over the individual samples (94 and 90) derive from a slight change, for the last item analysis, in the cutting points used to determine Alpha Highs and Alpha Lows.

Table 4. Summary Results of Item Analyses of Beta Highs versus Beta Lows

Sample	Number of Beta Highs	Number of Beta Lows	Number Significant at .05 Level	Percent Significant at .05 Level	Number Answered More Affirmatively by Beta Highs	Number Answered More Affirmatively by Beta Lows
A	20	20	50	8.83	6	44
B	20	21	49	8.66	24	25
C	17	17	53	9.36	21	32
D	20	20	46	8.13	19	27
E	16	17	27	4.77	18	9
Combined Samples	97	98	138	24.38	45	93

Note: The slight inconsistency between the N's reported for the combined samples (97 and 98) as compared to the N's calculated by summing over the individual samples (93 and 95) derive from a slight change, for the last item analysis, in the cutting points used to determine Beta Highs and Beta Lows.

or when factor analysis is applied at the scale rather than at the item or subscale level.

Looking next at the results polarized by the Alpha dimension, it may be seen that the item-analyses reveal an intrinsic imbalance in the constitution of the MMPI-item pool—in each of the five samples, many more items are answered affirmatively by Alpha Lows than are affirmed by Alpha Highs. The trend is consistent, strong, and highly significant statistically. If an MMPI scale to measure the Alpha dimension were comprised of the items discriminating Alpha Highs from Alpha Lows—a conventional and reasonable procedure for constructing personality scales—the resulting measure (if scored for Alpha Highs) would have about one-fourth of its items keyed for "true" and three-fourths of its items keyed for "false." Thus, although our procedures averted the influence of any effect of an agreement-response set, because the MMPI-item pool happens to contain relatively few items affirmable by Alpha Highs and many items declarable by Alpha Lows, Alpha Highs will appear to be "nay-sayers" and Alpha Lows "yea-sayers." A seeming manifestation of acquiescence has reappeared which, under less understood circumstances, might have been taken as evidence for the operation of this response set.

In the light of these results, it is retrospectively clear why the MMPI scales which relate to the Alpha dimension have, to a greater or lesser degree, an imbalance in their keying. The Sc scale, loading strongly on the Alpha dimension and aimed to measure the negative end of that continuum, contains 59 items keyed "true" and only 19 items keyed "false"; the SD scale, a superb measure of the positive end of the Alpha, contains 9 items keyed "true" but 30 items keyed "false." Both of these scales (and many others) have been claimed for acquiescence in the past and it is now clear how this misconstruction came about. By manipulating—deliberately or not—the loading of an MMPI scale on the Alpha dimension, the extent of item imbalance in that scale can also be expected to vary systematically.

The interpretation of the first factor of the MMPI in terms of acquiescence as once proposed by Messick and Jackson (1961a) may be seen now to have been seemingly feasible because of these intrinsic properties of the MMPI-item pool. The origins of this preponderance of items phrased in the one direction rather than in the other with respect to the Alpha dimension cannot be fully identified—it lies in part in some deliberate decisions made when constituting the item pool, in part in the extraordinary difficulty of phrasing certain statements in reverse form and, doubtless, in part in the way the MMPI just happened to evolve.

Although the result was foregone, the social desirability scale values of the items significantly related to the Alpha dimension were ascertained by making reference to the recent Messick and Jackson [1961b] social desirability scaling of the MMPI. In the main, the items affirmable by the Alpha Highs were highly desirable socially and the items "acquiesced" to by Alpha Lows were undesirable. Comparatively few items with intermediate social desirability values proved significant.

The analyses for the Beta dimension do not show so simple or potent a trend in the way the discriminating items are allocated to Beta Highs and Beta Lows, perhaps because the Beta dimension is not so weightily represented in the MMPI. There is a tendency for Beta Lows to be "yea-sayers" but the relationship is not so striking as for the Alpha dimension. The "yea-saying" ratios of Beta Lows are somewhat, but not greatly, accentuated if the Beta-related items which are highly desirable or highly undesirable socially are excluded from consideration. These latter items tend to be tinged heavily with Alpha. When only the items having SD scale values in the middle-two intervals of the eight-interval scaling continuum are considered, the number of affirmable items for Beta Highs and for Beta Lows becomes, for the five samples respectively, 1:23; 11:16; 7:14; 6:13; and 7:4. For combined samples, the ratio becomes 20:48.

It may well be that the characteristics of the MMPI-item pool, in conjunction with some other understandings, provides a basis for explaining the contentual core of "maladaptive under-control" which appears to underlie the Dy-3 scale of Jackson and Messick. In constituting the Dy-3 scale, they selected items falling within the mid-range of the social desirability continuum. Comparatively few items related to the Alpha dimension will be selected by this criterion while the likelihood of the selection of Beta-relevant items is increased. With the power of the Alpha dimension lessened (but by no means eliminated), the relatively underweighted Beta dimension is accentuated in importance and can take greater (but not complete) charge of the Dy-3 scale. Thus, when the correlations of Dy-3 with the *balanced* MMPI scales are calculated, it is found in all five samples that the Dy-3 scale falls within the Alpha Low-Beta Low quadrant.

As a consequence of the imbalance in keying of the Alpha-relevant and Beta-relevant items so that the low ends of *both* the Alpha and Beta dimensions are more densely represented by MMPI items than are the high ends, it follows that high scorers on a scale located in the Alpha Low-Beta Low quadrant (e.g., the Dy-3 scale) will—unless further controls are instituted—naturally be responding with "yesses" much more often than with "noes." That is, a scale located in the Alpha Low-Beta Low quadrant "fuses" or cumulates the response imbalances of both dimensions and therefore would be composed of items keyed primarily, but not exclusively, for "trues." This predicted description fits the Dy-3 scale well for it will be remembered that about one-third of the item intercorrelations in the Dy-3 scale were negative, indicating "true" keying for these items was inappropriate. Finally, if a low position on the Alpha dimension is viewed for the present as signifiying "neuroticism" and a low position on Beta is termed indicative of "under-control," then the contentual core of "maladaptive under-control" observed as the dominant factor in the Dy-3 scale is explained. This complicated rationale will perhaps achieve its final support in the next section, when the personological correlates of the Alpha and Beta dimensions are explored.

In summary, the analyses of Highs and Lows on the Alpha and Beta dimensions afford the following recognitions. There is probably an overweighting of the Alpha dimension within the MMPI and perhaps an underrepresentation of the Beta dimension. The difficulty in establishing sizable and reliable factors beyond the first two components when analyzing MMPI scales may be ascribed, in large part, to a redundancy of the basic item pool. This redundancy may redeem itself when the MMPI is applied solely to psychiatric populations; when used in nonpsychiatric settings, however, the MMPI-item pool appears to be too narrow in its coverage or weighting of dimensions beyond Alpha. Because of the structural properties of the MMPI-item pool, Alpha Lows particularly but also Beta Lows will appear—unfairly—to be acquiescent. The items related to the Beta dimension tend to be of intermediate social desirability value while the items related to the Alpha dimension usually are at extremes of the social desirability scale continuum. The contentual core of the Dy-3 scale can be viewed as a fortuitous function of the characteristics of the MMPI-item pool.

Having shown that acquiescence is not an important determinant of MMPI responses and how the credibility of the acquiescence interpretation happened to evolve as a function of the intrinsic characteristics of the MMPI-item pool, we may set this response style aside and focus now on social desirability.

Editors' Note:

The scale correlates of Beta will be taken up along with Alpha in the following article.

The Challenge of Response Sets: Social Desirability

J. Block

I

In this article, we describe the construction of a scale to measure the Alpha factor of the MMPI, the factor for which Edwards has proposed an interpretation in terms of social desirability. Although excellent measures of the Alpha dimension exist (e.g., SD, Pt), the dilemma posed by these scales is that they may be interpreted from either a characterological or a SD standpoint. The Alpha-measuring scale to be described and then evaluated measures the first factor of the MMPI exceedingly well but has been constructed so as to be "desirability-free." A scale that identifies the Alpha dimension although fairly excluding the influence of SD clarifies a formerly muddled situation since a "desirability-free" measure of Alpha is an untenable anomaly, given the SD hypothesis. It can arise if—and only if—the Alpha factor is a dimension thus far fortuitously linked to SD but not necessarily so. If the Alpha factor of the MMPI can be well measured without invoking the SD concept, then it follows that the SD interpretation does not intrinsically apply in this context.

Our strategy in the construction of this scale was to select Alpha-related items which concomitantly are neutral with respect to SD or are even keyed against the SD hypothesis. It proved possible to choose items meeting these dual criteria within the MMPI by virtue of some earlier analyses and a vast redundancy in representation of the Alpha factor.

It will be recalled, from the previous article (see II, 4), that in studying the properties of the MMPI-item pool, an item analysis was performed using as contrast groups the Alpha Highs (combined from Samples A through E, providing a total N of 95) and the Alpha Lows (combined from all 5 samples, the total N being 97). The three samples of men were combined with the two samples of women because separate analyses for the sexes indicated that with respect to the Alpha dimension, there were no distinguishable differences between men and women in regard to the psychological content of Alpha-discriminating items.

In these analyses of combined subgroups, 389 of the 566 MMPI items (68.7%) proved to discriminate at the .10 level of significance. At the .05 level, the figure was 355 items (62.7%) and at the .01 level, 292 items (51.6%). These are spectacular findings and testify to the extent of repetition within the MMPI-item pool of Alpha-relevant items. Because of the large sizes of the contrast groups employed, these figures, although still lower bounds, probably come close to the limiting (i.e., true) values.

Of the 389 items significant at the .10 level, 109 items (28%) are answered more affirmatively by the high scorers on the Alpha dimension and 280 items (72%) are responded to more frequently by low scoring individuals. As indexed by the SD scale values for MMPI items reported by Messick and Jackson [1961b] or by Heineman [1952], the vast preponderance of the differentiating items are at one extreme of the SD continuum or the other. The items affirmed by Alpha Highs tend to be socially desirable; the items affirmed by Alpha Lows tend to be socially undesirable.

But—and here is the potential we have tapped—there are a number of MMPI items significantly associated with the first MMPI factor which are in the neutral ranges of the SD continuum or even on the atypical side—given the particular contrast group—of the SD dimension. A scale comprised of such SD-neutral or SD-reverse-keyed Alpha items should measure the first factor of the MMPI but should not be vulnerable to an interpretation in terms of SD. As a matter of esthetic nicety but, as we have seen, by no means required, such a desirability-free Alpha scale should be constructed to have as many items keyed for a "true" response as are keyed for a "false" response, thus eliminating the intrusion (of the interpretation) of a possible acquiescence-response set.

Obviously, the logic of this approach depends on, besides the availability of a horde of Alpha-related items, an acceptable basis for identifying the scale position of these items on the SD continuum.

Unless the SD scale values (SDSVs) of the items selected to constitute the proposed scale are recognized as meeting the promised criteria, the scale and its correlates would roil instead of calm the contentious atmosphere.

The two most widely used and publicly available sets of SDSVs for the MMPI-item pool are those of Heineman [1952, reported also in Dahlstrom and Welsh, 1960] and Messick and Jackson [1961b, reported also in Volume II of Dahlstrom, Welsh, and Dahlstrom, 1975]. The Heineman scale values were developed using 108 college students as judges, a 5-point rating scale, and the method of equal-appearing intervals. The rating variabilities for each item are not published. The Messick and Jackson SDSVs were established employing 171 judges, a 9-point rating scale, and the method of successive intervals. Rating dispersions for each item were calculated. Messick and Jackson report a correlation of .964 between their scale values and those obtained by Heineman.

With the advent of the Messick and Jackson scale values, there has been a shift toward their use over the Heineman results, where such information is required. The grounds for this preference are multiple and cumulative: the Messick and Jackson results are more recent; a larger judge sample was used; finer discriminations are available; the scaling method employed was more sophisticated; and the additional, useful information about item-rating dispersions (i.e., item ambiguity) is available. Accordingly, in specifying the SDSVs of the Alpha-related items, the Messick and Jackson results were used.

A total of 40 items were selected according to the criteria and are defined as the Ego-Resiliency (Subtle) or ER-S scale. The label assigned to this scale is believed to follow from the behavioral correlates of the Alpha dimension, reported later. The ER-S scale consists of 20 items scored in the "true" direction and 20 items scored in the "false" direction. Each subset of 20 items contains items chosen almost exclusively from the middle intervals of the SD scaling continuum, and the two subsets have equivalent SDSV means and standard deviations. For the 20 items keyed "true," the mean SDSV is 5.11, with a standard deviation of .64; for the 20 items keyed "false," the mean SDSV is 5.21, with a standard deviation of .62. Moreover, the rating dispersions of the selected items are not unusual. For the 20 items keyed "true," the mean rating dispersion is 1.72; for the 20 items keyed "false," the mean rating dispersion is 1.48; the overall mean dispersion being 1.60. These figures may be compared with the mean rating dispersion of 1.64 based on the 40 MMPI items: 1, 51, 101, . . . 551, 2, 52, 102, etc. At the .01 level of significance, 36 of the ER-S items were related to the Alpha dimension. Of the remaining 4 items, all in the "true" subscale, 3 were Alpha-significant at the .05 level and 1 at the .10 level.

By virtue of the dual criteria employed in assembling items, we suggest that neither a "yea-sayer" nor an individual who responds in a socially desirable way can earn an extreme score on the full ER-S scale. The items defining the ER-S scale are reported in Table 1.

In Table 2 are presented the means, standard deviations, and Kuder-Richardson Formula 20 reliabilities of the ER-S scale, for nine different samples. Samples A through E have been previously described (see II, 4) and, when combined, formed the basis for the item analysis from which the ER-S items were selected. Samples F through I are additional samples employed to extend our knowledge of the functioning of the ER-S scale in samples fully independent of the scale's development. These latter samples may be briefly characterized:

Sample F consisted of 154 United States Marines, composed in about equal parts of recruits awaiting discharge because of their homosexual tendencies, recruits awaiting discharge for psychiatric reasons (but excluding homosexual involvement), and recruits satisfactorily completing their initial period of training. Sample F was a peculiar mélange, representing psychological disturbance more than psychological health.

Sample G contained 79 women seen at clinics of a university medical center. About half of this group were hypertensives, the remainder being clinic patients matched with the first half on a variety of nonmedical criteria.

Sample H consisted of 76 college women, half of them being defined as prehypertensive because of blood pressure lability and the remainder being matched with the first 38 subjects on a variety of nonphysiological criteria.

Sample I consisted of 87 female clinic patients, about half being hypertensive and the remainder being controls. The primary difference between Sample I and Sample G is that Sample I was collected more recently.

It will be seen from Table 2 that the ER-S scale enjoys adequate but not superb reliability. Samples A through E average a reliability slightly higher than the average earned by Samples F through I, a difference probably due to the slight capitalization on chance resulting from applying the ER-S scale to samples involved in its construction. But the reliability of the ER-S scale, even in totally new samples, is fully in keeping with the reliabilities usually attained by MMPI scales and may be compared with those reported in Table 1 in Article

Table 1. The Items Defining the MMPI *ER-S* Scale

Item No.	Item Text	Scoring Direction	Messick and Jackson SDSV
36.	I seldom worry about my health.	True	5.29
68.	I hardly ever feel pain in the back of the neck.	True	5.64
73.	I am an important person.	True	4.19
74.	I have often wished I were a girl. (Or if you are a girl) I have never been sorry that I am a girl.	True	4.57
91.	I do not mind being made fun of.	True	5.19
119.	My speech is the same as always (not faster or slower, or slurring; no hoarseness).	True	5.45
131.	I do not worry about catching diseases.	True	5.62
167.	It wouldn't make me nervous if any members of my family got into trouble with the law.	True	3.34
198.	I daydream very little.	True	5.60
222.	It is not hard for me to ask help from my friends even though I cannot return the favor.	True	4.66
235.	I have been quite independent and free from family rule.	True	5.19
242.	I believe I am no more nervous than most others.	True	5.82
270.	When I leave home I do not worry about whether the door is locked and the windows closed.	True	4.48
306.	I get all the sympathy I should.	True	5.10
329.	I almost never dream.	True	4.71
369.	Religion gives me no worry.	True	5.45
478.	I have never been made especially nervous over trouble that any members of my family have gotten into.	True	4.57
523.	I practically never blush.	True	5.68
528.	I blush no more often than others.	True	5.79
532.	I can stand as much pain as others can.	True	5.85
5.	I am easily awakened by noise.	False	4.34
71.	I think a great many people exaggerate their misfortunes in order to gain the sympathy and help of others.	False	4.84
89.	It takes a lot of argument to convince most people of the truth.	False	4.84
102.	My hardest battles are with myself.	False	4.99
112.	I frequently find it necessary to stand up for what I think is right.	False	7.50
134.	At times my thoughts have raced ahead faster than I could speak them.	False	5.51
201.	I wish I were not so shy.	False	5.47
279.	I drink an unusually large amount of water every day.	False	4.75
323.	I have had very peculiar and strange experiences.	False	5.10
327.	My mother or father often made me obey even when I thought that it was unreasonable.	False	5.11
382.	I wish I could get over worrying about things I have said that may have injured other peoples' feelings.	False	5.19
390.	I have often felt badly over being misunderstood when trying to keep someone from making a mistake.	False	5.00

Table 1. (continued)

Item No.	Item Text	Scoring Direction	Messick and Jackson SDSV
394.	I frequently ask people for advice.	False	5.77
402.	I often must sleep over a matter before I decide what to do.	False	5.07
425.	I dream frequently.	False	4.89
458.	The man who had the most to do with me when I was a child (such as my father, stepfather, etc.) was very strict with me.	False	5.05
465.	I have several times had a change of heart about my life work.	False	5.19
468.	I am often sorry because I am so cross and grouchy.	False	5.63
489.	I feel sympathetic toward people who tend to hang on to their griefs and troubles.	False	4.77
505.	I have had periods when I felt so full of pep that sleep did not seem necessary for days at a time.	False	5.18

II, 4. Comparatively, the ER-S scale is shorter than many MMPI scales, suggesting that the reliability of the scale might be appreciably increased if more items of the ER-S variety could be added. This possibility does not appear to exist within the constraints set by the MMPI-item pool.

It will be recalled from Article 4 that both the SD and Pt scales—the latter reversed—are collinear with the Alpha dimension. Let us see how the ER-S scale relates to these two measures. The relevant data are contained in Table 2 where it will be observed that the correlations between ER-S and SD, and between ER-S and Pt are extremely high.

Thus, for the nine samples, the correlations between ER-S and SD were, respectively: .70, .70, .64, .77, .79, .64, .67, .66, and .59. Corrected for the attenuating effects of the unreliabilities involved, these figures zoom to about the correlational limit, i.e., .99, .92, .92, .95, .99, .77, 1.00, .92, and .84. These are impressive correlations and indicate the ER-S scale—designed to exclude the influence of a SD response tendency—measures the same dimension indexed by the SD scale. That is, the Alpha dimension can be measured with no reference to the SD concept.

The relationship of the ER-S scale to the Pt scale must, of course, parallel the results obtained with the SD scale. For the nine samples, the correlations between ER-S and Pt were, respectively: $-.80$, $-.75$, $-.67$, $-.79$, $-.79$, $-.67$, $-.66$, $-.70$, and $-.61$. When due allowance is made for the attenuating effects of unreliability, these figures be-

Table 2. Descriptive Statistics for the *ER-S*, *SD*, and *Pt* MMPI Scales in Nine Different Samples

Sample	ER-S Scale (40 items)			SD Scale (39 items)					Pt Scale (48 items)				
	Mean	S.D.	K-R 20 Rel.	Mean	S.D.	K-R 20 Rel.	ER-S/ SD Cor.	ER-S/ SD Cor., Adj.	Mean	S.D.	K-R 20 Rel.	ER-S/Pt Cor.	ER-S/Pt Cor., Adj.
A	25.63	4.79	.704	34.89	3.22	.700	.698	.994	6.53	4.93	.810	−.795	−1.000
B	24.84	5.60	.775	34.01	3.85	.756	.701	.916	7.53	5.03	.801	−.752	−.954
C	24.52	4.27	.610	33.37	4.23	.790	.641	.923	9.07	5.72	.833	−.665	−.933
D	23.81	5.82	.781	31.16	5.31	.831	.765	.950	10.81	7.28	.884	−.792	−.953
E	23.27	5.36	.741	30.80	5.94	.864	.793	.991	12.51	8.25	.906	−.791	−.965
F	18.26	5.08	.674	22.56	7.96	.886	.638	.773	23.80	11.17	.929	−.673	−.851
G	21.18	4.31	.561	27.73	5.39	.792	.671	1.000	15.30	8.36	.888	−.658	−.932
H	23.08	4.82	.674	30.70	4.71	.759	.655	.916	12.17	6.22	.819	−.699	−.941
I	19.55	4.53	.609	26.51	5.76	.811	.592	.842	17.97	9.08	.902	−.610	−.823

come, respectively: —1.00, —.95, —.93, —.95, —.97, —.85, —.93, —.94, and —.82. Again, the ER-S scale proves to be collinear with a scale which in turn is a marker variable for the Alpha dimension. But where previously the marker variables for the Alpha factor were susceptible to an interpretation in terms of SD, the ER-S scale as a new marker variable for the Alpha dimension may *not* be conceived in SD terms.

Because of the logic of its design, we may expect the ER-S scale to be a more subtle measure of the Alpha dimension than either the SD or Pt scale and therefore, less affected by deliberate attempts to fake good. One of the problems with the SD and Pt scales has been their tendency to produce highly skewed score distributions, when applied to reasonably normal, nonpsychiatric subject samples. For the SD scale, scores tend to cluster around a rather high mean and are skewed downward; for the Pt scale, scores usually cluster around a low mean and are skewed upwards. The SD and Pt normative data for Samples A through E, all samples without an obvious taint of psychopathology, are available in Table 2 and exemplify this frequent finding.

The interpretive dilemma presented by highly skewed score distributions in nonpsychopathological samples is that we cannot distinguish between scores genuinely betokening psychological health and equivalent scores which have been earned by an intelligent person seeking to simulate adjustment. None of the items in the SD scale create any uncertainty in a would-be simulator, because the criterion for item selection was precisely that there be no disagreement among simulating judges. The Pt scale, although not based upon the criterion of clarity for simulation, proves nevertheless to contain items which are almost totally unambiguous.

The ER-S scale, however, generates score distributions which are rarely far from symmetrical and, as a result, provides discriminations among subjects unseparated by such Alpha markers as SD and Pt. The standard deviations developed by the SD and Pt scales vary widely and are especially small for the samples adjudged to be composed of healthy and generally intelligent individuals. The ER-S scale, on the other hand, develops appreciable standard deviations which fluctuate only slightly, and without any apparent order, over the nine samples. These psychometric properties, conjoined with (and doubtless a function of) the comparative contentual subtlety of the ER-S items suggest that this scale may not be so susceptible as earlier scales have been to the frequent, and often entirely reasonable, tendency to fake good.

Finally, after mustering the various statistical supports of the ER-S scale, we may dare to look at the content of its items. Projection of a personality formulation from inspection of item content is not without its hazards, especially when the interpretation is not consensually or empirically validated. Nevertheless, we suggest that the ER-S items, though on balance uninfluenced by social desirability as objectified by scaling methods, portray an individual with a sense of personal identity and sufficiency. The high scorer on ER-S evidences an absence of undue, persistent introspection about self, body, and others; he is not crabby about the world around him and is neither cynical nor gushily credulous about its inhabitants. He is autonomous but not adamantly so; he has direction and stability rather than being diffuse and oscillating. The low scorer on the ER-S scale, on the other hand, is fitful, touchy, ruminative, and acutely aware of and bothered by himself as he participates in life. These are conjectures, limited in depth and completeness; the extent to which they are valid empirically may be ascertained later.

II

Almost none of the recent work proposing reinterpretation of the MMPI in terms of acquiescence and of social desirability has sought to support these alternative views by reference to behavioral data independent of the MMPI. Instead, most of the reinterpreting arguments have been based upon the demonstration of relationships between the MMPI and *a priori* or scaling-constructed indices. However, where confounding continues to exist, or is intrinsic to the measure being employed, the demonstration of such relationships cannot provide differential support of competing interpretations. What is required is either unconfounding or resorting to fundamentally different domains of data wherein certain interpretations are no longer supportable.

We have already untied previously connected interpretive dimensions and shown that, within the MMPI, the response sets of acquiescence and social desirability are not required for predicting MMPI responses. The analyses of non-MMPI data now to be reported bring another and perhaps more powerful basis for evaluation to bear on the problem of response sets, particularly in regard to the usefulness of the SD concept. From such analyses can come the confluential recognitions which, when properly generalized back to situations where the confounding is inescapable or argued for as convenient, deny a previously irrepressible interpretation. In addition, in the protracted controversy which has surrounded the MMPI, there is something soul-satisfying in reality-testing the various interpretive contentions by concretely examining the behavior and personalities of individuals scoring high and scoring low on disputed dimensions. This method has proven powerful in the past [Block and Bailey, 1955b; Gough, McKee, and Yandell, 1955] and was also used by Couch and Keniston. Unfortunately, in the last instance, as noted earlier, the acquiescence measure Couch and Keniston studied is open to significant criticism and so the behavioral correlates found by them may be variously interpreted.

In the present study, subjects in Samples A through E had been observed in various contexts by psychologists who recorded their assessments of each individual by means of a Q sort. These Q judgments, of course, were expressed in complete absence of knowledge as to the MMPI responses of the subjects. Thus, these data reflect the social-stimulus value or essential personalities of the subjects as they were observed and understood by the participating psychologists. The analyses to be reported were based upon a simple average or composite of all the Q sorts available for each subject. The context of observation, the Q set employed, and the number of observers differed in the various samples.

In Sample A, the subjects were observed over the course of a three-day intensive assessment and were judged by no less than six and usually eight psychologists. The Q set employed contained 76 items and was oriented toward behavioral description with some items requiring deeper level inferences.

In Sample B, the subjects were observed for 1½ hours during the course of which they interacted with their wives in several standardized social situations. Only one observer—a clinical psychologist—was present. The 72-item Q set used was oriented toward description of the interaction of the subject with his wife.

In Sample C, the subjects were interviewed for an average of 12 hours each. Each subject was Q sorted by his interviewer and by another psychologist who had read the verbatim record of the interview sessions. The Q deck employed was the 100-item California Q set [Block, 1961], which is oriented toward a psychodynamic personality description.

In Sample D, the subjects were Q sorted by an interviewing psychiatrist and by a psychologist who had administered the Rorschach and TAT procedure. Two additional Q sorts were contributed by psychologists who formed an evaluation of the subject after studying the test protocols. The California Q set was employed.

In Sample E, the circumstances and procedures were as described for Sample C.

It is by no means suggested that these several procedures are of equal merit or optimal for the purposes of the present analysis. This kind of data is difficult to come by and considerations of availability have dictated their choice here.

Within each of the five samples, the Q sort composites of the Alpha Highs were contrasted, item by item, with the Q sort composites of the Alpha Lows using the t test to identify the discriminating Q variables. The results of these analyses are reported in Tables 3, 4, 5, 6, and 7. Parallel analyses of Beta Highs and Beta Lows were carried through to ascertain the behavioral significance of the Beta factor. The results are to be found in Tables 8, 9, 10, 11, and 12.

These tables require some comment. It should be noted that the number of Q items reaching the .05 level of significance varies widely from sample to sample. It is impossible (and unnecessary) to separate out the several reasons for this fluctuation. Certainly contributing are the differential reliabilities of the Q judgments as a function of the number of sorters involved and the scope of their observations (at least six judges observing over a three-day period contributed to the Q formulations of Sample A; one judge observing subjects for 90 minutes contributed to Q sorts analyzed for Sample B); the different degrees of extremeness of the comparisons being made (in Sample A, two groups of 20 were selected from a total pool of 100; in Sample E, groups of 16 and 17 were selected from a total pool of 49); and intrinsically different characteristics of the subject samples.

If we consider the *number* of statistically discriminating Q items as indicative of the behavioral potency of the MMPI factor involved, then in the three samples composed of males (Samples A, B, and C), the Beta dimension appears to have more consequence than the Alpha factor. For the two samples consisting of women (Samples D and E), the Alpha dimension has more behavioral ramifications than the Beta factor. Looking over the results from all five samples, it is clear that in nonpsychiatric samples, the Beta dimension is at least as behaviorally decisive as the Alpha factor, although the Alpha dimension is much more heavily emphasized within the MMPI. Doubtless, in samples containing individuals with a wider range of psychopathology — samples more appropriate to the initial intent and aspiration of the MMPI — the Alpha factor would enjoy the larger number of behavioral correlates. Overall, however, both MMPI factors possess independent behavioral correlates which are numerous, coherent, and of indisputable importance.

Table 3. Q Items Discriminating Alpha Highs from Alpha Lows, Sample A

Items More Characteristic of Alpha Highs (N=20)

Significant at the .01 level
None

Significant at the .05 level
4. Emphasizes success and productive achievement as a means for achieving status, power and recognition.
18. Efficient, capable, able to mobilize resources easily and effectively; not bothered with work inhibitions.
22. Is verbally fluent; conversationally facile.
64. Tends to become ego-involved; makes personally relevant many different contexts.
67. Is persuasive; tends to win other people over to his point of view.
71. Communicates ideas clearly and effectively.

Items More Characteristic of Alpha Lows (N=20)

Significant at the .01 level
None

Significant at the .05 level
9. Has slow personal tempo; responds, speaks, and moves slowly.
51. Is cold and distant in his relationships with others.
74. Is unaware of his social stimulus value.

Table 4. Q Items Discriminating Alpha Highs from Alpha Lows, Sample B

Items More Characteristic of Alpha Highs (N=19)

Significant at the .01 level
8. He expresses himself clearly.

Significant at the .05 level
6. He is proud of other.
29. He compliments other.
40. He trusts other.
42. He respects other.

Items More Characteristic of Alpha Lows (N=20)

Significant at the .01 level
None

Significant at the .05 level
15. He is demanding of other.
50. He is impatient with other.
51. He is stubborn.

Table 5. Q Items Discriminating Alpha Highs from Alpha Lows, Sample C

Items More Characteristic of Alpha Highs (N = 17)

Significant at the .01 level

75. Has a clear-cut, internally consistent personality. (*N.B. Amount* of information available before sorting is not intended here.)
84. Is cheerful. (*N.B.* Extreme placement toward uncharacteristic end of continuum implies gloominess.)

Significant at the .05 level

24. *Prides* self on being "objective," rational. (Regardless of whether person is really objective or rational.)
74. Is consciously unaware of self-concern; feels satisfied with self.

Items More Characteristic of Alpha Lows (N = 17)

Significant at the .01 level

47. Tends to feel guilty. (*N.B.* Regardless of whether verbalized or not.)

Significant at the .05 level

10. Anxiety and tension find outlet in bodily symptoms. (*N.B.* If placed high, implies bodily dysfunction; if placed low, implies absence of autonomic arousal.)
82. Has fluctuating moods.

Table 6. Q Items Discriminating Alpha Highs from Alpha Lows, Sample D

Items More Characteristic of Alpha Highs (N = 20)

Significant at the .01 level

2. Is a genuinely dependable and responsible person.
3. Has a wide range of interests. (*N.B.* Superficiality or depth of interest is irrelevant here.)
8. Appears to have a high degree of intellectual capacity. (*N.B.* Whether actualized or not.) (*N.B.* Originality is not necessarily assumed.)
15. Is skilled in social techniques of imaginative play, pretending and humor.
17. Behaves in a sympathetic or considerate manner.
26. Is productive; gets things done.
28. Tends to arouse liking and acceptance in people.
29. Is turned to for advice and reassurance.
54. Emphasizes being with others; gregarious.
63. Judges self and others in conventional terms like "popularity," "the correct thing to do," social pressures, etc.
66. Enjoys aesthetic impressions; is aesthetically reactive.
71. Has high aspiration level for self.
84. Is cheerful. (*N.B.* Extreme placement toward uncharacteristic end of continuum implies unhappiness or depression.)
86. Handles anxiety and conflicts by, in effect, refusing to recognize their presence; repressive or dissociative tendencies.
88. Is personally charming.
92. Has social poise and presence; appears socially at ease.
93. Behaves in a feminine style and manner. (*N.B.* The cultural or subcultural conception is to be applied as a criterion.)

Table 6. (continued)

Significant at the .05 level

6. Is fastidious.
18. Initiates humor.
20. Has a rapid personal tempo; behaves and acts quickly.
24. Prides self on being "objective," rational.
35. Has warmth; has the capacity for close relationships; compassionate.
51. Genuinely values intellectual and cognitive matters. (*N.B.* Ability or achievement are not implied here.)
64. Is socially perceptive of a wide range of interpersonal cues.
98. Is verbally fluent; can express ideas well.

Items More Characteristic of Alpha Lows (N=20)

Significant at the .01 level

10. Anxiety and tension find outlet in bodily symptoms. (*N.B.* If placed high, implies bodily dysfunction; if placed low, implies absence of autonomic arousal.)
22. Feels a lack of personal meaning in life.
30. Gives up and withdraws where possible in the face of frustration and adversity. (*N.B.* If placed high, implies generally defeatist; if placed low, implies counteractive.)
34. Over-reactive to minor frustrations; irritable.
38. Has hostility towards others. (*N.B.* Basic hostility is intended here; mode of expression is to be indicated by other items.)
39. Thinks and associates to ideas in unusual ways; has unconventional thought processes.
40. Is vulnerable to real or fancied threat, generally fearful.
45. Has a brittle ego-defense system; has a small reserve of integration; would be disorganized and maladaptive when under stress or trauma.
48. Keeps people at a distance; avoids close interpersonal relationships.
49. Is basically distrustful of people in general; questions their motivations.
55. Is self-defeating.
59. Is concerned with own body and the adequacy of its physiological functioning.
78. Feels cheated and victimized by life; self-pitying.
79. Tends to ruminate and have persistent, preoccupying thoughts.
82. Has fluctuating moods.
85. Emphasizes communication through action and non-verbal behavior.

Significant at the .05 level

16. Is introspective and concerned with self as an object. (*N.B.* Introspectiveness per se does not imply insight.)
46. Engages in personal fantasy and daydreams, fictional speculations.
50. Is unpredictable and changeable in behavior and attitudes.
62. Tends to be rebellious and non-conforming.
65. Characteristically pushes and tries to stretch limits; sees what he can get away with.
100. Does not vary roles; relates to everyone in the same way.

Table 7. Q Items Discriminating Alpha Highs from Alpha Lows, Sample E

Items More Characteristic of Alpha Highs (N=18)

Significant at the .01 level
15. The "light touch" as compared to the "heavy touch."
33. Is calm, relaxed in manner.
54. Emphasizes being with others; gregarious.
74. Is consciously unaware of self-concern; feels satisfied with self.
84. Is cheerful. (*N.B.* Extreme placement toward uncharacteristic end of continuum implies gloominess.)
92. Has social poise and presence; appears socially at ease.

Significant at the .05 level
'3. Has a wide range of interests. (*N.B.* Superficiality or depth of interest is irrelevant here.)
18. Initiates humor.
26. Is productive; gets things done. (Regardless of speed.)
28. Tends to arouse liking and acceptance in people.
29. Is turned to for advice and reassurance.
31. Is satisfied with physical appearance.
56. Responds to humor.
63. Judges self and others in conventional terms like "popularity," "the correct thing to do," social pressures, etc.
95. Tends to proffer advice.

Items More Characteristic of Alpha Lows (N=13)

Significant at the .01 level
22. Feels a lack of personal meaning in life. (Uncharacteristic end means zest.)
40. Is vulnerable to real or fancied threat, generally fearful.
68. Is basically anxious.
72. Over-concerned with own adequacy as a person, either at conscious or unconscious levels. (*N.B.* A clinical judgment is required here; number 74 reflects subjective satisfaction with self.)

Significant at the .05 level
39. Thinks and associates to ideas in unusual ways; has unconventional thought processes. (Either pathological or creative.)
47. Tends to feel guilty. (*N.B.* Regardless of whether verbalized or not.)
48. Aloof, keeps people at a distance; avoids close interpersonal relationships.
78. Feels cheated and victimized by life.
79. Tends to ruminate and have persistent, preoccupying thoughts (Either pathological or creative).
82. Has fluctuating moods.
87. Interprets basically simple and clear-cut situations in complicated and particularizing ways.
89. Compares self to others. Is alert to real or fancied differences between self and other people.

Table 8. Q Items Discriminating Beta Highs from Beta Lows, Sample A

Items More Characteristic of Beta Highs (N=20)

Significant at the .01 level

9. Has slow personal tempo; responds, speaks and moves slowly.
11. Is a conscientious, responsible, dependable person.
21. Is stereotyped and unoriginal in his approach to problems.
24. With respect to authority, is submissive, compliant and overly accepting.
28. Tends to side-step troublesome situations; makes concessions to avoid unpleasantness.
34. Conforming; tends to do the things that are prescribed.
35. Respects others; is permissive and accepting; not judgmental.
42. Is unable to make decisions without vacillation, hesitation or delay.
50. Over-controls his impulses; is inhibited; needlessly delays or denies gratification.

Significant at the .05 level

1. Derives personal reward and pleasure from his work; values productive achievement for its own sake.
7. Has a narrow range of interests.
8. Gets along well in the world as it is; is socially appropriate in his behavior; keeps out of trouble. (*N.B.* To be considered as conceptually separate from the subject's internal psychic state.)
17. Is rigid; inflexible in thought and action.
20. Lacks social poise and presence; becomes rattled and upset in social situations.
25. Is a likable person. (*N.B.* The subject's general acceptability rather than the rater's personal reactions is intended.)
31. Lacks confidence in his own ability.
41. Is natural; free from pretense; unaffected.
47. Is self-abasing; feels unworthy, guilty, humble, given to self-blame.
56. is pedantic and fussy about minor things.
74. Is unaware of his social stimulus value.

Items More Characteristic of Beta Lows (N=20)

Significant at the .01 level

4. Emphasizes success and productive achievement as a means for achieving status, power and recognition.
6. Is guileful and potentially deceitful.
12. Manipulates people as a means to achieving personal ends; opportunistic; sloughs over the meaning and value of the individual.
14. Is competitive with his peers; likes to be ahead and win.
15. Takes an ascendant role in his relations with others.
33. Tends to arouse hostility and resentment in other people.
45. Under-controls his impulses; acts with insufficient thinking and deliberation; unable to delay gratifications.
61. Is aggressive and hostile in his personal relations.
64. Tends to become ego-involved; makes personally relevant many different contexts.

Table 8. (continued)

65. Is sarcastic and cynical.
66. Emphasizes oral pleasure; self-indulgent.
72. Is rebellious toward authority figures, rules and other constraints.
73. Tends to be ostentatious and exhibitionistic.
76. Is an expressive, ebullient person; colorful.

Significant at the .05 level
2. Has a high degree of intellectual ability.
22. Is verbally fluent; conversationally facile.
48. Is self-defensive; rationalizes, excuses, blames.
52. Seeks and enjoys aesthetic and sensuous impressions.
60. Takes the initiative in social relations.
67. Is persuasive; tends to win other people over to his point of view.
71. Communicates ideas clearly and effectively.

Table 9. Q Items Discriminating Beta Highs from Beta Lows, Sample B

Items More Characteristic of Beta Highs (N=20)

Significant at the .01 level
7. He opposes other indirectly, without openly disagreeing or being frank.
19. He is deceiving and subtle in his manipulations of other.
66. He confuses other.

Significant at the .05 level
17. He hides his feelings from other.
35. He keeps other at a distance.
52. He belittles himself with other.
54. He apologizes for himself.
58. He is inhibited in this situation.

Items More Characteristic of Beta Lows (N=21)

Significant at the .01 level
9. When he disagrees, he tries to talk it over with other.
27. He is straightforward and frank with other.
31. He understands other as a person.

Significant at the .05 level
8. He expresses himself clearly.
24. He gives other help.
42. He respects other.
62. He is emotionally responsive to other.
70. He has a sense of humor.

Table 10. Q Items Discriminating Beta Highs from Beta Lows, Sample C

Items More Characteristic of Beta Highs (N=17)

Significant at the .01 level

2. Is a genuinely dependable and responsible person.
6. Is fastidious.
7. Favors conservative values in a variety of areas.
17. Behaves in a sympathetic or considerate manner.
25. Tends toward over-control of needs and impulses; binds tensions excessively; delays gratification unnecessarily.
26. Is productive; gets things done. (Regardless of speed.)
33. Is calm, relaxed in manner.
70. *Behaves* in an ethically consistent manner; is consistent with own personal standards.

Significant at the .05 level

5. Behaves in a giving way toward others. (*N.B.* Regardless of the motivation involved.)
16. Is introspective. (*N.B.* Introspectiveness per se does not imply insight.)
41. Is moralistic. (*N.B.* Regardless of the particular nature of the moral code.)
71. Has high aspiration level for self.
75. Has a clear-cut, internally consistent personality. (*N.B. Amount* of information available before sorting is not intended here.)
92. Has social poise and presence; appears socially at ease.
97. Is emotionally bland; has flattened affect.
100. Does not vary roles; relates to everyone in the same way.

Items More Characteristic of Beta Lows (N=17)

Significant at the .01 level

43. Is facially and/or gesturally expressive.
50. Is unpredictable and changeable in behavior and attitudes.
52. *Behaves* in an assertive fashion in interpersonal situations. (*N.B.* Item 14 reflects underlying submissiveness; this refers to overt behavior.)
53. Tends toward under-control of needs and impulses; unable to delay gratification.
62. Tends to be rebellious and non-conforming.
65. Characteristically pushes and tries to stretch limits; see what he can get away with.
67. Is self-indulgent.
73. Tends to perceive many different contexts in sexual terms; eroticizes situations.
82. Has fluctuating moods.
94. Expresses hostile feelings directly.
99. Is self-dramatizing; histrionic.

Significant at the .05 level

4. Is a talkative individual.
34. Over-reactive to minor frustrations; irritable.
45. Has a brittle ego-defense system; has a small reserve of integration; would be disorganized and maladaptive when under stress or trauma.
49. Is basically distrustful of people in general; questions their motivations.
58. Enjoys sensuous experiences (including touch, taste, smell, physical contact).
76. Tends to project his own feelings and motivations onto others.

Table 11. Q Items Discriminating Beta Highs from Beta Lows, Sample D

Items More Characteristic of Beta Highs (N=20)

Significant at the .01 level

7. Favors conservative values in a variety of areas.
9. Is uncomfortable with uncertainty and complexities.
40. Is vulnerable to real or fancied threat, generally fearful.
42. Reluctant to commit self to any definite course of action; tends to delay or avoid action.
70. Behaves in an ethically consistent manner; is consistent with own personal standards.
100. Does not vary roles; relates to everyone in the same way.

Significant at the .05 level

14. Genuinely submissive; accepts domination comfortably.
25. Tends toward over-control of needs and impulses; binds tensions excessively; delays gratification unnecessarily.
30. Gives up and withdraws where possible in the face of frustration and adversity. (*N.B.* If placed high, implies generally defeatist; if placed low, implies counteractive.)
48. Keeps people at a distance; avoids close interpersonal relationships.
75. Has a clear-cut, internally consistent personality. (*N.B.* Amount of information available before sorting is not intended here.)
97. Is emotionally bland; has flattened affect.

Items More Characteristic of Beta Lows (N=20)

Significant at the .01 level

3. Has a wide range of interests. (*N.B.* Superficiality or depth of interest is irrelevant here.)
4. Is a talkative individual.
8. Appears to have a high degree of intellectual capacity. (*N.B.* Whether actualized or not.) (*N.B.* Originality is not necessarily assumed.)
37. Is guileful and deceitful, manipulative, opportunistic.
98. Is verbally fluent; can express ideas well.

Significant at the .05 level

10. Anxiety and tension find outlet in bodily symptoms. (*N.B.* If placed high, implies bodily dysfunction; if placed low, implies absence of autonomic arousal.)
23. Extrapunitive; tends to transfer or project blame.
51. Genuinely values intellectual and cognitive matters. (*N.B.* Ability or achievement is not implied here.)
53. Various needs tend toward relatively direct and uncontrolled expression; unable to delay gratification.
59. Is concerned with own body and the adequacy of its physiological functioning.
62. Tends to be rebellious and non-conforming.
82. Has fluctuating moods.

Table 12. Q Items Discriminating Beta Highs from Beta Lows, Sample E

Items More Characteristic of Beta Highs (N=16)

Significant at the .01 level
70. Behaves in an ethically consistent manner; is consistent with own personal standards.

Significant at the .05 level
2. Is a genuinely dependable and responsible person.
7. Favors conservative values in a variety of areas.
41. Is moralistic. (*N.B.* Regardless of the particular nature of the moral code.)
47. Tends to feel guilty. (*N.B.* Regardless of whether verbalized or not.)
75. Has a clear-cut, internally consistent personality. (*N.B. Amount* of information available before sorting is not intended here.)

Items More Characteristic of Beta Lows (N=17)

Significant at the .01 level
92. Has social poise and presence; appears socially at ease.

Significant at the .05 level
4. Is a talkative individual.
46. Engages in personal fantasy and daydreams, fictional speculations.
56. Responds to humor.
67. Is self-indulgent.
73. Tends to perceive many different contexts in sexual terms; eroticizes situations.
88. Is personally charming.
99. Is self-dramatizing; histrionic.

III

Looking first at the results surrounding Alpha, it is apparent from Tables 3 through 7 that Alpha Highs are individuals perceived by psychologists as being genuinely psychologically healthy—they are evaluated as integrated and yet open to experience, able to cope resourcefully with their complex worlds. Alpha Highs are not feigning adjustment, as the SD formulation would require.

Alpha Lows, on the other hand, are in fact more disturbed and more brittle individuals—they are relatively vulnerable before life's inevitable stresses and, as a result, have chosen to participate less fully in their experience. Alpha Lows are not fairly construed simply as individuals in whom the tendency to emit socially desirable responses is reduced. It appears from these analyses that more than facade or an absence of facade was involved in the manner in which these several sets of subjects responded to the MMPI. In significant ways, these individuals conveyed some truths about themselves to which an interpretation in terms of SD does an injustice since the term, "social desirability," inevitably connotes pretense at some level. The present data indicate pretension cannot be assumed. On the other hand, the behavioral hypotheses which issue from a characterological view of Alpha as related to, say, differences along an adaptability-vulnerability personality dimension are well supported.

If the first MMPI factor is not to be understood profitably in terms of the SD concept, just how should this dimension be construed in the light of the current analyses? Welsh's [1956] earlier identification of this factor as "anxiety" would appear to be improved if changed to "susceptibility to anxiety." Anxiety is a *state* of the individual where this factor reflects a *characterological disposition*. In other factor analyses of the MMPI, this repeatedly found first component has been variously identified as, for example, "psychoticism" [Wheeler, Little, and Lehner, 1951] or "general maladjustment" [Tyler, 1951] and when reversed as "social appropriateness" [Block and Bailey, 1955] or "ego-strength" [Kassebaum, Couch, and Slater, 1959]. None of these labels seems conceptually satisfactory when referenced to the behavioral correlates of this factor, as reported here. Psychotics may well place low on the Alpha dimension but other, clearly nonpsychotic individuals also will be Alpha Lows. "General maladjustment" and "social appropriateness" perhaps are not incorrect as descriptive labels but they are labels with no conceptual properties, no position within a theoretical framework from which predictions will flow. The term, "ego-strength," is by now conceptually amorphous and used diversely, often simply as a jargonistic substitute for "adjustment."

The reader has before him the data from which he can form his own understanding of the first MMPI factor. However, the writer cannot forego the opportunity of indicating his own current conception of the significance of this MMPI dimension.

It is suggested that this factor be identified as "ego-resiliency." The word, resilient, implies the resourcefulness, adaptability, and engagement with this world that characterizes the individual placed high on this continuum; the word, ego, implies that an enduring, structural aspect of personality is involved. In conjunction, the term ego-resiliency, is intended to denote the individual's characteristic adaptation capability when under the strain set by new environmental demands. Alpha Highs appear to react to the press of new and yet unmastered circumstances in resourceful, tenacious, but elastic ways and so may be termed ego-resilient. Alpha Lows, on the other hand, have small adaptive margins and consequently react to their stresses in rigidified or chaotic ways. Because they are not ego-resilient, they are unable to respond effectively to the dynamic requirements of their situation.

An individual who is unresilient will not be in a *state* of anxiety if the circumstances in which he functions are for him safe and predictable. Yet, it may be expected that, inevitably, an adaptively inelastic individual will find a wider range of environmental happenings to be disruptive of his personal economy, and distressing. Accordingly, he will present himself as more anxious, more maladjusted, less appropriate, less attuned to this world and, not least, as possessing personal attributes which society agrees are undesirable.

Thus, the concept of ego-resiliency fits well the behavioral correlates of the first MMPI factor and can encompass the various interpretations previously offered of this dimension. The construct has the further advantages, moreover, of fitting into a theoretical framework, of not being tied to a particular evaluative society or culture as a referent, and of predicting to additional and diverse environmental contexts; e.g., ego-resilient individuals, as measured by the MMPI, should be able to track a dynamic stimulus more accurately than individuals who are inelastic; ego-resiliency, as measured by the MMPI, should relate—when relevant other variables are held constant—to both the ability to resist distractions and the ability to associate in distant, even bizarre ways when instructed to do so ("regression in the service of the ego"). For the several reasons, it is suggested that the first factor within the MMPI be identified as the Ego-Resiliency (ER) dimension.

For the present, the Alpha or Ego-Resiliency factor of the MMPI may be measured reasonably effectively by such established MMPI scales—scored in appropriate directions—as SD, Pt, Pn, and A. In the same tradition but with superior reliability is the Ego-Resiliency (Obvious) (ER-O) scale, listed and described in Appendix A of Block [1965]. The ER-O scale consists of 108 items, "true" and "false" balanced, all related at the .01 level of significance to the Alpha dimension but not selected with any reference to SD scale values.

All of these scales are susceptible to deliberate feigning attempts or to tendencies to deny—for reasons of which the responding individual may be unaware—actually existing personal frailties. Where the possibility of deliberate deception or personally unacknowledged defensiveness exists—that is, high L or K scores—the previously described ER-S scale is likely to be useful because of its content-subtlety and control for social desirability. Credence should be given to an individual's placement on the first factor of the MMPI only when it seems safe to presume that the tendency to "fake good" did not significantly affect his responses.

IV

Considering now the nature of the Beta-discriminating Q items (Tables 8 through 12), it may be seen that earlier clinical understandings of this MMPI component as related to the containment or expression of impulse are both solidified and extended. As we read the Beta analyses—and the reader has available before him the information on which he may base his own conclusions—in all five samples, in diverse yet coherent ways, the Beta Highs and Beta Lows appear to differ in the extent to which they suppress impulse or are spontaneous with it. There seem to be differences between the sexes in the way impulse is modulated, but that a dimension akin to impulse-control underlies these several comparisons does not appear in doubt. The results involving Sample B—although sparse perhaps because of the brevity of the observations and because only one observer was involved—are especially interesting in that they indicate the interpersonal consequences of different modes of impulse expression.

Earlier, Welsh [1956] labeled a similar MMPI dimension as "repression," a title that in view of the present analyses now seems overextended and only partially adequate. The notion of repression carries implications going well beyond simple impulse suppression, implications for which the current findings offer none of the special support required. To validate an interpretation in terms of repression necessitates demonstration of a specific sequence of intrapsychic events culminating in a discrepancy between awareness and intention on the one hand and behavior and expression on the other. Precisely because the concept of repression is complex, it requires special contrapositions of data for its support, and the personological correlates of the Beta dimension simply are insufficient for this task.

Kassebaum, Couch, and Slater [1959], having achieved the usual factor structure of the MMPI, interpret the Beta dimension in terms of "introversion-extroversion." They acknowledge the unusualness of this interpretation but are motivated to link their results to Eysenck's views on the dimensionality of human personality [1953]. Their reasoning stems primarily from the labels of the MMPI scales they analyzed and not further behavioral data.

Welsh's R scale, possessor of the highest loading on the Beta factor in the Kassebaum, Couch, and Slater analysis, is reinterpreted by these authors as a measure of cautiousness and inhibition, and hence of introversion. The introversion construction is considered further affirmed by the positive loadings earned by the D and Social Introversion scales and, less clearly, by scales labeled Achievement via Conformance and Originality Potential. As conceptual support for these loadings, Kassebaum, Couch, and Slater cite Eysenck citing Guilford and Guilford who say:

> It would seem that there is some basis for lumping together some characteristics bordering on seclusiveness with some implying a thinking person and still others that indicate depressed emotional tendencies and calling the resultant the introvert [Kassebaum, Couch, and Slater, 1959, p. 229; Eysenck, 1953, p. 104; Guilford and Guilford, 1939, p. 34].

The extrovert is viewed by Kassebaum, Couch, and Slater as one who is "expressive and labile, and cathects new activities easily" [p. 230] and who shows "id predominance over superego activities" [p. 229]. They also related the "yea-saying" tendency, as studied by Couch and Keniston [1961], to extroversion.

Conceptual preferences are in no small part esthetic preferences and in these latter terms, this writer finds the conceptualization of Kassebaum, Couch, and Slater, of Eysenck, and of Guilford and Guilford to be unsatisfying. Concepts should be integrates, not amalgams, and "lumping together" is hardly the way to achieve variables of unequivocal dimensionality. In particular, the formulation of introversion-extroversion advanced by Eysenck and accepted by Kassebaum, Couch, and Slater couples and confuses the dimensions of "constriction-expression" and "inward turning-outward turning" when both theoretically and empirically, as our Beta correlates show, these dimensions are separable. Impulsivity does not preclude the concomitant tendency for introspectiveness; constriction does not necessarily entail a rich inner life. If a distinction between impulse regulation and inner-outer orientation is held to be useful, as argued here, then it would be perhaps most faithful to the original and connotative meaning of the terms, introversion-extroversion, to restrict their definition to the focusing of attention on inner stimuli or on outer stimuli. In so doing, identification of the Beta dimension of the MMPI as introversion-extroversion no longer is tenable because this factor centrally relates to impulse monitoring per se.

Our own predilection—it may not be surprising—together with a desire for concepts that are not method-bound is to view the present behavioral results as arguing well for an interpretation in terms of over- and under-control as earlier formulated and experimentally studied [cf., J. Block, 1950; J. H. Block, 1951; Block and Block, 1951; 1952; Block and Thomas, 1955; Block and Martin, 1955]:

> The construct of ego-control relates to the individual's characteristic mode of monitoring impulse. When dimensionalized, the underlying continuum is conceived as representing excessive containment of impulse and delay of gratification at the one end (over-control) versus insufficient modulation of impulse and an inability to delay gratification at the other end (under-control). Behaviorally, an over-controller appears to be constrained and distant, with minimal expression of his personal emotions; he is highly organized and categorical in his thinking, tending to adhere rigidly to previous understandings; he can continue to work on uninteresting tasks for long periods of time; he is overconforming, indecisive, and with narrow and relatively unchanging interests; he delays gratification even when pleasure is a sensible course of action, not threatening of long range intents.
>
> Behaviorally, an under-controller is unduly spontaneous, with enthusiasms neither held in check nor long sustained; his decisions are made (and unmade) rapidly and his emotional fluctuations are readily visible; he disregards, if he does not disdain, social customs and mores; he tends toward immediate gratification of his desires even when such gratification is inconsistent with the reality of his situation or his own ultimate goals; his grooves for behavior are not deeply ingrained and, accordingly, his actions can frequently cut across conventional categories of response in ways that are (for better or for worse) original [Block and Turula, 1963].

Because the construct of ego-control fits the present data well and no clearly better conceptual alternative looms on the scene, we suggest that the second factor within the MMPI be identified as the Ego-Control (EC) dimension.

For the moment, reasonably adequate MMPI scales to measure the Beta or second dimension are the EC-3, EC-4 and R scales. The EC-5 scale, a fifth version of an MMPI scale to measure this component, is described in Appendix B of Block [1965] (see also Appendix I of Volume II of Dahlstrom, Welsh, and Dahlstrom, 1975) and may be preferable because of its generally higher reliability and because it is "true" and "false" balanced. But all of these scales are less than what is realizable because they all fail to respect some important differences between the sexes in the way over- and under-control is expressed.

Although there has been a general, and understandable, reluctance among scale constructors to employ different scales for men and for women, here is one instance, we believe, where a substantial improvement in the measurement of a dimension may result if separate scale construction is applied. With respect to ego-control, the culture tends to encourage or at least sanction impulsivity in the male while discouraging such behavior in the female. Thus, consider the items: "38. During one period when I was a youngster I engaged in petty thievery; 471. In school my marks in deportment were quite regularly bad." A response of "true" to these items is related to under-control in males but not in females.

As a further source of valid variance lost when sex differences are not respected, there are items which have one significance when responded to by males but rather different meanings in a feminine context. Thus, a response of "true" to the item: "441. I like tall women," is an indicator of under-control in men but is not a discriminator among women. A response of "true" to the item: "435. Usually I prefer to work with women," is scored for over-control in women but does not distinguish among men.

Because of cultural conditioning and the interaction of sex category with ego-control, separate EC scales for men and for women would appear to be desirable. Preliminary versions of such scales, labeled EC-5M and EC-5W are to be found in Appendix B of Block [1965], together with some of their descriptive statistics. Further work is continuing on developing sex-specific ego-control scales but not within the MMPI-item pool.

Do Face-Valid Items Have More Predictive Validity than Subtle Items? The Case of the MMPI Pd Scale

M. D. Gynther, B. R. Burkhart, and C. Hovanitz

For many years psychologists have argued about the relative merits of empirical versus intuitive-internal test construction strategies. Proponents of the former approach have emphasized the predictive validity of such inventories as the Minnesota Multiphasic Personality Inventory (MMPI) and the California Psychological Inventory (CPI) [Gough, 1968; Hathaway, 1972; Meehl, 1945a (see II, 1)], whereas opponents have criticized the heterogeneity of scale content, the item overlap, and the vulnerability of such instruments to response sets and styles [Jackson, 1971; Norman, 1972]. When inventories constructed by intuitive-internal methods are considered, however, psychometric elegance and interpretability of content often seem to have been given priority over concerns about empirical correlates [Gynther and Gynther, 1976].

Another distinction between these two orientations involves their susceptibility to faking or distortion. Empirically derived inventories invariably contain subtle as well as obvious items. For example, the relationship between responding *true* or *false* to "I am against giving money to beggars" and degree or type of psychopathology is obscure at best. Inventories constructed by means of factor analysis or some other intuitive-internal strategy, on the other hand, contain items whose scale membership is usually self-evident. Although distortion due to acquiescence or desirability can be controlled by technical means, inventories such as the Personality Research Form and the Sixteen Personality Factor Questionnaire are more open to faking because of the direct relationship between item content and criteria.

Subtle items contained in the MMPI and CPI are inherently resistant to faking [cf. Burkhart, Christian, and Gynther, 1978]. Although this may be a virtue, one can also ask whether responses to such items are related to criterion correlates. Many have argued or demonstrated that the answer is likely to be in the negative. Duff [1965], for example, found an inverse relation between MMPI item subtlety and item discriminating power. Goldberg and Slovic [1967] showed that "only scales built from items of the highest face validity had significant cross-validity" [pp. 466-467]. Koss and Butcher [1973] demonstrated that the MMPI items that characterized crisis situations displayed content clearly relevant to the particular situation. Jackson [1971], in a persuasive major article, argued that "most subtle items have been shown to correlate negatively with the rest of the items contained in a particular MMPI scale, raising the suspicion that they did not belong there in the first place" and that "a sample of item content most directly relevant to a particular trait will be the most efficient way of going about measuring it" [p. 234].

Despite these empirical and logical assertions, there has been no popular movement to discard the subtle items from the MMPI and CPI. A probable reason for the lack of reaction is the highly sporadic and noncumulative nature of the research on the subtle-obvious dimension. Some early work [Meehl and Hathaway, 1946 (see I, 9); Wiener, 1948] was followed many years later by a few other articles [e.g., Duff, 1965; Wales and Seeman, 1972]. Furthermore, despite Cronbach's [1970] plea for separate scoring of subtle and transparent MMPI items, no comprehensive scaling of all of these items on this dimension had been performed. Hence, no standard had been available for the development of subtle-obvious keys or the confirmation or disconfirmation of the discriminating power of the subtle items. Christian, Burkhart, and Gynther [1978], however, have recently obtained mean subtle-obvious ratings of all MMPI items answered true and false.

Questions pertaining to the relation between endorsement of subtle, obvious, and neutral items on certain MMPI scales and to external data that theoretically should be related to those scales can now be examined. This study, which is part of a series that analyzes such relationships, focuses on the relation of scores on the Psychopathic Deviate (Pd) subtle (S)-obvious (O) subscales to scores on a scale designed to assess nonconformity. If Jackson's position is correct, one should find that Pd-O scores are more highly related to admission of nonconforming behavior than are Pd-S scores and that the Pd-S nonconforming behavior correlation does not differ from zero. If, on the other hand, responses to subtle items have predictive power, the Pd-S-nonconformity correlation should be significantly different from zero. If both correlations differ from zero, examination of the relative contribution of each scale should reveal which kind of item carries most of the discriminative power.

Method

Subjects

Serving as subjects were 210 students (100 males, mean age=20.1 years, and 110 females, mean age=19.0 years) enrolled in introductory psychology courses. Extra credit was awarded for participation. Anonymity was assured by identifying all materials solely through the use of code numbers. Subjects were tested in groups that ranged in size from 12 to 25. Another sample of 40 males and 40 females was used to obtain test-retest data on the nonconformity scale described subsequently.

Instruments

Five questionnaires were administered to each subject: the MMPI [Hathaway and McKinley, 1967], the Profile of Mood States [McNair, Lorr, and Doppleman, 1971], the Beck Depression Inventory [Beck, 1967], an abbreviated version of the Pleasant Events Schedule [MacPhillamy and Lewinsohn, 1974], and a nonconformity scale. Only the results on the first and last named are germane to this study.

The nonconformity scale was made up of 30 items (see Table 1) designed to measure individual tendencies to break rules, laws, or regulations. Eight of the items consisted of the abbreviated form of Nye's [1958] scale used by Elion and Megargee [1975]: for example, Have you ever run away from home, taken things of medium value, or taken a car without the owner's knowledge? The other 22 items were added by the present authors to include a more comprehensive range of nonconforming behavior and ranged from such relatively innocuous items as: Have you ever "ignored fines for overdue books" and "cut or torn out pages of library books or journals?" to such serious offenses as: Have you ever "driven a car while intoxicated" or "phoned someone you didn't know and made obscene or suggestive proposals?"

Procedure

Each subject completed the first 399 items of the MMPI (Form R), but only responses to the L, K, and Pd scales were examined; L and K are validity indicators of 15 and 30 items, respectively, while Pd consists of 50 items designed to "cover a wide array of topics including absence of satisfaction in life, family problems, delinquency, sexual problems, and difficulties with life" [Graham, 1977a]. This scale was divided into obvious (N=19), neutral (N=19), and subtle (N=12) subscales according to the values obtained by Christian, Burkhart, and Gynther [1978]. In that study, items were rated from 1 (very subtle) to 5 (very obvious) according to the extent to which an item was indicative of a psychological problem. Table 2 lists the means and standard deviations of these ratings for each MMPI item.

For the purposes of this study, the categories of very subtle and subtle (1.000-1.799 and 1.800-2.599, respectively) were combined into a subtle category (Pd-S). The categories of obvious and very obvious (3.400-4.199 and 4.200-5.000, respectively) were combined into an obvious category (Pd-O). The neutral category consisted of those items with values from 2.600 to 3.399 (Pd-N). Table 3 gives the percentage of items in the standard MMPI scales falling in each of the subtle-obvious categories.

As shown in Table 1, the questionnaire measuring nonconforming behavior required subjects to rate the number of times (never, once or twice, several times, or very often) they had engaged in a given behavior since beginning grade school. A score was obtained for the inventory by assigning a value of 0 to items rated *never*, 1 to items rated *once* or *twice*, 2 to items rated *several times* and 3 to items rated *very often*.

Using templates designed for that purpose, subjects' scores on Pd-O, Pd-S, and Pd-N were calculated, in addition to their total scores on the Pd scale. Total scores on the nonconformity scale were obtained by adding scores on each of the 30 items. Reliability indices also were computed for this scale. Pearson product-moment correlations were then calculated between the total Pd + .4K, as well as the subtle, neutral, and obvious scores, and the nonconformity scores for males, females, and males and females combined. To determine the relative contribution of obvious, neutral, and subtle scores to the nonconformity score, semipartial and multiple correlations were calculated. Finally, relations among the standard MMPI *obvious* and *subtle* defensiveness scores (i.e., L and K, respectively), Pd subscores, and nonconformity scores were calculated.

Table 1. Nonconformity Questionnaire

Recent research has shown that everyone breaks some rules, regulations or laws during his or her lifetime. Some break them regularly, others less often. Below are some which are frequently broken, at least by some people. Check those that you have broken since beginning grade school. Have you:

*1. Driven a car without a driver's license or learner's permit (do not include driver training courses)?
   very often_____   several times_____   once or twice_____   no_____

*2. "Run away" from home?
   no_____   once or twice_____   several times_____   very often_____

*3. Taken things of medium value (between $2 and $50)?
   very often_____   several times_____   once or twice_____   no_____

*4. Taken things of large value (over $50)?
   no_____   once or twice_____   several times_____   very often_____

*5. Taken a car for a ride without the owner's knowledge?
   very often_____   several times_____   once or twice_____   no_____

*6. Bought or drank beer, wine or liquor under age (includes drinking at home)?
   no_____   once or twice_____   several times_____   very often_____

*7. Purposely damaged or destroyed public or private property that did not belong to you?
   very often_____   several times_____   once or twice_____   no_____

 8. Used marijuana?
   no_____   once or twice_____   several times_____   very often_____

 9. Sold marijuana?
   very often_____   several times_____   once or twice_____   no_____

10. Written bad checks?
   no_____   once or twice_____   several times_____   very often_____

11. Participated in illegal gambling?
   very often_____   several times_____   once or twice_____   no_____

12. Brought liquor into Alabama from out-of-state?
   no_____   once or twice_____   several times_____   very often_____

13. Been involved in fights?
   very often_____   several times_____   once or twice_____   no_____

14. Been involved in fights with deadly weapons (do not include wartime experience)?
   no_____   once or twice_____   several times_____   very often_____

15. Been suspended or expelled from school?
   very often_____   several times_____   once or twice_____   no_____

16. Cheated on an examination?
   no_____   once or twice_____   several times_____   very often_____

17. Used psychedelic drugs (e.g., LSD)?
   very often_____   several times_____   once or twice_____   no_____

18. Sold psychedelic drugs?
   no_____   once or twice_____   several times_____   very often_____

19. Driven a car while intoxicated?
   very often_____   several times_____   once or twice_____   no_____

Table 1. (continued)

20. Cut or torn out pages of library books or journals?
    no_____   once or twice_____   several times_____   very often_____

21. Looked in windows of persons of the opposite sex (i.e., "Peeping Tom")?
    very often_____   several times_____   once or twice_____   no_____

22. Had sexual relations with an "underage" person of the opposite sex (do not include occasions when you were also "underage")?
    no_____   once or twice_____   several times_____   very often_____

23. Not paid parking tickets?
    very often_____   several times_____   once or twice_____   no_____

24. Driven at speeds significantly above the legal limits?
    no_____   once or twice_____   several times_____   very often_____

25. Carried a concealed weapon?
    very often_____   several times_____   once or twice_____   no_____

*26. Used narcotic drugs (e.g., heroin)?
    no_____   once or twice_____   several times_____   very often_____

*27. Sold narcotic drugs?
    very often_____   several times_____   once or twice_____   no_____

28. Pretended to be someone you are not (e.g., physician, lawyer, etc.) to gain an unfair advantage or make a profit?
    no_____   once or twice_____   several times_____   very often_____

29. Ignored fines for overdue books?
    very often_____   several times_____   once or twice_____   no_____

30. Phoned someone you didn't know and made obscene or suggestive proposals?
    no_____   once or twice_____   several times_____   very often_____

Source: Nye (1958).

*These items adapted from Elion and Megargee (1975).

Results and Discussion

Coefficient alpha for the nonconformity scale was .83 (.85 for males and .75 for females). Split-half reliability for this scale was .86 (.87 for males and .79 for females). The test-retest correlation for a 2-week period was .94 (.91 for males and .92 for females) using a new sample of 80 subjects, equally divided by gender. These values are not surprising, considering the biographical nature of the inventory.

Means and standard deviations for males on the obvious, neutral, and subtle categories were 4.23 (SD=2.53), 7.31 (SD=2.21), and 5.18 (SD=1.86), respectively. For females, the corresponding figures were 4.13 (SD=2.81), 6.71 (SD=1.93), and 5.15 (SD=1.74). Nonconformity scores ranged from 2-41 for males and from 1-27 for females. Of the males, 11% had scores that exceeded the females' highest score. Means and standard deviations on the nonconformity

Table 2. Means and Standard Deviations of Obviousness Ratings for MMPI Items

Item No.	True M	True SD	False M	False SD	Item No.	True M	True SD	False M	False SD	Item No.	True M	True SD	False M	False SD	Item No.	True M	True SD	False M	False SD
1	1.11	.53	1.44	.86	37	1.87	.95	4.11	1.04	73	3.02	1.24	3.13	1.31	109	3.04	1.03	2.44	1.15
2	1.22	.55	2.91	1.15	38	2.89	1.04	2.17	1.17	74	3.11	1.66	2.71	1.46	110	4.28	1.03	2.40	1.38
3	1.37	.61	3.00	1.21	39	3.89	.95	2.33	1.06	75	1.76	1.04	3.24	1.25	111	1.96	1.12	3.09	1.30
4	1.83	.97	1.60	1.05	40	3.78	1.01	2.38	1.11	76	4.00	.82	2.06	1.30	112	1.63	.95	3.33	1.10
5	2.37	.95	1.88	1.15	41	4.11	.99	2.48	1.18	77	1.67	.79	2.46	1.21	113	1.39	.83	3.98	1.02
6	3.00	1.03	2.35	1.06	42	2.65	1.20	2.06	1.14	78	1.39	.68	1.88	1.00	114	3.52	1.15	2.17	1.22
7	1.83	1.02	2.67	1.25	43	4.17	.83	2.27	1.37	79	1.89	1.10	3.28	1.11	115	1.70	1.19	2.87	1.31
8	1.48	.86	3.46	1.11	44	3.94	1.00	2.15	1.27	80	3.09	1.09	2.17	1.24	116	2.96	1.01	2.15	1.23
9	2.04	1.05	2.91	1.09	45	3.28	1.30	2.17	1.24	81	1.35	.80	1.59	.88	117	2.80	1.28	2.46	1.30
10	3.41	1.07	2.02	1.26	46	1.94	.88	3.33	1.01	82	2.91	.84	2.11	1.08	118	2.41	1.13	2.15	1.14
11	2.38	1.03	2.58	1.21	47	3.52	1.03	2.13	1.16	83	1.30	.70	3.49	1.36	119	1.89	1.16	3.04	1.30
12	1.52	.81	2.09	1.23	48	4.09	1.17	2.54	1.29	84	3.07	1.37	2.81	1.31	120	1.76	1.04	2.22	1.19
13	3.22	1.15	2.21	1.02	49	4.07	.98	2.12	1.48	85	4.61	.75	2.25	1.48	121	4.41	.93	2.13	1.37
14	3.22	1.21	2.35	1.40	50	4.76	.71	2.27	1.43	86	3.44	1.03	2.38	1.32	122	1.67	.94	3.67	1.01
15	3.54	1.21	2.74	1.31	51	1.52	.86	2.76	1.06	87	1.39	.83	1.71	.91	123	4.22	.96	2.08	1.28
16	4.35	1.13	2.25	1.37	52	3.11	1.04	2.17	1.20	88	1.65	.70	4.26	1.10	124	3.02	1.13	2.50	1.03
17	1.50	.85	3.33	1.38	53	3.70	1.25	2.13	1.19	89	2.63	.95	2.56	1.17	125	3.11	1.18	2.06	1.30
18	1.76	1.12	2.54	1.30	54	2.02	1.16	4.24	.97	90	1.96	1.07	2.00	1.15	126	1.61	.98	2.02	1.18
19	3.13	1.02	2.39	1.06	55	1.74	1.10	2.96	1.25	91	2.74	1.34	2.65	1.25	127	3.35	1.29	2.75	1.28
20	1.87	1.09	3.35	1.23	56	2.70	1.20	2.02	.98	92	1.52	1.07	1.85	1.04	128	1.78	1.01	2.65	1.23
21	3.46	1.19	2.23	1.13	57	1.65	.77	3.15	1.17	93	3.25	1.12	2.59	1.22	129	2.89	.99	2.30	1.13
22	4.20	1.13	2.48	1.35	58	2.50	1.17	2.80	1.20	94	3.65	1.10	2.48	1.26	130	1.65	1.12	3.13	1.19
23	3.89	1.18	2.00	1.22	59	2.48	1.09	2.31	1.18	95	1.52	1.02	2.20	1.16	131	1.85	1.01	3.44	1.26
24	4.24	.99	2.50	1.36	60	1.44	.91	1.80	1.05	96	1.35	.67	3.35	1.27	132	1.41	.83	2.06	1.27
25	1.50	.98	1.52	.89	61	3.22	1.21	2.33	1.26	97	4.15	1.01	2.38	1.16	133	1.87	1.15	3.35	1.32
26	2.54	1.13	2.46	1.21	62	4.00	.97	2.52	1.31	98	1.63	1.12	2.67	1.52	134	1.76	.90	2.67	1.23
27	4.76	.71	2.31	1.57	63	1.72	1.19	3.26	1.26	99	1.89	1.04	2.98	1.25	135	2.87	1.15	1.80	1.00
28	4.02	1.00	1.78	1.05	64	3.22	1.05	2.07	1.14	100	2.59	1.12	2.75	1.10	136	3.50	1.24	2.46	1.35
29	3.30	1.15	1.92	1.12	65	1.53	1.01	4.17	1.12	101	1.63	1.02	3.29	1.29	137	1.59	.91	3.48	1.13
30	2.46	1.09	2.44	1.24	66	4.78	.73	2.33	1.52	102	2.76	1.21	2.75	1.28	138	2.98	1.22	3.00	1.14
31	3.67	1.05	2.23	1.23	67	3.65	1.10	3.46	1.21	103	1.65	.99	3.46	1.05	139	4.63	.74	2.27	1.43
32	3.50	1.00	2.12	1.04	68	1.89	1.12	3.00	1.16	104	4.33	.70	2.21	1.47	140	1.28	.72	1.98	1.08
33	3.54	1.05	2.44	1.33	69	4.15	1.10	2.54	1.72	105	2.11	.99	2.59	1.29	141	2.41	1.00	2.80	1.26
34	2.94	1.25	2.10	1.26	70	1.96	1.15	2.38	1.22	106	4.35	.85	2.52	1.42	142	3.24	1.06	2.07	1.00
35	4.54	.69	2.58	1.35	71	2.61	1.20	2.59	1.22	107	1.57	.94	4.02	1.15	143	1.96	1.07	2.52	1.13

Table 2. (Continued)

Item No.	True M	True SD	False M	False SD	Item No.	True M	True SD	False M	False SD	Item No.	True M	True SD	False M	False SD	Item No.	True M	True SD	False M	False SD
145	3.74	.98	1.98	1.04	181	2.28	1.05	2.79	1.38	217	3.50	1.13	1.59	1.39	253	2.67	1.32	2.54	1.20
146	3.11	.95	2.15	1.13	182	4.33	.97	2.42	1.41	218	4.13	.83	2.52	1.05	254	2.87	1.20	1.70	.89
147	3.09	.92	1.96	.97	183	2.26	1.04	1.61	.75	219	1.28	.72	1.63	.83	255	2.50	1.33	1.33	.67
148	2.94	1.04	2.04	1.07	184	4.61	.77	2.54	1.57	220	1.35	.80	4.02	1.00	256	2.46	1.05	1.85	1.19
149	1.54	.96	1.88	1.10	185	1.39	.61	2.46	1.17	221	1.28	.81	1.76	1.02	257	1.61	.83	4.04	.97
150	1.59	1.05	3.89	1.10	186	3.57	1.07	2.00	1.12	222	2.50	1.19	2.33	.98	258	1.39	1.09	2.85	1.49
151	4.52	.79	2.19	1.55	187	1.70	1.09	3.35	1.12	223	2.04	1.32	1.61	.83	259	2.72	.91	2.00	1.03
152	1.64	.88	3.50	1.17	188	1.28	.78	2.44	1.33	224	2.44	1.22	1.96	.97	260	2.72	1.03	1.33	.67
153	1.36	.65	3.59	1.07	189	3.35	1.16	1.87	1.10	225	2.02	.86	2.13	1.19	261	1.52	.81	1.94	1.24
154	1.44	.92	3.70	1.15	190	1.46	.84	3.44	1.00	226	2.72	1.22	2.13	1.17	262	1.80	.91	3.15	1.07
155	1.31	.73	3.24	1.16	191	2.70	1.25	1.80	.96	227	3.07	1.25	1.87	.95	263	2.72	1.05	1.46	.78
156	4.29	.94	2.42	1.53	192	1.57	1.11	3.37	1.02	228	1.72	.96	2.77	1.18	264	2.44	1.26	3.04	1.07
157	3.54	1.09	2.13	1.14	193	1.30	.63	2.27	1.23	229	1.80	.96	2.30	1.19	265	3.87	1.00	1.76	.85
158	3.24	.99	2.08	1.06	194	4.26	1.02	2.27	1.50	230	1.54	1.05	3.11	1.16	266	2.80	1.28	2.92	1.49
159	3.04	.94	2.13	1.16	195	2.00	1.16	2.46	1.31	231	2.94	1.16	2.49	1.24	267	2.80	.96	1.35	.77
160	1.35	.74	3.22	1.21	196	1.44	.78	3.00	1.19	232	2.35	1.18	2.35	1.03	268	2.00	1.94	3.07	1.08
161	1.28	.54	2.02	1.15	197	3.48	1.36	2.23	1.25	233	3.41	1.31	1.78	.88	269	3.91	1.05	2.12	1.32
162	2.78	1.03	2.50	1.26	198	1.85	.84	3.26	.98	234	2.87	1.15	1.89	.96	270	2.87	1.29	1.98	1.00
163	1.48	.78	2.85	1.05	199	1.96	1.15	2.91	1.19	235	1.96	.94	2.60	1.07	271	3.67	.99	1.61	.75
164	1.20	.62	3.15	1.17	200	4.20	.96	2.06	1.27	236	3.58	.97	1.92	1.01	272	1.67	1.01	2.59	1.26
165	2.94	1.08	2.83	1.27	201	2.22	1.07	3.22	1.10	237	2.83	1.29	2.49	1.20	273	3.37	1.25	1.85	1.07
166	3.22	1.20	1.91	1.13	202	4.54	.75	2.10	1.51	238	3.59	1.15	2.06	1.02	274	1.52	.89	2.04	1.13
167	3.28	1.19	2.44	1.43	203	1.41	.78	1.63	.82	239	2.54	1.31	2.54	1.34	275	4.76	.60	2.23	1.52
168	4.54	.84	2.52	1.46	204	1.26	.58	1.67	.98	240	2.46	.98	2.35	1.30	276	1.24	.64	3.09	1.31
169	1.61	1.02	3.74	.98	205	4.52	.91	2.29	1.29	241	2.98	1.29	1.83	.97	277	2.96	1.32	2.13	1.12
170	2.28	.98	2.91	1.21	206	2.20	1.31	2.13	1.21	242	1.94	1.02	3.35	1.16	278	3.59	1.13	2.50	1.24
171	2.48	1.09	2.24	1.18	207	1.22	.66	3.17	1.02	243	1.57	.83	3.54	1.05	279	2.15	.99	1.50	.81
172	2.74	1.14	2.00	.97	208	2.24	.95	1.85	.84	244	3.07	1.16	2.21	1.13	280	3.13	1.13	1.74	.93
173	1.37	.77	3.28	1.03	209	4.20	.93	2.04	1.28	245	3.61	1.11	2.12	1.25	281	1.98	1.13	3.78	.94
174	1.37	.88	3.09	1.05	210	3.57	1.17	1.88	1.25	246	2.83	1.31	1.75	1.14	282	3.26	1.31	2.21	1.30
175	1.52	.91	3.44	.98	211	3.78	.96	2.02	1.18	247	3.48	1.03	2.12	1.34	283	1.33	.76	1.67	.92
176	1.63	1.00	3.33	1.35	212	3.48	1.17	2.00	1.07	248	3.20	1.38	2.20	1.20	284	4.09	.90	2.17	1.15
177	1.39	.77	3.76	1.10	213	3.83	1.08	1.41	.83	249	1.91	1.15	2.27	1.21	285	1.89	1.08	2.44	1.21
178	1.57	.81	3.76	1.12	214	1.54	.89	2.52	1.17	250	2.89	1.22	2.50	1.32	286	3.78	.92	1.81	.99
179	3.26	1.10	2.38	1.07	215	4.22	1.03	2.04	1.39	251	4.26	1.18	2.12	1.29	287	2.33	1.02	3.48	1.07
180	2.61	.93	1.80	1.15	216	3.44	1.17	1.73	1.12	252	4.04	.99	2.13	1.31	288	3.44	1.05	1.88	1.18

Table 2. (Continued)

Item No.	True M	True SD	False M	False SD	Item No.	True M	True SD	False M	False SD	Item No.	True M	True SD	False M	False SD	Item No.	True M	True SD	False M	False SD
289	1.96	1.10	2.80	1.19	325	3.24	1.04	2.23	1.18	361	2.96	1.00	2.10	1.07	397	1.38	.86	2.87	1.02
290	3.17	1.16	2.08	1.15	326	4.15	1.05	2.29	1.40	362	3.11	1.05	2.08	1.12	398	3.58	.89	1.59	1.02
291	4.13	1.13	2.06	1.33	327	2.50	1.15	2.07	1.02	363	4.36	.93	2.23	1.54	399	3.16	1.04	2.79	1.36
292	2.98	1.06	1.44	.69	328	3.48	.98	1.96	1.01	364	3.83	1.04	2.10	1.18	400	2.58	1.37	2.83	1.27
293	4.30	.92	2.23	1.38	329	3.41	1.19	1.95	1.19	365	4.00	.94	1.87	1.09	401	2.02	1.20	2.65	1.31
294	1.48	.81	3.15	1.14	330	1.74	.98	3.13	1.29	366	4.22	.70	1.94	1.11	402	2.13	.89	2.12	1.04
295	1.74	1.00	2.00	1.07	331	4.28	.83	2.27	1.37	367	1.96	1.01	2.25	1.22	403	1.67	.88	3.00	1.14
296	1.98	1.16	2.52	1.07	332	3.11	1.10	1.83	1.14	368	2.37	1.04	2.50	1.16	404	2.61	1.15	2.21	1.18
297	3.28	1.26	2.88	1.31	333	4.24	.74	2.17	1.29	369	3.30	.87	2.56	1.26	405	1.57	.89	2.71	1.27
298	3.20	1.09	2.08	1.19	334	3.37	1.16	1.98	1.19	370	3.02	.95	2.50	1.34	406	3.04	1.19	2.17	1.32
299	2.80	.93	2.13	1.09	335	3.64	1.12	2.04	1.19	371	1.54	.94	2.04	1.12	407	1.59	.88	3.12	1.44
300	2.85	1.14	1.76	.92	336	3.44	.87	2.06	1.09	372	2.89	.95	1.75	1.03	408	2.94	1.20	2.38	1.09
301	4.13	.96	2.15	1.16	337	4.17	.85	2.02	1.11	373	3.22	1.01	2.38	1.29	409	2.37	1.06	2.21	1.09
302	1.72	1.09	3.54	1.10	338	3.87	.89	2.42	1.24	374	2.24	1.08	3.02	1.24	410	2.65	1.14	2.77	1.20
303	3.78	.87	2.17	1.22	339	4.78	.76	2.17	1.42	375	2.48	1.03	2.29	1.11	411	2.18	1.19	2.38	1.29
304	3.13	.98	1.94	1.19	340	2.57	1.17	2.27	1.25	376	3.59	.96	2.90	1.24	412	1.83	1.04	2.38	1.07
305	4.09	.69	2.04	1.19	341	3.39	1.18	1.96	1.03	377	2.33	1.16	1.71	.96	413	4.00	1.03	2.62	1.39
306	2.48	1.13	3.63	.97	342	3.94	1.02	1.98	1.11	378	2.46	1.09	2.25	1.20	414	3.89	.91	2.02	1.04
307	2.80	.98	1.94	1.07	343	3.20	1.13	2.15	1.14	379	2.20	.98	2.79	1.19	415	2.00	.95	2.27	1.14
308	3.20	1.13	3.15	1.13	344	3.44	1.00	2.13	1.17	380	1.57	.89	2.46	1.11	416	2.76	1.07	2.17	1.20
309	1.72	.96	3.39	.91	345	3.89	1.12	2.15	1.14	381	2.24	.82	1.77	.94	417	2.89	1.19	2.25	1.15
310	1.72	.86	3.46	1.01	346	3.09	1.17	1.98	1.18	382	1.54	.81	3.15	1.06	418	4.22	.77	2.37	1.28
311	2.80	1.17	1.87	1.10	347	2.00	1.01	3.83	1.12	383	1.65	.95	2.65	1.06	419	2.78	1.09	1.81	1.01
312	4.11	1.06	1.90	1.16	348	3.00	1.17	1.85	1.03	384	1.94	1.08	2.25	1.30	420	3.07	1.12	2.15	1.11
313	2.78	1.11	2.24	1.18	349	3.57	1.11	2.40	1.29	385	2.50	1.07	2.27	1.22	421	2.83	1.04	1.90	1.09
314	2.98	1.16	1.91	1.03	350	4.04	.92	2.25	1.14	386	2.24	.99	2.00	.97	422	3.33	1.01	1.81	1.01
315	4.31	.90	2.19	1.36	351	3.76	.92	1.87	1.05	387	1.89	1.14	2.17	1.28	423	1.49	.82	1.77	.96
316	3.13	.92	1.96	1.05	352	3.89	.96	2.23	1.28	388	2.89	1.11	1.90	1.03	424	3.17	1.20	1.92	1.10
317	2.98	1.01	2.02	.92	353	1.76	1.17	3.45	1.11	389	3.48	1.05	2.00	1.05	425	1.98	1.00	2.38	1.29
318	1.62	1.01	3.28	.78	354	3.80	1.03	2.06	1.24	390	1.46	.72	2.69	1.08	426	2.57	1.15	2.27	1.10
319	3.33	1.02	1.74	.95	355	4.64	.88	2.10	1.49	391	2.30	.96	1.76	1.08	427	2.00	.89	2.29	1.13
320	2.98	1.22	2.08	1.03	356	3.61	.88	1.88	.98	392	1.76	.95	2.12	1.15	428	1.54	.75	1.87	1.03
321	2.71	1.01	1.85	1.04	357	3.49	.99	2.19	1.21	393	3.67	.79	2.48	1.48	429	1.67	.76	1.77	1.00
322	2.63	.90	1.78	.91	358	3.83	.97	2.31	1.32	394	1.94	.98	2.40	1.14	430	1.33	.67	3.96	1.51
323	3.31	1.24	1.72	1.00	359	3.33	1.04	1.74	.88	395	3.15	1.25	2.17	1.25	431	3.41	.98	2.54	1.21
324	3.70	1.17	1.94	1.21	360	3.98	1.03	2.08	1.22	396	1.72	.91	2.15	1.30	432	1.76	.92	2.00	.95

Table 2. (Continued)

Item No.	True M	True SD	False M	False SD
433	3.67	1.35	2.08	1.33
434	1.65	.90	1.67	1.00
435	2.33	1.02	2.25	1.19
436	2.64	1.26	2.42	1.14
437	3.00	1.11	2.19	1.12
438	3.33	1.18	2.23	1.18
439	3.00	1.19	1.98	1.09
440	2.96	1.08	1.83	1.04
441	2.11	.97	1.90	.98
442	2.86	1.27	2.46	1.20
443	3.34	.91	2.42	1.21
444	2.15	1.01	2.42	1.19
445	1.76	.90	3.00	1.47
446	1.89	.90	3.00	1.23
447	2.98	1.04	2.25	1.23
448	3.96	.94	2.27	1.32
449	2.59	1.17	2.22	1.09
450	1.94	.93	3.46	1.30
451	2.28	1.05	2.72	1.19
452	3.57	1.13	2.33	1.30
453	2.94	1.20	2.08	1.99
454	3.09	1.23	1.88	1.00
455	3.35	1.06	1.92	1.06
456	3.61	1.00	2.23	1.37
457	3.09	1.07	2.04	1.20
458	2.50	1.19	2.23	1.21
459	3.89	1.02	2.31	1.26
460	1.89	.99	2.10	1.27
461	2.96	1.10	3.26	1.12
462	3.37	.97	2.20	1.31
463	1.41	.72	1.83	.98
464	2.07	1.04	2.46	1.42
465	2.22	1.09	2.21	1.23
466	1.65	.88	2.75	1.28
467	2.72	1.24	2.12	1.17
468	2.54	1.24	2.73	1.21
469	2.89	1.20	1.52	.96
470	4.28	.72	2.27	1.37
471	3.28	.91	2.04	1.12
472	3.65	1.14	2.06	1.09
473	3.17	1.14	2.10	1.01
474	1.80	.98	2.13	1.03
475	2.96	1.13	2.33	1.10
476	3.85	1.21	2.27	1.51
477	2.85	1.15	2.10	1.17
478	2.89	1.04	2.33	1.17
479	2.87	1.13	1.91	1.13
480	3.59	.88	1.98	1.06
481	3.61	1.04	1.57	1.05
482	3.44	.96	1.57	.91
483	1.67	.87	2.87	1.47
484	2.94	1.10	2.31	1.18
485	2.80	1.11	2.19	1.17
486	1.89	.99	2.37	1.28
487	2.22	1.11	2.06	1.21
488	1.61	.86	2.12	1.13
489	2.09	.99	2.58	1.19
490	1.78	1.01	2.23	1.20
491	3.07	1.14	1.90	.93
492	2.61	1.27	2.83	1.37
493	2.26	1.08	2.38	1.19
494	3.91	.99	2.19	1.33
495	2.44	1.07	2.42	1.02
496	1.87	.96	2.29	1.19
497	1.50	.75	2.13	1.05
498	1.96	.99	2.42	1.11
499	3.02	1.18	2.44	1.16
500	2.67	1.10	2.31	1.11
501	2.02	1.00	2.29	1.07
502	3.07	1.22	1.52	.94
503	2.59	1.13	2.37	1.22
504	2.71	.94	2.19	1.03
505	4.30	.99	1.89	1.35
506	3.35	1.08	1.98	1.08
507	3.02	1.04	1.96	1.08
508	1.72	.89	2.02	1.02
509	2.91	1.13	2.13	1.05
510	3.98	1.09	2.17	1.20
511	3.72	1.09	2.25	1.30
512	4.09	.87	2.02	1.32
513	2.22	1.13	2.08	1.01
514	3.65	1.23	2.21	1.18
515	1.72	.98	2.21	1.24
516	2.37	.97	1.88	.88
517	4.37	.88	2.44	1.33
518	3.41	.93	2.46	1.13
519	3.80	1.28	2.02	1.29
520	2.30	1.05	2.85	.96
521	2.24	1.02	2.41	1.09
522	1.96	1.07	2.35	1.25
523	2.07	.95	2.23	1.02
524	1.94	1.16	3.06	1.46
525	2.87	1.19	2.44	1.14
526	4.17	1.08	2.12	1.29
527	1.91	1.17	2.25	1.14
528	1.96	1.19	2.37	1.09
529	2.24	1.11	2.37	1.10
530	3.35	1.04	2.08	1.12
531	3.35	1.06	2.31	1.18
532	2.26	1.22	2.19	1.01
533	2.35	1.25	2.37	1.01
534	2.33	1.08	2.15	.96
535	3.26	1.16	1.83	.96
536	2.48	.96	2.25	1.14
537	2.17	1.16	1.88	1.04
538	1.87	1.05	1.81	1.03
539	1.87	1.00	2.23	1.23
540	1.83	1.12	2.50	1.42
541	2.83	1.12	2.02	1.15
542	2.22	1.21	2.31	1.23
543	4.02	.98	2.31	1.38
544	3.35	1.02	1.83	.94
545	3.15	1.01	1.98	1.08
546	1.54	.89	1.90	.98
547	3.15	1.17	1.78	1.05
548	2.74	1.24	2.60	1.30
549	3.72	1.00	2.35	1.15
550	2.00	1.16	1.77	.94
551	3.26	1.06	2.13	1.16
552	1.59	.98	1.85	.92
553	4.11	.91	2.21	1.21
554	1.98	1.13	1.88	1.06
555	3.91	.94	2.31	1.08
556	2.15	1.01	2.48	1.24
557	1.76	.99	1.81	1.01
558	3.33	1.06	2.65	1.15
559	3.15	1.10	2.27	1.16
560	3.28	1.15	2.29	1.47
561	1.44	.89	1.81	.99
562	2.07	1.16	1.96	1.03
563	1.73	.94	1.85	.98
564	1.80	.86	2.12	1.13
565	4.30	1.03	2.29	1.47
566	2.13	1.19	2.46	1.13

Source: Christian, Burkhart, and Gynther (1978).

Table 3. Percentage of Items in Subtle-Obvious Categories for MMPI Clinical Scales

Scale[a]	Very Subtle	Somewhat Subtle	Neither Subtle nor Obvious	Somewhat Obvious	Very Obvious
Hs	03	09	58	30	00
D	08	28	33	25	05
Hy	08	30	32	30	00
Pd	04	20	38	26	12
Mf	42	28	26	05	00
Pa	02	20	20	27	30
Pt	00	04	31	58	06
Sc	01	00	32	46	20
Ma	06	30	39	15	08
Si	12	34	35	17	00

Source: Christian, Burkhart, and Gynther (1978).

[a]The rating weight for an item was assigned within any particular scale in correspondence to the way that item was scored in the scale being considered. Therefore, if an item was scored false for that scale, then the false value was used, and if scored true for that scale, then the true value was used.

measure were 15.49 (SD=8.46) for males and 10.46 (SD=5.60) for females. Statistical analyses showed no significant difference associated with sex for the Pd subscale scores; however, males' nonconformity scores significantly exceeded those obtained for females, $t(208)=5.09, p<.001$.

The correlations between the full Pd scale (with the usual correction weighting of .4K) and the nonconformity scale were: .36 for male subjects, .39 for female subjects, and .38 for both sexes combined. All of these values are significantly different from zero at beyond the .001 level. Of special interest, however, are the relationships among the Pd-O, Pd-N, and Pd-S scores and the scores obtained on the nonconformity scale. For males, zero-order correlations of these relationships (in the order given in the preceding sentence) were .33 $(p<.001)$, .18 (ns), and .26 $(p<.01)$. Both obvious and subtle item endorsements were significantly related to scores on the nonconformity scale. Furthermore, this particular comparison indicated that there was no difference in their predictive power, $t(97)=$ .51, ns. These results are not consistent with the hypothesis that obvious (i.e., face-valid) items will account for all or nearly all of the discriminative power in a predictor-criterion relationship.

For females, zero-order correlations among nonconformity scores and Pd-O, Pd-N, and Pd-S scores were .40 $(p<.001)$, .21 $(p<.05)$, and .16 (ns), respectively. In this instance, obvious and neutral scores were significantly related to the criterion. However, the subtle score-nonconformity score relation did not differ significantly from zero.

Furthermore, statistical analysis showed a difference in the predictive power of obvious and subtle scores, $t(107)=1.68, p<.05$, one-tailed. These results clearly confirm Jackson's [1971] hypothesis.

Semipartial and multiple correlations were run to determine the relative contributions of the separate subscales with the other(s) controlled. For males, the multiple correlation of obvious and neutral scores with scores on the nonconformity scale was .33. This information in conjunction with the zero-order correlations previously reported indicates that the obvious items contributed a substantial amount over and above the neutral items $(.33^2 - .18^2 = .08)$, $F(1, 97) = 8.71$, $p<.01$. It also indicates that neutral items contributed very little variability beyond that attributable to the obvious items. Given these results, we will not consider the neutral items in the context of evaluating the relative contribution of the subtle items to the obvious items. The multiple correlation of the subtle and obvious items with the nonconformity scores was .41. If one considers this finding in conjunction with the zero-order correlations, it is clear that the obvious items contributed a substantial amount over and above the subtle items $(.41^2 - .26^2 = .10)$, $F(1, 97) = 11.72, p<.001$. The subtle items, on the other hand, added a statistically significant although relatively small contribution over and above the obvious items $(.41^2 - .33^2 = .06)$ $F(1, 97) = 6.88$, $p<.05$. This analysis indicates that given the choice of subtle, neutral, or obvious items as predictors, the obvious items are preferable.

For females, the same general pattern was found. In this case, the multiple correlation between obvious and neutral items and the nonconformity scores was .40. Since the zero-order correlation between obvious items and nonconformity scores was also .40, it is clear that neutral items contributed nothing to this relationship. The multiple correlation between subtle and obvious items and nonconformity scores was .44, which clearly shows that obvious items contribute substantially more unique variance than do subtle items (the zero-order correlation between subtle items and nonconformity scores was .16).

The multiple correlations show that, for males and females, obvious items have more predictive power than subtle items and, further, that neutral items contribute little, if anything, to an understanding of the predictor-criterion relationship. What are the correlations among Pd-O, Pd-N, and Pd-S scores? Only correlations for the total sample are given, since there were no significant sex differences in response to these categories. Correlations between Pd-O and Pd-N, Pd-O and Pd-S, and Pd-N and Pd-S scores were .45 $(p<.001)$, −.01 (ns), and

.21 ($p<.01$), respectively. It is especially interesting to note the lack of relationship between Pd-O and Pd-S scores, a finding that is consistent with the results of the multiple correlation analysis. Although subtle items do not contribute as much predictive variance as obvious items, the two sets of items are relatively independent of each other and consequently in combination make for good prediction.

Relationships among Pd subscores, nonconformity scores, and scores on MMPI scales L and K were also examined. Since L and K are considered to be measures of defensiveness, one would anticipate negative correlations between L and K and Pd-O scores and positive correlations between L and K and Pd-S scores, with the L, K, and Pd-N correlations falling somewhere between these extreme values. For all subjects, K's correlation with Pd-O scores was $-.52$ ($p<.001$). The K-Pd-N correlation was $-.20$ ($p<.01$) and the K-Pd-S correlation was .39 ($p<.001$). The L-Pd-O correlation was $-.42$ ($p<.001$), the L-Pd-N correlation was $-.18$ ($p<.01$), and theL-Pd-S correlation was $-.02$ (ns). All these relationships are in line with expectations except for the L-Pd-S correlation. The discrepancy between the K-Pd-S and the L-Pd-S correlations probably reflects the difference in the type of defensiveness measured by L and K. The L scale is composed of items that have psychologically unambiguous and generally socially unfavorable content (e.g., "I do not always tell the truth"). The K scale includes a much broader range; some items resemble those on the L scale, whereas the relationship of others to defensiveness is much more obscure (e.g., "I have never felt better in my life than I do now," keyed *false*). Thus, it is not surprising the K covaries with Pd-S and Pd-O, whereas L, with its restricted range of content, is associated only with the rejection of Pd-O items.

Relations among L, K, and nonconformity scores were also investigated. These values are differentiated by sex, since males and females responded significantly differently to the nonconformity measure. The correlations between L scores and nonconformity scores were $-.37$ ($p<.001$) for males and $-.49$ ($p<.001$) for females. In other words, the higher the L scale score, the less nonconforming behavior was admitted. Correlations between K scores and nonconformity scores were $-.09$ (ns) for males and $-.36$ ($p<.001$) for females. When one considers that the correlation between Pd-O and K was $-.50$ for males and that the correlation between Pd-O and nonconformity scores for this subgroup was .33, the lack of relationship between K and nonconformity scores in males is difficult to understand. Perhaps males are less defensive (in the K scale sense) about reporting nonconforming behavior than are females.

For the most part, relationships found among Pd subscale scores and MMPI scales L and K followed predictable patterns, which tends to augment the construct validity of both the new and standard scales. Also, relations among the various MMPI measures and the nonconformity measure suggest that this latter instrument does get at the dimension it was designed to tap. We do not argue that responses to this nonconformity scale are a veridical reflection of the nonconforming behaviors a person has engaged in. However, we do claim, as did Elion and Megargee [1975] that "the more delinquent behavior a student reported, the more antisocial he was, whether or not these reports were completely accurate" [p. 168].

To summarize, this study offers support for the position that subscales composed of items clearly related to the criterion have more discriminative power than subscales composed of items not clearly related to the criterion. Neutral items appear to have no discriminative power beyond that already contained by the obvious items. Subtle items, on the other hand, do have a unique contribution to make and, in combination with obvious items, give more predictive power than does either set alone. These results probably would not have been anticipated by those familiar with the work of Ashton and Goldberg [1973] and Jackson [1975]. However, those studies did not indicate that scales composed of empirically derived items have no validity. What they did show is that content-coherent intuitive scales have superior validity to empirical scales. The comparative validities of obvious and subtle subsets of items that constitute the empirical scales were not examined. Whether the pattern described above will be found for other MMPI scales remains to be seen. The present authors are currently investigating the predictive powers of obvious, neutral, and subtle components of MMPI scales D, Hy, Pa, and Ma, the only other clinical scales with enough subtle items to permit such an analysis.

MMPI Performance, Response Set, and the "Self-Concept Hypothesis"

J. B. Taylor, M. Carithers, and L. Coyne

Perhaps because of the atheoretic and empirical history of Minnesota Multiphasic Personality Inventory (MMPI) development, it is only in the past 2 decades that systematic research has examined the processes that mediate responses to specific MMPI items. The major empirical attacks on this problem have attempted to demonstrate either that (a) item responses are importantly governed by a respondent's tendency to give positive or negative responses irrespective of content (the original "acquiescence response set hypothesis") or that (b) item responses are governed by a respondent's tendency to endorse socially desirable items (the original "social desirability set hypothesis"). A third view, that item responses are mediated by a general tendency toward "deviant" or atypical behavior (one facet of the "deviation hypothesis"), may be seen as subsuming the above hypotheses as special cases.

A decade of controversy, and much experimentation, has led to significant modification of the original acquiescence and social desirability hypotheses. Thus, several forms of acquiescent response set have been posited [Bentler, Jackson, and Messick, 1971; Jackson, 1967; Messick, 1967; Morf and Jackson, 1972]. Similarly, several studies suggest that different forms of social desirability response set exist [Boe, Gocka, and Kogan, 1966, 1967; Messick and Jackson, 1972]. The controversy between these views now appears on the wane, seemingly more from exhaustion than from resolution.

228

[For recent reviews, cf. Bentler, Jackson, and Messick, 1971; Block, 1971; Fiske and Pearson, 1970; Wiggins, 1968].

Recently, Wiggins [1966] has suggested that the MMPI may be usefully viewed as a communication device that the respondent uses to transmit information about himself to the tester or institution. The MMPI, in this view, is seen as a medium for self-presentation. Presentation of self necessarily implies a preexisting set of self-concepts to be presented. We therefore suggest, as an extension of Wiggins' view, that responses to specific items may be mediated by more abstract concepts of the self, with each self-concept serving as a criterion against which items are evaluated. Thus the individual answering a number of specific MMPI items may do so in such a manner as to communicate that he is physically disabled, morally impeccable, a victim of circumstances, etc. We refer to such discrete and cognitive views of the self as "self-concepts," and the hypothesis that they mediate and organize specific responses to inventory items is referred to as the "self-concept hypothesis."

The notion of "self-concept" has posed major problems for psychological theory since the time of William James. Currently the term is often used in a limited way as a synonym for "self-evaluation." Our usage is somewhat broader. By self-concept we are referring to one or another abstract category used by an individual in encoding his or her behavior. Any individual uses a number of such categories and hence may be seen as having a variety of self-concepts.

Any particular category, any particular self-concept, may be described as a point or a region along some more general dimension. Thus the examples cited above may be described as points or regions along dimensions of health-sickness, moral goodness-badness, and controlling-victimized, respectively. Self-evaluation is one dimension among many, although (as we shall later see) it may have unique importance.

In accord with most self-concept theories, we assume that self-concepts provide a source of behavioral consistency. Individual actions (including responses to test items) are chosen so as to be concordant with existing self-categorizations. This assumption does not deny that transient happenings may also influence self-concept presentation; it does not deny that self-concept may be changeable; and it does not deny that individuals may differ in their tendency toward self-consistency. It only assumes that some degree of stability and consistency of self-concepts exists in most individuals.

These assumptions, as applied to test-taking behavior, suggest that responses to a large number of specific scale items may be chosen so as to be consistent with a much smaller number of abstract self-concepts. Thus consistency among item responses is neither viewed as reflecting the influence of personality "traits" nor as reflecting the influence of "response sets." Rather, it is considered an outcome of a particular communicative process in which item responses are consistently chosen so as to communicate information about more abstract self-concepts [cf. Carson, 1969].

Some support for the self-concept hypothesis is given by Wiggins' [1966] demonstration that MMPI items can be organized into scales of homogeneous content with reasonable consistency among items of similar content. Each of these content scales may be seen as transmitting one or another type of self-concept. However, Wiggins' findings fall short of demonstrating that the standard MMPI scales in fact reflect the respondent's more general self-concepts. Three objections arise. First, the demonstration of correlation among items of similar content may be explainable as a function of trait consistency. Second, correlations between items may be attributable in part to response sets. A more adequate demonstration would measure self-concept in a manner free of acquiescence or other response sets and then relate these self-concept reports to the standard MMPI scales. Third, factor analysis of Wiggins' scales emerged with only three factors, the two major ones being similar in implication to the A and R factors of the MMPI first reported by Welsh [1956] and since often replicated. If responses are organized by differentiated self-concepts, then a more differentiated set of factors would be expected. The failure to find additional factors may of course arise if additional factors are not present. On the other hand, it might also arise if major self-concept dimensions are tapped only by a single scale, so that a differentiated factor solution cannot emerge. In this connection, it is noteworthy that factor analyses of MMPI *item* responses typically emerge with a large number of content-specific factors—a result attributable to the large number of items typically included in such analyses.

Study 1 of this article tests the self-concept hypothesis. Eighty-three psychiatric patients were asked to respond to a set of rating scales measuring cognitive concepts of the self, using mainly the conceptual dimensions suggested by Wiggins. Responses to these self-concept scales were correlated wth MMPI scores on the standard clinical and validity scales. These correlations were factor analyzed, and the results are interpreted as showing the amount of variance in the standard MMPI scales that may be attributable to mediation by cognitive concepts of the self. It was found that the inclusion of self-concept markers produces an unusually differentiated factor solution, with self-concept dimensions accounting for two thirds of the explained MMPI variance.

Study 2 is a replication of Study 1 with a larger and more hetero-geneous group of respondents and additional self-concept measures. The major conclusions of Study 1 are supported; no evidence was found for important additional self-concept dimensions within the MMPI item pool.

Study 1

Method

Subjects and Procedure. Eighty-three patients newly admitted to the inpatient or outpatient facilities of Topeka State Hospital served as subjects. These subjects were drawn from the larger respondent sample reported in Taylor, Ptacek, Carithers, Griffin, and Coyne [1972]. All cases with scale scores missing or a significant number of MMPI items left unanswered were eliminated. Thirty-eight were male; 38 were outpatients; and 69% were between the ages of 14 and 29. Ninety-five percent of the subjects were Caucasian, and all were resi-dents of the Topeka metropolitan area.

Testing was done in two sessions, with 1-3 days intervening between sessions. The MMPI, plus one set of self-concept scales, was adminis-tered at the first session; at the second session a comparable set of self-concept scales, with different items but devised to measure the same content domains, was administered in counterbalanced order, along with the Marlowe-Crowne Social Desirability Scale [Crowne and Marlowe, 1964].

Measures. The MMPI was scored for the standard clinical and valid-ity scales, the Welsh A and R factor scales, and the Edwards Social Desirability Scale [Edwards, 1957]. The K correction was not in-cluded in scoring the clinical scales. In addition, the clinical and cor-rection scales of the MMPI were further scored from keys eliminating item overlap [Adams and Horn, 1965; Dahlstrom, Welsh, and Dahl-strom, 1972]. Also scored was the Marlowe-Crowne Social Desirabil-ity Scale, measuring the tendency to endorse desirable but unlikely items.

The self-concept measures consisted of 24 self-rating scales (listed in Table 1), designed to tap 10 of the Wiggins [1966] MMPI content domains plus two additional domains (anxiety and moralism). Thus, each of 12 domains was tapped by two different but comparable rating scales. (Hence there are two numbers in Table 1 for each self-concept scale.) All scales, constructed by a technique described in Taylor [1968a, 1968b], used a thermometer-like line, with the self-concept dimension specified in a single question at the top, the ends of the scale anchored by a single adjective or phrase, and the points along the scale anchored by a set of defining items. Figure 1 presents an illustrative example. A multitrait-multimethod analysis [Taylor, Ptacek, Carithers, Griffin, and Coyne, 1972] has shown these scales to be relatively free of response-style variance, to have discriminant

Table 1. Self-Concept Rating Scales: 1-24

	Scale Question	Polar Anchor	Related Wiggins Scale (1966)
1, 2	How self-confident do you usually feel?	Very self-confident vs. not very self-confident	Poor Morale
3, 4	How smoothly do your thoughts run?	Thoughts run smoothly vs. thoughts disrupted	Organic Symptom
5, 6	How good is your health?	Good health vs. poor health	Poor Health
7, 8	How anxious do you feel?	Very anxious vs. very calm	—
9, 10	How much satisfaction & contentment do you feel?	Dissatisfaction with family, friction and disharmony vs. contentment	Family Problems
11, 12	How much do you experience mental problems?	Troubled by mental problems vs. not troubled by mental problems	Psychoticism
13, 14	How conscientious do you think you are?	Extremely moral, conscientious and virtuous vs. not highly moral or virtuous	—
15, 16	How willing are you to express anger?	Strong tendency to express anger vs. unwilling to express anger	Manifest Hostility
17, 18	How religious are you, in a fundamentalist sense?	Strongly religious vs. not very religious, in a fundamentalist sense	Religious Fundamentalism
19, 20	In general, how cheerful do you usually feel?	Cheerful vs. depressed	Depression
21, 22	How comfortable and confident do you feel with other people?	Comfort, confidence, enjoyment around people vs. discomfort, self-consciousness and worry around people	Social Maladjustment
23, 24	How would you describe your kinds of interests in terms of toughness or sensitivity?	Tough vs. sensitive	Feminine Interests

HOW COMFORTABLE AND CONFIDENT DO YOU FEEL WITH OTHER PEOPLE?

Comfort, confidence, and
enjoyment around people

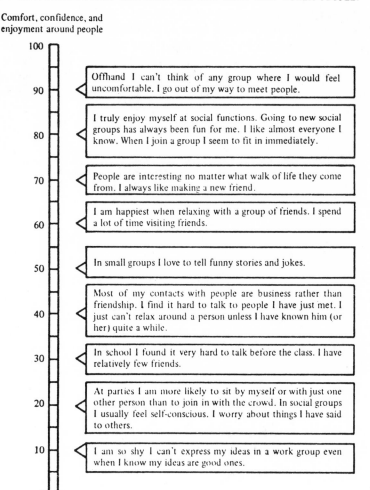

100

90 — Offhand I can't think of any group where I would feel uncomfortable. I go out of my way to meet people.

80 — I truly enjoy myself at social functions. Going to new social groups has always been fun for me. I like almost everyone I know. When I join a group I seem to fit in immediately.

70 — People are interesting no matter what walk of life they come from. I always like making a new friend.

60 — I am happiest when relaxing with a group of friends. I spend a lot of time visiting friends.

50 — In small groups I love to tell funny stories and jokes.

40 — Most of my contacts with people are business rather than friendship. I find it hard to talk to people I have just met. I just can't relax around a person unless I have known him (or her) quite a while.

30 — In school I found it very hard to talk before the class. I have relatively few friends.

20 — At parties I am more likely to sit by myself or with just one other person than to join in with the crowd. In social groups I usually feel self-conscious. I worry about things I have said to others.

10 — I am so shy I can't express my ideas in a work group even when I know my ideas are good ones.

0

Discomfort, self-
consciousness and
worry around people

Figure 1. Example-Anchored Self-Concept Scale.

validity superior to multiitem measures similar in content, and to adequately mark eight factors tapped also by the Wiggins scales. The self-concept scales listed in Table 1 include the major factor markers from Taylor et al. [1972].

Analysis. The scores from all scales were intercorrelated, and four blocks of correlations were factor analyzed. The four blocks consisted of correlations between (a) standard MMPI scales only, (b) abbreviated MMPI scales only, (c) standard MMPI scales and self-concept scales, and (d) abbreviated MMPI scales and self-concept scales. Correlations with the independently administered Marlowe-Crowne Social Desirability Scale were included in each block. These procedures allow a comparison of factor solutions with and without item overlap and with and without independent self-concept information.

Each block was factored by the principal-component method (R^2 in the diagonals) followed by normal varimax rotation. Adopting the usual criterion, all factors with eigenvalues $\geqslant 1$ were rotated: Three factors were rotated for Blocks 1 and 2 and nine factors for Block 4. By this criterion, eight factors would have been rotated for Block 3, but in the interest of comparability, nine factors were rotated there also.

Since this article is concerned with self-concept mediation of MMPI responses, and since item overlap leads to heightened and "spurious" shared variance, we focus on the factor results and implications of correlations among self-concept markers and nonoverlapping MMPI scales. Results of the other analyses are cited briefly for comparative purposes.

Results

Table 2 presents the factor loadings when nonoverlapping MMPI scales and self-concept scales are analyzed jointly. Seven factors are clearly marked by one or more sets of self-concept measures (see the boxed values in Table 2). Of the two remaining factors, one is marked predominantly by MMPI scales, the other, equally by self-concept and MMPI measures.

A prior factor analysis—using a larger set of self-concept markers, the Wiggins MMPI content scales, and additional multiitem scales— extracted nine factors [Taylor et al., 1972]. A comparison of factor solutions between Taylor et al. [1972] and this study (using the self-concept scales common to the two studies) indicates essential agreement for eight of the nine factors. Factor I is essentially equivalent to the earlier factor labeled as "Confident Cheer *versus* Depressive Anxiety and Self-Doubt." It is marked in this analysis most strongly by self-concept scales of "Self Confidence," "Efficiency of Thinking," and "Comfort with People" and has major loadings on the MMPI scales D, Mf, Pt, Sc, Si, and Edwards Social Desirability. The second factor, earlier labeled as a "Family Harmony" dimension, is marked here by loadings on the "Family Satisfaction and Comfort" self-concept scales, with a loading also on the MMPI Pd scale. The third factor of this analysis, marked almost entirely by various MMPI scales, is similar to a factor tentatively described earlier as a "method set factor." Factor IV, in this and the prior solution marked (and labeled) by the "Masculine Interests" self-concept scales, is marked here also by the Mf scale of the MMPI. Factor V, a "Religious Fundamentalism" dimension in both solutions, was marked by religiosity self-concept scales; here it is marked for the MMPI scales only by a negligible loading on Ma. Factor VII, in this and the earlier solution marked by the "Mental Problems" self-concept scales, has in this solution surprisingly few MMPI scales with even a negligible loading. Factor VIII, a replicated "Physical Health" dimension, is marked here by the F, Hs, Pa, Sc, and SD scales of the MMPI. Factor IX in this study and Taylor et al. [1972] is clearly loaded on two self-concept scales asking about "moral virtue and conscientiousness"; surprisingly, it here has no major loading even on the MMPI validity scales.

Although these eight factors are essentially similar to the factors extracted previously, in this solution Factor VI is new. Its marker loadings are small and scattered; its interpretation is therefore doubtful.

Table 2 also shows the percentage of variance accounted for by each factor, both within the self-concept scales and within the MMPI scales. For the MMPI scales, factors clearly marked by self-concept measures account for 68.3% of the shared variance; the presumed methods-set factor and the "unexplained" factor together account for 31.7%. The method-set factor alone accounts for 26.6% of the shared variance.

In this analysis, the Edwards Social Desirability Scale is split between two self-concept dimensions—Confident Cheer and Physical Health—and has a lesser loading on the third, methods-set, dimension. In prior research the Edwards scale has been held to measure a single unitary response style influencing a variety of personality measures. In view of past findings, we might expect social desirability to mark the major dimension in a general factor solution. The first principal component of the present analysis may be regarded as an analogue of a general factor solution: On it, the Edwards Social Desirability Scale

Table 2. Rotated Factor Loadings, h² Values, and Variance Components of Selected Sets of Self-Concept Measures and Non-Overlapping MMPI Scales: Study 1. (N = 83)

Scale	I	II	III	IV	V	VI	VII	VIII	IX	h²
SELF-CONCEPT										
Self-Confidence (1)	.760	−.076	.030	.108	.088	.000	−.004	−.190	.230	.692
Self-Confidence (2)	.739	.134	.093	.001	.016	.017	−.145	−.156	.097	.629
Thoughts (1)	.705	−.002	−.008	.053	.151	−.066	.015	−.379	.162	.698
Thoughts (2)	.531	−.023	.158	−.133	−.102	−.253	−.352	−.239	.126	.596
Health (1)	.341	.025	−.173	.012	−.185	.047	.039	−.540	.249	.539
Health (2)	.342	−.192	.080	.225	−.060	−.061	.045	−.680	.022	.683
Anxious (1)	−.480	.393	.048	−.006	.140	.025	.410	.093	−.106	.596
Anxious (2)	−.365	.263	−.471	.105	.130	.402	.058	.203	−.004	.658
Family (1)	−.206	.749	.090	−.033	−.040	−.035	.054	.082	−.012	.625
Family (2)	−.005	.507	−.102	.071	−.104	.162	.256	.060	−.340	.494
Mental Problems (1)	−.317	.095	−.088	.042	−.064	.000	.647	.085	.071	.553
Mental Problems (2)	−.313	.025	−.058	.087	.012	.147	.607	.298	−.222	.638
Conscientious (1)	.165	−.165	.115	.049	−.022	.080	.002	−.084	.787	.702
Conscientious (2)	.126	−.116	.179	.183	.048	.422	−.194	−.005	.484	.547
Anger (1)	−.108	.164	−.230	−.143	.083	−.097	.481	−.011	−.255	.425
Anger (2)	−.082	−.064	−.175	.154	−.136	.047	.207	.248	−.464	.405
Religious (1)	.082	−.073	.015	−.210	.794	.006	−.052	.139	−.016	.710
Religious (2)	.133	−.010	.027	−.140	.829	.032	.112	.079	.092	.753
Cheerful (1)	.573	−.274	.073	−.017	.213	−.119	−.074	−.259	.115	.555
Cheerful (2)	.618	−.216	.221	−.183	.112	−.210	−.145	−.187	.235	.679
Comfort (1)	.729	−.118	.095	.077	.016	.166	−.176	.070	.196	.662
Comfort (2)	.839	.055	.169	.059	−.030	.146	−.068	.098	.032	.776
MF (1)	.127	−.050	−.065	.633	.011	.024	−.287	−.126	.011	.523
MF (2)	.152	.040	−.115	.618	−.173	−.087	.131	.049	.113	.489

MMPI

L	.088	.182	.653	.112	.150	.093	.094	.085	.140	.546
F	-.337	.213	-.201	.121	-.138	-.309	.424	.547	-.065	.811
K	.133	.119	.620	-.153	-.178	.032	-.017	-.057	.051	.479
Hs	-.394	.223	-.226	-.130	.103	.173	.152	.652	.005	.763
D	-.648	.130	-.188	-.145	-.233	.253	.246	.306	.067	.771
Hy	-.026	.055	.017	-.273	.058	.554	.284	.330	-.015	.579
Pd	-.135	.443	-.503	.080	-.161	.039	.123	.265	-.212	.631
Mf 1	-.544	.248	-.447	.153	.041	.200	.027	.120	.050	.640
Mf 3	.229	.106	.388	-.268	-.057	.552	-.115	-.141	.257	.694
Mf 4	.211	-.233	-.067	-.587	.177	-.007	-.067	.113	.150	.519
Mf 5	-.150	.353	.087	-.508	.180	.163	-.103	.029	-.017	.483
Pa	.078	-.148	-.029	.010	.177	.144	.356	.590	-.157	.580
Pt	-.515	.173	-.601	-.031	.058	.016	.235	.338	-.036	.831
Sc	-.624	.269	-.324	.069	-.089	-.164	.180	.432	-.089	.834
Ma	.248	-.117	-.296	.318	-.353	-.284	.259	.185	-.030	.571
Si	-.718	.239	-.106	-.032	.050	-.121	.127	.032	-.132	.653
Welsh A	-.486	.172	-.651	.015	.088	.053	.106	.324	-.051	.820
Welsh R	-.040	.008	.623	-.111	.093	.093	-.110	.021	.026	.433
Edwards SD	.497	-.288	.392	-.003	-.014	.058	-.245	-.482	-.022	.780
Marlowe-Crowne SD	.293	-.182	.543	.007	.245	-.009	-.271	.071	.252	.615

% of explained variance within method

Self scales	32.90	9.11	3.86	7.38	10.71	4.08	11.37	9.58	11.01
MMPI	23.14	7.40	24.88	7.97	3.40	8.37	6.28	16.75	1.81

Note: Total percentage of variance accounted for 60.95 and 65.27 for the self-concept and MMPI scales, respectively. The boxes indicate those factors marked by one or more sets of self-concept measures.

has a loading of .832. Those self-concept scales implying direct self-evaluation also all have principal-component loadings ⩾.65. Thus, social desirability (which Ford and Meisels, [1965], have shown to be equivalent to the Osgood "evaluation" dimension) may be regarded as marking a higher order factor of self-evaluation, a general dimension that partially subsumes several discrete self-concept dimensions. This view is in accord with a suggestion by Lecky [1945], who argued that item responses (and other behaviors) show consistency because "all of an individual's values are organized into a single system, the preservation of whose integrity is essential. The nucleus of the system, around which the rest of the system revolves, is the individual's valuation of himself" [p. 109].

The elimination of overlapping items leads to a shortening of all MMPI scales, with a consequent reduction in reliable variance. Further, the elimination of item overlap inevitably decreases the amount of variance common to different scales. It is therefore of interest to note that factoring the *full* MMPI scales, with self-concept scales also included, results in a set of factors highly similar to those found for the abbreviated scales, generally identified by the same major markers. As might be expected, given their greater length and spuriously shared variance, the factor loadings and the commonalities for the full MMPI scales were generally higher than for the abbreviated scales. When self-concept scales are excluded from the factor analysis, both the abbreviated and full scale solutions emerged with three factors: two factors marked in each case by the Welsh A and R scores and a third dimension marked by loadings on the F and Pa scales.

Discussion

Guilford [1952] has noted three problems with factor analysis of the standard MMPI scales: The standard scales are too few to lead to a good rotational solution, they are factorially complex, and item overlap leads to spuriously shared variance. Acquiescence and other response sets further complicate analysis since their influence is hard to assess independently of scale content. The present study has surmounted these difficulties by eliminating item overlap, by introducing at least two convergent self-concept measures for every anticipated dimension, and by using self-concept measures that have been shown to be reasonably free of response-set variance. The inclusion of replicated self-concept markers has led to an unusually differentiated factor solution for the MMPI scales. Most factor studies of the MMPI have isolated two main factors, A and R, often with one or two additional and minor factors that disappeared on replication. Such findings are reported both with normal and with deviant respondents. In contrast, the present solution emerges with nine factors, seven of which are clearly marked by repeated self-concept measures, so that interpretation is less problematic. As has long been known, clear factors cannot be expected to emerge unless several measures clearly tap each factor. The greater number of factors here obtained results entirely from the inclusion of the self-concept scales that provide clear and replicated markers for the factor space. The results show that the MMPI scales are indeed factorially complex and so intertwined in their complexity that a differentiated solution is unlikely when they are analyzed alone. The problem of item overlap among scales seems less important since similar solutions and loadings emerged with the full and the abbreviated scales.

The self-concept hypothesis suggests that the shared variance among MMPI scales is attributable to a number of discrete dimensions of self-presentation. The findings reported here are generally supportive of the hypothesis. About two-thirds of the shared MMPI variance is assigned to one or another self-concept dimension. Acquiescence response set and/or the particular response set tapped by the Crowne-Marlowe scale may account for about one-quarter of the shared MMPI variance.

It is possible, of course, that Factor III is more than a methods-set dimension—it may also reflect additional self-concepts not measured in this study. To examine this possibility, factor scores were computed for each respondent on Factor III; these scores were then correlated (point biserial) with 129 items from eight abbreviated MMPI scales. Table 3 shows the 11 statements with correlations $\geqslant .45$. These items generally seem to communicate a self-concept dimension describable as "difficulty in coping with the ordinary demands of life." Thus, a self-concept interpretation of the so-called method-set factor is not entirely ruled out. Although the known self-concept factors adequately explain the bulk of systematic variance within the MMPI, further explorations of other self-concept domains may clarify the nature of the remaining variance.

Study 2

In Study 1 we have shown that the inclusion of 24 example-anchored self-concept scales significantly clarified the nature of the MMPI factor space. However, these results were found with a relatively small sample of respondents, all were neuropsychiatric patients, and there was some evidence that additional and untapped self-concept dimensions were also present in the MMPI scales. It seemed useful therefore to replicate the essential features of Study 1, this time testing a larger and more heterogeneous group of respondents and adding several additional self-concept measures. Study 2 provides data on the replicability of the earlier factor solution and tests the possibility that other self-concept dimensions may have contributed to the method-set factor.

Method

Subjects and procedure. The MMPI and two sets of self-concept

Table 3. Marker Items for the Presumed Method-Set Factor

Item	MMPI item	r_{xy}
I have sometimes felt that diffi-culties were piling up so high that I could not overcome them. (F)	397	.587
At periods my mind seems to work more slowly than usual. (F)	374	.524
I almost never dream. (F)	329	−.521
I am apt to pass up something I want to do because others feel I am not going about it in the right way. (T)	443	−.518
Sometimes some unimportant thought will run through my mind and bother me for days. (T)	359	−.513
I must admit that I have at times been worried beyond reason over something that really did not matter. (T)	499	−.485
My plans have frequently seemed so full of difficulties that I have had to give them up. (T)	389	−.484
Even when I am with people I feel lonely much of the time. (T)	305	−.460
I have had periods of days, weeks, or months when I couldn't take care of things because I couldn't get going. (T)	41	−.482
Once in a while I think of things too bad to talk about. (F)	15	.460
At times I have very much wanted to leave home. (T)	308	−.460

scales were administered to 201 subjects. Included were 95 neuro-psychiatric patients at Topeka State and Topeka Veterans Adminis-tration hospitals; 47 participants in Veterans Administration and state alcoholism treatment programs; and 59 students at Washburn Uni-versity, Topeka. The sample was predominately Caucasian (92%) and predominantly male. In the clinical settings, testing was done over a 2-day period, with the final set of self-concept scales administered on the second day. Students were tested in single sessions, with the MMPI intervening between the two sets of self-concept scales. In all testing, the self-concept scales were presented in counterbalanced order.

Measures. As in Study 1, the MMPI was scored for the standard clinical and validity scales, for the Welsh A and R factor scales, and for the Edwards Social Desirability Scale. The clinical and validity scales for the MMPI were scored also from keys eliminating item overlap [Adams and Horn, 1965].

The self-concept scales included the 24 measures reported in Study 1 plus the 12 additional scales listed in Table 4. (There are two

Table 4. Self-Concept Rating Scales: 25-34

	Scale Question	Polar Anchors	Sample Item(s)
25, 26	How restless or excited do you become?	Restless, enthusiastic, easily excited vs. placid and calm.	"When I get bored I like to stir up some excite-ment."
27, 28	How much is your life disrupted by fears?	Strong tendency to fear-fulness, fears interfere much with life vs. rela-tive lack of fears, fears don't interfere with life.	"I have so many fears that I dread leaving my house." "The sight of blood bothers me."
29, 30	How much do you feel you are guided by the usual standards of right and wrong?	Not guided by usual stan-dards of right and wrong vs. guided by usual standards of right and wrong.	"I don't blame a person for taking advantage of someone who lays himself open to it."
31, 32	How do you feel about your life as it is now?	Feel on top of life vs. feel overwhelmed by life.	"I can usually handle the problems I meet." "Sometimes I feel so bad that everything goes to pot."
33, 34	How have people and life treated you?	Treated badly vs. treated well.	"I've found that people are only interested in you for what they can get."

numbers for each scale question because each of 12 domains was tapped by two different but comparable rating scales.) It was hoped that the added scales would tap such self-concept variance as existed within the method-set factor.

Analysis. As in Study 1, scores from all scales were intercorrelated, and four blocks of correlations were factor analyzed. The four blocks consisted of correlations between (a) standard MMPI scales only, (b) abbreviated MMPI scales only, (c) standard MMPI scales and self-concept scales, and (d) abbreviated MMPI scales and self-concept scales. As stated before, these procedures allow a comparison of factor solutions with and without item overlap and with and without independent self-concept information.

Factor-analytic methods were as reported previously: A principal-components analysis (with R^2 in the diagonals) was followed by varimax rotation. All factors with eigenvalues $\geqslant 1$ were rotated. Three factors were rotated for the matrices including only MMPI scales; and nine factors were rotated for the combined MMPI and self-concept scales.

As in Study 1, we focus here on the factor results from the block of abbreviated MMPI scales and self-concept markers, briefly citing other results for comparative purposes.

Results

Table 5 presents the factor loadings when nonoverlapping MMPI scales and self-concept scales are analyzed jointly. It will be noted that seven of the factors are marked by one or more sets of replicated self-concept scales; one factor (III) is marked only by three MMPI scales; and the final factor (VII) is marked by five MMPI scales and minimally by a single-concept scale.

In spite of the very different sample of subjects, and in spite of the incorporation of new scales, findings are similar to those of Study 1. As summarized in Table 6, five factors are clearly replicated; two factors are partially replicated; and two factors are newly emergent. Of the two new factors, one (Factor VII) replaces a previously uninterpretable factor and the other (Factor VI) incorporates additional variance provided by new self-concept scales.

It should be noted that contrary to expectation increasing situational heterogeneity among respondents did not increase the variance of scale scores nor the level of correlations—in fact, the opposite effect occurred.

Our anticipation that the new self-concept scales would reduce the MMPI variance attributable to the method-set factor was disappoint-

Table 5. Rotated Factor Loadings, h² Values, and Variance Components of an Extended Set of Self-Concept Measures and Nonoverlapping MMPI Scales: Study 2. (N = 201)

Scale	I	II	III	IV	V	VI	VII	VIII	IX	h²
SELF-CONCEPT										
Self-Confidence (1)	.666	-.061	.030	.165	.027	-.086	.098	.136	.072	.517
Self-Confidence (2)	.609	-.054	.000	-.052	.179	.039	-.144	-.035	.090	.440
Thoughts (1)	.735	-.083	-.039	.059	.077	.034	.032	.026	-.011	.561
Thoughts (2)	.730	-.195	-.010	.015	-.030	-.012	-.041	-.124	.040	.591
Health (1)	.424	-.126	.052	-.037	.001	-.086	.019	-.492	-.105	.460
Health (2)	.345	.072	.000	.001	-.135	-.133	-.174	-.526	.068	.472
Anxious (1)	-.600	.187	-.268	-.111	-.031	.097	-.054	.094	.006	.501
Anxious (2)	-.600	.119	-.092	-.022	-.042	.310	.040	.066	-.034	.488
Family (1)	-.192	.614	-.131	-.025	.031	.036	.046	-.190	.024	.473
Family (2)	-.072	.525	.042	-.039	.022	.199	.088	-.109	-.176	.375
Mental Problems (1)	-.414	.242	.012	-.270	-.073	.349	.248	.055	.084	.502
Mental Problems (2)	-.474	.212	-.212	-.143	-.015	.343	.371	.065	.154	.618
Conscientious (1)	.061	-.091	.007	-.020	.108	.039	-.009	.013	.503	.279
Conscientious (2)	.159	-.264	-.073	.041	.055	-.123	-.029	-.184	.352	.279
Anger (1)	-.144	.259	-.199	-.001	-.038	.502	.129	-.118	-.104	.422
Anger (2)	-.035	.101	.037	-.003	.046	.480	.073	.044	-.301	.344
Religious (1)	.028	.090	-.089	-.023	.741	-.052	.002	.067	.109	.585
Religious (2)	.079	-.087	.002	-.143	.738	.028	.075	.081	.074	.597
Cheerful (1)	.720	-.043	.072	.000	-.073	-.158	-.063	-.121	.137	.594
Cheerful (2)	.653	-.029	.045	-.102	.028	-.119	-.111	-.147	.109	.500

Table 5. (continued)

| | Factor | | | | | | | | | |
Scale	I	II	III	IV	V	VI	VII	VIII	IX	h²
Comfort (1)	.661	−.039	−.035	−.120	.003	.107	−.274	.093	.076	.555
Comfort (2)	.632	−.055	−.046	−.058	−.001	−.080	−.218	−.117	.012	.476
MF (1)	.079	−.086	.114	.734	−.060	.078	−.061	−.014	−.027	.580
MF (2)	.110	.022	−.112	.464	−.041	.238	.102	−.212	.065	.359
Restless (1)	−.055	.178	.011	−.170	−.104	.217	.346	−.317	−.124	.357
Restless (2)	−.075	.184	−.089	.011	−.148	.153	.272	−.271	−.116	.253
Fears (1)	−.469	.098	−.200	−.119	.069	.093	.252	.066	.085	.372
Fears (2)	−.412	.167	−.217	−.130	.018	.295	.337	−.053	.254	.530
Standards (1)	−.058	.560	−.070	−.006	−.156	.270	.086	.185	−.014	.507
Standards (2)	−.045	.145	−.006	.069	−.135	.646	.089	.146	.031	.494
Feelings re Life (1)	.696	−.051	−.014	−.015	−.119	−.025	−.015	−.076	.220	.557
Feelings re Life (2)	.714	−.123	−.025	−.030	.002	−.217	−.057	−.213	.094	.631
Life Treated (1)	−.200	.490	−.003	−.017	.096	.371	.167	.172	.126	.501
Life Treated (2)	−.308	.325	−.091	.085	.054	.486	.073	.021	.149	.483
Strong Temper (1)	−.335	.338	.120	.022	.130	.319	.112	−.061	−.345	.495
Strong Temper (2)	−.255	.080	−.049	.197	.244	.474	.123	−.073	−.314	.516

MMPI

L	.183	−.018	.249	.124	.106	−.041	.119	.126	.544	.450
F	−.331	.397	−.088	.064	.026	.208	.639	.113	−.001	.744
K	.224	−.153	.662	.030	−.114	−.060	.017	.002	.117	.544
Hs	−.521	.169	−.163	.059	.129	.194	.302	.508	−.029	.734
D	−.678	.064	−.024	−.065	−.211	.155	.144	.086	.021	.565
Hy	−.212	−.284	.271	−.218	−.034	.001	.300	.089	.289	.429
Pd	−.405	.525	−.115	.049	.076	.093	.200	.001	−.229	.599
Mf 1	−.525	.155	−.324	−.321	−.040	.075	.207	−.127	−.264	.644
Mf 3	.166	−.458	.411	−.052	.040	−.087	−.084	−.243	.130	.501
Mf 4	.123	−.050	−.196	−.490	.181	−.013	.099	−.057	−.074	.347
Mf 5	−.057	−.030	.229	−.610	−.057	.109	.038	−.188	.092	.489
Pa	−.120	−.016	.228	−.045	.173	.087	.532	.036	.143	.410
Pt	−.661	.253	−.244	−.146	.032	.137	.437	.115	−.179	.837
Sc	−.479	.281	−.128	−.092	.005	.199	.620	.107	−.058	.771
Ma	−.467	.212	−.150	.062	−.147	.074	.228	.044	−.191	.406
Si	−.798	.111	−.026	−.042	−.042	.056	.087	−.076	−.126	.686
Welsh A	−.670	.091	−.299	−.088	.135	.115	.248	.068	−.231	.706
Welsh R	−.031	.186	.383	−.084	−.012	−.231	.081	−.012	.515	.515
Edwards SD	.636	−.321	.232	.086	−.026	−.129	−.351	−.156	.109	.745

% of explained variance within method

Self scales	40.14	11.54	2.13	6.17	7.99	14.22	5.27	6.48	6.06
MMPI	34.57	10.37	12.83	7.69	1.84	2.72	16.50	4.30	9.19

Note: Total percentage of variance accounted for 47.83 and 58.55 for the self-concept and MMPI scales, respectively. The boxes indicate those factors marked by one or more sets of self-concept measures.

Table 6. Factors, Markers, and Loadings

Factor	Designation	Self-Concept Markers and Loadings		MMPI Markers and Loadings
		Fully Replicated Factors		
I (I)[a]	Confident cheer vs. depressive anxiety and self-doubt	1, 2	Self-confident (.67)(.61)[b]	Hs (−.52)[b] D(−.68)[b]
		3, 4	Thought order (.73)(.73)[b]	Pd (.40) Mf 1 (−.53)[b]
		5	Health (.42)	Pt (−.66)[b] Sc (−.48)[b]
		7, 8	Anxiety (−.60)(−.60)[b]	Ma (−.47) Si (−.80)[b]
		11, 12	Mental problems (−.41)(−.47)[b]	Welsh A (−.67)[b]
		19, 20	Cheer (.72)(.65)[b]	Edwards Social Desirability (.64)[b]
		21, 22	Comfort with people (.66)(.63)[b]	
II (II)[a]	Family Harmony	25, 26	Fears (−.47)(.41)[c]	F (.40) Pd (.53)[b]
		29, 30	Feelings re life (.70)(.71)[c]	
		9, 10	Family satisfaction (.61)(.53)[b]	
IV (IV)[a]	Masculine Interests	29	Standards (.56)[c]	Mf 3 (−.46)
		33	Treatment by life (.49)[c]	
		23, 24	Tough-tender interests (.73)(.46)[b]	Mf 4 (−.49)[b] Mf 5 (−.61)[b]
V (V)[a]	Religious Fundamental	17, 18	Religious (.74)(.74)[b]	—
VIII (VIII)[a]	Physical Health	5, 6	Health (−.49)(−.53)[b]	Hs (.51)[b]

		Partially Replicated Factors	
IX (IX)[a]	Moral virtue	13, 14	Conscientiousness (.50)	L (.54) Welsh A (.51)
(III)[a]			(.35)[b]	
III (III)[a]	Method-set	—		K (.66)[b] Mf 3 (.41)[b] Welsh R (.38)[b]

		New Factors	
VI	Hostility	15, 16	Anger (.50)(.48)	—
		30	Standards (.65)[c]	
		34	Treatment by life (.49)[c]	
		36	Temper (.47)[c]	
VII	?	12	Mental Problems (.37)	F (.64) Mf 5 (.53) Pa (.44) Pt (.62) Edwards Social Desirability (−.35)

[a] Factor number in Study 1.
[b] Replicated factor marker.
[c] New scale.

ed. Instead, the new scales contributed mainly to Factors I and VI. The earlier method-set factor in this solution split into two parts, providing MMPI variance to Factor IX (marked in this and the earlier solution by equivalent self-concept scales of conscientiousness) and to Factor III, a residual method-set dimension.

The amount of variance attributable to each factor is shown in Table 5. As in Study 1, about two-thirds (70.7%) of the explained MMPI variance is attributable to factors marked by equivalent self-concept measures; the remaining variance is attributable to the truncated method-set Factor III and to the uninterpretable Factor VII. As before, factoring the full MMPI scales with self-concept markers produced a highly differentiated factor structure essentially equivalent to that found with the abbreviated scales. Factoring either group of MMPI scales alone resulted in a three-factor solution, with two of the factors being marked by the Welsh A and R factor scales. The Edwards Social Desirability Scale marked the first principal component (.84) in all solutions, as did other scales implying general "self-evaluation."

This replication supports the major conclusions of Study 1. The bulk of shared MMPI variance is attributable to various self-concept dimensions rather than to response set. Some of these self-concepts may be organized by a higher order dimension of self-evaluation. No evidence was found for additional and important self-concept dimensions in the MMPI beyond those extracted previously.

Implications

These two studies suggest that more complexity resides in the MMPI scale scores than has been indicated in prior factor research. The finding of this complexity, and the clarification of its nature, has resulted entirely from the inclusion of direct and very obvious self-rating scales that tap different dimensions of self-concept. About two-thirds of the explained MMPI variance falls within factors defined clearly and unambiguously by such scales, thus lending support to the notion that specific item responses in the MMPI are mainly mediated and organized so as to communicate more abstract concepts of the self.

However, we also found that about 30% of the consistent MMPI variance is not captured by the self-concept scales but is instead spread across several indeterminant factors, the most important being marked by the Marlowe-Crowne Social Desirability Scale, the K scale, and Welsh's Factor R. Although responses to MMPI items may be largely mediated by abstract self-concepts, other processes also appear to be operative. Self-concept scales based on item analyses failed on replication to clarify what these "other processes" might be.

Perhaps a further clue may be found in the research on the Marlowe-Crowne Social Desirability Scale. Persons scoring high on this measure are described as "conforming," "cautious," "persuasible," "amenable to social influence," "other directed" and "conflict avoidant." Leaving aside the deeper dynamics, these characterizations suggest that item responses of high scorers on the Marlowe-Crowne scale may be less influenced by stable and firmly held self-concepts and more influenced by a general quest for approval [Crowne and Marlowe, 1964, pp. 189-191]. In other words, the factor marked by the Marlowe-Crowne scale may capture a particular exception to the self-concept hypothesis.[1]

Apart from this problem, it still remains true that the bulk of MMPI variance appears to reflect a few underlying self-concepts. The MMPI may be using 566 items to get at variables that could be assessed more efficiently—and with much greater conceptual clarity—by using self-rating scales. Discriminant function analysis of the data from Study 2 indicates that the full clinical scales of the MMPI and the example-anchored self-concept scales are both equally effective in distinguishing between normal, alcoholic, and patient subgroups [Taylor, Coyne, and Carithers, 1973]. Thus, the findings reported here may have practical implications for the construction of more cost-effective instruments in survey and screening applications.

Besides these practical implications, the findings may also have implications for other problems in personality psychometrics. The self-concept hypothesis seems applicable to other "personality" inventories besides the MMPI, so an approach similar to the one exemplified here might prove helpful in resolving contradictions between divergent analyses of "personality factors" [e.g., Cattell, 1965; Guilford, 1959]. Another implication lies in test theory. We have elsewhere [Taylor, 1977] provided data showing that the present approach, coupled with elementary notions drawn from self-theory, may clarify some aspects of what Loevinger [1957] has called the "characteristic correlation" of a trait or behavior domain. And since

---

1. Alternatively, the presumed "method-set Factor III may be interpreted as tapping "acquiescence response set." The correlation between MMPI loadings on Factor III and "per cent of scale items keyed false" in the nonoverlapping scales is .758 in the initial study and .782 in the replication ($p \leqslant .01$ for both). This is not necessarily incongruent with the discussion above, since the compliant personality attributes described by Crowne and Marlowe may characterize individuals who respond to scale items in an acquiescent manner. (footnote added, 1979)

(as we have noted earlier in this article) self-concepts may be considered to be abstract categories used by an individual in encoding his or her behavior, the self-concept hypothesis lends support to Mischel's [1968] notion that factor analyzing self-report data does *not* elucidate "underlying dimensions of personality"; rather, such analyses may be expected to elucidate the linguistic categories and structures shared among a set of respondents. This is not necessarily a trivial accomplishment, since one venerable tradition in personality psychology would view "self-concepts"—and thus, self-concept categories—as having an important influence on behavior. In fact, the self-concept hypothesis suggests that the major conceptual problem in personality psychometrics may lie in clarifying the relationships between the more or less stable self-concepts held by the individual and the social behavior that the same individual exhibits in the blooming, buzzing, and ever-changing world in which he lives.

Section III
Special Personality Scales

Parallel to the development of profile patterns and configural rules for guiding inferences to be made from the basic MMPI scales, there has been a competing line of research leading to the construction of additional scales. Although these two lines of test development seem to be quite antithetical, the basic rationale for each is the same. The number of different characteristics that a personologist may wish to try to evaluate or predict by means of a psychometric instrument is very large relative to the number of component scales that any practical multiscale instrument is likely to offer. Each such specific real-world criterion is also likely to reflect both different components of variance and combinations of those variances that are different from those captured in any one general test scale. Therefore, in an effort to approximate the combinations that are needed for the best assessment of any new criterion, the personologist may seek to capture those components of variance (and the optimal combination or pattern of variances) either by combining item answers in a new arrangement (a special scale) or by combining the existing measures of those components in some new configural pattern of basic scale scores (a new interpretive rule). The former method may permit more precise tailoring of the variances to the criterion, and the second usually provides more stable bases for estimating particular variances. A number of the configural and patterning methods employed for special research and clinical purposes have been gathered in Chapter 3 of Dahlstrom, Welsh, and Dahlstrom [1972]. Here,

251

some of the most widely used special clinical and research scales are presented, together with their developmental rationale and derivational data. (See also Graham's recent review of special scales [1977b].)

In this set of scales, each of the major methods of scale construction are represented: intuitive judgments of item content, internal consistency by interitem correlation, and empirical keying against external criteria. As was made clear in the articles in Section I, the primary method of construction of the basic MMPI scales has been reliance upon external criterion separation. In this approach judgments about people and their particular behavioral characteristics are employed to establish criterion groups; the kinds of answers that characterize each criterion group are then found by item analysis. The nature of the item content separating these criterion groups usually has not been given much consideration in locating the items. (See Gynther et al. 1979 in II, 6.) That is, the material the subject is reporting in these item endorsements has not had any necessary bearing upon the characteristics used to separate the criterion groups in the first place. Of greater interest has been whether the new scale does as well in separating new criterion groups formed on the same basis as the original samples.

In the intuitive approach, judges make judgments about items, not people. Here the determination is what the item may be revealing about an individual who answers it in a particular way; all items that the judges think reflect some common attribute are collected together into a judgmentally based scale. Clearly, subsequent research has to be directed to the nature of the non-test correlates of such a scale to appraise the wisdom and insights of the judges in identifying some common feature generating these item answers.

The internal consistency method uses some elements of each of the other approaches: an intuitive formulation of the kinds of items to be studied guides the selection of items to be intercorrelated, but empirical data are gathered about which items actually go together. Intuitive judgments about which items to include in the final scale are generally superseded by statistical evidence on their internal consistency rather than by content considerations. Like the intuitive scales, internal consistency scales do not have any direct relationship to non-test characteristics; the same process of establishing external validity that the judgmental scales require has to be employed in subsequent research work on these internal consistency scales as well.

The first selection in this section reports the work of Janet Taylor Spence on a judgmental measure of manifest anxiety which was developed as part of her dissertation at the University of Iowa. This scale has been incorporated into a very large number of studies under a variety of designations (e.g., Taylor anxiety scale, Iowa manifest anxiety scale (MAS), At, etc.). It also served as the basis for the development of the Duke Anxiety Checklist which has now evolved into the Spielberger State-Trait Anxiety Index (STAI) [Spielberger, Lushene, and McAdoo, 1977]. In some of these applications it is clear that investigators using this anxiety scale were unaware of its origins in the MMPI item pool. The present selection makes clear in what specific ways the item content has been altered for use as a separate measure outside of the regular MMPI administration; most of the applications of the scale, however, have been by means of a supplementary scoring key for use with the MMPI answer sheet. Professor Spence has written a thoughtful and reflective paper [Spence, 1971] on the long line of research that has flowed from the first experimental studies carried out at Iowa in collaboration with Kenneth W. Spence. The scale has also been employed in numerous clinical assessments and research studies [cf. Dahlstrom, Welsh, and Dahlstrom, 1975]. It is important to note that this scale bears strong similarity to Welsh's first factor scale, A [Welsh, 1965], Eichman's scale I [Eichman, 1962], and Block's Alpha factor (see II, 5) as measured by the ER scale.

The second selection reports the empirical derivational and validational work on the ego-strength scale by Frank Barron. Although primary criteria for the item analyses for this measure came from ratings of outcome of brief, psychoanalytically oriented psychotherapy carried out on patients in the psychiatric clinics of the Kaiser Foundation in Oakland, California [Barron and Leary, 1955], the underlying dimension reflected in the scale is conceived to be one with broad personological implications. Thus, the scale is included now in the most routine computerized scoring and interpretive services for the MMPI because of its clinical utility, and it has been employed as a basic independent variable in a large number of experimental laboratory investigations as well. In this selection Barron reports his findings on the Es scale with both patients and normal populations.

The starting point for the development of the repression-sensitization scale, as reported in the third selection, was a configural patterning of basic MMPI scales. In this work, therefore, Donn Byrne proposes substituting a special scale for an interpretive index. This method pits the two major approaches against each other. In support of his new scale, the author reports a number of different research studies, each of which has continued to stand up under cross-validation in the lengthy research literature that has followed his lead. The present selection is the original derivational article based on the long version of the R-S scale. A revised form based on about two-thirds of the items was published by Byrne, Barry, and Nelson [1963]; this is the form of the scale that was included in Appendix I of Dahlstrom, Welsh, and Dahlstrom [1975]. This personality dimension appears to have broad implications for human behavior, in and out of the research laboratory.

In the fourth selection, a lengthy excerpt from a detailed monograph, Jerry Wiggins applies a combination of intuitive and internal consistency methods of scale development to the MMPI item pool. The research supplements the empirical development of scales against external criteria that was conducted originally by the test authors. It also carries forward in much greater detail the research on critical items [cf. Lachar and Wrobel, 1979] in which the primary focus is on the direct communications from test subject to test examiner via MMPI item endorsements. That is, in place of more ambiguous single-item messages, each of the content scale scores provides a summary of the extent of an individual's concerns in a given area of life experience. These scales have both clinical implications [cf. Lachar and Alexander, 1978] and general personological relevance [Wiggins, Goldberg, and Appelbaum, 1971]. (It should be noted in regard to this last reference, however, that the content-scale statistics on the Minnesota adult samples included in this publication are somewhat in error; more accurate values have been provided in Appendix I of Dahlstrom, Welsh, and Dahlstrom, 1975.)

The last selection is an original article prepared for this volume by George S. Welsh, one of the editors of the original volume of *Basic Readings on the MMPI* [1956]. In the present research, a continuation of the investigations reported in Welsh [1975], the author pursues a novel line of study of the relationships of personality characteristics to creative activities. Early research in this area was largely restricted to the search for personality deficiencies which served to prevent people from realizing their full potential. In place of this focus on underachievement and failure, Welsh has identified personality characteristics that are associated with intellective and creative potentialities. In addition, he has employed an unusual scale development method which generates separate MMPI scales for the four quadrants of a two-dimensional surface rather than two linear scales to be used conjointly. Comparable quadrant scales have been developed for other personological instruments (e.g., CPI, ACL, SVIB, and the Welsh Figure Preference Test). This line of research goes a long way toward establishing the generality of the MMPI as a personality instrument as opposed to a narrowly conceived psychiatric or psychopathological test.

The articles in this section came from the following sources: article 1 from J. A. Taylor (Spence). A personality scale of manifest anxiety. *Journal of Abnormal and Social Psychology*, 1953, 48, 285-90; article 2 excerpted from F. Barron. An ego-strength scale which predicts response to psychotherapy. *Journal of Consulting Psychology*, 1953, 17, 327-33, and original material prepared for the first edition of the *Basic Readings on the MMPI* in 1956; article 3 excerpted from D. Byrne. The Repression-Sensitization scale: rationale, reliability, and validity. *Journal of Personality*, 1961, 29, 334-49; article 4 excerpted from J. Wiggins. Substantive dimensions of self-report in the MMPI item pool. *Psychological Monographs*, 1966, 80, 22 (Whole #630); article 5 is an original manuscript prepared by G. S. Welsh for this volume. We are indebted to the authors and to the publishers of the journals for permission to reproduce these articles in this form.

A Personality Scale of Manifest Anxiety

Janet Taylor Spence

A series of recent studies [Lucas, 1952; Peck, 1950; Spence and Taylor, 1951; Taylor, 1951; Taylor and Spence, 1952; Wenar, 1950; Wesley, 1950] has shown that performance in a number of experimental situations, ranging from simple conditioning and reaction time to a "therapy" situation involving experimentally induced stress, is related to the level of anxiety as revealed on a test of manifest anxiety. Most of these investigations were concerned with the role of drive or motivation in performance, drive level being varied by means of selection of subjects on the basis of extreme scores made on an anxiety scale rather than by experimental manipulation (e.g., electric shock, stress-producing instructions, etc.). The use of the anxiety scale in this connection was based on two assumptions: first, that variation in drive level of the individual is related to the level of internal anxiety or emotionality, and second, that the intensity of this anxiety could be ascertained by a paper and pencil test consisting of items describing what have been called overt or manifest symptoms of this state.

Since the scale has proved to be such a useful device in the selection of subjects for experimental purposes, a description of the construction of the test and the normative data that have been accumulated in connection with it may be of interest to other investigators in the field of human motivation.

Development of the Scale

The manifest anxiety scale was originally constructed by Taylor [1951] for use in a study of eyelid conditioning. Approximately 200 items from the Minnesota Multiphasic Personality Inventory were submitted to five clinicians, along with a definition of manifest anxiety that followed Cameron's [1947] description of chronic anxiety reactions. The judges were asked to designate the items indicative of manifest anxiety according to the definition. Sixty-five items on which there was 80 percent agreement or better were selected for the anxiety scale. These 65 statements, supplemented by 135 additional "buffer" items uniformly classified by the judges as nonindicative of anxiety, were administered in group form to 352 students in a course in introductory psychology. The measures ranged from a low anxiety score of one to a high score of 36, with a median of approximately 14. The form of the distribution was slightly skewed in the direction of high anxiety.

Subsequently, the scale went through several modifications [cf. Bechtoldt, 1953]. At present it consists of 50 of the original 65 items that showed a high correlation with the total anxiety scores in the original group tested. Furthermore, the buffer items have been changed so that the total test, which has been lengthened from 200 to 275 items, includes most of the items from the L, K, and F scales of the MMPI and 41 items that represent a rigidity scale developed by Wesley [1950]. The 50 anxiety items are reproduced in Table 1, along with the responses to these items considered as "anxious" and the ordinal numbers of the statements as they appear in the present form of the test.

Table 1. Item Composition of the Manifest Anxiety Scale

MAS #	MMPI #	Item
4	163	I do not tire quickly. (False)
5*	23, 288	I am troubled by attacks of nausea and vomiting. (True)
7*	242	I believe I am no more nervous than most others. (False)
11	190	I have very few headaches. (False)
13*	13, 290	I work under a great deal of tension. (True)
14	335	I cannot keep my mind on one thing. (True)
16	322	I worry over money and business. (True)
18	186	I frequently notice my hand shakes when I try to do something. (True)
24*	528	I blush no more often than others. (False)
25*	14	I have diarrhea once a month or more. (True)
26*	431	I worry quite a bit over possible misfortunes. (True)
27	523	I practically never blush. (False)

Table 1. (continued)

MAS #	MMPI #	Item
33	530	I am often afraid that I am going to blush. (True)
35	31	I have nightmares every few nights. (True)
36	7	My hands and feet are usually warm enough. (False)
37	263	I sweat very easily even on cool days. (True)
38*	191	Sometimes when embarrassed, I break out in a sweat which annoys me greatly. (True)
41*	230	I hardly ever notice my heart pounding and I am seldom short of breath. (False)
43	424	I feel hungry almost all the time. (True)
44*	18	I am very seldom troubled by constipation. (False)
48	125	I have a great deal of stomach trouble. (True)
51*	442	I have had periods in which I lost sleep over worry. (True)
54*	43	My sleep is fitful and disturbed. (True)
56*	241	I dream frequently about things that are best kept to myself. (True)
66	321	I am easily embarrassed. (True)
67*	317, 362	I am more sensitive than most other people. (True)
77*	217	I frequently find myself worrying about something. (True)
82*	67	I wish I could be as happy as others seem to be. (True)
83	407	I am usually calm and not easily upset. (False)
86	158	I cry easily. (True)
87*	337	I feel anxiety about something or someone almost all the time. (True)
94	107	I am happy most of the time. (False)
99	439	It makes me nervous to have to wait. (True)
100*	238	I have periods of such great restlessness that I cannot sit long in a chair. (True)
103	340	Sometimes I become so excited that I find it hard to get to sleep. (True)
107*	397	I have sometimes felt that difficulties were piling up so high that I could not overcome them. (True)
112*	499	I must admit that I have at times been worried beyond reason over something that really did not matter. (True)
117*	287	I have very few fears compared to my friends. (False)
123	352	I have been afraid of things or people that I knew could not hurt me. (True)
136	142	I certainly feel useless at times. (True)
138	32, 328	I find it hard to keep my mind on a task or job. (True)
145* **	371	I am not unusually self-conscious. (False)
152*	361	I am inclined to take things hard. (True)
153*	506	I am a high-strung person. (True)
163*	301	Life is a strain for me much of the time. (True)
164	418	At times I think I am no good at all. (True)
168*	86	I am certainly lacking in self-confidence. (True)
183*	555	I sometimes feel that I am about to go to pieces. (True)
187*	549	I shrink from facing a crisis or difficulty. (True)
190*	264	I am entirely self-confident. (False)

*These statements were rewritten for subsequent revision. (See Table 2.)

**In transcribing from the MMPI, the author inadvertently omitted the word "not" from this item; hence, the item was scored True in the Manifest Anxiety Scale.

Normative Data

Under the innocuous title of *Biographical Inventory*, the test in its present form has been administered to a total of 1971 students in introductory psychology at the State University of Iowa during five successive semesters from September, 1948 to June, 1951. The distribution for this sample is presented in Figure 1. As can be seen by inspection, the distribution shows a slight positive skew, as did the original scale. The fiftieth percentile falls at about 13, the eightieth at about 21, and the twentieth at about 7. The mean of the distribution is 14.56.

Sex Differences

A comparison of the scores of males and females in this total sample revealed that the mean score of the women was somewhat higher. The difference between the two means however was not statistically significant. For this reason, both sexes have been included in a single distribution.

Different Populations

Scores on the scale are also available for samples drawn from

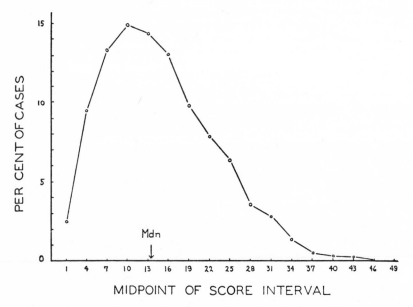

Figure 1. Frequency Polygon Showing Per Cent of the 1971 University Students Receiving the Indicated Scores on the Manifest Anxiety Scale.

somewhat different populations. Distributions for 683 airmen tested at the beginning of basic training at Lackland Air Force Base and for 201 Northwestern University night-school students of introductory psychology show essentially the same form as the group reported above, while the quartiles are in close agreement.

Consistency of Scores

In order to determine the stability of the anxiety scores over time, groups of individuals have been retested on the scale after various intervals. In one instance, the results of retesting 59 students in introductory psychology after a lapse of three weeks yielded a Pearson product-moment coefficient of .89.

In a second test-retest study [cf. Bechtoldt, 1953], the scale was given to 163 students in an advanced undergraduate psychology course who had previously taken the test as introductory students. For 113 of these cases 5 months had elapsed since the first testing, while an interval of 9-17 months had intervened for the remaining 50. The test-retest coefficient was found to be .82 over 5 months and .81 for the longer period. Furthermore, no systematic change, upwards or downwards, was found in these distributions, i.e., the means of each of the three sets of scores remained essentially the same after retesting. Thus, for all groups tested, both the relative position of the individual in the group and his absolute score tended to remain constant over relatively long periods of time.

Relationship of the Biographical Inventory to the MMPI

Since it might be desired to obtain anxiety scores for individuals who have been given the complete MMPI rather than the Biographical Inventory, it is necessary to consider the effects of the different sets of filler items on the 50 anxiety statements. There is some evidence [cf. Bechtoldt, 1953] to suggest that the distribution of anxiety scores given in the form of the MMPI will differ significantly from that obtained from the Biographical Inventory. The Biographical Inventory was administered to 282 freshmen males, and approximately 18 weeks later the group MMPI was given to the same students. The correlation between the two sets of measures, obtained by determining the scores on the 50 anxiety items on each test, was .68. This, it will be noted, is a slightly lower figure than that obtained by test-retest on the Inventory after a comparable length of time. In addition, the forms of the distributions were statistically different, as indicated by a chi-square test of homogeneity. Since the initial scores of this group, obtained from the Biographical Inventory, were similar to those found with other groups, the discrepancy of the results between the Inventory and the MMPI suggests that the radical change in filler items may exert a definite influence on the anxiety scores. Before anxiety scores obtained from the MMPI can be evaluated it would appear to be necessary to have more normative data concerning the scale scores obtained from this form.

Revision of the Scale

A further revision of the scale is now being carried out by the writer. This variation represents an attempt to simplify the vocabulary and sentence structure of some of the anxiety items that appear to be difficult to comprehend, especially for a noncollege population. Toward this end, the 50 anxiety items were first submitted to 15 judges who were instructed to sort them into four piles according to comprehensibility, the first position representing the simplest to understand and the fourth the most difficult. It was found that 28 of the items had a mean scale value of 2.00 or more. These 28 items were selected for revision and rewritten in at least two alternate forms. (In rewriting the items, the Thorndike word count [cf. Thorndike and Lorge, 1941] was consulted. These counts primarily determined substitution of words within an item whenever this was done.) Each set of alternatives was then ranked by a different set of 18 judges, first for ease of understanding and then for faithfulness of meaning to the original statement. For most of the items, the alternative judged to be simplest was also chosen as being closest in meaning to the original item and was therefore selected for the new scale. For those items in which a discrepancy occurred, faithfulness of meaning was chosen over simplicity. However, in every case, the new statement selected for inclusion on the scale was judged simpler than the original. These 28 rewritten items are shown in Table 2.

Relationship between the Old and New Versions of the Scale

To demonstrate the relationship between the old and new versions of the test, both forms were administered to students in introductory psychology at Northwestern University College. A sample was selected from the college population for this purpose since it was thought that this group would show the least confusion in interpreting the original versions of the difficult items and, therefore, better demonstrate the comparability of the two forms than less verbally sophis-

Table 2. Items Rewritten for the Revised Form of
the Manifest Anxiety Scale

MAS #	Item
5	I am often sick to my stomach. (True)
7	I am about as nervous as other people. (False)
13	I work under a great deal of strain. (True)
24	I blush as often as others. (False)
25	I have diarrhea ("the runs") once a month or more. (True)
26	I worry quite a bit over possible troubles. (True)
38	When embarrassed I often break out in a sweat which is very annoying. (True)
41	I do not often notice my heart pounding and I am seldom short of breath. (False)
44	Often my bowels don't move for several days at a time. (True)
51	At times I lose sleep over worry. (True)
54	My sleep is restless and disturbed. (True)
56	I often dream about things I don't like to tell other people. (True)
67	My feelings are hurt easier than most people. (True)
77	I often find myself worrying about something. (True)
82	I wish I could be as happy as others. (True)
87	I feel anxious about something or someone almost all of the time. (True)
100	At times I am so restless that I cannot sit in a chair for very long. (True)
107	I have often felt that I faced so many difficulties I could not overcome them. (True)
112	At times I have been worried beyond reason about something that really did not matter. (True)
117	I do not have as many fears as my friends. (False)
*145	I am more self-conscious than most people. (True)
152	I am the kind of person who takes things hard. (True)
153	I am a very nervous person. (True)
163	Life is often a strain for me. (True)
168	I am not at all confident of myself. (True)
183	At times I feel that I am going to crack up. (True)
187	I don't like to face a difficulty or make an important decision. (True)
190	I am very confident of myself. (False)

*See note in Table 1.

ticated individuals. Scores obtained from 59 students showed a Pearson product-moment correlation of .85 between the old and new versions, the latter being administered three weeks after the initial testing. This figure is quite comparable to the test-retest coefficient found for the previous form of the scale after a similar time interval. Considering only the 28 rewritten items, the correlation becomes .80.

While the correlation coefficient shows the high degree of relationship between the old and revised forms, the question still remains as to whether rewriting the 28 items has reduced the difficulty level of these statements so as to minimize confusion and misinterpretation. In an attempt to determine this, the scores of the 59 students given both versions were analyzed into two components: that for the 28 difficult items and that for the 22 items left intact. For each form, scores on the 28 items were correlated with the remaining 22. It was reasoned that if the original forms of the 28 items were confusing, then the rewritten items, if attempts to simplify were successful, would show a higher correlation with the 22 items left intact than would the original statements. The actual correlations obtained in this manner were .81 for the old version and .83 for the new. Although the difference between the coefficients was in the desired direction, a t test indicated that it was statistically insignificant. However, a significant difference in correlations might be obtained with subjects of lesser educational attainment since misinterpretation of the 28 original items would be more likely to occur with such a group.

Normative Characteristic of the New Scale

To determine further characteristics of the distribution of scores on the new version, 229 students in introductory psychology were given only the revised form of the scale [Ahana, 1952]. It was found that the shape of the distribution and the values of the quartiles did not differ significantly from those obtained with the previous form.

Retest scores are also available for 179 individuals from the sample described above. A product-moment correlation of .88 was found after an intertest interval of four weeks. However, while the position of the individuals in the group tended to remain the same, a downward shift in the absolute scores of the entire distribution was noted from test to retest. The difference between means (14.94 vs. 12.92) was significant at the .01 level of confidence, as indicated by a t test.

Relationship of the Anxiety Scale to Other Measures

The anxiety scale was developed for, and has been used exclusively as, a device for selecting experimental subjects, without regard to the relationship of the scores to more common clinical definitions (e.g., clinical observation). While defining degree of anxiety in terms of the anxiety-scale scores is a perfectly legitimate operational procedure, determining the relationship between this definition and clinical judgments might extend the applicability of both the scale and the experimental results found in the studies utilizing the scale.

In order to determine the relationship between the scale and clinical judgments, it would be necessary to have ratings made by trained observers for a large, randomly selected group of individuals and to correlate these with the anxiety-scale scores. Such an investigation has not yet been carried out. However, some indirect evidence on this point is provided by the anxiety scores of patients undergoing psychiatric treatment [Spence and Taylor, 1953]. The anxiety scale used with these patients is essentially the same as the unrevised Biographical Inventory except that it is being administered in an individual form.

Anxiety scores are available for 103 neurotic and psychotic individuals, drawn from both an in- and outpatient population. As can be seen from Figure 2, the distribution of scores is highly skewed toward the low anxiety end of the scale. The median score is approximately 34, a score equivalent to the 98.8 percentile of the normal subjects shown in Figure 1. Thus the distributions of scores for the patient and the normal group are markedly different.

On the assumption that psychiatric patients will tend to exhibit more manifest anxiety symptoms (as determined by direct observation) than do normal individuals, this difference between the two groups appears to indicate that there is some relationship between the anxiety-scale scores and clinical observation of manifest anxiety.

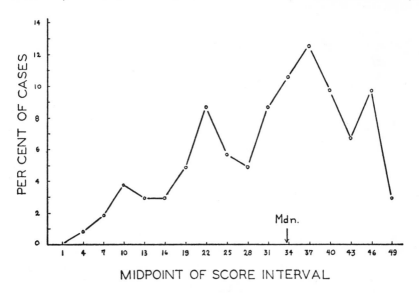

Figure 2. Graph of the Frequency Distribution of Manifest Anxiety Scores
Received by 103 Psychiatric Patients.

Summary

A manifest anxiety scale, consisting of items drawn from the Minnesota Multiphasic Personality Inventory judged by clinicians to be indicative of manifest anxiety, was developed as a device for selecting subjects for experiments in human motivation.

After statistical analysis the original 65-item scale was reduced to the 50 most discriminating statements. These items, supplemented by 225 statements nonindicative of anxiety, are given under the title of the Biographical Inventory. Normative data and test-retest correlations found with scale scores taken from the Biographical Inventory are presented.

A further revision of the scale was undertaken in which certain items were rewritten in an attempt to simplify their vocabulary and sentence structure. Characteristics of the scores obtained from this revised version were found to be similar to those of the previous form.

In an attempt to determine the relationship between the anxiety-scale scores and manifest anxiety as defined and observed by the clinician, the anxiety scores for groups of normal individuals and psychiatric patients were compared.

The Ego-Strength Scale and Its Correlates

F. Barron

This paper reports the development and cross-validation of a scale which was originally designed to predict the response of psychoneurotic patients to psychotherapy. Consideration of the scale content and its correlates, however, suggests that a somewhat broader psychological interpretation be placed upon it, making it useful as an assessment device in any situation where some estimate of adaptability and personal resourcefulness is wanted. It appears to measure the various aspects of effective personal functioning which are usually subsumed under the term "ego-strength."

The scale consists of 68 items from the MMPI, selected from the total pool of 550 items on the basis of significant correlation with rated improvement in 33 psychoneurotic patients who had been treated for six months in a psychiatric clinic. The test responses of the patients were obtained before psychotherapy began, so that the scale, so far as logic of construction is concerned, is designed to predict whether or not after about six months of therapy the patient will have improved.

The sample of 33 patients was divided into two groups: 17 patients who were judged to have clearly improved, and 16 patients who were judged to be unimproved. Although the sample is small, the cases were intensively studied, and two skilled judges who had thoroughly acquainted themselves with the course of the therapy (although not themselves involved in it otherwise) were in considerable agreement (r of .91) in their independent ratings of degree of improvement. While one would not ordinarily base scale development on a sample of this size, it was reasoned here that a small number of well-studied cases who were classified with high reliability, and, as collateral evidence indicated [Barron, 1950], with high accuracy as well, would serve better than the practical alternative, which was to get a large sample in which the therapist's rating of outcome was accepted uncritically.

When the improved and unimproved groups were scored on this 68-item scale, the mean of the improved group proved to be 52.7, that of the unimproved group 29.1, a difference which is significant well beyond the .01 level (t of 10.3). The odd-even reliability of the scale in a clinic population of 126 patients is .76. Test-retest reliability after three months in a sample of 30 cases is .72.

The 68 items of the scale are presented in Table 1, arranged in groups according to the kinds of psychological homogeneities which, in the judgment of the writer, are involved in the item content. The direction of the response for improved cases is given in parentheses after each item. The item numbering is taken from the booklet form of the MMPI.

The pretherapy characteristics of patients who improve in therapy, as compared with those who do not improve, might be summarized as follows:

Improved: (a) good physical functioning; (b) spontaneity, ability to share emotional experiences; (c) conventional church membership, but nonfundamentalist and undogmatic in religious beliefs; (d) permissive morality; (e) good contact with reality; (f) feelings of personal adequacy and vitality; (g) physical courage and lack of fear.

Unimproved: (a) many and chronic physical ailments; (b) broodiness, inhibition, a strong need for emotional seclusion, worrisomeness; (c) intense religious experiences, belief in prayer, miracles, the Bible; (d) repressive and punitive morality; (e) dissociation and ego-alienation; (f) confusion, submissiveness, chronic fatigue; (g) phobias and infantile anxieties.

From an inspection of these differences, one might easily be led to envy the mental salubrity of psychoneurotic patients who are about to improve. Their actual mental distress, however, has been detailed in case material presented in two previous reports [Barron, 1950, 1953b], and will not be repeated here. What the group comparison really reveals, of course, is the *dimension* on which the improved and unimproved groups differed. Had the improved patients been compared with an exceptionally healthy nonclinic group of subjects, the same items might well have emerged as descriptive of the difference between the groups, but with the characteristic responses of the improved patients being exactly opposite to those listed above. In other words, the nature of the criterion behavior determines the nature of the dimension which the item analysis will reveal, but the question of the strength of that variable in the criterion groups must be answered separately.

In this case, it is suggested that what is being measured is a general factor of capacity for personality integration, or ego-strength. The greater vividness of psychopathology often tends to obscure the ego-synthetic or constructive forces in the behavior of a psychologically disturbed individual, so that a prognostic evaluation is generally more difficult to make than a diagnostic evaluation. Nevertheless, in spite of the saliency of psychopathology in the clinical picture, it may be presumed that the patient has certain latent strengths which will gradually show themselves, particularly as the psychological crisis which brings him to therapy subsides. What the item content of the prediction scale seems to indicate is that these strengths are of the sort that are generally ascribed to a well-functioning ego, and that it is latent ego-strength which is the most important determinant (within the patient) of response to brief psychotherapy.

Such an interpretation would, of course, have relatively little warrant without supporting evidence from other samples. The obvious next step is to inquire into the relation of the scale to other measures in new populations. Support for this interpretation can be found in the results obtained in a number of different studies carried out either at the Institute of Personality Assessment and Research (IPAR) at the University of California, Berkeley, or at the Langley-Porter Neuropsychiatric Institute in San Francisco.

Correlates of the Prediction Scale

In this further inquiry, one clinic sample and two nonclinic samples were studied. The clinic sample consisted of 77 women and 50 men who were seen for diagnostic studies on the psychology service at the Langley-Porter Clinic during a given term of work. The nonclinic samples consisted of 160 male air force officers and 40 male graduate students.

The first step was to obtain adjective descriptions, by objective and skilled observers, of high and low scorers on the prediction scale. This was made possible by administering the MMPI to graduate students who were participating in intensive three-day psychological assessments being conducted at the Institute of Personality Assess-

Table 1. Item Composition of the Ego-Strength Scale

MMPI #	Item

Physical functioning and physiological stability.

153	During the past few years I have been well most of the time. (True)
51	I am in just as good physical health as most of my friends. (True)
174	I have never had a fainting spell. (True)
189	I feel weak all over much of the time. (False)
187	My hands have not become clumsy or awkward. (True)
34	I have a cough most of the time. (False)
2	I have a good appetite. (True)
14	I have diarrhea once a month or more. (False)
341	At times I hear so well it bothers me. (False)
36	I seldom worry about my health. (True)
43	My sleep is fitful and disturbed. (False)

Psychasthenia and seclusiveness.

384	I feel unable to tell anyone all about myself. (False)
489	I feel sympathetic towards people who tend to hang on to their griefs and troubles. (False)
236	I brood a great deal. (False)
217	I frequently find myself worrying about something. (False)
100	I have met problems so full of possibilities that I have been unable to make up my mind about them. (False)
234	I get mad easily and then get over it soon. (True)
270	When I leave home, I do not worry about whether the door is locked and the windows closed. (True)
359	Sometimes some unimportant thought will run through my mind and bother me for days. (False)
344	Often I cross the street in order not to meet someone I see. (False)
241	I dream frequently about things that are best kept to myself. (False)

Attitudes toward religion.

95	I go to church almost every week. (True)
488	I pray several times every week. (False)
483	Christ performed miracles such as changing water into wine. (False)
58	Everything is turning out just like the prophets of the Bible said it would. (False)
420	I have had some very unusual religious experiences. (False)
209	I believe my sins are unpardonable. (False)

Moral posture.

410	I would certainly enjoy beating a crook at his own game. (True)
181	When I get bored, I like to stir up some excitement. (True)
94	I do many things which I regret afterwards (I regret things more or more often than others seem to). (False)
253	I can be friendly with people who do things which I consider wrong. (True)
109	Some people are so bossy that I feel like doing the opposite of what they request, even though I know they are right. (True)
208	I like to flirt. (True)
430	I am attracted by members of the opposite sex. (True)

Table 1. (continued)

MMPI #	Item
548	I never attend a sexy show if I can avoid it. (False)
231	I like to talk about sex. (True)
378	I do not like to see women smoke. (False)
355	Sometimes I enjoy hurting persons I love. (True)

Sense of reality.

33	I have had very peculiar and strange experiences. (False)
349	I have strange and peculiar thoughts. (False)
251	I have had blank spells in which my activities were interrupted and I did not know what was going on around me. (False)
48	When I am with people, I am bothered by hearing very queer things. (False)
22	At times I have fits of laughing and crying that I cannot control. (False)
192	I have had no difficulty in keeping my balance in walking. (True)
62	Parts of my body often have feelings like burning, tingling, crawling, or like "going to sleep." (False)
541	My skin seems to be unusually sensitive to touch. (False)

Personal adequacy, ability to cope.

389	My plans have frequently seemed so full of difficulties that I have had to give them up. (False)
82	I am easily downed in an argument. (False)
32	I find it hard to keep my mind on a task or job. (False)
244	My way of doing things is apt to be misunderstood by others. (False)
555	I sometimes feel that I am about to go to pieces. (False)
544	I feel tired a good deal of the time. (False)
261	If I were an artist, I would like to draw flowers. (False)
554	If I were an artist, I would like to draw children. (False)
132	I like collecting flowers or growing house plants. (False)
140	I like to cook. (False)
380	When someone says silly or ignorant things about something I know, I try to set him right. (True)

Phobias, infantile anxieties.

367	I am not afraid of fire. (True)
525	I am made nervous by certain animals. (False)
510	Dirt frightens or disgusts me. (False)
494	I am afraid of finding myself in a closet or small closed place. (False)
559	I have often been frightened in the middle of the night. (False)

Miscellaneous.

221	I like science. (True)
513	I think Lincoln was greater than Washington. (True)
561	I very much like horseback riding. (False)
458	The man who had most to do with me when I was a child (such as my father, stepfather, etc.) was very strict with me. (True)
421	One or more members of my family is very nervous. (True)
515	In my home we have always had the ordinary necessities (such as enough food, clothing, etc.). (True)

ment and Research, University of California, Berkeley. Following the assessment periods, the staff members of the Institute filled out an adjective check list with the purpose of describing each one of the subjects in the assessment, on the basis of the subject's socially observable behavior in situational procedures, interviews, and informal social interaction. A composite staff impression was thus assembled.

The 10 highest and 10 lowest scorers on the psychotherapy prediction scale were then compared by item-analyzing the composite adjective list for the two groups. The adjectives which showed a statistically significant difference (.05 level) between high and low scorers are listed below. (The staff observers were, of course, in ignorance of the test scores of the subjects.) The adjectives checked more frequently about high-scoring subjects were: alert, adventurous, determined, independent, initiative, outspoken, persistent, reliable, resourceful, responsible. The adjectives checked more frequently about low-scoring subjects were: affected, dependent, effeminate, mannerly, mild. The general impression conveyed is of greater resourcefulness, vitality, and self-direction in the high scorers, and effeminacy, inhibition, and affectation in the low scorers. This picture is supported by staff ratings of these same subjects on a number of psychological variables which it was thought could be inferred from social behavior in the assessment setting. The psychotherapy prediction scale correlated significantly with vitality (.38), which was defined simply as "general energy level," and with drive (.41), defined as "persistence, resolution, perseverance, *directed* energy." In addition, the scale showed low but positive correlation with several other variables descriptive of effective functioning. These are self-confidence (.24), poise (.24), and breadth of interest (.25). Significant negative correlations are with submissiveness (−.40), effeminacy (−.34), and intraceptiveness (−.34). As in the adjective descriptions, the high scorers on the scale emerge as more adequate physically, more at ease socially, and somewhat broader culturally. Low-scoring men are effeminate, submissive, and inclined to turn inwards rather than to be emotionally outgoing.

The relationship of the prediction scale to intelligence was next investigated. Among the functions of the ego, as described by psychoanalytic writers and summarized by Fenichel [1945], are perceiving, planning, synthesizing, and, in general, bringing the subject into an adaptive relationship to reality. Ego-determined behavior is what we are accustomed to call *intelligent* behavior. Any scale which purports to measure ego-strength should be positively correlated with standardized measures of intelligence.

In the sample on which the scale was developed, its correlation with Wechsler-Bellevue IQ is .44. In the air force officer sample, the scale correlates .36 with total score on the Primary Mental Abilities Test, and .47 with the intellectual efficiency scale of the California Psychological Inventory. In that same sample it correlates .48 with the potential success scale developed at the Institute of Personality Assessment and Research against a criterion consisting of faculty ratings of the probable professional success of the doctoral candidates studied. In the graduate student sample itself, the psychotherapy prediction scale correlates .39 with intelligence as measured by the Miller Analogies Test. Further, in the latter sample it correlates .52 with the intellectual efficiency scale. Thus it relates to general intelligence, as measured by a variety of tests, even in highly restricted ranges of intelligence. Certainly the ego-strength interpretation of the scale is supported.

The scale also is related to tolerance and lack of ethnic prejudice. In the standardization sample it correlates $-.47$ with the ethnocentrism (E) scale of Form 60 of the University of California Public Opinion Study Questionnaire. In the graduate student sample it correlates $-.35$ with the prejudice scale [Gough, 1951] of the MMPI, and $-.46$ with the E scale. Its correlation with the E scale in the air force officer sample is $-.23$, and its correlation with the tolerance scale of the CPI in that sample is .42.

Again, these findings lend some weight to the notion that what is being measured is general excellence of ego-functioning. The authors of *The Authoritarian Personality* [Adorno et al., 1950], in their successful search for the character defects which accompany ethnocentrism, found that high scorers on the E scale show "lack of differentiation of the ego." This is manifested among clinic patients [Levinson, 1950], in "a narrow range of experience, emotionally and intellectually," together with "rigidity and constriction," "stereotyped thinking," and so on. All these things are thus, by inference, negatively related to scores on the psychotherapy prediction scale.

The relationship of the scale to the diagnostic and validity scales of the MMPI was determined in both the graduate student sample and the diagnostic study cases. The results are shown in Table 2. Surprisingly high negative correlations are found with most of the measures of psychopathology, averaging in the neighborhood of $-.60$ with hypochondriasis, depression, hysteria, psychasthenia, and schizophrenia, and around $-.50$ with paranoia in the clinical samples. What this suggests is that the prediction scale is picking up a general factor of psychopathology in the MMPI, reflecting degree of maladjustment or ego-dysfunction irrespective of differential diagnosis. In other words, it is related to general elevation of the profile, regardless of the pattern.

The correlations are, of course, partly a function of overlap of items (generally scored in the reverse direction) between the prediction scale and the diagnostic scales. The amount of net overlap for each scale is shown in Table 3. The very fact of overlap itself testifies to the character of the scale as a measure of general excellence of ego-functioning, manifested in this instance by absence of chronic psychopathology.

The Es scale has been put into T-score form that is comparable to the scores in the standard MMPI profile; see Appendix F in Dahlstrom, Welsh, and Dahlstrom [1972]. The raw score means and standard deviations from a number of samples are presented in Table 4. The values from the clinical samples are quite consistent, with somewhat higher means for the graduate students and the air force officers. It would be justifiable, of course, to determine T scores on the basis of the clinic samples alone, provided that the scale is to be interpreted solely as a psychotherapy prognosis scale for use in an outpatient clinic. In Table 5, a chart is given for conversion of raw scores into T scores when the scale is used only for such prediction purposes rather than as a measure of ego-strength in the general population.

Cross-Validation of the Scale as a Prediction Instrument

The prediction scale was tested on three new samples of psychotherapy patients, in order to see whether it was doing the job for which it was designed. The patients were psychoneurotic, the psychotherapy was brief (very close to six months in all cases), and the clinical setting was similar to that in which the scale was developed. All the patients took the MMPI at the beginning of therapy, and all were rated as to degree of improvement at some date following termination of therapy. The three cross-validating samples are described below:

1. Fifty-three patients who were given psychotherapy because of delayed recovery from injury or physical disease. Ratings of improvement were made by expert judges (who had not taken part in the therapy) on the basis of terminal interviews. At a final rating conference, these 53 patients were ranked in terms of degree of improvement. This sample of patients had been studied some six years earlier by Harris and Christiansen [1946], who showed that patterns of test scores on both the Rorschach and the MMPI were predictive of improvement. The same pretherapy MMPI's were now scored on the

Table 2. Relationship of the Ego-Strength Scale to Clinical and Validity
Scales of the MMPI in Clinic and Student Populations

Scale	Male Clinic Patients (N = 50)	Male Graduate Students (N = 36)	Female Clinic Patients (N = 77)
F	−.49	−.36	−.47
K	.31	.31	.31
Hs	−.62	−.67	−.63
D	−.60	−.53	−.67
Hy	−.39	−.61	−.63
Pd	−.48	−.07	−.34
Mf	−.04	−.43	.07
Pa	−.62	−.07	−.49
Pt	−.71	−.54	−.71
Sc	−.55	−.44	−.64
Ma	−.04	−.33	−.21

Table 3. Item Overlap of the Ego-Strength Scale and MMPI Diagnostic Scales

Scale	Items Scored in Same Direction	Items Scored in Opposite Direction	Net Overlap
Hs	None	2, 43, 51, 62, 153, 189, 192	Seven items, scored opposite
D	58, 241	2, 32, 36, 43, 51, 153, 189, 208, 236, 270	Eight items, scored opposite
Hy	253	2, 32, 43, 51, 109, 153, 174, 189, 192, 234	Nine items, scored opposite
Pd	82	32, 33, 94, 231, 244	Four items, scored opposite
Pa	None	109, 341	Two items, scored opposite
Pt	None	22, 32, 36, 94, 189, 217, 344, 349, 359	Nine items, scored opposite
Sc	None	22, 187, 192, 241, 251, 349	Six items, scored opposite
Ma	109, 181	22, 100, 251	One item, scored opposite

Table 4. Ego-Strength Scale Statistics

Sample	N	Range	Mean	SD
Standardization sample	33	15-62	41.94	13.30
1st cross-validation sample[a]	53	26-58	40.10	7.62
2nd cross-validation sample	52	23-60	41.04	8.18
3rd cross-validation sample	46	22-61	42.06	9.32
Clinic diagnostic cases	127	23-60	41.97	7.36
VA mental hygiene clinic patients	52	22-59	41.79	7.38
IPAR graduate students	40	37-60	50.92	5.62
Air force officers	160	38-60	52.73	4.05

[a]Scores on the abbreviated scale are prorated for length of scale.

prognosis scale. Only 39 items of the 68 could be used, however, as these patients had been given a shortened form of the MMPI, containing only the items which make up the clinical and validity scales of the test. The correlation with terminal rating is .42.

2. Fifty-two patients who had received brief psychotherapy during the preceding five years at the Langley-Porter Clinic. The sample was obtained by asking therapists who had worked at the clinic during that period of time to nominate patients whom they remembered as clear examples of exceptional improvement, complete lack of improvement, and moderate improvement. The latter group consisted of 27 patients, while the two extreme groups numbered 9 and 16 respectively.The degree of relationship between pretherapy prognosis scale scores and this trichotomy, as determined by computation of eta, is .54. The means were as follows: unimproved, 32.75; improved, 43.07; exceptional improvement, 49.66.

3. Forty-six patients who were part of the current patient load on the psychiatric service of a general hospital. All these patients had had approximately six months of psychotherapy at the time the rating was obtained. Ratings were made by the therapists themselves, on a 9-point scale of improvement. The correlation with pretherapy prognosis scale scores is .38.

These correlation coefficients are of about the magnitude that one would expect for a scale which is giving a valid measure of patient variables related to outcome of psychotherapy. It is reasonable that there should remain considerable unaccounted-for variance, quite apart from whatever error variance is contributed by the fallible criterion and predictor measure; for there are many important determinants of outcome of therapy besides the personality of the patient.

Table 5. Conversion Table for Use of Ego-Strength Scale in Clinic Samples

Raw Score	T Score	Raw Score	T Score	Raw Score	T Score	Raw Score	T Score
22	25	34	42	46	57	58	72
23	27	35	43	47	58	59	73
24	29	36	44	48	59	60	74
25	30	37	45	49	60	61	75
26	32	38	47	50	62	62	76
27	33	39	48	51	63	63	78
28	34	40	49	52	64	64	79
29	36	41	50	53	65	65	80
30	37	42	52	54	67	66	82
31	38	43	53	55	68	67	83
32	39	44	54	56	69	68	85
33	40	45	56	57	70		

The personality of the therapist, for example, is also important, and, in addition, there is a subtle interactional factor which results from the combination of a particular patient with a particular therapist, which is not infrequently the crucial determinant of outcome in a given case. Then there are, of course, life-situational variables outside of the therapy, affecting both patient and therapist, individually or jointly. It seems safe to say that no standardized test is likely to achieve any very high order of correlation with therapeutic outcomes. At the same time, the effort to construct measures of the different sources of variance tends to advance the research problem somewhat, and to make new questions answerable. If the scale presented here continues to prove effective upon further investigation, it opens the way to an inquiry into the effect of the therapist's personality, intelligence, and social attitudes upon therapeutic results, with the effect of patient variables held constant. Beyond that question, of course, lies the more difficult problem of measuring interactional effects, and their unique influence on the therapeutic relationship.

Relationship to the Management of Aggression

In the present study, the scale was found to correlate positively with independence of judgment in a group situational test based on the Asch experiment [1950], with resistance to illusion, and with ability to orient oneself in darkness in a situation in which there is not only a minimum of external support but also a deliberately introduced distorting influence (the Witkin rod and frame experiment, 1954). Es was also correlated positively with several tests of social judgment, and negatively with the fascism scale [Adorno et al., 1950]. Thus, the ego-strength scale may be presumed to have sufficient validity and consistency so that the unexpected findings to be described later may properly be considered as requiring explanation in terms of the theory of ego development.

The men who constituted the sample for study in this investigation were 100 United States Air Force officers, of the rank of captain. They were observed for three days in a program of living-in assessment at the Institute of Personality Assessment and Research in Berkeley.

The majority of these men were combat veterans, and many of them had been decorated for valor during World War II. Of the 100, 96 were married, and most of these were fathers as well. In general, the sample was well above average in personal stability, intelligence and physical health. This fact, of course, showed itself on the Es scale:

the average T score for the sample was 63, with a standard deviation of 5.7.

In an effort to achieve a personality description of each subject which would allow room for the expression of clinical inference and which would at the same time be readily amenable to statistical analysis, a set of 76 Q-sort statements descriptive of personal functioning was assembled. These 76 statements were used by each staff member at the conclusion of the three days of living-in assessment to sum up his impressions of each person studied; the statements were sorted on a nine-point scale, the frequencies at each point being such as to make the final distribution conform closely to the normal curve. The objective was to obtain an ordering of the traits according to saliency within the person, rather than to order the persons in relation to one another on a given dimension. These staff observer Q-sorts were then composited for all staff raters (ten in all). It is thus the averaged staff judgments with which the individual subject is finally characterized.

These Q-sort descriptions were of course given without knowledge of the objective test performances of the subjects. No rater knew the Es scores of any of the subjects at the time he did the Q-sort.

A word concerning the method of study may be appropriate here. The distinctive feature of living-in assessment as a research instrument is that it provides a great variety of informal social interaction, in which the psychological staff members sit down to meals with the subjects, participate in a social hour before dinner, and are fairly called participant observers. In addition, considerable emphasis is placed upon situational tests, and also upon interviews, group discussion, improvisations, charades, and the like. Thus the social characteristics of the subjects have much opportunity to manifest themselves, and the raters are in a position to observe significant behavior.

Results with the Q-Sort

The relationship between Es scores and each one of the 76 Q-sort statements was determined. A total of 40 of the 76 statements proved to be correlated to a statistically significant (.05 level) degree with Es. (This was an unusually large number of Q-sort correlates for an MMPI scale in the present study; most of the standard clinical indicators on the MMPI were significantly correlated with only two or three Q-sort items, the average for the entire test being fewer than 5 per scale.)

A Tryon-type cluster analysis of the entire Q-sort item-pool was carried out to discover what communities of variance existed among the items. This cluster analysis is reported elsewhere [Block, 1954].

In listing the 40 Q-sort items correlated with the Es scale, we have grouped variables according to their own intercorrelations; that is, clusters of interrelated items are presented together.

Cluster I. Items Descriptive of General Effectiveness
1. Efficient, capable, able to mobilize resources easily and effectively; not bothered with work inhibitions.
2. Derives personal reward and pleasure from his work; values productive achievement for its own sake.
3. Is self-reliant; independent in judgment; able to think for himself.
4. Is an effective leader.
5. Is counteractive in the face of frustration.
6. Takes the initiative in social relations.
7. Communicates ideas clearly and effectively.
8. Is persuasive; tends to win other people over to his point of view.
9. Is verbally fluent; conversationally facile.

Cluster II. Items Descriptive of Aggressiveness, Power-Orientation, and Disregard of the Rights of Others
1. Takes an ascendant role in his relations with others.
2. Is competitive with his peers; likes to go ahead and to win.
3. Emphasizes success and productive achievement as a means for achieving status, power, and recognition.
4. Is aggressive and hostile in his personal relations.
5. Manipulates people as a means for achieving personal ends; opportunistic; sloughs over the meaning and value of the individual.
6. Is rebellious toward authority figures, rules, and other constraints.
7. Is sarcastic and cynical.

Items in clusters not substantially represented among Es scale correlates
1. Is masculine in his style and manner of behavior.
2. Is active and vigorous.
3. Prefers action to contemplation.
4. Undercontrols his impulses; acts with insufficient thinking and deliberation.

The Q-sort items which have a significant (.05 level) negative association with Es are these:

Cluster III. Items Descriptive of Personal Inferiority, Lack of Inner Resources
1. Lacks social poise and presence; becomes rattled and upset in social situations.
2. Lacks confidence in his own ability.

3. Is unable to make decisions without vacillation, hesitation, or delay.

4. Would become confused, disorganized, and unadaptive under stress.

5. Is suggestible; overly responsive to other people's evaluations rather than his own.

6. Is rigid; inflexible in thought and action.

7. Has a narrow range of interests.

8. Has slow personal tempo; responds, speaks, and moves slowly.

9. Tends not to become involved in things; passively resistant.

10. Is pedantic and fussy about minor things.

Cluster IV. Items Descriptive of Excessive Conformity and Personal Constriction

1. Overcontrols his impulses; is inhibited; needlessly delays or denies himself gratification.

2. With respect to authority, is submissive, compliant, and overly accepting.

3. Conforming; tends to do the things that are prescribed.

4. Tends to side-step troublesome situations; makes concessions to avoid unpleasantness.

5. Is stereotyped and unoriginal in his approach to problems.

6. Is self-abasing; feels unworthy, guilty, humble; given to self-blame.

7. Is pessimistic about his professional future and advancement.

Items in clusters not substantially represented among Es scale correlates

1. Sympathetic; feels for and with other people.

2. Respects others; is permissive and accepting; not judgmental.

3. Is effeminate in his style and manner of behavior.

Discussion of Q-Sort Results

Most of the results from the use of the Q-sort technique are quite consistent with findings from other procedures and from other studies. High scorers on Es, it would seem, are effective and independent people, with easy command over their own resources. They are intelligent, stable, and somewhat original, and they make their presence felt socially. Men who score high are appropriately masculine in their style of behavior. Low scorers, on the other hand, are confused, unadaptive, rigid, submissive, and rather stereotyped and unoriginal; low scorers among men tend to be somewhat effeminate as well.

This much is readily assimilable to the concept of ego-strength as it is generally used by psychologists. The observations which are the central concern of this report, however, point either to inadequacies in the scale or to some theoretical difficulties in relation to the concept itself. The Q-sort items in Cluster II appear to describe certain features, in the characters of at least some high scorers, which are not usually associated with strength of the ego. There is a good deal of aggression, perhaps even unethicality and destructiveness, implied in these items. There are at least some persons among the high scorers who are hostile and competitive, rebellious toward authority, opportunistic and manipulative, and sarcastic and cynical. If one thinks of a strong ego as one which is well integrated with a rational superego, then these persons might be considered to be improperly classified by the scale. Briefly, they appear to be manifesting more egoism than ego-strength.

The essential question here has to do with the existence and the management of aggression and hostility. Broadly speaking, hostility may be turned either inward, against the self, or outward, against objects; in an effective person, theory would hold, it is turned inward, in the service of the superego, to just the extent necessary for easy socialization; and outward, in the service of the ego, to just the extent necessary for the vigorous prosecution of one's own interests in gaining goods and prospering in life. Excesses in either direction would presumably characterize the weak ego; either extreme intropunitiveness or rampant hostility which draws retaliation is an inefficient solution in the management of aggression.

However, there is an economic consideration which must be borne in mind, and which may be crucial in explaining the present finding. Individuals differ in the amount of hostility and aggression which they carry about with them, and which it is the business of the ego to handle effectively. In persons with an excess of hostility, originating perhaps in more than the usual amount of frustration and disharmony in childhood, it might be expected that the question essentially resolves itself into this: will hostility be turned characteristically against the self, with the ego adopting a masochistic position in relation to the superego, or will the hostility be turned characteristically against objects other than the self?

The externally directed aggressiveness which we have observed in some high scorers on Es might then be explained as an economic solution, and a mark of greater rather than less ego-strength, if indeed it can be shown that these persons were subjected in childhood to experiences of frustration and disharmony, more so than what one finds in other high scorers on the scale. Fortunately, there are some data which bear on this hypothesis, and which permit at least a partial check on it. Each person studied had been interviewed for two hours by a psychiatrist concerning his background, with particular attention to childhood history. The interviewer, at the conclusion of the study, then rated all subjects relative to one another, using a nine-point scale, on various psychiatric variables, including one called "pathogenicity of childhood." This was defined as "the presence in childhood of circumstances which commonly produce mental illness or psychological upset." (The interviewers, it should be mentioned, did not see the subjects at any time except during the interview, and knew nothing of objective test performances or of the assessment staff's reactions to the subjects.)

To check the hypothesis that "hostile" high scorers on Es had more pathogenic childhoods, average scores of each subject on the Q-sort items in Cluster II were determined. Then all subjects who had earned T scores of 60 or more on the Es scale were ranked in terms of their Cluster II scores. This group consisted of 61 subjects. The top and bottom third of these (20 in each group, high Cluster II scorers being *more* aggressive and low scorers *less*) were now selected for comparison on life-history background factors, particularly the rating on pathogenicity of childhood. The latter comparison is presented in Table 6.

Considered in relation to the total sample, high scorers on both Es and Cluster II have had more pathogenic childhoods than the average subject, while persons who score high on Es but low on Cluster II have had less than the average amount of difficulty in childhood. The difference is statistically significant when the two groups are compared with one another. The interpretation seems justified that

Table 6. Comparison of High Ego-Strength, High Aggressiveness S's with High Ego-Strength, Low Aggressiveness S's on Ratings of Pathogenicity of Childhood

Item	Subjects High on Es, Low on Aggressiveness (Cluster II)		Subjects High on Es, High on Aggressiveness (Cluster II)
Mean	4.4		5.8
SD	2.11		1.99
F		4.45	
p		<.05	

persons high on ego-strength, who nevertheless manifest considerable hostility toward others, are those who actually have more aggression in themselves to manage as a result of disturbing events in childhood.

Results supporting this interpretation are obtained when specific background information from the life-history interviews is considered. The interviewers, immediately upon the conclusion of each interview, used an "interview check list" to record what they had learned of the subject and his background. The 267 check list items were analyzed for differences between high Es scorers who were *high* and those who were *low* on Q-sort Cluster II. Thirty-three items showed differences significant at the .05 level. An over-all description based on this analysis is given below.

Lows on Cluster II (hostility and aggression) were warmer in relating to the interviewer, were dressed both more comfortably and more inconspicuously, and appeared to be both more masculine and more reserved. Highs were described as more assertive, more self-assured, and more verbose. Highs also appeared more military, and held themselves straighter. As children, the lows were quieter, and tended more to play with other boys. The highs were more aggressive, and their play was described as more rough-and-tumble. The highs expressed negative affect toward their parents, while lows had more positive affect, and were more dutiful as children. The lows were more often described as having had stable homes. The highs, on the other hand, reported much more family friction. Highs describe their mothers more often as practical, while lows describe their mothers as warm and home-making. No differences emerged in the description of the father. In general, however, the lows idealized their parents more. To the lows, religion was personally meaningful and important, and they spoke favorably of it more often than did the highs. Highs had more often been separated or divorced from their wives. Highs also had more frequently had premarital intercourse with their wives.

The over-all picture from the life-history interview would seem to support the generalization that aggressiveness in persons of excellent ego-strength stems from life circumstances marked by relatively greater discord in the home during childhood, and friction in significant personal relations.

Summary and Conclusions

To recapitulate: an MMPI scale was developed for the purpose of predicting response to psychotherapy, and upon inspection of its item content and its personality and intelligence test correlates it was interpreted as being essentially a measure of ego-strength. It is here proposed that the scale be known as the ego-strength scale of the MMPI, and that the conventional abbreviation for it should be Es.

The relationship of the scale scores to therapeutic outcomes in several cross-validating samples led to the conclusion that a significant determinant of personality change in psychotherapy is strength of the ego before therapy begins. Among the characteristics which are collectively referred to as ego-strength are physiological stability and good health, a strong sense of reality, feelings of personal adequacy and vitality, permissive morality, lack of ethnic prejudice, emotional outgoingness and spontaneity, and intelligence.

Since the patients who seek psychotherapy are almost invariably in some sort of psychological difficulty, it must be evident that these characteristics are usually not salient features of the clinical picture at first contact. The evidence suggests, however, that such strengths are latent in the personality, and that they emerge as therapy progresses. By implication, it seems probable that the kind of personal crisis which brings the person of good ego-strength to the clinic is more situation-linked and less characterologically based (i.e., less chronic) than the personal difficulties of the person with poor ego-strength.

The scale should be useful both as a research instrument and as an additional clinical indicator on the MMPI. The present writer would suggest, however, that considerable caution should be exercised in the clinical use of the scale. Certainly it should not serve as the basis for categorical recommendations to treat or not to treat certain patients; the grounds for such action in a clinic should properly involve values as well as facts, and in any event the kind of crude measuring device presented here represents a fairly low order of "fact." Any prognostic assertions made on the basis of this scale should be quite tentative, and probably should be accompanied by a visual image of the kinds of scatter plots which may give rise to correlations in the general neighborhood of .45.

As a research instrument, the scale should prove useful in giving some assessment of the role of "patient variables" in determining the complex outcome which is involved in response to psychotherapy. It may also be of some value in assessing the kind of change that occurs in therapy. One may ask, for example, whether there is actually an enhancement of ego-strength as a consequence of therapy, and get an answer by comparing pretherapy with post-therapy scores on the scale. Or one might inquire whether the therapy itself is causing the change for the better in patients who improve; evidence on the issue might be obtained by setting up a research design which would use as a control group a sample of patients who are matched with the therapy sample in terms both of Es scores and of present need for psycho-therapy, but who differ in that they do not receive psychotherapy.

In addition, the scale may be useful as an assessment device quite apart from the clinical situation. Its correlates with personality vari-ables in normal samples are similar to the pattern of relationships seen in clinic samples, and in general it seems to be measuring construc-tive forces in the personality. Thus it may serve as a predictor in any situation in which an estimate of personal adaptability and resource-fulness is called for. An unexpected finding that some high scorers on the scale were notably aggressive and hostile was explained in terms of the economic management of hostility engendered by disturbing childhood circumstances. The more aggressive subjects who had earned high scores on the scale reported more instability and family friction in their homes during their childhood, and they also expressed more negative feelings toward their parents; the less aggressive high-scoring subjects came of homes marked more by stability and warmth.

The Repression-Sensitization Scale: Rationale, Reliability, and Validity

D. Byrne

For over a decade, work in the area of perceptual defense has gener-ated widespread interest and a deluge of empirical data. Since the Harvard studies in the late forties [Bruner and Postman, 1947a; Bruner and Postman, 1947b; Postman, Bruner, and McGinnies, 1948], articles dealing with this topic have been primarily of three varieties: the demonstration of differential recognition thresholds for matched pairs of neutral and emotionally-toned stimuli, attempts to explain (or explain away) these data, and the investigation of the cor-relates of individual differences in responding to such tachistoscopic tasks. While articles of the first two varieties have been the focus of a good deal of controversy, the third has involved a consistent and steadily growing body of evidence. The relevance of these findings to personality theory and their freedom from the earlier criticisms of work on perceptual defense has periodically been stressed [Eriksen, 1954b; Lazarus, 1954].

Repression-Sensitization as a Behavior Dimension

Though terminology has varied somewhat across experiments, re-sults with many different response measures suggest that individuals fall along a continuum with respect to the characteristic way in which they respond to threatening stimuli. At one extreme of this continu-um are behavior mechanisms of a predominantly avoiding (denying, repressing) type, while at the other extreme are predominantly approaching (intellectualizing, obsessional) behaviors. Research utilizing differential recognition thresholds for emotionally-toned vs. neutral stimulus material has frequently employed the terms represser and sensitizer to describe representatives of the respective ends of this dimension. Individuals in the former category are defined as those exhibiting a relatively elevated threshold for emotional material (defense, disruption) and in the latter as those exhibiting a relatively lowered threshold for such material (vigilance, facilitation).

In several studies, a relationship was found between differential threshold scores and other behavior. Compared with sensitizers, individuals who respond repressively in a perceptual task also tend to be identified as repressers on the basis of case history and interview material [Lazarus, Eriksen, and Fonda, 1951], to be classified by psychiatric personnel as internalizers [Shannon, 1955], to remember successes better than failures in a scrambled-sentence task [Eriksen, 1952a], to forget an anxiety-arousing Blacky picture [Perloe, 1960], to prefer avoidance and forgetting defenses on the Blacky Defense Preference Inquiry [Nelson, 1955], to express less sexuality and hostility on a sentence-completion test [Lazarus et al., 1951], to respond to a sentence-completion test with blocking, avoidance, denial, and clichés [Carpenter, Wiener, and Carpenter, 1956], to give evidence of inhibition and constriction on the Rorschach and a figure-drawing task [Kissin, Gottesfeld, and Dickes, 1957], and to give fewer TAT stories with aggressive themes [Eriksen, 1951]. Negative results were reported by Kurland [1954] who found no relationship between therapist ratings of defense mechanisms and differential threshold scores.

Another series of studies dealing with this behavior dimension has utilized response measures other than threshold determination. In contrast to behavior which could be labeled repressing, sensitizing defenses are suggested by behavior in which individuals tend to recall failures and material associated with painful shock [Lazarus and Longo, 1953], to recall incompleted tasks in a threatening situation and learn affective words as easily as neutral ones [Eriksen, 1952b], to be able to verbalize the pattern of electric shock applied during a learning task and to be able to avoid the punished responses deliberately [Eriksen and Kuethe, 1956], to have a shorter latency for aggressive and succorant words on a word-association test and to accept such concepts on the Rorschach [Eriksen and Lazarus, 1952], to give more emotional words in response to appropriate TAT cards and to give more Rorschach responses [Ullmann, 1958], to respond to a sentence-completion test with admission of inadequacy and failure, rationalization, intellectualization, and humor [Wiener, Carpenter, and Carpenter, 1956], and to be sharpeners rather than levelers in a neutral psychophysical task [Holzman and Gardner, 1959].

An implicit assumption with a personality variable such as repression-sensitization is that individuals are consistent in their defensive reactions to threatening stimuli over a period of time. Attempts to establish intra-individual consistency have met with both success [Stein, 1953] and failure [Spence, 1957]. However, because almost every E devises his own methodology and seldom pauses to investigate the reliability of his measuring devices [Byrne and Holcomb, 1962], negative findings are not as damaging as they might be.

Most of the evidence is positive and indicates that repression-sensitization is a meaningful behavior dimension. A series of hypotheses, involving this dimension both as an independent and as a dependent variable, has emerged from work in this area. In order to further this line of research, it would be helpful to have an easily administered, reliable, valid method by which these defenses could be measured. While several possibilities (including differential perceptual thresholds, Rorschach, TAT, Blacky, sentence completion test, and behavior ratings) have been utilized in the investigations just discussed, an MMPI approach seemed to meet the criteria most effectively.

An MMPI Scale to Measure Repression-Sensitization

MMPI defense indicators. From time to time various scales of the MMPI have been used to measure defenses. Sensitizing behavior has been found to be characteristic of Ss scoring low on K and L [Page and Markowitz, 1955], high on the F minus K index [Ullmann, 1958], low on Hy [Eriksen, 1954a; Mathews and Wertheimer, 1958], low on the Hy denial scale [Carlson, 1954; Gordon, 1957; Gordon, 1959], high on the Hy admission scale [Gordon, 1959], low on the Hy minus Pt index [Eriksen and Davids, 1955; Truax, 1957], high on Pt [Carlson, 1954; Eriksen, 1954a; Eriksen and Browne, 1956; Eriksen and Davids, 1955; Eriksen, Kuethe, and Sullivan, 1958], and high on the MAS [Eriksen and Davids, 1955; Gordon, 1959]. Repressive behavior is indicated by scores which lie in the opposite direction. In addition, a clinical interpretation of the total profile has been successfully used as an index of repression [LaForge, Leary, Naboisek, Coffey, and Freedman, 1954].

The repression-sensitization scale. Altrocchi, Parsons, and Dickoff [1960] reported the use of a defense measure which was made up of a combination of six MMPI scales. Their measure of the repression-sensitization dimension was an index, representing the common theme of many previous measures of the dimension, in which the total of the D plus Pt plus Welsh Anxiety scores was subtracted from the L plus K plus Hy denial total. High positive scores were defined as indicative of repressive behavior while high negative scores were defined as sensitization.

Several potential measurement difficulties arise with this measure because of item overlap among the six MMPI scales which are combined in it. For example, item 32 contributes to D, Pt, and Welsh Anxiety scores, thereby giving it an arbitrary weight of three. More confusing possibilities also arise. For example, item 30 contributes to D *and* to L, K, and Hy denial; thus, it is included in opposing halves of the index with a net weight of two for repression. While such differential item weights could conceivably prove to be the optimum ones, their accidental nature in this instance is clear.

To overcome these possible deficiencies, the author substituted a repression-sensitization scoring system in which each of the items comprising the six scales is scored only once; in addition, all inconsistently scored items were eliminated. In this new scale, high scores indicate sensitization and low scores repression. The items and scoring are given in Table 1.

In order to establish the reliability and validity of this scale for a college population, a questionnaire was designed which contained all 182 items of the six original scales in the order in which they appear in the MMPI. The questionnaire consists of 156 scorable and 26 buffer items.

Reliability and Norms

Coefficient of internal consistency. To determine the split-half reliability of the scale, the test booklet was administered to 133 students (60 males, 73 females) enrolled in introductory psychology courses at the University of Texas. Scores on odd and even items constituted the two halves of the test. The coefficient of internal consistency was found to be .88, corrected by the Brown-Spearman formula.

Coefficient of stability. Another sample of students from the same population was utilized to establish the stability of the score over time. The test was administered to a group of 75 students (37 males, 38 females) and then readministered six weeks later. The coefficient of stability was also found to be .88. These two reliability estimates are of sufficient magnitude to warrant the further use of this scale in research.

Norms. Because the most immediate research contemplated with the test involves the use of college students as Ss, the normative data obtained up to the present time are limited to this group. It is quite unlikely that these norms would be appropriate for other populations such as neuropsychiatric patients. In addition, to the extent that introductory psychology students at the University of Texas represent a special group, the reported figures may be inappropriate for other college populations.

With these limitations in mind, the material presented in Table 2 consists of summary data for the total of 624 Ss to whom the test has been administered. The difference between the mean scores of male and females Ss is not statistically significant.

Concurrent and Construct Validity

The studies described below involve a correlational approach to test validation. Since there is no definitive criterion measure of the repression-sensitization behavior dimension, each of the studies is best conceptualized as relevant to the establishment of concurrent and/or construct validity. The purpose of this research was not to test hypotheses growing out of a theory of defensive behavior. Rather

Table 1. Scoring of the MMPI Items (Group Form) in the
Repression-Sensitization Scale

True

5	6	10	12	15	22	26	32	41	43	45	52	60
67	71	75	76	86	90	93	94	102	104	105	106	109
120	124	129	130	134	135	136	138	141	142	147	148	150
158	159	162	165	170	171	172	180	182	183	189	193	195
201	213	217	225	234	236	238	255	259	265	266	267	278
279	288	289	290	292	301	304	305	316	321	322	336	337
340	342	343	344	345	346	349	351	352	356	357	358	359
360	361	362	374	382	383	384	389	396	397	398	406	411
414	418	431	443	461	465	499	502	511	518	544	555	

False

2	3	8	9	18	36	46	51	57	58	64	80	88
95	96	98	107	122	131	145	152	153	154	155	164	178
191	207	208	233	241	242	248	253	263	270	271	329	353
379												

Note: A revised version of the R-S scale made up of 127 of these items [Byrne, Barry, and Nelson, 1963], together with additional normative data based on Minnesota normal men and women, may be found in Appendix I of Dahlstrom, Welsh, and Dahlstrom [1975].

there was an effort to determine whether or not scores obtained on the R-S scale are (*a*) consistent with scores on an instrument designed to measure a similar behavior dimension and (*b*) related to various response measures in a manner consistent with previously reported indices of repression-sensitization.

Ullmann's Facilitation-Inhibition Scale

Background. Shannon [1955] defined three types of defensive reaction as internalization (avoidance of anxiety by denial), external-ization (avoidance of anxiety by projecting the motivation onto others), and acting-out (avoidance of anxiety by immediate expres-sion of the conflict in verbal or nonverbal behavior). With neuro-psychiatric patients classified according to these definitions, he found a highly significant relationship between defensive behavior as judged by hospital personnel and defensive behavior as measured by a tachis-toscopic task. Internalizers responded to sexual, aggressive, and dependency stimuli with perceptual repression while externalizers and acters-out responded with perceptual sensitization. In subsequent work with Shannon's defense categories, the latter two defensive re-actions are usually grouped together as facilitators in contrast to in-hibitors (internalizers). On the basis of the perceptual differences, inhibition-facilitation appears to correspond with repression-sensiti-zation.

Table 2. Normative Data for Repression-Sensitization Scale

	Frequency Distribution	
	Males	Females
110-119	2	1
100-109	9	2
90-99	31	6
80-89	35	25
70-79	51	39
60-69	72	48
50-59	100	53
40-49	66	40
30-39	26	13
20-29	1	3
10-19	1	—
Mean	63.08	61.80
Standard deviation	17.71	16.20
N	394	230

Following up Shannon's investigation, Ullmann [1958] devised a reliable scale for rating case history records for these types of behavior mechanisms. In order to increase the objectivity of measurement and to obtain a more economical measuring system, he developed [Ullmann, 1962] an empirical MMPI scale to measure facilitation-inhibition. With case history ratings as the criterion, 43 cross-validated MMPI items were found to discriminate patients in the two defense categories and to constitute a reliable test. (See Appendix I in Dahlstrom, Welsh, and Dahlstrom, 1975.)

The origin of Ullmann's scale suggests that it is measuring the same behavior dimension as the R-S scale. Since the two tests are scored in the opposite direction, it is hypothesized that they will be negatively correlated.

Procedure. A total of 64 students (40 males, 24 females) were given the R-S scale and the Facilitation-Inhibition scale several weeks apart.

Results. A difficulty arises in correlating the two sets of scores because both scales utilize MMPI items, and 20 of these are common to both instruments. Thus, simply ascertaining the relationship between the total scores should yield a spuriously high coefficient. On the other hand, removing the common items from both instruments would shorten each, decrease the reliability of measurement, and probably yield a spuriously low correlation. There are also intermediate possibilities in which the overlapping items are removed from one scale and not the other. The results of each of these types of comparison are reported in Table 3. There is a statistically significant negative relationship between scores obtained on the two scales, whether or not the overlapping items are excluded. The hypothesized relationship was confirmed. Ullmann [1962] has carried out a similar correlational study, using a population of 64 male hospitalized patients. He

Table 3. Relationship between Regular and Abridged
Facilitation-Inhibition and Repression-Sensitization Scales

Scales Correlated	r
F-I and R-S	−.76**
F-I* and R-S	−.71**
F-I and R-S*	−.81**
F-I* and R-S*	−.71**

    * Overlapping items omitted.
  ** $p < .01$.

found that the Facilitation-Inhibition scale correlates —.94 with the R-S scale (both scales unabridged). Greater variability in defensive behavior within the hospital group probably accounts for the greater magnitude of the correlation coefficient in Ullmann's study. Using a sample of 132 psychiatric patients, Ullmann also found that 72 of the 156 R-S scale items significantly differentiate facilitators and inhibitors identified on the basis of case history material.

Self-Ideal Discrepancy

Background. The degree of congruency between an individual's description of himself as he is and as he would like to be has frequently been used as a measure of psychological adjustment. However, a person who characteristically utilizes repressive defense mechanisms might be considerably less likely to verbalize negative self descriptions (to himself or to E) than a person whose defenses are characteristically sensitizing. And, on at least one such measuring instrument—Worchel's [1957] Self Activity Inventory—the self-ideal discrepancy score is primarily a function of differences in self descriptions. With a sample of 57 students, the author found that negative self descriptions on the test correlated .74 ($p<.01$) with the discrepancy score while negative ideal-self descriptions correlated —.08 (n.s.). Therefore, defense mechanisms should be expected to influence self scores (and hence discrepancy scores) but not ideal-self scores.

There is some evidence that repressing individuals tend to describe themselves more positively on Leary's Interpersonal Check List [Altrocchi et al., 1960] and in a Q-sort task [Block and Thomas, 1955; Chodorkoff, 1954] than do individuals who utilize sensitizing defenses. On the basis of these studies, it is hypothesized that the R-S scale is positively related to negative self-descriptions, positively related to the degree of discrepancy between descriptions of self and ideal-self, and unrelated to negative ideal-self descriptions.

Procedure. In two independent investigations, students enrolled in introductory psychology courses at the University of Texas were given the R-S scale and Worchel's SAI on different days by different Es. The SAI is a measure of self-ideal discrepancy which consists of 51 statements describing hostile, achievement-oriented, sexual, and dependency behavior. S indicates on a five-point scale the degree to which the statement describes him as he is and the degree to which it describes the sort of person he would like to be. The discrepancy score consists of the total absolute difference between self and ideal ratings for each item. In the first study, Ss consisted of 98 students (48 males, 50 females) for whom only the discrepancy scores from the SAI were available. In the second, Ss consisted of 57 students (37 males, 20 females) for whom self, ideal-self, and discrepancy scores were available.

Results. In the first sample, repression-sensitization correlated .62 ($p<.01$) with self-ideal discrepancy. In the second sample, the R-S scale correlated .55 ($p<.01$) with self-ideal discrepancy, .66 ($p<.01$) with self description, and .25 (n.s.) with ideal-self description. Again, the hypothesized relationships were confirmed.

Sex, Aggression, and Emotionality on the TAT

Background. Eriksen [1951] has argued that the patterns of defensive responses which are elicited by perceptual tasks should be reflected in projective test responses. Using male neuropsychiatric patients, he found that Ss with low recognition thresholds for aggressive stimuli gave more TAT stories with aggression as a main theme than did Ss with high recognition thresholds for such stimuli. Ullmann [1958] made a similar argument with respect to inhibitors and facilitators. Classifying male neuropsychiatric patients on the basis of case history material, he found that facilitators responded to appropriate TAT cards with more emotional words than did inhibitors.

Several assumptions were tentatively made in planning the following investigation. It was assumed that the R-S scale measures a general tendency to approach or avoid threatening stimuli; that sexual, aggressive, and emotional responses represent some degree of threat to almost everyone in our culture; and that individual differences in defensive behavior are sufficiently great in a normal population to yield differences in fantasy productions comparable to those found in hospital populations. If these assumptions are tenable, Ss with high scores on the R-S scale should respond to TAT cards with more sexuality and aggression and with a greater proportion of emotional words than Ss with low scores.

Procedure. From a total group of 213 introductory psychology students whose R-S scores were available, 29 with high scores (78 to 110) and 24 with low scores (18 to 47) were selected. In groups of 2 to 15 they were shown nine TAT cards (20, 12BG, 14, 6GF, 6BM, 18GF, 7BM, 3BM, 13MF) according to Atkinson's [1958, pp. 836-837] administration procedure. Without knowledge of each S's R-S score, the protocols were scored for sexual content

[Mussen and Scodel, 1955], aggressive content [Feshbach, 1955], and the number of emotional words [Ullmann, 1957]. Scoring by two independent judges resulted in correlations of .94, .87, and .998 which indicates high interscorer reliability for each scoring system.

Results. For the three sets of scores, the data were examined for males and females separately to compare sensitizers and repressers. In Table 4 the means and standard deviations are shown. A series of *t* tests were computed in order to compare the two defense groups for each TAT score. Neither the aggression score nor the percentage of emotional words were found to be related to the defense measure. However, the male sensitizers had significantly higher sexual scores than the male repressers ($t = 2.86$, $df = 38$, $p < .01$). Sex scores for the female sensitizers and repressers differed in the same direction, and the magnitude of the difference was slightly greater than for the male Ss. However, the difference was not statistically significant ($t = 1.42$, $df = 11$, $p < .20$). It should be noted that there were only 13 female Ss in contrast to 40 males.

In brief, the hypothesis relating sexual fantasy productions and defenses was partially confirmed; those concerning aggressive fantasy and the use of emotional words were not.

Deviant Response Bias

Background. Berg [1955] has proposed that deviant response patterns (responses which differ from the modal response of the group) constitute a general personality characteristic. Therefore, the tendency to respond deviantly to any stimulus should be related to the tendency to engage in any deviant behavior, including those which we label abnormal. A considerable amount of evidence has been presented to support this contention [e.g., Berg, 1955; Berg, 1959].

Following Berg's lead, Grigg and Thorpe [1960] used Gough's

Table 4. TAT Scores for Sex, Aggression, and Emotional Words

	Males				Females			
	Repressers (N=18)		Sensitizers (N=22)		Repressers (N=6)		Sensitizers (N=7)	
	M	SD	M	SD	M	SD	M	SD
Sex	4.39	3.13	7.91	4.39	1.50	3.57	5.29	5.58
Aggression	1.70	.48	1.89	.61	1.76	.69	1.74	.56
Percentage of Emotional Words	8.88	4.15	9.62	2.30	9.18	1.84	9.77	2.32

Adjective Check List and established modal and deviant responses for university freshmen. They then constructed a scale made up of the 33 most commonly and 39 least commonly checked adjectives. The deviant response score equals the number of the latter words checked plus the number of the former words not checked. It was found that the mean deviant response score of students seeking psychiatric and personal counseling was significantly higher than that of unselected students and those seeking vocational counseling.

If deviant response set on this instrument is a general measure of maladjustment, the R-S scale should be related to it in a curvilinear fashion. However, if defense mechanisms are operative in influencing the checking of adjectives, it would be hypothesized that a positive, linear relationship exists between defense scores and deviant response scores.

Procedure. In two separate investigations, students in introductory psychology courses were given both the R-S scale and the 72-item Adjective Check List. In the first study a group of 50 males and in the second a group of 63 Ss (40 males, 23 females) were given the two tests on separate testing sessions.

Results. In both instances, a positive correlation between the two sets of scores was found with no evidence of curvilinearity. For the first group the correlation was .42 ($p<.01$) and for the second .33 ($p<.01$). The second of the two hypotheses was thus confirmed. There seems to be a small but statistically significant tendency for the most deviant responses to be made by sensitizers and for the most repressive Ss to make modal responses.

Intelligence

Background. In investigating construct validity, the absence of a relationship with a theoretically irrelevant construct can be as important as the presence of predicted relationships. In the case of the repression-sensitization dimension and intelligence, neither theory nor empirical findings would lead to the postulation of a relationship.

Procedure. Two separate studies, using different measures of intelligence, were carried out. In the first, 132 students (60 males, 72 females) were given the R-S scale and the Shipley-Hartford scale. In the second, 26 males were given the R-S scale, and their standard scores (based on a University of Texas freshman population) on a college entrance test were obtained.

Results. In neither study was a relationship found between repression-sensitization and a measure of intellectual ability. Correlation with the Shipley-Hartford was −.15 (n.s.) and with the entrance test scores .25 (n.s.).

Independence of Samples

In this portion of the paper, dealing with validity, eight different studies were reported. It should be noted, however, that it was not possible to secure eight independent samples of Ss. Actually, students were drawn by a variety of Es from three distinct subject pools. In the first, 132 Ss participated in the first IQ study, and 98 of these individuals also took part in the first SAI study. In the second, 50 Ss were drawn for the first deviant-response-bias investigation, and 26 of them also took part in the second IQ study. In the third, 127 Ss participated in the work on the remaining four studies. Of these Ss, 23 participated in only one study (21 for the TAT, and one each for the Ullmann and second deviant-response-bias investigations) while 13 took part in all four. Of the remaining Ss in this pool, in various combinations, three of the tests were given to 27 Ss, and two to 18 Ss.

Even though the use of eight different populations would have been a preferred procedure, it is well to remember that four of the six reported relationships were replicated on independent samples.

Discussion

The body of findings reported here lend support to the propositions that the R-S scale is a reliable measuring instrument and that it is a measure of defense mechanisms as defined by previous work in the area.

Also, some additional problems have been touched upon. Two proposed measures of maladjustment (self-ideal discrepancy and deviant-response bias) were found to be positively related to the repression-sensitization dimension. There appears to be a strong possibility that psychodiagnostic instruments which rely on self-ratings in one form or another tend to identify as maladjusted those who respond to stress with sensitizing mechanisms while overlooking the repressing individuals. An alternate possibility is that scores on the repressing end of this dimension represent optimum adjustment.

The lack of relationship between the defense measure and aggressive and emotional TAT responses points up the difficulty in generalizing across populations as different as hospitalized patients and university freshmen. Perhaps the positive results reported by Eriksen [1951] and Ullmann [1958] with neuropsychiatric patients depended on the degree of anxiety evoked by such cues in emotionally disturbed individuals. The fact that the sexual responses did yield positive results in this study for the male Ss is possibly a function of a greater degree of anxiety arousal by sexual than by aggressive and emotional cues in a college population. In addition, female Ss might well be found to yield similar results if (a) a female E is used to decrease the possible tendency of female sensitizers to suppress sexual responses deliberately and (b) a larger sample is used.

In future work, an attempt will be made to refine the R-S scale in order to increase its reliability as a measuring device. It seems likely that in a college population many of the MMPI items are inappropriate. One approach to increasing the reliability of this instrument will be that of an item analysis in which the goal will be greater homogeneity of the scale. Additional research plans call for a presentation of theoretical and empirical material dealing with (a) the antecedent childhood conditions which result in individual differences in defensive behavior, (b) defensive response tendency as an intervening variable in a number of stimulus-response relationships, and (c) the possibility of bringing about either permanent or temporary changes in defense mechanisms.

Summary

Work in the area of perceptual defense has led to the concept of a behavior dimension comprising psychological defenses ranging from repression to sensitization. Several scales of the MMPI have been found to be related to this dimension, and the present test consists of a combination of six of these scales. In a college population, the coefficient of internal consistency was found to be .88, and the coefficient of stability was also .88. Normative data were presented.

A series of studies were undertaken in order to contribute to the establishment of concurrent and construct validity for the repression-sensitization scale. It was found that the R-S scale is negatively correlated with Ullmann's Facilitation-Inhibition scale; positively correlated with self-ideal discrepancy and with negative self descriptions but unrelated to ideal-self descriptions; negatively correlated with the California F scale; positively related to the expression of sexual responses on the TAT for male Ss only and unrelated to the expression of aggression and emotionality for either sex; positively correlated with deviant-response bias on an Adjective Check List; and unrelated to measures of intellectual ability.

Thus, the R-S scale appears to be a reliable test, and, with minor exceptions, the evidence suggests that it is a measure of defensive behavior.

Content Dimensions in the MMPI

J. Wiggins

The concept of item *content* has enjoyed neither precise specification nor active empirical exploration in the recent history of objective personality assessment. This situation may, in part, be attributed to the general disrepute into which "face validity" has fallen as a validity criterion [APA, 1954; Stagner, 1958] and to the tendency to regard responses to ambiguous items as reflecting "dynamic" aspects of personality. Meehl's now classic empirical manifesto [1945a (see II, 1)] raised the hope that dynamic aspects of personality might be assessed by means of true-false item pools superficially bearing little resemblance to the criterion at hand. A not infrequently encountered corollary of this belief is the superstition that knowledge of the content of an empirical scale may somehow vitiate the mysterious mediating process that links scale scores to empirical criteria.

Jackson and Messick's [1958] influential distinction between content and style in personality assessment was partly motivated by their desire to measure the former class of variables with more precision. Their methodological innovations enabled them to separate, within limits, components of content and style in the MMPI [Jackson and Messick, 1961]. Several studies later, Jackson and Messick's view [1962a (see II, 3)] of content has a wistful tone: "Actually, we are very much concerned with measuring content, but content—like a tarpon being hunted by a spear fisherman at ten fathoms—usually appears somewhat closer, larger, and more easily captured than is actually the case." Without denying the rather poor showing that

300

content made in their studies, it should be noted that their criterion for content demanded interitem consistencies within the MMPI clinical scales that survived the partialing out of two potent sources of content-confounded stylistic variance—"acquiescence" and "social desirability." As will be indicated later, the assessment strategy of contrasted criterion groups [Wiggins, 1962b] that was employed in the development of the MMPI clinical scales cannot be expected to ensure content homogeneity within empirical scales.

The most nihilistic position with respect to personality test item content has been taken by Irwin Berg [1955, 1959, 1961], the originator of the deviation hypothesis. The assessment *strategy* of statistical differentiation between deviant and normative groups has impressed Berg as being so fundamental to personality measurement as to render unimportant the item *content* whereby this differentiation is achieved [Berg, 1959]. In many ways this position is a restatement of the pragmaticism of the empirical movement [Meehl, 1945a] with a *non sequitur* corollary which makes the blindness of blind empiricism a virtue. Berg's main point with respect to content seems to be that any given content may be considered *in principle* to be as effective for a predictive task as any other content and that recourse should be made to empirical evidence as the final arbiter. Berg [1959] is careful to note that this does not mean that "any item is just as good as every other for discriminative purposes" [p. 89]. However, he tends to overstate his case:

> One should be able to construct the MMPI scales from the Strong interest blank and the Strong occupational scales from the MMPI items by using the same technique. Or, for that matter, one should be able to develop the scales of both tests from almost any hodge-podge of a similar number of items. . . . Given enough deviant responses and clean criterion groups, one should be able to duplicate any existing personality, interest, occupational and similar scales without regard to particular item content [Berg, 1955, p. 70].

The basis of the above inference is not clear since Berg is unable to provide even a rudimentary rationale whereby one might be able to predict the suitability of a given content for a given assessment. Similarly, when Berg [1961] states, "The carefully described 26 categories of test item content employed by the MMPI are probably irrelevant for clinical measurement purposes" [p. 361], it is not clear how one might know this in advance of empirical test. One may argue that, *in principle*, alternative and equally effective item pools might be discovered for any given prediction situation, and such a principle cannot be disproved. To prejudge a given item pool requires a theory of content, however, and Berg's contribution to this enterprise has been mainly a negative one [Norman, 1963].

In light of the foregoing discussion it is not surprising that the 26 content categories involved in the original classification of the MMPI item pool have received little attention in the literature [Wiggins and Vollmar, 1959]. The test authors themselves [Hathaway and McKinley, 1940] were reluctant to attribute much significance to either selection or classification of item content, although their aim "that more varied subject matter be included to obtain a wider sampling of behavior of significance to the psychiatrist" seems clearly to have been met. The content categories themselves have not excited the curiosity of many of the authors who have contributed to the nearly 1,000 articles [Dahlstrom and Welsh, 1960] on the MMPI that have since appeared.

Although the academic and professional community has seen fit to ignore or denigrate the content of the MMPI, other segments of our society ("subjects") have been less quiescent [Brayfield, 1965]. Viewed from the other side of the desk, the 566 items of the MMPI appear to represent a massive invasion of privacy. Appeals to the principles of empiricism [Gordon, 1965] serve only to emphasize the insensitivity of the professionals involved, and such appeals hardly justify the use of any particular set of items for a given selection purpose. Attempts to placate the public by removing the more "offensive" items from the MMPI pool [Braaten, 1965; Butcher and Tellegen, 1966 (see IV, 3)] cannot be justified on a scientific basis. In short, a legitimate issue has been raised concerning the content of personality inventory items, and the scientific and professional community has been stirred from an undeserved complacency. The viewpoint that a personality test protocol represents a communication between the subject and the tester (or the institution he represents) has much to commend it, not the least of which is the likelihood that this is the frame of reference adopted by the subject himself.

The present study represents a first step in the direction of clarifying the content of the MMPI item pool. Starting with the original content classifications of Hathaway and McKinley, both psychometric and intuitive procedures were employed in the development of a set of scales designed to be internally consistent, moderately independent, and representative of the major substantive clusters that appeared to exist in the total MMPI item pool.

There have been a number of previous attempts to provide bases for regrouping MMPI items in ways other than that provided by the standard empirical scales. For the most part, these studies have used existing empirical scales as the basis for further regrouping. Homogeneous subgroupings of items within each of the standard empirical scales have been identified on a rational basis by Harris and Lingoes [1955] and on a factor-analytic basis by Comrey [1957a, 1957b, 1957c, 1958a, 1958b, 1958c, 1958d] and Comrey and Marggraff [1958]. Among other things, these studies have indicated that the standard MMPI empirical scales are far from homogeneous in item content and that the dimensionality of the MMPI item pool might be greater than that suggested by factorial studies of the individual scales [Lingoes, 1960]. It is important to note, however, that the substantive dimensions which emerged in these studies are dimensions which are defined in relation to the original empirical scales. These clusterings are based on only a portion of the total MMPI and represent subclusters of content "filtered through" the strategy of contrasted groups employed in the construction of the original scales. Such clusterings, no doubt, contain meaningful dimensions of item content; but, in addition, they contain variance peculiar to all dimensions along which the originally contrasted normal and psychiatric groups differed [Wiggins, 1962b].

Attempts at more efficient measurement through factorially derived scales have also been conducted within the limited context of the original empirical scales. Welsh [1956] cluster-analyzed nonoverlapping clinical scales to obtain markers for his item-analytic procedures that yielded the well-known A and R scales. Similarly, Eichman [1961, 1962] used the results of a factor analysis of clinical scales to derive his factor scales. Although working on the item level, Mees [1959] employed only 119 items selected from the standard clinical scales in developing his item factor scales. The fact that only subsets of items defined by the clinical scales were employed in these factorial studies probably does not seriously detract from their goal of more efficient measurement. Factor scales for the MMPI can be developed from almost any subsample of items [Wiggins and Lovell, 1965] and possibly from just a few direct statements [Peterson, 1965]. Unfortunately, the factorial homogeneity of MMPI items has made the test particularly vulnerable to interpretations in which stylistic [Edwards and Diers, 1962; Jackson and Messick, 1961; Messick and Jackson, 1961] and method [Wiggins and Lovell, 1965] components are involved or contaminated with substantive components. The extent of this contamination cannot be fully assessed until a serious effort has been made to illuminate the substantive dimensions of the total item pool rather than simply that portion of it which is most responsive to the strategy of contrasted groups.

Original Content Categories

In selecting items for possible inclusion in the final version of the MMPI, the "universe of content" [Loevinger, 1957] was deemed to be "behaviors of significance to the psychiatrist" [Hathaway and Mc-Kinley, 1940; see I, 1]. With this in mind, "the items were supplied from several psychiatric examination direction forms, from various textbooks of psychiatry, from certain of the directions for case taking in medicine and neurology, and from the earlier published scales of personal and social attitudes" [Hathaway and McKinley, 1940]. The names of the 26 categories suggested by the test authors as descriptive of item clusters in the MMPI pool are given in Table 1. To these 26 labels have been added phrases that are descriptive of the item content within each category.

Internal Consistency

As a first step in the investigation of the contribution of the original content categories to test variance, each category was considered to be a "scale" composed of n items that could be combined to yield

Table 1. Original Content Categories of the MMPI

Affect-Depressive (32 items): Sadness, despair, pessimism, futility; loneliness; guilt and expectation of punishment; worrying and brooding; sensitivity; anxiety; psychomotor retardation.

Social Attitudes (72 items): Introverted, seclusive; withdrawn; shy; non-outgoing; non-fun-loving; overly sensitive; irritable; feels misunderstood; lacking in self-confidence; social rigidity; uncommunicative; lacking in social aggressiveness; critical and resentful of others.

Morale (33 items): Lacks self-confidence; low self-esteem; works and lives under tension; difficulties in concentrating, planning, making decisions, completing tasks; expects failure and resents success of others; suggestible and immature; feels misunderstood and unappreciated; sensitive and pessimistic.

Political Attitudes—law and order (46 items): Sees world as jungle; identification with criminal code; distrust of motives of others; discipline problem in school; delinquent childhood; thrill seeking; resentment and distrust of authority; competitive and vindictive; independence from norms; lack of concern for family members' misbehaviors; opinionated.

Obsessive and Compulsive States (15 items): Obsessions, compulsions, rumination; destructive impulses; covert defiance; overt compliance.

Table 1. (continued)

General Neurologic (19 items): Headaches, nausea; seizures; lability; poor judgment; distractability; poor memory.

Vasomotor, Trophic, Speech, Secretory (10 items): Hot and cold sensations; sweating; blushing; dry mouth; poor reading comprehension.

Delusions, Hallucinations, Illusions, Ideas of Reference (31 items): Delusions of persecution and grandeur; ideas of influence; suspiciousness; hallucinations; bizarre experiences; malevolent forces in environment.

Phobias (29 items): Admission of general fearfulness and worry; specific irrational fears of animals, states of nature, disease, heights, crowds, etc.

Family and Marital (26 items): Lack of affection for parents; domination by parents; lack of parental support; desire to leave home; poverty; strife within family; disapproval, resentment, ambivalence, and annoyance at family members; disappointment in love; never been in love.

Lie Items (15 items): Naïve and improbable claims to virtue with venial sins such as procrastination, vanity, gossip, citizenship, mild anger, bad thoughts, competitiveness, etc.

Masculinity-Femininity (55 items): Feminine interest pattern in literature, hobbies, and childhood games; preference for feminine as opposed to masculine vocations; confused sexual identity; admission of weakness, fears, worries, and distress.

General Health (9 items): Poor health; worry about health; high strung; weight fluctuation; easily tired.

Motility and Coordination (6 items): Muscular paralysis, contraction, tremor, weakness, and lack of coordination.

Gastrointestinal System (11 items): Excessive and poor appetites; stomach trouble; constipation and diarrhea; lump in throat.

Affect-Manic (24 items): Excitement, euphoria, high energy; restless and impulsive; irritability, quick temper, destructive impulses; optimism; flight of ideas; unpredictable; short memory; wide and short-term interests; unusual hearing.

Occupational (18 items): Rigid work habits; distractability; sensitivity to opinions and criticisms of others; obstinance; indecisiveness; timidity; lack of self-confidence and concern about work; resentment of boss.

Cardiorespiratory System (5 items): Chronic cough; asthma or hay fever; chest pains; vomiting or coughing blood; pounding heart and shortness of breath.

Habits (19 items): Sleep disturbance; sensitivity to dreams; absence of dreams; excessive drinking and use of alcohol; abstinence from alcohol; giving in to bad habits.

Cranial Nerves (11 items): Disturbances in vision, speech, audition, olfaction, and swallowing; facial paralysis.

Sensibility (5 items): Hypersensitivity to pain, touch, numbness; tingling skin sensations.

Educational (12 items): Dislike of reading—both fiction and nonfiction, likes funny papers and articles on crime; slow learner, disliked school.

Religious Attitudes (19 items): Fundamentalist beliefs; rejection of fundamentalist beliefs; unusual religious experiences; religiosity; magical beliefs; lack of praying and church attendance.

Sadistic, Masochistic Trends (7 items): Enjoys hurting and being hurt by loved ones; cruelty to animals; enjoys frightening people; fetishism.

Sexual Attitudes (16 items): Anxiety over sex; sexual preoccupation; sexual perversion; suppressive attitudes toward sex; permissive attitudes toward sex; disgust and embarrassment about sex.

Genitourinary System (5 items): Disturbance in urination; skin rash; something wrong with sex organs.

a single total score for any individual. As a preliminary scoring method, each item was keyed in the direction of "deviance" as determined by the *infrequent* item option chosen in the Minnesota normal population [Hathaway and McKinley, 1951, pp. 26-29]. It should be emphasized that this scoring procedure is not entirely consistent with the empirically determined keying direction of the MMPI clinical scales, since several of the clinical scales contain items that are keyed in the popular direction. More important, such a scoring procedure in no way ensures optimal scale homogeneity since both ends of an attitudinal continuum may be deviant with respect to population norms. In the case of sexual attitudes, for example, items admitting *both* antisexual attitudes and sexual acting out are deviant; hence both are keyed in the same direction although such keying is intuitively inconsistent. In the absence of detailed information concerning such things as interitem correlations, however, the preliminary scoring method was considered the one most compatible with the original purpose of the item pool.

The internal consistency of content categories thus formed was assessed from the full-scale MMPI protocols of 500 Stanford University students in introductory psychology. Total scores on odd and even items within each of the 26 content categories were obtained separately for 250 men and 250 women students. Correlations between odd- and even-item totals, corrected by the Spearman-Brown formula for double test length, are given in Table 2.

The internal consistencies of the original content categories can be seen to vary from near-zero coefficients to coefficients in the .80s. Directly comparable internal consistency appraisals of the standard MMPI clinical scales have not been reported for college students taking the group form [Dahlstrom and Welsh, 1960, p. 474]. The most comparable data available [Gilliland and Colgin, 1951] suggest, however, that the majority of content categories have internal consistency coefficients equal to or greater than those reported for the standard MMPI clinical scales. As indicated in Table 2, the internal consistencies of many of the content categories are hampered by containing small numbers of items. Hathaway and McKinley [1940] were not explicit about the extent to which the number of items in a given category can be taken as representative of the relative significance of the category to a psychiatrist. Whether arising from implicit, explicit, or fortuitous circumstances, there are definite psychometric restrictions on the extent to which 5-item content categories may contribute to total test variance as contrasted with 55- or 72-item categories. When all content-category internal-consistency coefficients are corrected to the common base of the largest category (72 items), there is little to discourage an investigator from developing an expanded pool of items for any of the categories simply because some of them happen to be underrepresented in the MMPI. The obtained reliabilities are even more impressive in light of the previously mentioned fact that the scoring procedures which were employed did not ensure scale homogeneity.

It is of interest to note that the three content categories which have the highest internal consistencies for both men and women are Affect-Depressive, Social Attitudes, and Morale. As previously reported [Wiggins and Vollmar, 1959; see also Dahlstrom, Welsh, and Dahlstrom, 1972, Table 7-3, p. 235], these three categories account for some 70% of the item content of Welsh's A scale, the empirically

Table 2. Corrected Odd-Even Reliability Coefficients for 26 Original Content Categories of the MMPI

Category	n	r_{xx} (N = 250 Men)	r_{xx} (N = 250 Women)
Affect-Depressive	32	.865	.851
Social Attitudes	72	.850	.775
Morale	33	.802	.738
Political Attitudes	46	.727	.632
Obsessive-Compulsive	15	.668	.601
General Neurologic	19	.644	.693
Vasomotor	10	.632	.628
Delusions	31	.624	.470
Phobias	29	.622	.728
Family and Marital	26	.581	.471
Lie Items	15	.550	.652
Masculinity	55	.547	.505
General Health	9	.476	.307
Motility and Coordination	6	.475	.553
Gastrointestinal	11	.470	.353
Affect-Manic	24	.454	.510
Occupational	18	.436	.396
Cardiorespiratory	5	.422	.477
Habits	19	.418	.588
Cranial Nerves	11	.417	.538
Sensibility	5	.338	.397
Educational	12	.333	.261
Religious Attitudes	19	.258	.184
Sadistic-Masochistic	7	.244	.302
Sexual Attitudes	16	.216	.249
Genitourinary	5	.169	.176
Total	550		

derived marker of the potent first factor of the MMPI [Welsh, 1956].
A decade ago such an observation would have lent encouragement to
a substantive interpretation of the first factor of the MMPI. It is now
generally recognized that an unfortunate confounding of item characteristics and content mitigates against any such straightforward interpretation [Block, 1965 (see II, 4, 5); Dicken, 1967; Wiggins, 1962b;
Wiggins and Goldberg, 1965].

Factorial Structure

Despite the fact that some of the original content categories are
not reliably represented and that the present scoring method is less
than optimal, it is of considerable interest to inquire into the number
and kinds of substantive dimensions represented in the total MMPI
item pool. Such an analysis would be the first to be based on a mutually exclusive and exhaustive classification of MMPI items.

Accordingly, product-moment intercorrelations among the 26 total
scale scores were computed separately in the college samples of 250
men and 250 women. The matrices of content-category intercorrelations were factored by the method of principal components [Harman,
1960]. Latent roots that exceeded unity were retained and rotated
analytically to a varimax criterion [Kaiser, 1958].

The method of analysis employed yielded seven factors for men
and six for women that accounted respectively for 60.9% and 55.1%
of the total variance. The rotated factor matrices for men and women
are presented in Tables 3 and 4. Factor loadings less than .33 have
been omitted, and the matrices have been arranged in such a way as
to facilitate comparison. Factor interpretation will be further facilitated by consulting the content-category descriptions provided in
Table 1.

Factor I appears to be the familiar general maladjustment dimension of the MMPI clinical scales. The content categories that load
this factor most heavily reflect subjectively experienced distress on
the part of the respondent. Low self-esteem, depressed mood, and
feelings of inadequacy are coupled with social uneasiness and introversion. Anxiety is experienced directly with its usual physiological
manifestations. This factor is loaded moderately by items reflecting
irrational fears, restless irritability, and obsessional thinking. In men,
this general maladjustment is also reflected in poor work habits and
feminine interests. In women, maladjustment includes an unsatisfactory family background and a greater emphasis on poor physical
health and undesirable habits.

Factor II is loaded by an intriguing combination of contents that have heretofore been observed to covary only in highly specialized instruments. The Political Attitudes category reflects authority conflict and authoritarian attitudes toward law and order. A sadomasochistic orientation is combined with obsessive-compulsive symptoms and overt compliance. Naive and improbable claims to virtue may further suggest rigidity. Together these categories provide an almost classic description of the authoritarian personality syndrome that has been described in a variety of other contexts [Adorno, Frenkel-Brunswik, Levinson, and Sanford, 1950; Loevinger, 1962; Rokeach, 1960; Stern, Stein, and Bloom, 1956]. Although this factor is most clearly defined for women, the additional categories that load it for men are compatible with the areas of maladjustment often associated

Table 3. Rotated Factor Matrix of 26 Original Content Categories
(N = 250 Men)

	I	II	III$_a$	III$_b$	IV	V	VI	h^2
Morale	.74							.81
Vasomotor	.74							.66
Social Attitudes	.70			−.34				.68
Affect-Depressive	.61	−.41		−.33				.82
Occupational	.45	−.53						.54
Phobias	.41		.39	−.39				.59
Affect-Manic	.40	−.54						.58
Obsessive	.40	−.52						.58
Masculinity	.33	−.35				.44	−.54	.62
Political Attitudes		−.63						.49
Sadistic		−.61						.53
Lie		.54						.61
Delusions		−.40	.39					.59
Sensibility		−.40	.53					.59
Cranial			.73					.61
Gastrointestinal			.55					.50
Genitourinary			.52		−.50			.56
General Neurologic			.50			.33		.63
Cardiorespiratory			.49	−.44				.51
Habits			.35			.45		.48
Motility				−.79				.69
General Health				−.68				.56
Sexual Attitudes					−.73			.64
Family and Marital					−.67			.62
Religious Attitudes						.74		.57
Educational							.85	.80
Variance, %	20.3	18.9	16.8	11.8	9.6	8.2	14.4	

with authoritarianism. In men, the mood disturbances, poor work habits, sensitivities, delusional thinking, and feminine interests may reflect a more deep-seated personality disturbance than is the case with authoritarianism in women.

Two dimensions of physical symptoms in men (factors IIIa and IIIb) appear to be combined in a single dimension of physical complaint for women (factor III). Factor IIIa in men is loaded by a variety of complaints presumably representative of disturbance in cranial nerve, gastrointestinal, sensibility, genitourinary, neurologic, and cardiorespiratory systems. Factor IIIb appears to center around general health concerns, symptoms of fatigue, and cardiorespiratory complaints. Both these factors are loaded slightly by categories of psychological symptoms as well. In women, fatigue and general health concern are combined with the aforementioned systemic symptoms

Table 4. Rotated Factor Matrix of 26 Original Content Categories
(N = 250 Women)

	I	II	III	IV	V	VI	h^2
Morale	.75						.74
Vasomotor	.44						.52
Social Attitudes	.80						.70
Affect-Depressive	.78			.34			.81
Occupational				.55			.52
Phobias	.41			.52			.56
Affect-Manic	.41		−.41				.53
Obsessive	.47	.37	−.33				.59
Masculinity			−.33	.42		−.44	.57
Political Attitudes		.51	−.33		−.34		.58
Sadistic		.80					.66
Lie		−.35		−.56			.46
Delusions			−.57		−.34		.60
Sensibility			−.65				.52
Cranial			−.64				.43
Gastrointestinal			−.44				.44
Genitourinary			−.33			.44	.38
General Neurologic	.47		−.63				.63
Cardiorespiratory			−.56				.43
Habits	.37		−.38				.37
Motility			−.76				.71
General Health	.51		−.35				.50
Sexual Attitudes				.69			.50
Family and Marital	.54						.45
Religious Attitudes					−.84		.73
Educational						.63	.42
Variance, %	26.9	11.4	26.6	16.6	9.5	9.0	

into one general factor of somatic complaint. With the exception of the Manic category reflecting fast tempo and irritability, the psychological symptom categories appear quite secondary in their contribution to this factor.

Factor IV is highly and uniquely loaded by the category of Sexual Attitudes. Categories associated with deviant sexual attitudes vary remarkably for men and women. In men such attitudes are associated with family conflict and specific genitourinary complaints. In women, this factor is negatively loaded by improbable claims to virtue and positively loaded by feminine interests. Psychological symptoms in women take the form of irrational fears, poor work habits, and feelings of depression and guilt.

Factor V is strongly and uniquely loaded by deviant religious attitudes. In men, sleep disturbance, drinking habits, feminine interests, and, to a lesser extent, some somatic complaints tend to have loadings on this factor. In women, authoritarian attitudes and delusional thinking have very slight loadings on the deviant religious attitudes factor.

Factor VI is defined by deviant educational attitudes. In both men and women, antieducational attitudes are associated with masculine interests. In women, this factor is also loaded by the category of Genitourinary complaints.

In summary, a principal component analysis of the 26 mutually exclusive and exhaustive content categories of the MMPI yielded six interpretable factors in both men and women. The first three of these factors appear to represent general syndromes of complaint, while the last three appear to center around more specific substantive categories. The factors of general maladjustment and somatic complaint are familiar ones that might be anticipated on the basis both of clinical scale development and of the overrepresentation of such categories in the MMPI item pool. The factor of authoritarianism appears to represent a theoretically meaningful combination of substantive categories that has, until now, been obscured by the strategy employed in the development of the clinical scales. Deviant attitudes toward sex, religion, and education have likewise not been previously stressed as important substantive components of the MMPI item pool.

Revision of Original Content Categories

Given the encouraging internal consistencies and factorial structure of the original content categories, it seemed fruitful to attempt a more substantively consistent grouping of items within categories as a basis for subsequent development of actual content *scales*. Although many strategies of scale construction were possible at this point, the one chosen placed primary emphasis on the "rational" or substantive considerations involved in the classification of item content. Since this strategy is so antithetical to the traditional approach to MMPI scale construction, a brief justification seems required.

For better or (more likely) for worse, the MMPI represents a *fixed* item pool. Examination of the interrelationships among many characteristics of this item pool led Wiggins and Goldberg [1965] to conclude:

> Over- and under-representation of certain classes of desirability, endorsement, ambiguity, and grammatical characteristics tends to make the item pool unnecessarily homogeneous and may, in part, contribute to rather severe restrictions in criterion group discriminations. The fortuitous confounding of such item characteristics with substantive dimensions [Block, 1965; Wiggins, 1962b] has created interpretative problems [Edwards, 1957a; Jackson and Messick, 1961] which may never be satisfactorily resolved within any fixed item pool [pp. 394-395].

Although these authors stress the importance of basic research in item development, such research will not be of immediate value to the practical consumer of the MMPI. The present attempt to develop substantive scales for the MMPI was not initiated with the hope of overcoming the built-in shortcomings of the item pool. It was predicated, however, on the assumption that the interaction of item characteristics and stylistic tendencies with substantive dimensions might be better understood than the interaction of such sources of variance with the complex and poorly understood dimensions yielded by the strategy of contrasted groups (e.g., "hysteria").

The method whereby the original MMPI content categories were revised involved the collapsing of several categories into single categories, reassignment of items from one category to another, elimination of original categories, creation of new ones, and rekeying of item options within categories. Procedures were, with one minor exception, completely intuitive, and no claim is made for their replicability.

The major item regroupings involved physical symptoms, interests, and items reflecting manifest hostility. Items from General Health, Cardiorespiratory, Gastrointestinal, and Genitourinary were combined in the single revised category of Poor Health. Items from General Neurologic, Cranial Nerves, Motility and Coordination, and Sensibility were combined into a single category of Organic Symptoms. Items reflecting hostility from the Sadistic-Masochistic category formed the nucleus of a new category of Manifest Hostility, to which 21 items from seven other original categories were added. A small group of items from the Habits category was considered separately as an Addiction category.

The Occupational Attitudes category was judged to be too heterogeneous, and items from this category were regouped under Obsessive-Compulsive, Poor Morale, and four other revised categories. Original categories that were retained were purified around a central theme and items eliminated or borrowed from other categories in light of this theme. The category of Habits, for example, was redefined as Sleeping Habits, which eliminated seven of the original items and added three from other categories.

The categories of Educational Attitudes and Masculinity-Femininity were placed in a common pool, and from this pool preliminary attempts were made to differentiate feminine interest patterns from tendencies toward sexual inversion. When this differentiation was judged to be unsuccessful, a general category of Feminine Interests was developed which proved to be ambiguous with respect to keying direction. In the absence of a clear-cut rationale, the empirical norms of Drake [1953] were used as a basis for item keying. Items in the Feminine Interest category that significantly differentiated men and women in Drake's sample were retained and keyed in the female direction.

Internal Consistency of Revised Categories

A more consistent arrangement of items into content categories should be reflected in increased internal consistencies in the revised set. Total scores on odd and even items were computed for each of the 18 revised categories in samples of 250 men and 250 women students from Stanford University. Since these samples had, in part, inspired the reclassification, odd and even totals were also computed in a mixed group of 203 men and women introductory psychology students from the University of Oregon. Table 5 presents Spearman-Brown corrected internal consistency coefficients for the Stanford and Oregon samples. Since new content categories were created and old ones were considerably altered in the revision of the content categories, the success of the revision procedures cannot, in all cases, be directly assessed by comparison of each category with its revised counterpart. A slight decline in internal consistency occurred in depression, obsessive-compulsive, and vasomotor categories. This is more than offset by the increases in internal consistency which occurred in 14 categories which can be compared with their original counterparts. The most dramatic increase occurred in the category of Religious Attitudes, in which *deletion* of four items and rekeying of those remaining resulted in internal consistency increases from the low .20s to the high .80s. Regrouping sadistic-masochistic items into the more general category of Manifest Hostility resulted in increases from the low .30s to the middle .70s. Other increases may be noted by comparing Table 5 with Table 2.

Construction of Final Content Scales

On the basis of the data presented in Table 5, it was decided that there were 15 substantive dimensions in the MMPI pool which possessed promising internal consistencies and sufficient numbers of items to warrant further exploration. These 15 dimensions appear as the first 15 categories in Table 5. The categories of Addiction, Lie, Vasomotor, and Sexual were dropped from further consideration at this point. The categories of Feminine Interests, Sleeping Habits, and Obsessive-Compulsive were carried along a very tentative basis.

Table 5. Corrected Odd-Even Internal Consistency Coefficients of Revised Content Categories in Two College Populations

Revised Category	n	Stanford Men (N = 250)	Stanford Women (N = 250)	Oregon Men and Women (N = 203)
Religious	15	.87	.86	.81
Social	56	.84	.83	.80
Depression	33	.83	.82	.78
Morale	40	.84	.79	.74
Authority	43	.77	.71	.80
Phobias	27	.72	.80	.75
Hostility	27	.75	.73	.75
Organic	36	.71	.79	.72
Psychoticism	48	.75	.72	.71
Family	27	.74	.67	.73
Hypomania	25	.72	.71	.66
Health	28	.76	.70	.52
Feminine	56	.55	.60	.82
Sleep	15	.56	.58	.52
Obsessive	27	.52	.55	.50
Addiction	6	.67	.53	.42
Lie	15	.55	.65	.55
Vasomotor	10	.62	.60	.58
Sexual	16	.34	.51	.53

The Stanford sample was randomly divided into two groups of 300 and 200 subjects, with an equal number of men and women within each group. The group of 300 Ss served as an item analysis group for scale purification, and the group of 200 Ss was used for an independent assessment of the homogeneity of scales formed by item analysis.

Point-biserial correlations were computed between the 550 items of the MMPI and each of the 15 total scale scores of the revised content categories. An item was retained in a given content scale if (1) its point-biserial correlation with the total scale of the category of which it was a member exceeded .30 and (2) its correlation with the total scale of the category of which it was a member exceeded its correlation with all 14 remaining revised content category scores.

Table 6 shows the number of items eliminated by each of the two criteria of item analysis. Among the Social Maladjustment items, for example, 26 items were eliminated because their correlation with the Social total scale score was less than .30. Three additional items were eliminated because their item-total correlations, although greater than .30, were equaled or exceeded by item-total correlations with one or more of the 14 additional content categories.

It can be seen from Table 6 that item selection was made primarily on the basis of internal consistency. Only 20 items were elimi-

Table 6. Number of Items Eliminated by Item Analysis
of Revised Content Categories

Scale	Original	r < .30	Non-Independent	Final n
Religious	15	3	0	12
Social	56	26	3	27
Depression	33	12	2	20*
Morale	40	15	3	23*
Authority	43	21	2	20
Phobias	27	7	1	19
Hostility	27	7	1	20*
Organic	36	13	0	23
Psychoticism	48	31	4	13
Family	27	11	0	16
Hypomanic	25	5	0	20
Health	28	15	0	13
Feminine	56	26	0	30
Sleep	15	3	1	11
Obsessive	27	14	3	10

*Includes one additional item from another content category.

nated on the basis of their being correlated with categories other than their own. Note, however, that the criterion of scale independence employed was quite minimal. Three items were judged to have been initially misclassified after examination of their correlations with other categories. Thus, one Obsessive item was transferred to the Depression category, one Social item to the Morale category, and one Psychoticism item to the Hostility category.

The 15 revised content categories and the 15 content scales formed by item analysis were then scored in the group of 200 Ss originally set aside for this purpose. As a more general measure of scale homogeneity, Cronbach's [1951] coefficient alpha was computed for the 15 categories and 15 scales. Content scales were judged to be improved by item analysis if their alpha coefficient increased despite the elimination of substantial portions of items.

Table 7 presents alpha coefficients for the revised categories and the scales formed by item analysis. The contaminated correlation between the two sets of measures is presented in the final column. The Religion, Social, Morale, Authority, Family, and Feminine Interests scales were judged to be improved by item analysis. Scale purification was extreme in several instances and resulted in improved alphas despite elimination of almost half the items in the scale.

Table 7. Coefficient Alpha Internal Consistency Estimates for
Revised Categories and Item-Analyzed Content Scales
(N = 200 Men and Women)

Category	Revised	n	Final	n	Revised vs. Final
Religious	81	(15)	83	(12)	98
Social	83	(56)	86	(27)	95
Depression	84	(33)	82	(20)	96
Morale	81	(40)	84	(23)	93
Authority	77	(43)	78	(20)	92
Phobias	70	(27)	67	(19)	96
Hostility	72	(27)	69	(20)	97
Organic	76	(36)	70	(23)	96
Psychoticism	76	(48)	61	(13)	85
Family	72	(27)	72	(16)	94
Hypomanic	69	(25)	67	(20)	97
Health	69	(28)	59	(13)	90
Feminine	77	(56)	84	(30)	96
Sleep	56	(15)	56	(11)	97
Obsessive	56	(27)	57	(10)	82

Increased homogeneity was not achieved by item analysis for Depression, Phobias, Hostility, Organic, Psychoticism, Hypomania, or Health. Subsequent attempts to improve these scales by less stringent item-analytic criteria were not successful. It was decided, therefore, to retain these scales in their revised form. The Sleeping Habits and Obsessive scales were abandoned at this point on the grounds of unpromising homogeneity.

The foregoing procedures resulted in the adoption of 13 mutually exclusive scales that were considered internally consistent, moderately independent, and representative of the major substantive clusters of the MMPI. All these scales were based on rational regroupings of the original content categories proposed by Hathaway and McKinley. Six of these scales were further refined by item-analytic procedures. This final set of 13 scales will be referred to as the MMPI content scales. (Item lists may be found in Wiggins, 1966.) The content of the items in the scales is described in Table 8.

Table 8. Description of MMPI Content Scales

SOC *Social Maladjustment:* High SOC is socially bashful, shy, embarrassed, reticent, self-conscious, and extremely reserved. Low SOC is gregarious, confident, assertive and relates quickly and easily to others. He is fun-loving, the life of a party, a joiner who experiences no difficulty in speaking before a group. This scale would correspond roughly with the popular concept of "introversion-extraversion."

DEP *Depression:* High DEP experiences guilt, regret, worry, unhappiness, and a feeling that life has lost its zest. He experiences difficulty in concentrating and has little motivation to pursue things. His self-esteem is low, and he is anxious and apprehensive about the future. He is sensitive to slight, feels misunderstood, and is convinced that he is unworthy and deserves punishment. In short, he is classically depressed.

FEM *Feminine Interests:* High FEM admits to liking feminine games, hobbies, and vocations. He denies liking masculine games, hobbies, and vocations. Here there is almost complete contamination of content and form, which has been noted in other contexts by several writers. Individuals may score high on this scale by presenting themselves as *liking* many things, since this item stem is present in almost all items. They may also score high by endorsing interests that, although possibly feminine, are also *socially desirable,* such as an interest in poetry, dramatics, news of the theatre, and artistic pursuits. This has been noted in the case of Wiggins's Sd scale. Finally, of course, individuals with a genuine preference for activities that are conceived by our culture as "feminine" will achieve high scores on this scale.

MOR *Poor Morale:* High MOR is lacking in self-confidence, feels that he has failed in life, and is given to despair and a tendency to give up hope. He is extremely sensitive to the feelings and reactions of others and feels misunderstood by them, while at the same time being concerned about offending them. He feels useless and is socially suggestible. There is a substantive overlap here between the Depression and Social Maladjustment scales and the Poor Morale scale. The Social Maladjustment scale seems to emphasize a lack of social ascendance and poise, the Depression scale

Table 8. (continued)

feelings of guilt and apprehension, while the present scale seems to emphasize a lack of self-confidence and hypersensitivity to the opinions of others.

REL *Religious Fundamentalism:* High scorers on this scale see themselves as religious, churchgoing people who accept as true a number of fundamentalist religious convictions. They also tend to view their faith as the true one.

AUT *Authority Conflict:* High AUT sees life as a jungle and is convinced that others are unscrupulous, dishonest, hypocritical, and motivated only by personal profit. He distrusts others, has little respect for experts, is competitive, and believes that everyone should get away with whatever he can.

PSY *Psychoticism:* High PSY admits to a number of classic psychotic symptoms of a primarily paranoid nature. He admits to hallucinations, strange experiences, loss of control, and classic paranoid delusions of grandeur and persecution. He admits to feelings of unreality, daydreaming, and a sense that things are wrong, while feeling misunderstood by others.

ORG *Organic Symptoms:* High ORG admits to symptoms that are often indicative of organic involvement. These include headaches, nausea, dizziness, loss of motility and coordination, loss of consciousness, poor concentration and memory, speaking and reading difficulty, poor muscular control, tingling skin sensations, and disturbances in hearing and smelling.

FAM *Family Problems:* High FAM feels that he had an unpleasant home life characterized by a lack of love in the family and parents who were unnecessarily critical, nervous, quarrelsome, and quick tempered. Although some items are ambiguous, most are phrased with reference to the parental home rather than the individual's current home.

HOS *Manifest Hostility:* High HOS admits to sadistic impulses and a tendency to be cross, grouchy, competitive, argumentative, uncooperative, and retaliatory in his interpersonal relationships. He is often competitive and socially aggressive.

PHO *Phobias:* High PHO has admitted to a number of fears, many of them of the classically phobic variety such as heights, darkness, and closed spaces.

HYP *Hypomania:* High HYP is characterized by feelings of excitement, well-being, restlessness, and tension. He is enthusiastic, high-strung, cheerful, full of energy, and apt to be hotheaded. He has broad interests, seeks change, and is apt to take on more than he can handle.

HEA *Poor Health:* High HEA is concerned about his health and has admitted to a variety of gastrointestinal complaints centering around an upset stomach and difficulty in elimination.

Note: Item composition of these content scales may be found in Wiggins [1966] or in Appendix I of Dahlstrom, Welsh, and Dahlstrom [1975].

Internal Consistency of Content Scales in Normal Populations

Since virtually all of the preliminary investigation and development of the MMPI content scales was based on a single college population, it was necessary to gather additional data from other populations to assess the psychometric characteristics of the final scales.

Accordingly, complete MMPI protocols were obtained from the samples listed in Table 9. A group of Air Force enlisted men served as a noncollege normal population, while remaining samples were college students of both sexes from several geographical regions.

Table 9. Composition of Normal Sample (N = 1368)

Group	Men	Women
Air Force enlisted men*	261	
Stanford University	250	250
University of Minnesota	96	125
University of Oregon	95	108
University of Illinois	100	83
Total	802	566

*Chanute Air Force Base, Rantoul, Ill.

The internal consistency of the MMPI content scales was assessed by computing alpha coefficients in samples not involved in scale derivation. These data are presented in Table 10. Reliability coefficients from the college samples are, with one notable exception, generally in accord with expectations gained from the derivation samples. The exception is Feminine Interests which, although among the most internally consistent scales in the derivation sample, is the least reliable scale in other college and Air Force samples. More in line with expectations are the generally high internal consistencies of Social Maladjustment, Religious Fundamentalism, Depression, and Poor Morale in the college groups. As before, Hypomania and Poor Health are among the lowest in internal consistency, but the obtained alpha coefficients are quite respectable in comparison with the majority of MMPI scales in use today.

With the exception of Feminine Interests, the alpha coefficients obtained in the Air Force sample are substantial, indicating a generality beyond college populations. Several differences in the relative internal consistencies of the content scales in an Air Force, as opposed to a college, population may be noted. Whereas Psychoticism and Organic Symptoms are only moderately reliable in college groups, they are among the most internally consistent scales in the Air Force sample. This may reflect, in part, the greater heterogeneity of the Air Force sample. It is also of interest to note that, whereas Religious Fundamentalism is consistently among the most reliable scales for college groups, it is one of the least reliable scales in the Air Force sample.

Table 10. Coefficient Alpha Internal Consistency Estimates for
MMPI Content Scales in Seven Normal Samples

	Air Force Enlisted Men	University of Minnesota		University of Oregon		University of Illinois	
		Men	Women	Men	Women	Men	Women
	(N = 261)	(N = 96)	(N = 125)	(N = 95)	(N = 108)	(N = 100)	(N = 83)
SOC	.829	.856	.835	.830	.862	.856	.843
DEP	.872	.860	.831	.821	.756	.842	.854
FEM	.585	.523	.505	.594	.566	.650	.542
MOR	.857	.866	.825	.804	.753	.867	.804
REL	.674	.892	.861	.842	.756	.817	.793
AUT	.681	.794	.772	.743	.669	.766	.698
PSY	.877	.794	.687	.738	.662	.763	.806
ORG	.863	.772	.645	.652	.695	.749	.731
FAM	.707	.712	.789	.712	.694	.806	.643
HOS	.764	.819	.794	.788	.651	.776	.765
PHO	.765	.663	.721	.568	.701	.705	.770
HYP	.671	.701	.715	.682	.632	.679	.667
HEA	.743	.557	.713	.555	.537	.673	.651

Factorial Structure of Content Scales

Unlike the standard MMPI clinical scales, the MMPI content scales do not share common items and were constructed in such a way as to maximize the homogeneity of each scale. Nevertheless, the criterion employed for scale independence (in the correlational sense) during item analysis was quite minimal, and the number of separate substantive dimensions involved in this set of scales is certainly fewer than 13. It is of interest, therefore, to examine the nature of the factor structure underlying the content scales.

Two factor analyses were performed on samples of 250 men and 250 women from Stanford University. In addition to the 13 MMPI content scales, six marker variables were included to define the traditional MMPI clinical scale space. Four of these markers are subject to stylistic interpretation, while the remaining two are not. Welsh's [1956] factor scales A and R were included as markers of the first two factors of conventional MMPI space. Wiggins's Sd [Wiggins, 1959] and the Cof of Cofer, Chance, and Judson [1949] were included to permit investigation of the possible convergence of the third content factor with the third stylistic dimension previously mentioned [Edwards, Diers, and Walker, 1962]. Block's [1965] ER-S and EC-5 were included as desirability-free and acquiescence-free measures of the factors he describes as "ego resiliency" and "ego control," respectively. The intercorrelation matrices were factored by the method of principal components, and factors with latent roots greater than unity were rotated analytically to a varimax criterion. The rotated factor matrices for samples of Stanford men and women are presented in Table 11. Factor loadings less than 0.33 have been omitted and the matrices have been arranged to facilitate comparison.

Table 11. Rotated Factor Matrices of Content Scales plus Six Marker Variables

	Stanford Women (N = 250)						Stanford Men (N = 250)					
	I	II	III	IV	V	h^2	I	II	III	IV	V	h^2
MOR	81	...	...	...	...	80	79	...	36	...	...	77
A	80	...	37	...	...	88	85	...	40	...	...	91
SOC	79	−36	...	...	...	81	62	−56	...	...	...	81
DEP	78	...	38	...	...	81	78	...	42	...	...	82
ER-S	−57	−42	−37	...	...	67	−69	...	−34	...	...	63
PHO	53	...	...	...	34	49	47	...	58	...	...	57
HOS	40	72	...	...	...	69	68	37	...	...	...	69
Cof	−40	...	...	75	...	79	−44	...	...	71	...	78
FAM	37	34	...	...	...	33	...	40	40	...	...	47
PSY	33	37	56	...	...	59	53	...	61	...	...	69
R	...	−83	...	...	...	74	−38	−72	...	...	...	78
HYP	...	70	...	...	...	66	52	58	...	...	...	71
EC-5	...	−70	...	40	...	80	...	−80	...	...	...	83
AUT	...	55	...	...	...	49	48	33	34	...	−35	59
ORG	...	...	82	...	...	75	34	...	77	...	...	71
HEA	...	...	78	...	...	74	...	...	76	...	...	69
Sd	...	...	...	88	...	78	...	...	...	83	...	77
REL	...	...	...	72	...	58	...	...	...	75	...	62
FEM	...	...	...	...	85	74	...	...	...	...	87	80
Variance, %	50	18	15	9	8		36	17	22	16	9	

Five factors emerge from the matrix of the content scales and the six marker scales. These five factors account for 69% and 72% of the total variance in the female and male samples, respectively. The first three factors are recognizable as the same obtained in the earlier analysis. The fourth factor is a "stylistic" factor determined by the inclusion of Sd and Cof. These stylistic scales have little in common with content scales other than Religious Fundamentalism, although this, in itself, is an intriguing finding. The present space is such that Feminine Interests emerges as a fifth quite specific factor distinct from factor II.

Factor I. Anxiety Proneness versus Ego Resiliency. The first factor in both samples is clearly and unambiguously marked by Welsh's A, which coordinates the first factor of content scales with the first factor obtained in all studies of clinical scales to date. Although scale A provides a statistical identification of the factor, it does not allow a choice between stylistic and substantive interpretations. Block's ER-S, which does not admit of stylistic interpretation, has a substantial, but not unique, loading on this factor in the present analyses. It will not be argued that the present factor is free of the contaminating influence of social desirability. However, the nature of the content scales that load this particular factor is of more than passing interest. Poor Morale, Social Maladjustment, and Depression have high loadings on the first factor in both groups. The item content of these scales (Table 8) suggests an individual lacking in self-confidence who is socially inhibited and given to feelings of guilt and apprehensiveness. An individual at the other end of the implied continuum would be characterized by self-confidence and optimism, social ascendance and poise, and a confident, resilient approach to the future. The item content of the scales that mark this factor is so close to the independent behavior descriptions obtained by Block [1965] for individuals with high and low scores on the same psychometric dimension that Block's suggested label of "ego resiliency" is here applied to the first factorial dimension of MMPI content scales.

Factor II. Impulsivity versus Control. The second factor is marked by Welsh's R and Block's EC-5, with R predominating in the sample of women and EC-5 marking the factor in the sample of men. Although R is highly subject to stylistic interpretation, EC-5 is not. In light of the recent criticisms directed at the interpretation of this dimension as "acquiescence" [Block, 1965; McGee, 1962; Rorer, 1965; Rorer and Goldberg, 1965], the burden of proof of the utility of such an interpretation is shifted to its proponents. More germane to the present analyses is the nature of the content scales that load this factor. Hypomania has high loadings on the second factor in both samples. The items that constitute this scale emphasize excitement, restlessness, hotheadedness and overcommitment. Such items are suggestive of impulsivity or lack of control at one pole of the dimension and control, or possibly, overcontrol at the other. Manifest Hostility and Authority Conflict have high loadings on this factor in the female sample. The items in these scales reflect the free expression of aggressiveness and the cynical, distrustful attitude that everyone should get away with what he can. Such items are seen as consistent with the lack of impulse control suggested by the Hypomania scale. In the male sample, Manifest Hostility and Authority Conflict have smaller loadings, while Social Maladjustment and Family Problems contribute more. Again, the constellation of content scales marking the second factor is highly similar to the independent behavior descriptions obtained by Block [1965] for this dimension which caused him to label the factor a "control" dimension. It is also of interest to note that Block [1965] has argued that the control dimension is expressed differently in men and women, which also appears to be the case in the present analyses.

Factor III. Health Concern. In both samples, the third factor is characterized by high loadings on Organic Symptoms and Poor Health. The relationship between these two scales is rather obvious and would seem to warrant the general label of "health concern" for the factor. In college populations, at least, there appears to be an underlying factor of concern with health that includes both the headaches, dizziness, etc., from the Organic Symptoms content scale and the gastrointestinal complaints from the Poor Health content scale. Lacking the independent behavior descriptions that were available for the first two factors and lacking a factor marker that would relate the present dimension to previous ones, it seems best to view this factor as one involving "reported poor health." Considering the large number of items in the MMPI pool that relate to health, it is not surprising that such a factor should emerge. A "poor physical health" factor has emerged from factor analysis of items from several of the standard MMPI clinical scales [Comrey, 1957a, 1957b, 1957c, 1958c; Comrey and Marggraff, 1958]. Factor analysis of groups of MMPI scales has also yielded a "somatization" factor [Eichman, 1961; Fisher, 1964].

Factor IV. Social Desirability Role Playing. This factor was rather clearly determined by the inclusion of the stylistic role-playing scales which define it: Wiggins's [1959] Sd and the Cof of Cofer et al. [1949]. As previously indicated, a considerable number of studies attest to the behavioral correlates of these scales, namely, the tendency to modify answers to the MMPI in a socially desirable direction when instructed to do so. The content scale of Religious Fundamentalism has a high and unique loading on this factor in both samples. The most conservative interpretation of this finding would be that the items in the Religious Fundamentalism scale are those which are most subject to change under conditions which encourage faking. However, in view of the fact that the Marlowe-Crowne Social

Desirability Scale [Crowne and Marlowe, 1960] is known to load this factor [Edwards et al., 1962; Edwards and Walsh, 1964; Liberty, Lunneborg, and Atkinson, 1964], a further inference seems justified. On the basis of the extensive documentation of the correlates of the Marlowe-Crowne scale [Crowne and Marlowe, 1964] that is known to load this factor, it seems likely that, in these college samples, individuals who describe themselves as religious, churchgoing people may be operating under a strong motive to gain social approval [Crowne and Marlowe, 1964]. Such a phenomenon may be quite specific to these particular samples, however.

Factor V. Feminine Interests. When the present set of marker scales are included in the factor analysis of MMPI content scales, Feminine Interests emerges as a specific factor. In the earlier factor analyses of content scales in several male samples, the Feminine Interests scale was seen to vary from sample to sample in its factorial contribution. Such a factor is reminiscent of the "feminine interests" factor which has been reported from time to time in the literature [Cook and Wherry, 1950; Cottle, 1949; Kassebaum, Couch, and Slater, 1959; Wheeler, Little, and Lehner, 1951] and which has exhibited considerable fluctuation from sample to sample. Interpretation of this factor must be restricted to the content of the items in the Feminine Interests scale (Table 8) since its non-MMPI correlates have not been investigated.

In summary, when the factorial dimensions of the MMPI content scales were aligned with previously reported dimensions of MMPI clinical scales, considerable convergence was evident. In a college population, the first two factors were clearly marked by Welsh's [1956] A and R which permitted their identification as the first two factors of previously reported studies. Although the possible contaminating effect of "social desirability" could not be ruled out, the first factor was interpreted as reflecting "anxiety-proneness versus ego resiliency." The second factor was interpreted as "impulsivity versus control" with less concern for the possible alternative interpretation of "acquiescence." The third factor appeared to reflect "health concern" as judged from the item content of the scales that loaded it. A relatively specific factor of "feminine interests" was identified, although its generality across populations was questioned. The possibility that high scores on the Religious Fundamentalism content scale may be associated with high approval motivation [Crowne and Marlowe, 1964] was also raised.

Discussion

To encourage further investigation of the empirical properties of the content scales is to imply that they possess advantages over the currently employed clinical scales. Since such a position is taken by the present investigator, it seems appropriate to review these claimed advantages and to discuss their relevance for both clinical and research applications of the MMPI.

Viewed from the convenient hindsight of 25 years, the MMPI appears to have been poorly conceived for the purposes it was eventually to serve. The Kraepelinian categories to which it was committed were soon to pass into disfavor. Moreover, the predictive success of the individual scales in making such psychiatric categorizations was considerably less than had been anticipated. Under the impetus of an unprecedented amount of research, there was a shift of emphasis from the psychiatric to the personological implications of the clinical scales, and the application of the scales was extended far beyond the original context of personnel decisions.

The MMPI clinical scales are poorly equipped to serve as personality trait scales for several reasons. Several of the scales lack the internal consistency that is usually taken as evidence of an organized pattern of behavior. Also, an interpretative ambiguity exists with respect to the meaning and significance of low scores on the scales, since "normal" subjects rarely achieve a score of zero [Wiggins, 1962b]. Indeed, the hodgepodge of content that contributes to a high score on a given clinical scale is not suggestive of any consistent personality trait or structure. The fact that this makes the inventory difficult to fake would seem, at best, a mixed blessing. Given the substantive heterogeneity of the clinical scales, a configural "pattern" may be achieved in a wide variety of ways, and it seems cavalier to apply standard "blind" interpretations to such patterns, as is done in clinical practice. Finally, a minor but irritating characteristic of the scales is the extensive degree of item overlap that exists among them [Adams and Horn, 1965; Shure and Rogers, 1965].

It seems likely that the MMPI item pool, which was once considered so rich and untapped, may be too limited as a source of items for building general purpose personality scales [Wiggins and Goldberg, 1965]. This may be true with respect to both content and item characteristics and is certainly true of the extent to which the two are confounded. Nevertheless, in the absence of any immediate replacement, it would seem unwise to abandon an inventory that has the empirical virtues, however limited, of the MMPI. Rather, it would seem appropriate to explore the utility of supplemental measures that are not encumbered by all the substantive and psychometric shortcomings of the clinical scales.

The MMPI content scales possess a respectable degree of internal consistency. This internal consistency must, in part, be attributed to homogeneous organization of psychological, physical, and social complaints that seem appropriately combined by a cumulative scoring model [Loevinger, 1957]. Although no claim is made for scale unidimensionality or Guttman-type item properties, each scale has a compelling, though prosaic, feature. Subjects who achieve high scores on the scales do so by admitting to, or claiming, an unusual amount of the substantive dimension involved. Subjects who achieve low scores claim a small amount and, by so doing, may or may not be similar to certain abnormal groups. But subjects who say they are hostile are saying just that and not that they have organic symptoms or strong religious convictions. A return to this type of Woodworthian simplicity has been long overdue.

Although apparently heterogeneous in content, covariation among content scales may be reduced to three underlying factors. The first two of these factors were found to be colinear with the first two factors consistently found in analyses of the MMPI clinical scales. This result is not surprising within the domain of MMPI items and may even reflect an upper limit on the number of parsimoniously interpretable factors within the conventionally defined questionnaire realm [Peterson, 1965]. However, the content scales tend to clarify the specific manner in which the ubiquitous two factors of personality questionnaires manifest themselves within the MMPI item pool. The item content of the scales that mark these two factors lends itself readily to the substantive interpretations placed upon these dimensions by Block [1965]. This is especially important when it is recognized that Block's interpretations were buttressed by independently obtained empirical evidence.

Coming from the same item pool, the content scales are no less free than the clinical scales of confounding item characteristics that lend themselves to stylistic interpretations. The tenor of recent critical thinking on this issue suggests, however, that the burden of proof of the utility of stylistic interpretations has been shifted to the proponents of such styles. In any event, *what* is being confounded by item characteristics in the case of the content scales seems clearer. Future studies of item characteristics would do well to examine their effects on substantive dimensions rather than on the poorly understood dimensions yielded by the scale construction strategy of contrasted groups. Such research would naturally be facilitated by scales composed of nonoverlapping items.

The case for further investigation of substantive aspects of the MMPI may best be presented by calling attention to a basic feature of assessment situations that has tended to be ignored or belittled by sophistic arguments. Regardless of psychologists' views of a test response, the respondent tends to view the testing situation as an opportunity for *communication* between himself and the tester or institution he represents [Carson, 1969; Leary, 1957]. Obviously, the respondent has some control over what he chooses to communicate, and there are a variety of other factors which may enter to distort the message, many of them attributable to the testing media themselves [Cattell, 1961; LaForge, 1963]. Nevertheless, recognition of such sources of "noise" in the system should not lead us to overlook the fact that a message is still involved. The MMPI content scales may be closely attuned to this message and, as such, may provide a useful supplement to the standard clinical scales.

Relationship of Creativity/ Intelligence Scales to MMPI Profiles of Gifted Adolescents

G. S. Welsh

The MMPI was one of several personality tests employed in a study of the relationship between measures of creativity and intelligence in gifted adolescents. Special MMPI scales emerged from the study and may be interpreted in the framework of a two-dimensional model proposed to account for the original empirical findings of this research. Since the model has been shown to have implications for many different areas of psychological interest in addition to creativity and intelligence, the special MMPI scales should be of value for personality assessment in these areas as well.

Origence/Intellectence Model

The personality model proposes two independent dimensions, "origence" and "intellectence." The vertical dimension, origence, contrasts persons preferring a structured, orderly, and systematic approach with those more at home in situations which are unstructured, open-ended, and susceptible of being re-ordered in different ways. The horizontal dimension, intellectence, differentiates persons preferring literal, concrete, and practical kinds of tasks from those who find congenial abstract, conceptual, and theoretical modes of problem-solving. The dimensions are orthogonal and generate four distinct personality types which are summarized in Table 1.

Table 1. A Two-Dimensional Model for Personality Study

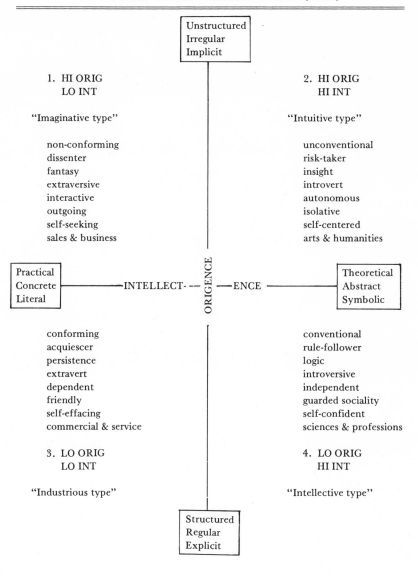

Unstructured
Irregular
Implicit

1. HI ORIG
   LO INT

"Imaginative type"

    non-conforming
    dissenter
    fantasy
    extraversive
    interactive
    outgoing
    self-seeking
    sales & business

2. HI ORIG
   HI INT

"Intuitive type"

    unconventional
    risk-taker
    insight
    introvert
    autonomous
    isolative
    self-centered
    arts & humanities

Practical
Concrete
Literal

——INTELLECT- - - ORIGENCE - —ENCE ——

Theoretical
Abstract
Symbolic

    conforming
    acquiescer
    persistence
    extravert
    dependent
    friendly
    self-effacing
    commercial & service

    conventional
    rule-follower
    logic
    introversive
    independent
    guarded sociality
    self-confident
    sciences & professions

3. LO ORIG
   LO INT

"Industrious type"

4. LO ORIG
   HI INT

"Intellective type"

Structured
Regular
Explicit

Development of Scales

Development of these special scales in the creativity/intelligence study has been given in detail elsewhere [Welsh, 1975] but may be easily summarized. Subjects, highly talented and gifted high-school students attending a special summer program, were selected in terms of their pattern of scores on two standard tests. Groups of students were selected who scored either extremely high or extremely low on a difficult intelligence test, Terman's Concept Mastery Tests [Terman, 1956], and at the same time either high or low on a noncognitive measure, the Revised Art Scale of the Welsh Figure Preference Test (WFPT), widely used in creativity research [Welsh, 1959, 1979]. There were thus available for MMPI item analysis four groups: (1) high on the creativity measure but low on the intelligence test; (2) high on both; (3) low on both; and (4) low on creativity but high on intelligence.

The MMPI item pool was then searched to find items that differentiated each group from the other three groups considered conjointly. For example, an item such as "When someone does me a wrong I feel I should pay him back if I can, just for the principle of the thing," showing a True response pattern of 82% for group 1, 57% for 2, 54% for 3, and 55% for 4 is a good item for this kind of analysis. The item typifies the one group but does not differentiate the other groups. "Some of my family have habits that bother and annoy me" shows a pattern of 43% True for group 2 with 23% for group 1, 21% for 3, and 24% for 4. "I frequently ask people for advice" is more often answered True by group 3 than by the other groups. Typical of group 4 is a True response to "I find it hard to make talk when I meet new people."

The items typifying each of the four groups can be organized in terms of meaningful psychological clusters [see Welsh, 1975, pp. 245-57] and can be consulted to see the specific item content characterizing each group, but the essential personological nature of the content is indicated by the summary of clusters given in Table 2. It may be of interest to compare these particular item groupings derived from the MMPI with the general features of the four origence/intellectence types shown in Table 1 which are based on items from the Adjective Check List (ACL) and the Strong Vocational Interest Blank (SVIB) as well as the MMPI.

Scoring of Scales

The items typifying each group can, of course, be construed as a scale and scored on that basis. Item numbers for the four scales are given in Welsh [1975, p. 244] and also in Dahlstrom, Welsh, and Dahlstrom [1975, pp. 329-30]; these lists may be used in the construction of scoring keys. For convenience, as well as to ensure con-

Table 2. Summary of Item Clusters for Special MMPI Scales

High Origence/Low Intellectence M-1	High Origence/High Intellectence M-2
Misanthropic and negative attitude toward others	Asociality, lack of social interests
Tension and excitement	Introversive withdrawal, emotional subjectivity
Need for stimulation and change	Denial of physical, mental symptoms and fears
Variable energy level	
Worry, pessimism, indecision	Interest in serious matters, lack of interest in trivia
Impulsivity and compulsivity	Permissive morality, attitudinal frankness
Lack of resentment of others, permissive morality	Recognition and acceptance of basic id urges and impulses
Family difficulties	Rejection or denial of conventional religiosity
Regressive attitude toward childhood	
Lack of serious interests	Rejection of home and family

Low Origence/Low Intellectence M-3	Low Origence/High Intellectence M-4
Sociable and gregarious, personal objectivity	Positive regard for others, philanthropic and altruistic attitudes
Conventional, orthodox, fundamental religiosity	Denial of somatic symptoms, fears, and worries
Admission of symptoms, fears, and phobias	Decisive and self-confident
Mental alertness and practicality	Denial of basic id urges and impulses
Denial of basic id urges and impulses	Social ineptness, lack of social ease
Conventional and practical interests	Lack of aesthetic interests
Dependence on and acceptance of family	

tinuity in nomenclature, the convention used is to refer to the MMPI scales as M-1, M-2, M-3, and M-4. The counterpart scales for the ACL are referred to as A-1, A-2, A-3, and A-4; those for the Strong VIB use the initial letter S, and those developed subsequently for the California Psychological Inventory (CPI) are designated by C.

A table of T scores based on statistics for the gifted adolescents used in developing the origence/intellectence scales is given in Welsh [1975, p. 260]. For those who wish to use the Minnesota normals for the generation of T scores, means and standard deviations are reported in Dahlstrom, Welsh, and Dahlstrom [1975, pp. 329-30]. It should be noted, however, that these statistics are based on a somewhat reduced set of items, as indicated there.

The scales themselves can be interpreted as a four-scale profile but in most cases they are more meaningful when converted into dimensional scores. The raw scores for the scales are first expressed as T scores and then converted into difference scores showing the location in the two-dimensional personality model.

The dimensional score for origence is calculated by subtracting the sum of the two low origence T scores (M-3 + M-4) from the sum of the two high origence T scores (M-1 + M-2). Similarly, the dimensional score for intellectence is obtained by subtracting the two low intellectence T scores (M-1 + M-3) from the sum of the two high intellectence T scores (M-2 + M-4). Examples illustrating this method of converting the four typological scale scores into dimensional scores are shown in Table 3. It should be noted that for the norm group the mean difference is zero with a standard deviation of 20. Thus it can be seen that a representative group of architects falls slightly below the average of gifted adolescents on origence but falls one standard deviation above the students on intellectence. Creative architects, on the other hand, exceed them on both dimensions, scoring better than a standard deviation higher on origence and a standard deviation and a half higher on intellectence.

Implications for Creativity

The location of the two groups of architects in the personality model indicated by their difference scores on the two dimensions illustrates very nicely one of the hypotheses set forth in the original gifted-adolescent study: "A person is likely to be judged as creative if he falls high on origence and high on intellectence *relative* to the central tendency of his own peer status group" [Welsh, 1975, p. 198]. It is clear that the creative architects with scores of +21 on

Table 3. Computation of Dimensional Scores from Quadrant Values of Origence
and Intellectence on Two Groups of Architects

Representative Architects N = 41		Creative Architects N = 40	

Mean Raw Scores

M-1	M-2
13	29

M-3	M-4
25	28

Mean T Scores   Sum

M-1	M-2
44	57

101⌐
      ⌐ −2
103⌐   ⌐ ORIG

M-3	M-4
48	55

Sum   92   112
         ⌐___⌐
         +20
         INT

Mean Raw Scores

M-1	M-2
14	32

M-3	M-4
20	25

Mean T Scores   Sum

M-1	M-2
45	63

108⌐
      ⌐ +21
87⌐   ⌐ ORIG

M-3	M-4
37	50

Sum   82   113
         ⌐___⌐
         +31
         INT

Example: Computation of origence score is as follows:

$T_{(M-1)} + T_{(M-2)}$ = High origence; 44 + 57 = 101.

$T_{(M-3)} + T_{(M-4)}$ = Low origence; 48 + 55 = 103.

ORIG = (High origence) − (Low origence); 101 − 103 = −2.

origence and +31 on intellectence do indeed fall higher than the
representative architects on both dimensions, since the latter show
scores of only −2 on origence and +20 on intellectence. These loca-
tions for the MMPI scores are consistent with findings based on
composite scores for the dimensions which include difference scores
for the ACL and the SVIB as well as the MMPI. For a total of 124
architects, rated creativity correlated .47 with composite ORIG and
.30 with composite INT.

Implications for Intelligence

In the original study of gifted adolescents the composite score
for intellectence was highly correlated with the verbal Concept Mastery Test (CMT), with values of .74 for males and .72 for females;
composite origence showed only .02 for males and .09 for females.
A somewhat different relation appears for a nonverbal intelligence
test, the D-48 [Black, 1963; see also Welsh, 1969, pp. 34-37]. Although INT is positively correlated, .41 for males and .32 for females,

a negative correlation is found with ORIG, −.18 and −.13. The D-48 is a timed test with few items and seems to be susceptible to the effects of careless errors. Thus, the high origent person may earn a lower score than he/she should because he/she is careless, fails to follow instructions, or responds impulsively.

CMT scores were available for the creative architects discussed above and correlations were calculated for MMPI origence and intellectence. Values of .17 and .28 did not attain significance because of the small N (40) but are of interest since INT shows a stronger relationship than ORIG to verbal intelligence.

Diamond [1971] used MMPI origence/intellectence scales to select subjects high and low on origence. Following brainstorming instructions, the high origent subjects improved their scores on some of Guilford's structure of intellect measures [1967] while the low origent group did not.

An extensive correlational analysis of regular MMPI scales as well as the MMPI origence/intellectence scales with measures of intelligence and teacher ratings may be found in Welsh [1977].

Other Areas of Research

The MMPI was employed in a study of delinquency by Koszalka [1976], and data were analyzed in the origence/intellectence framework. A sample of 167 subjects ages 16-17 from a training school had a mean IQ of 95. As expected, most of them fell below the mean of the gifted adolescents on intellectence (93.5%), but more than half (58%) were higher on origence. Percentages in the quadrants are: high origence/low intellectence (55%), high/high (3%), low/low (38.5%), and low origence/high intellectence (3.5%). Despite this departure from the norms for the gifted, the internal relationships with other variables were consistent. That is, those delinquents with higher IQs fell higher on intellectence than their lower IQ peers. Although the typical delinquent MMPI profile was obtained, those higher on origence showed more saliency of Pd than those relatively lower.

A nondelinquent sample of 40 subjects with a mean IQ of 87 was reported by Baughman and Dahlstrom [1968]. Although they also fell low on intellectence, they had fewer subjects high on origence. Percentages in the quadrants were: high origence/low intellectence (40%), high/high (2.5%), low/low (50%), and low origence/high intellectence (7.5%).

Adult criminals also fall low on intellectence but are close to the norm for the most part on origence. MMPI data were made available by James A. Panton (personal communication) for six different types of crimes ranging from white-collar crimes to first-degree murder; origence scores fell between +2 and −7, while those on intellectence ranged from −22 to −29. In another study a group of drug abusers was contrasted with a control group of prisoners; the former were at +12 on origence and −14 on intellectence, while the controls were lower on both dimensions (−1 on origence and −23 on intellectence). This is consistent with other studies showing an association of drug use and origence [Welsh, 1975, p. 221].

Dogmatism in college students has been investigated by Faschingbauer and Eglevsky [1977] and Faschingbauer, Moore, and Stone [1978]. MMPI scales for origence/intellectence were correlated with Rokeach's scale of dogmatism [1960]. For 30 North Carolina and 40 Texas undergraduates, correlations with ORIG were .02 and .07, while highly significant negative correlations appeared for INT of −.61 and −.59. Thus, the high intellectent person may express less dogmatism than the low, but the dimension seems unrelated to origence.

Two Methods of Analysis

Analyses of results with origence/intellectence scales have been carried out in two different ways. The first emphasizes the hypothetical personality *dimensions* themselves as exemplified by correlation of the difference scores with other variables. The second method of analysis utilizes the *typology* generated by these dimensions. Rather than a fourfold typology based on extreme scores alone, as employed in the initial study, a method was developed so that medium-scoring groups could be accommodated as well. To this end a scatter plot was made with orthogonal axes for origence and intellectence since the difference scores were uncorrelated; in this bivariate space each student was located in terms of his or her scores on ORIG and INT. Cutting scores were then used to divide each dimension into three equal parts — low, medium, and high. In principle such a conjoint tripartition necessarily yields nine sections or "novants" with exactly one-ninth of the cases (11.11%) in each novant. (The term "novant" is used here in a general descriptive sense, not in the special meaning indicated when it was first employed by Welsh [1965].) Although this ideal distribution was not obtained precisely, it was closely approximated, as may be judged by the novant frequencies given in Tables 4 and 5.

For consistency in nomenclature the extreme "corner" novants follow the same numerical system as before, i.e., high ORIG/low INT = 1, high ORIG/high INT = 2, low ORIG/low INT = 3, and low ORIG/high INT = 4. The middle novants are designated by composite numerals to indicate their novant location: high ORIG/medium INT = 1-2, medium ORIG/low INT = 2-3, medium ORIG/high INT = 2-4, and low ORIG/medium INT = 3-4. The central novant, medium ORIG/medium INT, is given the designation 0 to show its location at the origin of both dimensions.

Novant Profiles

Figures 1 and 2 show the mean MMPI profiles for the male and female gifted adolescents grouped in terms of novant location based on composite scores for origence and intellectence. In addition to the validity scales and the regular clinical scales, a two-scale configuration at the right shows scores for factor scales A and R [Welsh, 1956, 1965]. Profile codes for the clinical scales are given in Tables 4 and 5 with the noncorrected code shown first and the K-corrected code second. The former is drawn with a solid line in the figures, and the K-corrected scale values are indicated by the dashed line. Emphasis will be placed on the profiles without K since previous analyses of these subjects by the present writer have been based on noncorrected scale scores.

MMPI profiles for the entire sample are available in Welsh [1969]; profiles are also given separately there for subgroups according to areas of interest, i.e., English, science, art, music, etc.

Most striking in the profile configurations shown in Figures 1 and 2 is the dramatic shift in slope of the factor scales. A is positively related to origence and negatively related to intellectence, but R follows the opposite pattern. Thus, there is a drop in A and a rise in R as one progresses across the novants from 1 to 4.

A similar kind of diagonal progression may be seen in the validity scales. In novant 1 there is a clear spike on F, with L and K below average; this shifts in novant 4 to a peak on K, with L and F right at the average.

Elevation of the clinical profile follows a similar pattern and is consistent with the usual association of F and profile height. Novant 1 has a mean T-score elevation of 63.9 for males but novant 4 is only 52.5. Females are slightly lower in absolute elevation but show

Table 4. Origence/Intellectence Novant Mean Profile Codes
for Gifted Adolescent Males

Novant 1 High ORIG/Low INT N = 61	Novant 1-2 High ORIG/Med INT N = 37	Novant 2 High ORIG/High INT N = 57
8'94576-3210	5'49867-3210	5'489 62-7301
879'546-3210	5'89476-3210	5'849762-301
Novant 1-3 Med ORIG/Low INT N = 58	Novant 0 Med ORIG/Med INT N = 75	Novant 2-4 Med ORIG/High INT N = 59
59-4876312/0	5-946837 120	5-63 9824 07/1
9587-46312/0	5879-463120	58-67439201
Novant 3 Low ORIG/Low INT N = 59	Novant 3-4 Low ORIG/Med INT N = 68	Novant 4 Low ORIG/High INT N = 50
95 436782/10	5-36429708/1	5-36204/9871
9-47583612/0	5-78346 92 01	5-38 47 62 019

Note: The first code in each novant is based on uncorrected scores; the second is K-corrected.

Table 5. Origence/Intellectence Novant Mean Profile Codes
for Gifted Adolescent Females

Novant 1 High ORIG/Low INT N = 68	Novant 1-2 High ORIG/Med INT N = 63	Novant 2 High ORIG/High INT N = 67
94867-3120/5	49 68-73201/5	69-480732/15
98476-3120/5	98 467-3201/5	689-47 032/15
Novant 1-3 Med ORIG/Low INT N = 69	Novant 0 Med ORIG/Med INT N = 73	Novant 2-4 Med ORIG/High INT N = 65
9-46873 0/215	69438072/15	64930 827/15
98-746310/25	89467302/15	68479 302/15
Novant 3 Low ORIG/Low INT N = 74	Novant 3-4 Low ORIG/Med INT N = 85	Novant 4 Low ORIG/High INT N = 53
6934 782/015	63094 7/2815	6304/295781
967843 21/05	786 4390 1/25	6783401/925

Note: The first code in each novant is based on uncorrected scores; the second is K-corrected.

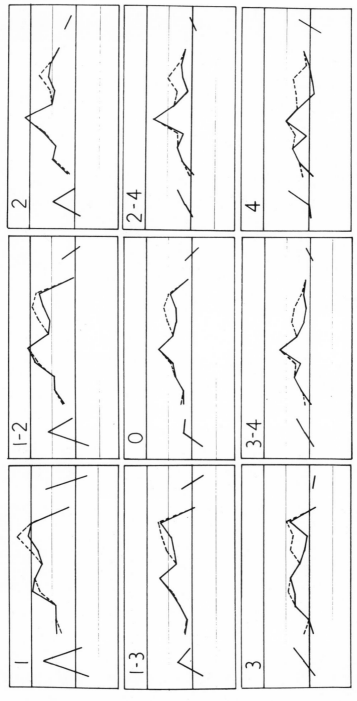

Figure 1. Mean Values on Basic MMPI Scales (+A and R) for Male Adolescents Falling in Each Novant.

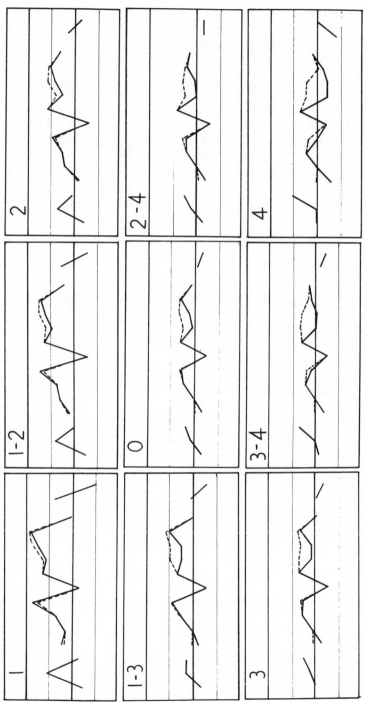

Figure 2. Mean Values on Basic MMPI Scales (+A and R) for Female Adolescents Falling in Each Novant.

the same progression. The mean T for novant 1 is 59.5 and for novant 4, 50.3. (For comparative purposes, the mean T scores for Mf have been subtracted from 100 to reverse the scoring direction.)

Mf shows some interesting sex differences in terms of both absolute elevation and relative salience in the profile. For females the diagonally opposite novants of 1 and 4 have Mf scores over 46, and the remaining novants fall in the 43 to 44 range. Yet novant 4 is the only one in which Mf is not the lowest scale in the profile code; Pt, Sc, and Hs drop below it.

For males there is a marked increase in Mf with origence and a slight increase with intellectence. Thus novant 3 is lowest with a T score of 58.2 and novant 2 is highest with 72.1. The salience of Mf, however, seems to be more strongly associated with intellectence. An index was calculated using the following formula: $2(Mf) - (Pd + Pa)$. The lowest index was earned by novant 1 with only 2.9; the highest appeared for novant 2-4, 22.6, even though it ranked fourth in absolute elevation. This index of Mf salience was calculated for architects studied by MacKinnon [1961] and showed the most creative group highest at 29, a middle group next at 27, and a representative group lowest at 20.

For females Pa seems to follow a similar pattern of relationship to intellectence. An index of the salience of Pa was calculated with the formula $2(Pa) - (Mf + Pt)$. The three low intellectent novants have a mean index of 16.7, the novants medium on intellectence average 18.5, and the high intellectent novants fall highest at 23.4.

Many other implications of the novant profiles for personality assessment can be inferred from a study of the figures and the tables of codes. For example, Sc is greater than Pt for the high and the medium levels of origence, but for all three novants low on origence Pt exceeds Sc. This relationship holds for both sexes. It may be pointed out that Sc was one of the few MMPI scales to be significantly correlated with rated creativity in architects [Hall and MacKinnon, 1969].

The neurotic triad shows mild elevation, with Hy the leading scale in all novants for females and for all but novant 2 for males, where D is most elevated. The order of the neurotic triad scales is consistently Hy > D > Hs for females and for six of the male novants.

There seems to be a sex difference in the role of D. For males there is an increase with intellectence and with origence so that novant 3 has the lowest mean (50.2) and novant 2 has the highest

(60.0). For females, however, D rises only in the three high origent novants and is close to the norm for medium and low origence.

Finally, one last example will be given which is related to impulsivity and impulse control. An index of inhibition/exhibition was calculated from the formula $(Hy + Pa) - (Pd + Ma)$. Positive values indicate capacity for restraint and modulation, and negative values are associated with intemperance and acting-out behavior. The index is positively related to intellectence and negatively to origence. Thus, the greatest negative values fall in novant 1, -15.1 for males and -15.2 for females; the highest positive values appear for the opposite novant 4, 11.0 for males and 14.5 for females. It may be pointed out that in a study of careless errors made in answering intelligence test items [Welsh, 1968] it was the high origent/low intellectent individuals who committed the most, and the least were made by those low on origence and high on intellectence.

By way of comparison it may be noted that a representative sample of prisoners reported by Panton [1976] scored -12.1, a value somewhat lower than novant 1 students. Consistent with the implications of the inhibition/exhibition index, a sample of prisoners age 60 years or more had an index of only -2.1. The three groups of architects [Hall and MacKinnon, 1969] did not differ on this index; for the most creative to the least the scores are 7, 8, and 8.

In summary, it is our contention that many phenomena of interest in human behavior in addition to personality characteristics related to creativity and intelligence, the original focus of our study, may be susceptible to investigation in terms of the concept of origence and intellectence and the fourfold typology generated by this two-dimensional personality model. If the model proves feasible, then we should expect formulations to generate specific predictions within the framework of the general hypotheses of psychological similarity, categorical congruity, and the consistency corollary.

Section IV
Professional Issues

Efforts to make the MMPI convenient to use and economical of the psychologist's time and energy helped to ensure its wide acceptance and utilization in numerous contexts and settings. Unfortunately, these same features have led to careless or insensitive uses, even frank abuses of the test. Since nonprofessionals can easily be trained to administer, score, and record the results of the MMPI, necessary professional supervision may tend to become less vigilant, testing routines may deteriorate, safeguards be neglected, and established procedures lose relevance and sensitivity to the feelings, reactions, and concerns of test subjects, clients, or patients. The articles in this section take up some of the many issues involved in the proper use of any psychological test. These writers discuss the ways in which the effectiveness of the MMPI may be undermined and the welfare of the individual being tested may be less adequately served, if not actually harmed rather than helped. Only a few of these important problems can be covered by these selections, however; all users of the MMPI should be thoroughly familiar with the relevant publications of the American Psychological Association [1974, 1977] and such general discussions as Gredler (1975) and Westin [1967].

It will be readily apparent that there is another common theme running through these articles: the items of the MMPI, their content, their role in diagnostic and personological assessment, their indispensability or lack thereof, as well as their intrusiveness and controversiality. These articles supplement material presented earlier on

343

response sets that may be triggered by some test items and on the importance of item subtlety (in section II) and item content (in section III). The issue of primary interest here is the elimination of particular items or the reduction of the total item pool of the MMPI. It should be pointed out that some who work with the test have advocated augmenting the item pool to cover content areas not adequately sampled by the existing inventory [Schofield, 1966].

The first article began as a letter written in reply to a layman who had become concerned about items in the MMPI that seemed to be related less to personality than to fundamental religious beliefs and commitments. He had written to Starke Hathaway to find out from the author of the test why such material should be covered. After preparing and sending his reply, Hathaway circulated the letter to several colleagues for their information and general reactions. At their urging this reply was published in the *American Psychologist*. It has subsequently been reprinted in other collections and is included here because it covers so many aspects of this problem in its sensitive and detailed recounting of the decisions that Hathaway and McKinley made as they constructed the inventory.

Toward the end of his letter, Hathaway states: "As for psychologists who are those most widely employing such tests, I am aware that the public will look with increasing seriousness upon those who are entrusted with problems of mental health and the assessment of human actions." A little over a decade later the trial in the United States District Court of New Jersey that is reported in the second article took place, involving the very issues that Hathaway had discussed. It is unlikely that this suit will be the last one in which psychological tests and their uses will be challenged. We hope that the focus will continue to be on the specific uses, practices, and procedures of psychologists and not on the test instruments per se.

Articles 3 and 4 in this section report empirical studies of one alternative solution that has been advanced to get around the adverse reactions that some test subjects have to the content of some items in the MMPI: namely, simply dropping those items from the test. The authors provide data on the extent of the objections, the kinds of items under fire, and the impact of such proposed deletions upon the discriminative power of the inventory. In light of these findings, it seems clear that important test variance would have to be sacrificed if the item pool were bowdlerized to meet all objections that have been raised. Accordingly, test users have been urged to take greater care in preparing test subjects for the material in such inventories as the MMPI, to set up safeguards against possible violations of security of the test answer sheets and reports together with appropriate communication to the subjects concerning these protective measures, and to monitor the work of those who are involved in handling and filing test materials and reports to ensure that professional standards are preserved.

The last article takes up another major development in the use of the MMPI in personality research and clinical practice: efforts to shorten the testing time and reduce the item coverage of the test. As the private practice of psychology has increased and become more diversified, the temptation has grown to abbreviate psychodiagnostic procedures, bypass efforts to study and appraise the status of clients as they present themselves for help, and move quickly to direct interventions more narrowly focused and goal-limited. Time is money in such a practice, and the professional may quite understandably yield to temptations to pursue various shortcuts in his or her contacts: four-card Rorschach administrations, three-subtest Wechsler batteries, and shortened interviews and diagnostic workups. Efforts to develop short forms of the MMPI are a natural extension of this trend. Unfortunately, the full extent of the sacrifices that are required for such abbreviations of the inventory has not been fully appreciated. The serious weakening of the basic scales and the loss of all of the special diagnostic scales that are summarized in article 5 should be sobering to any worker who may be contemplating using one or another of the current short forms of the MMPI for either research or clinical application. Whatever value the MMPI may possess as a clinical or personological instrument is seriously attenuated in any short-form version.

The articles in this section came from the following sources: article 1 from S. R. Hathaway. MMPI: professional use by professional people. *American Psychologist*, 1964, 19, 204-10; article 2 is an original manuscript prepared by W. G. Dahlstrom for this volume; article 3 from J. N. Butcher and A. Tellegen. Objections to MMPI items. *Journal of Consulting Psychology*, 1966, 30, 527-34; article 4 from C. E. Walker. The effect of eliminating offensive items on the reliability and validity of the MMPI. *Journal of Clinical Psychology*, 1967, 23, 363-66; article 5 is an original manuscript prepared by W. G. Dahlstrom for this volume. We are indebted to the authors and to the publishers of the journals for permission to reproduce these articles in this form.

MMPI: Professional Use by Professional People

S. R. Hathaway

This long letter was prompted by a courteous inquiry that I received. The inquiry referred to the use of the MMPI as an aid in the selection of policemen from among applicants. It was pointed out that there are laws against inquiry about religious affiliation and the specific issue was the presence in the MMPI of items relating to religion.

Letter to Mr. R.

First I would like to express my appreciation of your reasonably expressed inquiry about the MMPI as possibly offensive in the statements that relate to religious activities and which might provide personal information on which discriminatory acts might be based. Because of sporadic public antagonism to psychological testing, and in view of our mutual concern for our civil liberties, I am going to answer you at considerable length and with unusual care. I shall send copies of this answer to the Psychological Corporation and to others who may be concerned. Let me assure you at the outset that I believe I am proceeding from a considered position rather than from a defensive attitude that could lead me to irrationally protect the MMPI, other such tests, or psychologists in general. I believe that I would be among the first to criticize some of the uses to which tests are put, and some of those who use them improperly. I must also immediately make it clear that I am antagonistic to ignorant attacks upon tests. Tests are not offensive elements; the offensive elements,

347

if any, come with the misuse of tests. To attack tests is, to a certain extent, comparable to an attack upon knives. Both good and bad use of knives occurs because they are sharp instruments. To eliminate knives would, of course, have a limiting effect upon the occurrence of certain hostile acts, but it would also greatly limit the activities of surgeons. I simply discriminate between the instrument and the objectives and applications of the persons who wield it. I am calling attention to the difference between a switchblade knife, which is good for nothing but attack, and a scalpel knife, good for healing purposes but which can also be used as a weapon. I hope that no one will think that any test was devised in the same spirit that switchblade knives were devised. It is absurd if someone holds the belief that psychologists malignantly developed instruments such as the MMPI for use against the welfare of man, including of course man's personal liberties and rights. But if the MMPI and such tests have origins analogous to the scalpel, and are really perversely used to man's disadvantage, we are properly concerned. Let me turn to a history of the MMPI items about which you have inquired.

I should begin with an account of the origin of the MMPI itself. I believe I am competent to do this, and I hope you will see that its origins were motivated toward virtue as I have suggested above. In about 1937, J. C. McKinley, then head of the Department of Neuropsychiatry of the Medical School at the University of Minnesota, supported me in a venture which grew out of a current problem in our psychopathic hospital. The problem lay in the fact that insulin therapy as a treatment method for certain forms of mental disease had just become a widespread method of treatment. Different clinics were finding highly varied values. Some reported the treatment to be exceedingly effective; others said it was ineffective. The treatment was somewhat dangerous to patients, and it was exceedingly expensive in terms of hospitalization and nursing care. McKinley happened to be one of the neuropsychiatrists of the time who felt that more careful investigation should be undertaken before such treatments were applied, and in particular before we used them on our patients.

It occurred to us that the difficulty in evaluation of insulin treatment lay largely in the fact that there was no good way to be assured that the patients treated by this method in one clinic were like those treated in another clinic. This was due to the fact that the estimations of the nature of a person's mental illness and of its severity were based upon professional judgment, and could vary with the training background of the particular psychiatrist as well as with his personal experiences. Obviously, if the patients treated at one center were not like those treated at another center, the outcome of treatment might be different. At that time there was no psychological test available that would have helped to remove the diagnostic decisions on the patients in two clinics from the personal biases of the local staffs. There was no way that our hospital staff could select a group of patients for the new treatment who would be surely comparable in diagnosis and severity of illness to those from some other setting. It became an obvious possibility that one might devise a personality test which, like intelligence tests, would somewhat stabilize the identification of the illness and provide an estimate of its severity. Toward this problem the MMPI research was initiated.

I have established that decisions about the kind and severity of mental illness depend upon the psychological examinations of the psychiatrists and other professional persons. The items upon which the judgments are based constitute the symptoms of mental maladjustment or illness. Such symptoms have for many, many years been listed in the textbooks of psychiatry and clinical psychology that treat with mental disorder. These symptoms are verbal statements from or about the patient. The simplest and most obvious form of these symptoms are statements that confess feelings of unhappiness, depression, and the like. The statements may also be less personal, as in complaints about one's lot in life and about the inability to find employment or the mistreatment by others.

In summary, the symptoms of mental illness and unhappiness are represented in verbal complaints or statements that relate to personal feelings or personal experiences or reactions to job and home. It should be immediately apparent that unlike most physical illnesses, these verbally presented complaints or symptoms usually do not permit direct observation by others. If a patient reports a painful nodule or abdominal pain, the reported pain can usually be observed by some physical or nonverbal means that lends credence to the complaint. Many symptoms of mental illness are contrastingly difficult to observe by nonverbal means. It is almost impossible to establish that the person presenting the symptom is actually suffering from a distortion of his psychologically healthy mental state by some psychological complex. There is much arbitrariness even in the statement, "I am unhappy." Frequently no physical observation can be brought to bear upon the statement. The complainant may look unhappy and may even add that he is suicidal, yet friends and the examiner can agree that he is "just asking for sympathy, is no worse off than the average." There is no way of solidly deciding what the words really mean. This point is crucial to what I am writing. If it is not clear at this point, reference books on semantics should be consulted. S. I. Hayakawa would be a good source.

I know of no method which will permit us to absolutely assess unhappiness or mental illness, either as to kind or severity, unless we start from inescapable symptoms that are verbally expressed and subject to the vagaries in the personal connotations of words and phrases. In initiating the research upon what was to produce the MMPI, we collected as many as we could find of the symptomatic statements recognized by authorities as indicative of unhappiness and mental illness. There were hundreds of these statements. We had at one time well over a thousand of them. Every one of these symptomatic statements had already been written into the literature or had been used as a practical bit of clinical evidence in the attempt to understand patients. I repeat this because I want to thoroughly emphasize that every item in the MMPI came from assumed relationships to the assessment of human beings for better diagnosis and treatment of possible mental illness.

Now with all this preamble I am prepared to discuss the particular items that you have highlighted in your letter. It happens that, among the many items collected and finally selected to make up the MMPI, there were at least 19 relating to religion in one way or another. I have listed these items to remind you again of the ones you cited, and I have added others that may further illustrate what I am saying (see Table 1). Now you have asked why we included these statements on religion among the possible symptoms of psychological maladjustment. Why should these items still appear in the MMPI?

In the first instance, the subject matter evidenced in the symptoms of depressed or otherwise mentally disturbed persons often largely centers in religion. There is a well-recognized pattern of psychological distortion to which we apply the term religiosity. When we use the word "religiosity," we indicate a symptomatic pattern wherein the process of an intercurrent psychological maladjustment is evidenced by extremes of religious expression that are out of the usual context for even the deeply religious person. A bishop friend of mine once illustrated the problem he sometimes had in this connection by his account of a parishioner who had routinely given a tithe as his offering toward support of the church, but who, within a few weeks, had increased the amount he gave until it was necessary for him to embezzle money for his weekly offering. Surely, my friend said, there is more here than ordinary devotion; there is something which

Table 1. List of MMPI Items Related to Religion with Percentage Endorsements by Normal Men and Women

	Male		Female	
	True	No Answer	True	No Answer
I am very religious (more than most people).	8	9	11	9
Religion gives me no worry.	83	4	70	4
I go to church almost every week.	42	3	52	4
I pray several times every week.	50	3	83	2
I read in the Bible several times a week.	21	5	30	3
I feel sure that there is only one true religion.	49	8	51	11
I have no patience with people who believe there is only one true religion.	56	4	47	10
I believe there is a God.	92	5	96	2
I believe there is a devil and a hell in afterlife.	63	14	67	14
I believe in a life hereafter.	76	12	87	7
I believe in the second coming of Christ.	57	18	68	12
Christ performed miracles such as changing water into wine.	69	16	77	15
The only miracles I know of are simply tricks that people play on one another.	37	10	27	14
A minister can cure disease by praying and putting his hand on your head.	4	10	5	11
Everything is turning out just like the prophets of the Bible said it would.	52	29	54	32
My soul sometimes leaves my body.	8	18	5	12
I am a special agent of God.	14	13	16	21
I have had some very unusual religious experiences.	20	5	13	2
I have been inspired to a program of life based on duty which I have since carefully followed.	42	14	50	15

should be considered from another frame of reference. In this anecdote there is an element of the symptomatic pattern, religiosity. But, as is true of nearly every other aspect of human personality to which the MMPI refers, no one item will ordinarily establish this distortion of the ordinarily meaningful position of religion. And no one item can be used to detect the problem as it occurs in various persons. Two persons rarely express even their usual religious feelings in identical ways.

It never occurred to us in selecting these items for the MMPI that we were asking anything relative to the particular religion of our patients. It obviously did not occur to us that there were other than the Christian orientation wherein religiosity might be observed. Because of this oversight on our part, several of our MMPI symptoms that we assumed were indicative of religiosity happen to be obviously related to the Christian religion, although we find that most persons simply translate to their own orientation if it is different. I should hasten to add that although these symptoms were hoped to be specific to persons who suffer from religiosity, they have not all turned out that way. Not every aspect of religion is at times a symptom of mental illness. Certainly it is obvious that there is nothing symptomatic in admitting to one's personal acceptance or rejection of several of the items. The point at which a group of items becomes consistent in suggesting symptoms is subtle to distinguish. As my bishop friend's story illustrated, it is not unusual that one contributes to religious work even though there exists a doubtful extreme. As I will show below, all these items are endorsed or rejected by some ordinary, normal people. If any of the items have value toward clinical assessment, the value comes in combination with other items which probably will not seem to relate to religion.

The MMPI, which started out so small and inconspicuously, has become a world-known and -used instrument. We did not expect this outcome. If I were to select new items, I would again include items that related to religiosity. I would this time, of course, try to avoid the implication that the religiosity occurred only among adherents to the Christian faith. I am obviously unhappy about the limited applicability of these items, but I am, in the same sense, unhappy about other items in the MMPI. A considerable number of the items have been challenged by other groups from other standpoints. By this I mean only to remind those concerned about these religiosity items that there are frankly stated items on sex, there are items on body functions, there are items on certain occupations; in fact, there are items on most every aspect of psychological life that can be symptomatic of maladjustment and unhappiness. If the psychologist cannot use these personal items to aid in the assessment of people, he suffers as did the Victorian physician who had to examine his female patients by feeling the pulse in the delicate hand thrust from behind a screen. I shall come back to this point later, but it is obvious that if we were making a new MMPI, we would again be faced either with being offensive to subgroupings of people by personal items they object to or, if we did not include personal items and were inoffensive, we would have lost the aim of the instrument.

One may protest that the MMPI is intended for the patient, the mentally ill person, not applicants to schools, high-school children, or to those being considered for jobs. I cannot give a general defense of every such use, but this is a time when preventive health is being emphasized. We urge everyone to get chest X rays and to take immunizing shots. We are now beginning to advocate general surveys with such psychological instruments as the MMPI. The basic justification is the same. We hope to identify potential mental breakdown or delinquency in the school child before he must be dragged before us by desperate parents or by other authority. We hope to hire police, who are given great power over us, with assurance that those we put on the rolls should have good personal qualities for the job. This is not merely to protect us, this also is preventive mental health, since modern job stability can trap unwary workers into placements that leave them increasingly unhappy and otherwise maladjusted. If the personality of an applicant is not appropriate to the job, neither employer nor applicant should go ahead. We have always recognized the employer's use of this principle in his right to personal interview with applicants. Since the items and responses are on record, the MMPI and such devices could be considered to be a more fair method of estimation than the personal interview, and, when they are machine scored, they make possible much greater protection from arbitrary personal judgments and the open ended questions that are standard for personal interviews.

It seems to me that the MMPI examination can be rather comparable to the physical examination for selection of persons. One would not wish to hire a person with a bad heart when the job required behavior that was dangerous to him. I think it would be equally bad to hire a person as a policeman whose psychological traits were inappropriate and then expect him to do dangerous things or shoot to kill as a policeman is expected to do. There is, from physical and psychological examinations, a protection to the person being hired as well as to those hiring him. This is not meant as an argument for the use of the MMPI in every placement that requires special skills or special personality traits. I am arguing a general point.

I would next like to take up MMPI items to bring out a new line of evidence which, I am sorry to say, is not familiar to some psychologists, but which is of importance in giving you an answer to your questions. Turn again to the above items, particularly to the "True" response frequencies. We will look at implications about the people taking the MMPI as we interpret the True frequencies of response for these items. Before we do so, we should consider the source of the frequency figures. The males and females who provided these standard data, which are the basis for all MMPI standards, were persons who came to the University Hospitals bringing patients or who were around the hospitals at the time when we were collecting data. Only those were tested who were not under a doctor's care and who could be reasonably assumed to be normal in mind and body. These persons, whom we call the normal adult cross-section group, came from all over Minnesota, from every socioeconomic and educational level; there is reason to believe that they are a proper representation of the rank and file people of Minnesota. It is probably well known that, in the main, Minnesota population was drawn from North European stock, is largely Christian in background, and has a rather small number in the several minority groups. Certainly, it can hardly be said that this population is unduly weighted with extremists in the direction of overemphasis upon religion or in atheism or in other belief characteristics. Probably one would expect this population to be rather more religious than the average for all the states. Finally, the majority of the persons who provided these basic norms were married persons and most were parents. Data given in the table can be found in the fundamental book on the MMPI, *An MMPI Handbook* by Dahlstrom and Welsh [1960].

But now consider the items. Let us assume, as is often naively assumed, that when one answers an item one tells the truth about oneself. Of course, there is no requirement that those who take the MMPI should tell the truth, and this is a very important point. Also, I have tried to establish that truth is a very complicated semantic concept. But let us assume for the moment that people do tell the truth as they see it. Take the item, "I go to church almost every week." According to the data given, 42% of the men and 52% of the women go to church almost every week. Now these data are representative of the whole state. I am sure that ministers of the state would be gratified if all these people were reporting accurately. Parenthetically, I suppose that "church" was read as "synagogue" or "temple" without much trouble. But I do not know what percentage of people are actually estimated to go to some church almost every week. At any rate I cannot conceive that 42% of the men of the state of Minnesota are in church nearly every week even if 52% of the women are. I even cannot conceive that half of the men in Minnesota and 83% of the women actually pray several times a week. I might imagine that 21% of the men and 30% of the women would read in the Bible several times a week. This would represent about one-fifth of all the men and about one-third of all the women. My real impression is that people simply do not know that much about the Bible. However, take the next item. Here it says that one feels sure there is only one true religion. To this about half of the men and half of the women answered True. Perhaps these might be considered bigoted, but what of the ones who have obviously answered false? There seems to be a great deal of religious tolerance here; about half of the persons of Minnesota do not even express a belief that there is only one true religion.

It is true that a high percentage say they believe there is a God. This seems to be a noncommittal item, since most people are aware that God has many meanings. The item which follows it, however, which permits denying or accepting a belief in a devil and hell in afterlife, is quite interesting. Twenty-three percent of men and 19% of women reject this belief. By contrast, a life hereafter is denied by 24% of men and by 13% of women. The second coming of Christ is expected by only 57% of men and 68% of women if we accept what these figures seem to say. Again, with reversal, Christ as a miracle worker is doubted by 31% of men and 23% of women. Stated more directly, 37% of men and 27% of women come straight out and say that miracles were not performed. The item apparently includes Old and New Testament sources among others. On down in the list, one finds that only 14% of men and 16% of women believe themselves to be special agents of God.

I think I have gone over enough of these items to provide a suggestion of what I am going to next point out. But I would like to add two more MMPI items in sharper illustration of the point. These two additional items have nothing obvious to do with religion. The first of them is, "I almost never dream," and the second is, "I dream frequently." One of the first things we found in the early studies of MMPI items was that the same person frequently answered True to both these items. When asked about the seeming contradiction, such a person would respond, among other possibilities, by saying to the first item that surely he had very few dreams. But, coming to the next item, he changed his viewpoint to say that he dreamed frequently as compared to some of the people he knew. This shift of emphasis led us to recognize that, in addition to the general semantic problem developed above, when people respond to items, they also do not usually respond with the connotations we expect. Apparently even if the people are telling a truth of some kind, one would need an interview with them to know what they really intend to report by answering True or False. I suppose this is similar to the problem of the oath of allegiance over which some people are so concerned. One may state that he is loyal to the United States, for example, yet really mean that he is deeply convinced that its government should be overthrown and that, with great loyalty to his country, he believes revolution to be the only salvation for the country. However much we might object to it, this belief would permit a person to swear to his loyalty in complete honesty. I think most everyone is aware of this problem about oaths, and it is a routine one with MMPI item responses.

In summary of all this, if one wished to persecute those who by their answers to these items seemed inconsistent with some religious or atheistic pattern of beliefs, there would be an embarrassingly large number of ordinary people in Minnesota who would be open to suspicion both ways. In reality, the responses made to these items have many variations in truth and meaning. And it would betray considerable ignorance of the practical psychology of communication if any absolute reliance were placed on responses.

As a final but most significant point relative to these items, I should point out that administration of the MMPI requires that those who are taking the test be clearly informed that they may omit any item they do not wish to answer for whatever purpose. I have never seen any studies that have drawn conclusions from the omission of particular items by a particular person. We found that items among these that are being considered were unusually frequently omitted. You may notice this in the No Answer columns. One-third of all the respondents failed to answer the item relative to the Bible and the prophets, for example. This is a basic fact about the MMPI and such tests, and I cannot see why this freedom will not permit to each person the latitude to preserve his privacy if he is afraid. Still again I would add that, in many settings, possibly nearly every setting, where the MMPI is used in group administration, those who take it are permitted to refuse the whole test. I admit that this might seem prejudicial, and I suspect that if any one chooses to protect himself, he will do it by omitting items rather than by not taking the test at all. Is refusal to take the test any different from refusing to subject oneself to an employment or admission interview by a skilled interviewer? I think that some people who have been writing about the dangers of testing must have an almost magical belief in tests. Sometimes, when I feel so at a loss in attempting to help someone with a psychological problem, I wish that personality tests were really that subtle and powerful.

Groups of items called scales, formed into patterns called profiles, are the useful product of tests like the MMPI. I note that in your inquiry you show an awareness that the MMPI is usually scored by computers. The scales that are used for most interpretation include 10 "clinical" scales. These are the ones that carry most of the information. Several other scales indicate whether the subject understood and followed the directions. No one of these main scales has less than 30 items in it and most of them have many more than 30. The scores from the machine come back not only anonymously indicating the number of items answered in a way that counts on the scale, but the scores are usually already transformed into what we call T or standard scores. These T scores are still more remote from the particular items that make up a scale. The graphic array of T scores for the scales are finally printed into the profile.

In this connection, there is a very pretty possibility offered by the development of computer scoring. If we wish to take advantage of the presumed advantages of the use of tests, yet be assured that particular item responses shall not be considered, then we only need to be assured that those using the test do not score it, must send it straightway to the computer center, and, in the end, receive back only the profiles which are all that should be used in any case. The original test may be destroyed.

The scales of the profile were not arbitrarily set up. The MMPI is an experimentally derived instrument. If an item counts on a scale, I want to make it very clear that that item counts, not because some clinician or somebody thought that the item was significant for measuring something about human personality, but it counts because in the final analysis well-diagnosed groups of maladjusted, sometimes mentally ill persons answered the item with an average frequency differing from the average frequency of the normative group that I have used for the above illustrative data. This is an exceedingly significant point and is probably least often understood by those who have not had psychometric training. No one read or composed these items to decide what it meant if one of them were answered True or False. The meanings of the items came from the fact that persons with a certain kind of difficulty answered in an average way different from the "normal" standard. For example, the item "I go to church almost every week" is counted on a scale for estimating the amount of depression. We did not just decide that going to church was related to depression. We had the response frequencies from men who complained that they were depressed. They answered True with a frequency of only 20%. You will note that the normals answered True with a frequency of 42%—22% more often. Now this difference also turned up for women who were depressed. We adopted a False response to this item as a count on the depression scale of the MMPI. We do not even now know why depressed people say they go to church less often. Note that you are not depressed if you say False to this one item. Actually, 55% of the normals answered False. Use of the item for an MMPI scale depended on the fact that even more of the depressed persons answered False and so if you say False you have added one item more in common with depressed people than with the normals despite the fact that more than half the normals answered as you did.

Even psychologists very familiar with the MMPI cannot tell to which scale or scales an item belongs without looking it up. People often ask for a copy of a test so they can cite their objections to items they think objectionable, and they assume that the meaning of the item is obvious and that they can tell how it is interpreted. I am often asked what specified items mean. I do not know because the scoring of the scales has become so abstracted that I have no contact with items.

One more point along this line. Only 6 of the above 19 items are counted on one of the regular scales that are mostly used for personality evaluation. Four more are used on a measure that is only interpreted in estimation of the ability of the subject to follow directions and to read well enough. In fact, about 200 of the whole set of items did not end up on any one of the regularly used scales. But, of course, many of these 200 other items occur on one or another of the many experimental MMPI scales that have been published.

We cannot change or leave out any items or we lose an invaluable heritage of research in mental health. To change even a comma in an item may change its meaning. I would change the words of some items, omit some, and add new ones if I could. A new test should be devised, but its cost would be on the order of $100,000 and we are not at this time advanced enough so that the new one would be enough better to compensate for the loss of the research and diagnostic value of the present MMPI even in view of its manifest weaknesses.

The subject of professional training brings me to my next line of response. It is appropriate that the public should be aware of the uses of such tests as the MMPI, but I have repeatedly pointed out that it is far more important that the public should be aware of the persons who are using the test and of the uses to which it is put. In this context, the distributor of the MMPI, the Psychological Corporation of New York City, accepts and practices the ethical principles for test distributors that have been promulgated by the American Psychological Association. These rules prohibit the sale of tests to untrained or incompetent persons. Use or possession of the MMPI by others is prohibited but, since this carries no present penalty, the distributor is helpless except for his control of the supply. Tests, as I have said above, are not like switchblade knives, designed to be used against people; they offer potential contributions to happiness. And I cannot believe that a properly accredited clinical psychologist or psychiatrist or physician who may use the MMPI would under any circumstances use it to the disadvantage of the persons being tested. If he does so, he is subject to the intraprofessional ethical-practice controls that are explicit and carry sanctions against those of us who transgress. The MMPI provides data which, like certain medical data, are considered by many to be helpful in guidance and analysis and understanding of people. Of course in the making of this point, I am aware that there is no absolute meaning to what is ethical. What one group may think should be done about a certain medical-examination disclosure may be considered by another group to be against the patient's interest. I cannot do more than extend this ubiquitous ethical dilemma to the use of the personality test.

The essential point is that such tests should not be used except in professional circles by professional people and that the data it provides should be held confidential and be protected within the lawful practice of ethics. When these requirements are not met, there is reason for complaint. I hope I have made it clear that it is also my conviction that the MMPI will hurt no one, adult or child, in the taking of it. Without defending all uses of it, I surely defend it, and instruments like it, when they are in proper hands and for proper purposes. Monachesi and I have tested 15,000 ninth-grade school children with the MMPI. This took us into public schools all over the state, even into some parochial schools. In all of this testing, we had no difficulties with children, parents, or teachers except for a few courteous inquiries. We are now publishing what we hope will be significant data from this work, data bearing on delinquency and school dropout. We believe that this work demonstrates that properly administered, properly explained, and properly protected tests are acceptable to the public.

At the beginning of this statement I warned that I was going to make it quite long because I felt deeply on the matter. I hope I have not sounded as though I were merely being defensive, protecting us from those who would burn tests and who for good reasons are exceedingly sensitive about psychological testing. I am apologetic if I have sounded too much like the professional scientist and have seemed to talk down to the issue or to be too minutely explicit. I have not meant to insult by being unduly simple, but I have felt that I had to expand adequately on the points. As for psychologists who are those most widely applying such tests, I am aware that the public will look with increasing seriousness upon those who are entrusted with problems of mental health and the assessment of human actions.

I will end with a repetition of my feeling that, while it is desirable for the public to require ethical practices of those using tests, the public may be reassured that the psychologists, physicians, and others who use these new tests will be even more alert to apply the intraprofessional controls that are a requisite to professional responsibility. But I must emphasize that it is not to public advantage to so limit these professional judgments that we fail to progress in mental-health research and applications from lack of freedom to use the best instruments we have and to develop better ones.

Screening for Emotional Fitness: The Jersey City Case

W. G. Dahlstrom

In his "Letter" about the role of controversial items in the MMPI (IV, 1), Hathaway proved to be prophetic. In the summer of 1977, a trial was held in Newark, New Jersey that directly involved the MMPI and questions about the constitutionality of its use in screening candidates for positions as fire fighters in the Fire Department of Jersey City, New Jersey.

Briefly, five men (two firemen already on the force, two men who were on the eligibility list but had yet to take the psychological battery, and one unsuccessful candidate for a position in the Fire Department) sued two officials in the Jersey City government (the chief of the Fire Department and the director of Public Safety) and Stevens Institute of Technology, the parent institution of the Laboratory of Psychological Studies (LPS), which held a contract with Jersey City for the screening for emotional fitness of potential fire fighters. It was a civil suit in the United States District Court of New Jersey, joined early by the American Civil Liberties Union of New Jersey and later by other civil liberties organizations, charging that the use of psychological tests like the MMPI, the Edwards Personal Preference Schedule, the Rorschach, the Thematic Apperception Test, and other minor projective techniques, together with a personal interview, were intrusive upon the applicants' privacy and in violation of their rights of freedom of belief protected under the First and Fourteenth Amendments to the Constitution. Some 133 items from the MMPI and the EPPS, including those alluding to religious,

361

political, or sexual attitudes and experiences, were specifically cited.

Proceedings in the case were protracted, beginning in 1974 with one of the plaintiffs seeking a restraining order from the Court to halt the testing program, followed by hearings about the Court's jurisdiction, appeals, and other actions leading up to the actual trial during June and July of 1977. Senior Judge James A. Coolahan heard the case and issued his opinion nearly a year later [McKenna v. Fargo, 451 F. Supp. 1355 (1978)]. The issues involved in this case and its initial outcome will be briefly summarized here. The interested reader is urged to consult the full opinion on this landmark case.

Although officials in the Fire Department in Jersey City had been using psychological techniques to screen candidates for the Fire Department since the spring of 1966 (after many new problems with members of the force arose during the riots of 1965), the LPS screening program under attack in this suit had been in operation only since 1972. Under this contract, arrangements had been made to examine individual applicants for positions in the Fire Department who had already passed several previous steps in the selection process: a Civil Service test, a medical examination, and an agility battery. The staff at the LPS, several full-time and part-time doctoral and/or licensed psychologists, put each candidate through group and individual testing, interviewed each person at some length about background experiences and current interests and attitudes, and prepared a report on each with a recommendation as to the fitness of the candidate for service in this hazardous duty. At first, group procedures like the MMPI or the EPPS were hand scored; but after 1974 the MMPIs, at least, were machine scored by computer. After the individual tests were scored, the results of the total battery were gone over by one of two senior supervising psychologists. Test data were retained at LPS, and only the written report with a final recommendation was sent to the Jersey City officials. The LPS reports were based on individualized psychodiagnostic assessment of each candidate; the applicant was not appraised in terms of any arbitrary cutting scores or single grading standard.

If either a negative or a qualified opinion were rendered, a referral was made for further evaluation by a psychiatrist. Concurrence from the psychiatrist concerning the liabilities of the candidate would lead Fire Department officials to remove the individual's name from the eligibility rolls. An appeal mechanism was established by the Civil Service Commission by means of which an unsuccessful applicant could be put back on the list and considered for some later opening in the fire brigade. Part of this appeal procedure was further psychological assessment. Although the initial report from LPS at Stevens to the Jersey City officials contained no raw test data, the appeal procedures before the Civil Service Medical Review Board did require that complete files of raw test data and findings be supplied to both sides in the proceedings, allowing for rebuttal.

In June of 1977, before the start of the trial, I was asked to serve as an expert witness for the defense. I traveled to Newark twice. The first visit involved a deposition in which my qualifications were explored, the areas of my testimony were covered, and a list of my "authorities" was filed. These discovery procedures enabled the lawyers for the plaintiffs to prepare questions for my cross-examination. The second trip to Newark was for the trial itself.

My testimony on direct examination was rather straightforward, covering the various instruments employed in the test battery at LPS, their scientific acceptability, their relevance to the kinds of assessments required by the contract with the Jersey City Fire Department, and the kinds of training I thought necessary for psychologists who were to use them in this kind of psychological appraisal. The cross-examination was much longer and more wide-ranging. It covered methods of validation of tests, the opinions of various authorities in the field (e.g., L. J. Cronbach, A. Anastasi, J. P. Guilford, and J. S. Wiggins) about instruments, procedures, and practices in psychological assessment, differences between proximal and ultimate criteria in evaluating the accuracy of a given assessment method, as well as the implications of using tests for the purposes stated in the case as these procedures might affect the welfare of the applicants themselves. One of the points that I tried to make in my testimony was the distinction elaborated by Cronbach and Gleser [1965] between individual decisions and institutional decisions. Since the same instruments may be employed in both contexts, opportunities for misunderstanding might easily arise as to who is the client, what purposes are being served by the tests in each setting, and what questions are under investigation. In considering the procedures used by the staff psychologists at the LPS in these assessments, I felt that the needs of the citizenry of Jersey City were being safeguarded, the potential dangers to other members of the fire brigades in case of psychological breakdown on the part of the new member were being anticipated as well as they could be by current psychological techniques, and the possibility of mistaken placement of a candidate in a position in which his or her own life might be endangered was being minimized by the screening procedures. More-over, the possibility of error in judgment by the LPS staff in turning down a candidate who did in fact possess the necessary emotional fitness seemed to be well offset by the back-up referral and the ap-peal mechanisms.

A great deal of testimony was recorded in the month-long trial (16 volumes of transcript), and further motions and petitions were entered into the record until February of 1978. In May, the case was decided. The opinion that was issued by Judge Coolahan is well worth studying in its entirety, but it is hoped that a few excerpts can convey the care with which it was prepared. It was wide-ranging, thoughtful, and sensitive to the many nuances involved in the profes-sional use of psychological tests for screening candidates for jobs that involve life-threatening hazards. Judge Coolahan stated in his preamble: "Rarely does a case involve conflicting interests as impor-tant and as difficult to reconcile as those in this litigation." After disposing of technical issues involving jurisdiction, standings of the plaintiffs to sue, efforts of the Stevens Institute of Technology to divest itself of involvement in the case by canceling the contract that LPS had with Jersey City, and moves by lawyers of the plaintiffs to obtain a partial summary judgment to the effect that any questioning of the applicants was on its face unconstitutional (both of the latter two efforts being unsuccessful), the opinion reviewed the facts of the case and then dealt with the two sets of opposing concerns in this litigation.

The job of fire fighter was acknowledged to be an unusual occupa-tion, like work on the police force but unlike most lines of work that do not involve direct life-threatening risks to self and co-workers, as well as to the citizens of the Jersey City community who may be exposed to fires, disasters, or accidents of all kinds. In general, screening efforts were recognized as being designed "to detect emo-tional flaws in applicants that could lead to failures in performance or poor decisions at critical moments and to check for psychosis or imminent emotional breakdown" [p. 12]. From the testimony, Judge Coolahan abstracted a number of details about ways in which fire fighters had manifested such flaws and deficiencies: freezing halfway up ladders during rescue efforts, refusing orders or failing to carry them out at the scene of a fire, becoming so disorganized as to be unable to turn on a hydrant, or becoming panicked and unable to find one's way out of a burning structure. In addition to tolerance of stress, danger, and risks to life and limb, obeying reason-able orders from superiors, and making decisions under pressure, the officials of the Fire Department expressed concerns about a fire fighter's tolerance for boredom and strains of close living with other members of the fire brigade. "Thus, Chief Fargo's characterization of fire fighting as a life-endangering profession in which psychological elements play a crucial role is entirely credible" [p. 27]. Accordingly, the judge acknowledged that "the State interest is compelling, indeed, and is served by the challenged evaluation and hiring procedure" [p. 60].

Judge Coolahan nevertheless was equally sensitive to the issues of privacy and freedom of belief raised by the use of psychological tests. He stated: "It is difficult to imagine what more private information could be required by the Government than that involved in this case" [p. 58]. He amplified his view of this kind of intrusion further: "In this case, the degree and character of the disclosure is far greater and more intrusive. The evaluation looks deeply into an applicant's personality, much as a clinical psychologist would if requested to do so by an applicant. Fire-fighter candidates are called upon to reveal the essence of their experience of life, the collective stream of thoughts and feelings that arise from the ongoing dialogue which individuals carry on between the world and themselves in the privacy of their being. It involves a loss of the power individuals treasure to reveal or conceal their personality or their emotions as they see fit, from intimacy to solitude" [p. 58]. He saw the heart of this case as being the unique kind of "involuntary disclosure" made by these job applicants to the staff psychologists at LPS, acting as an agent of the city government of Jersey City, New Jersey.

Judge Coolahan was also responsive to the issue of abridgment of freedom of belief. He stated: "While the issue of privacy is presented by the facts of this case, the problem of protection of freedom of belief is not" [p. 50]. He found further that "the facts do not begin to suggest that applicants were tested for social, political, and religious beliefs or sexual attitudes in conformity with an orthodoxy mandated by Jersey City. In fact, Jersey City did not see the raw testing data and relied primarily on the LPS summary. The LPS evaluation was made for the purpose of selecting firemen who had a high probability of withstanding the psychological pressures of fighting fires and living in close quarters. The behavioral potentials which LPS referred to in making a recommendation were obviously relevant psychological and emotional factors, and not an orthodoxy of faith or political belief" [pp. 50-51]. He further stated: "The Court does not dismiss lightly the potential for abuse of personality testing; it simply is not found in this case."

In weighing these two rights, of privacy and freedom from self-disclosure on the part of each citizen and of the need for the state to protect its interests, Judge Coolahan determined "that the constitutional protection afforded privacy interests is not absolute. State interests may become sufficiently compelling to sustain State regulations or activities which burden the right of privacy" [p. 59].

As for the use of tests to meet this compelling need, Judge Coolahan stated: "The large and perhaps crucial part that psychological factors play in the job of fire fighting certainly establishes the relevance of a psychological evaluation.... The use of clinical techniques does not appear to be a fundamentally unsound premise for selection of firemen or conceptually without support in psychological principles" [p. 32].

When Judge Coolahan's opinion appeared on May 25, 1978, it was: "that the defendants' psychological testing is constitutional." Since that time, appeal of this ruling has been heard and the judge's opinion has been upheld by the Circuit Court of Appeals in Philadelphia (June, 1979). The ultimate disposition of this case and future developments in this area of litigation will be matters of vital interest to professionals and the public alike in the years ahead.

Objections to MMPI Items

J. N. Butcher and A. Tellegen

In recent months, a great deal of criticism has been leveled against industrial and governmental use of structured personality tests, particularly the Minnesota Multiphasic Personality Inventory (MMPI). Critics of the MMPI, for example, consider items relating to sexual practices and religious beliefs offensive and the policy of requiring potential employees to disclose this information about themselves an invasion of privacy. This controversy has become so intense that one entire issue of the *American Psychologist* [Brayfield, 1965] was devoted to it.

There are at least four ways in which psychologists may react to these criticisms: Some psychologists have felt that continuing use of personality tests in an essentially unrestricted manner is necessary for effective clinical and industrial practice and for the development of future instruments, and tend to ignore the criticism. Others have taken the opposite extreme and recommended that the MMPI be dropped from assessment procedures. Still others have considered a compromise to be in order and have recommended adapting personality tests by deleting offensive items. Finally, there are advocates of a continued use of structured personality tests, but under appropriate restriction and with more discriminating "professional" application.

The fairly widespread criticism of psychological tests (some communities have taken action to put an end to psychological testing) draws attention to the remarkable fact that psychologists have

367

made little effort to make a direct study of objections to their procedures.

It is true, of course, that "test-taking attitudes" and "defensiveness" have been studied extensively, especially in connection with the MMPI, as factors affecting the validity of the test results. The occurrence of omissions (or "question marks") in a person's answer sheet has also been mentioned as a possible indication of sensitivity in particular areas. Furthermore, willingness or unwillingness to disclose one's self to individuals in different roles has been investigated in exploratory studies by Jourard [1964], Willerman [1962], and others. Jourard, in his studies on self-disclosure, found that people are much more unwilling to disclose information relating to "personality" than to other aspects of behavior, for example, interests, and that the person asking for the information often determines how much information is disclosed. At the same time, it remains true that no direct study appears to have been made of objections to questions asked in the context of psychological evaluation. This is the more remarkable as psychologists are, broadly speaking, certainly aware of the importance of attitudes toward self-disclosure as determinants of the interaction between themselves and their clients or patients.

This study was designed to provide empirical data relevant to the problem of objectionability of MMPI items. The following questions were of interest:

1. What is the influence of situational factors? The strongest criticism of the MMPI has been against its use in the selection of employees. Thus, one question of interest was whether an especially large number of objections would be raised in a hypothetical selection situation.

2. What is the role of item content? Are types of content, other than sex and religion, considered objectionable?

3. What are the effects of "purging" the MMPI of its most objectionable items? This is an important practical issue. Any alteration in the MMPI structure at this time would drastically change interpretative procedures which have grown out of extensive research with the instrument in its current form. The deletion of items without explicit consideration of gains and losses would be irrational. Would the objection rate for various MMPI scales be greatly decreased if items that elicit many objections are deleted? What information would be lost (which MMPI scales would be most affected) under such a policy?

Method

Subjects

Subject (Ss) were 139 students (58 males) from consecutive summer sessions of the introductory psychology course. All Ss were volunteers and received course credit for participation. One S refused to participate when he learned that the task involved taking the MMPI, and one foreign student was excluded because of language difficulty. Two experimental conditions were employed: a "General" and a "Selection" condition, with N = 68 and N = 69, respectively.

General Condition

Instructions for this condition were designed to communicate to Ss that they were to take the MMPI in the usual way except that they could omit items which they would be unconditionally opposed to answering. The instructions were as follows:

> As you know, the MMPI is used in many different settings for various purposes (counseling, psychiatric evaluation, personnel selection, etc.). We would like to determine which (if any) of the MMPI items might raise objections on the part of people who take the MMPI in such settings. Therefore, we would like you to proceed as follows: Read and answer each question in the usual manner (True or False), *except* in the following case: Do *not* answer questions which you would feel *generally* opposed to answering. In other words, do *not* answer items which, in your opinion, should *never* be included in this kind of questionnaire, *regardless* of the setting.

Selection Condition

The Ss in the Selection condition were instructed to respond to the MMPI as though they were being administered the inventory by a prospective employer in a selection situation. The Ss were told that they could omit items they would object to answering in this situation. The instructions were as follows:

> Many business and industrial firms use the MMPI in the selection of employees. We would like to determine which (if any) of the MMPI items might raise objection on the part of prospective employees asked to take the MMPI. Therefore, we would like you to proceed as follows: Read and answer each question

in the usual manner (True or False), *except* in the following case: Do *not* answer questions which *in the situation just described* you would feel opposed to answering. In other words, do *not* answer items that in your opinion should *not* be included in this kind of questionnaire, *when given to a prospective employee.*

The MMPI was group administered in four sessions during two consecutive quarters of summer school. In both summer sessions, one group of Ss was administered the MMPI under one set of instructions and on the following evening a second group was administered the MMPI under the other instructions. In the second summer session, the order of the conditions was the reverse of that in the first summer session.

Mimeographed instruction sheets were distributed to Ss and were also read aloud by E. All Ss with questions about the task were asked to raise their hands and an E would answer them individually. All questions were answered noncommittally and usually referred S back to the printed instructions.

The Ss were instructed to sign their names on the answer sheets. After the first administration each quarter, Ss were asked not to discuss the study with their classmates until the study was completed the following evening.

Results

Individual Reactions

The first step of the analysis was to examine the number of objections made by individuals in the two conditions. The following statistics describe some characteristics of the two distributions. The median number of objections was 10 in the General condition and 21 in the Selection condition. The variability in both groups, however, was marked and the frequency distributions were quite skewed; in both groups about 15% of the Ss made no objections, but several Ss in the upper half of both distributions made very large numbers of objections. This was especially evident in the Selection condition, with 20% of the Ss making more than 100 objections. The variability in number of objections was, as a result, larger in the Selection condition. An F test on square-root-transformed objection scores showed the difference in variance between the two groups to be significant ($p < .001$).

An analysis of variance classifying Ss according to sex and condition was carried out. A square-root transformation was again used, and through random elimination the number of Ss was reduced to 25 in each of the four cells. Sex differences were not significant ($p < .25$). The number of objections in the Selection condition, however, was significantly larger than in the General condition ($p < .05$).

In brief, Ss differed widely in the extent to which they considered the MMPI items objectionable. More objections were made when Ss were asked specifically to imagine themselves in a job-selection situation; here, one-fifth of the subjects objected to about one-fifth or more of the items.

Relationship between Item Content and Objection Rate

Next the attention was directed to items, rather than individuals. The objection rates in both conditions were determined first. In the Selection condition, the average rate per item was .116, in the General condition it was .051. The higher objection rate for the Selection condition was, of course, already implied in the earlier analysis of individual differences. The question of interest in this analysis was whether items differ appreciably in objection rate and whether these differences are associated with identifiable types of content. This question required some form of item-content analysis. Two different approaches were followed.

First, those items were singled out which elicited the largest number of objections. An item-objection rate of .20 or larger was arbitrarily set as a criterion for being an Objectionable Item (OI). This resulted in 12 OIs in the General condition and 76 OIs in the Selection condition. These items were read through several times by the authors in search for types of content. Four major content categories emerged quite clearly. They were labeled: "Sex," "Religion and Religious Beliefs," "Family Relationships," and "Bladder and Bowel Function." Most items clearly fitted in one of these four categories. The remaining items were placed in an "Other" category. Subsequent inspection of the "Other" category brought to light a small but interesting cluster of statements (Nos. 15, 241, 303, 511) each of which admits mental processes which S does not, should not, or cannot reveal to others; for example, "Once in a while I think of things too bad to talk about."

Table 1 lists the OIs belonging to each of the five categories for both the General and Selection condition. An analysis was under-

Table 1. Content Classification of MMPI Items
with Objection Rates of .20 or More

Category	Items	
	General Condition	Selection Condition
Sex	20, 133, 297	20, 37, 69, 101, 133, 179, 199, 208, 231, 239, 297, 302, 310, 320, 324, 427, 441, 470, 485, 514, 519, 548, 558, 566
Religion and religious beliefs	58, 483	27, 50, 53, 58, 95, 98, 115, 206, 249, 258, 369, 373, 387, 413, 420, 464, 476, 483, 488, 490, 491
Family relationships	237	65, 216, 220, 224, 237, 325, 421, 478, 562
Bladder and bowel function	14, 63, 542	14, 18, 63, 462, 474, 486, 542
Other	61, 287, 513	15, 61, 311, 19, 70, 73, 127, 184, 232, 241, 287, 303, 358, 511, 513, 533

taken to determine whether a high objection rate was indeed a general characteristic of items falling in any one of the four positive content categories. All 550 MMPI items were classified by an independent judge (nonpsychologist) as belonging or not belonging to one of these four. Cutting points were also adopted for both of the conditions, dividing the distribution of objection rates of all MMPI items into an upper and lower half. Each item could now be classified as Positive when it belonged to one of the four positive content categories, or as Negative when it did not, and as falling above or below the objection-rate cutting point of a given condition. The resulting two fourfold tables (one for each condition) were evaluated by means of X^2 tests. The results were highly significant (well below $p = .001$) and clearly indicate that a consistent association exists between high objection rate and judged positive content in both the General and Selection condition.

A second approach to the content analysis was to make use of the a priori item classification by Hathaway and McKinley. (A list of items belonging in each category was made available by S. R. Hathaway.) Since this classification categorizes only 495 out of 550 items the remaining 55 items were examined and a cluster of 15 was placed in an additional category labeled "Occupational Interests."

For categories consisting of 11 or more items, the following analysis was carried out. For each category, and for both conditions, the proportion of items with objection rates above the earlier mentioned cutting point was compared through the use of X^2 tests with the expected proportion derived from the total item pool. For the categories used in the analysis, the mean item objection rates and the p values based on the X^2 tests (corrected for continuity where needed) are shown in Table 2.

Table 2. Mean Item Objection Rates and Direction of Difference for Item Content Categories

Content Category	General Condition		Selection Condition	
	Mean	p[a]	Mean	p[a]
2. General neurologic (19 items)	.035	n.s.	.087	n.s.
3. Cranial nerves (11 items)	.036	n.s.	.105	n.s.
8. Gastrointestinal—	.107⎱		.219⎱	
9. Genitourinary (16 items)	.141⎰	n.s.	.243⎰ +	< .05
10. Habits (19 items)	.042	n.s.	.117	
11. Family and marital (26 items)	.055	n.s.	.179+	< .001
12. Occupational attitudes (18 items)	.034	n.s.	.060−	< .01
13. Educational attitudes (12 items)	.015−	< .05	.075−	< .01
14. Sexual attitudes (16 items)	.131+	< .01	.298+	< .001
15. Religious attitudes (19 items)	.148+	< .001	.292+	< .001
16. Political attitudes—law and order (46 items)	.055	n.s.	.124+	< .05
17. Social attitudes (72 items)	.036	n.s.	.097−	< .02
18. Affect, depressive (32 items)	.046−	< .05	.106	n.s.
19. Affect, manic (24 items)	.039	n.s.	.087−	< .01
20. Obsessive, compulsive (15 items)	.040	n.s.	.123	n.s.
21. Delusions, hallucinations, illusions, ideas of reference (31 items)	.070+	< .001	.154+	< .001
22. Phobias (29 items)	.030−	< .01	.103	n.s.
24. Morale (33 items)	.044	n.s.	.082−	< .01
25. L scale	.045	n.s.	.120	n.s.
26. Occupational interests (15 items)[b]	.007−	< .001	.059−	< .02
Total item pool	.051		.116	

[a] Based on X^2 tests; see text.

[b] A group of items not categorized by Hathaway.

Inspection of Table 2 reveals that in both conditions the objection rates are significantly higher for Categories 14 (Sexual Attitudes), 15 (Religious Attitudes), and 21 (Delusions, etc.), while the rates are significantly lower for Categories 13 (Educational Attitudes) and 26 (Occupational Interests).

The contingency tables furthermore showed very similar patterns in the two conditions, although significant only in one of them, for Categories 8-9 (Gastrointestinal-Genitourinary) and 16 (Political Attitudes, etc.) which show comparatively high objection rates, and for Categories 17 (Social Attitudes) and 18 (Affect, depressive), both of which have relatively low rates in both conditions. It was noted that a small group of items in Category 18 had distinctly higher objection rates than the others. One (518) is a "sex" item; four others (61, 202, 209, 413), interestingly, are statements in which S describes himself as reprehensible, sinful, condemned (e.g., Item 61, "I have not lived the right kind of life."). True-False questionnaires apparently do not have special appeal to normal Ss as a format for possible self-accusation or confession; these four items are perhaps also seen as related in some way to the religious and political attitude items.

This part of the results, then, suggests that Ss would under any circumstances, including selection situations, tend to make particular objection to items stating religious and political attitudes, to "confession"-type items, to sexual items or items dealing with bladder and bowel function, and to items describing peculiarities of mentation and experience. On the other hand, Ss appear to view as inherently more acceptable, even in selection situations, those items that deal with school performance, reading habits, and the like (Category 13); items stating occupational interests; items concerning the individual's interpersonal response (Category 17 which contains many of the *Social Introversion* scale items); and items expressing lack of energy, worry, etc. of the kind found in Category 18. These results are more detailed than, but certainly consistent with, the outcome of the first content analysis.

Table 2 also shows some interesting differential outcomes for the two conditions, over and above the overall differences in objection rates. Items dealing with family and marital situations (Category 11) have, comparatively speaking, a high objection rate in the Selection condition, while the relative rate in the General condition is about average, indicating that questions in this area are not necessarily unacceptable, but are definitely so in selection situations. On the other hand, the objection rates for Categories 12, 19, and 24 are well (and significantly) below average in the Selection condition, but not in the General condition. In other words, items concerned with behaviors and attitudes in work situations and such traits as independence and self-confidence (Categories 12 and 24) are, in comparison to other items, seen as particularly appropriate for selection situations. The same appears true for items describing such ostensible hypomanic symptoms as poor control of temper, restlessness, etc. found in Category 19.

The overall difference in objection rate between the two conditions, as well as the observed interaction between item content and condition, indicate that Ss did respond differentially under the two instructional sets. This is not too surprising. On a priori grounds, one could expect certain items to be acceptable in at least certain settings—and therefore have relatively low objection rates in the General condition—but be regarded as quite inappropriate if the setting happens to be a job-selection situation—and therefore have high objection rates in the Selection condition.

In this connection it is relevant, however, to state to what extent item-content variables might influence objection rates *independently* of situational considerations. In terms of the present study one could find out to what extent the relative objection rates of items and item groupings in a specific situation, the Selection condition, would be predictable from the relative objection rates generated by telling Ss to disregard the special situational factors, as was done in the General condition. To the extent that the two sets of objection rates covary, one could assert that in addition to situational factors certain "transsituational" factors determine the objections to items with a given content. The present data in fact indicate a substantial degree of correspondence. The correspondence for individual items is reflected in a product-moment correlation of .85 between the objection rates, in the two conditions, of the first 50 MMPI items. Furthermore, the corresponding correlation for the average objection rates of all 25 Hathaway-McKinley categories, plus the Occupational Preferences category, was found to be .95. These correlations indicate that relative objection rate of item content in the Selection condition is predictable to a perhaps surprising degree from objection rates observed in the General condition. The results support the notion that dos and don'ts exist that influence in a rather generalized fashion, across situations, the willingness to accept certain inquiries about one's self. The results indicate, as one might expect, that such dos and don'ts involve a diversity of content and seem to reflect the "general culture" and its standards of what is privileged, relevant, shameful, etc.

Consequences of Item Elimination

One frequently made suggestion has been to "purge" the MMPI of its most offensive items. Several analyses were undertaken to determine the effects of this approach. Questions of interest were: (*a*) Would the elimination of the most objectionable items affect some MMPI scales more than others? (*b*) Would elimination of the OIs reduce the mean item-objection rate sufficiently to be of practical value? The percentage of OIs for various MMPI scales is shown in column 3 of Table 3. The F scale and three clinical scales, Pd, Mf, and Sc, contain a high percentage of OIs (17-22%). Other scales, like the K scale, consist of items that are more innocuous and produce relatively little negative reaction.

Table 3. Item Objection Rates for Basic and Special Scales
and Effect of Eliminating Objectionable Items

Scale	General Condition	Selection Condition		
	Mean IOR[a]	Mean IOR	% OI[b]	Mean IOR without OI
L	04	12	06	11
F	05	14	19	11
K	03	09	00	09
Hs	04	11	06	08
D	04	11	12	08
Hy	03	08	03	07
Pd	06	13	22	10
Mf	05	13	18	09
Pa	05	13	08	12
Pt	04	09	06	08
Sc	05	13	17	11
Ma	05	11	09	10
Si	04	09	06	08
A	04	08	02	08
R	03	11	02	11
So-r	04	10	05	09

[a]IOR = Item Objection Rate.

[b]OI = Objectionable Items, a group of 76 items with objection rates ⩾ .20.

The results are suggestive. If one were to attempt to construct a personality questionnaire with a lower objection rate out of the MMPI item pool, the selective loss of items, particularly affecting certain scales concerned with behavior and thought disorder, might well reduce its usefulness for making decisions.

Moreover, deletion of the 76 OIs still has only a limited effect on the average objection rate of the MMPI in the Selection situation. The data presented in Column 4 of Table 3 reflect changes in the mean item-objection rate after deletion of the 76 OIs in the Selection condition. Even after deleting a large number of items, the objection rate in the employment situation tends to remain quite high. In other words, a solution to the problem of objectionability to the MMPI which is directed toward the removal of offensive items will *not* appreciably reduce objections in an employment situation but *will* lead to selective loss of important behavioral information.

There is the additional consideration that any scale from which items have been eliminated on a nonrandom basis has changed sufficiently in nature to require revalidation. Past studies bearing on the interpretation of these scales could no longer be relied on. Hathaway [1964; see IV, 1] emphasizes a similar consideration, and points in addition at the considerable cost involved in restandardization and revalidation.

Relationship between Objections and ?

When Ss are given the option of omitting items they do not wish to answer (a part of the original instructions to the MMPI which has in recent years been discouraged), do they tend to delete items which this study has found to have the highest objection rates?

Correlations between number of objections and frequency of omission [Hathaway and Briggs, 1957] on 100 randomly selected MMPI items for males and females in the General and Selection condition were obtained; they are shown in Table 4.

Table 4. Relationship between Item Omissions
and Number of Objections over 100 Items

	General		Selection	
	r	p	r	p
Males	.33	< .05	.19	< .10
Females	.56	< .01	.31	< .05

In combination, these data suggest that a significant correlation exists between objection frequency and omission frequency. One might infer that Ss, when given the option, will to some degree omit items they find objectionable. The reported correlations do not, however, indicate a particularly strong relationship. Several factors probably enter here: (*a*) there has been a change in values over the 20 or so years separating the two populations; (*b*) Ss tend to answer some questions even though they may strongly object; (*c*) Ss may have difficulty answering certain items without considering their content objectionable. One might venture the guess that explicit permission to omit objectionable items could reduce the incidence of negative reactions to the test.

Conclusions

The use of the MMPI in any setting, including selection situations, is a sensitive matter. If its use is necessary, explicit consideration of S's possible reaction is called for.

One suggested precaution, elimination of offensive items, is believed to be unfeasible. Not only was deletion found to involve selective, rather than random, loss of information, but the overall objection rate for various scales was shown to remain quite high in the Selection condition.

Another way of possibly reducing objection rates might be to allow S in so many words to omit items he does not wish to answer. This was the procedure in the earlier days of the MMPI. In some individuals this would result in such a high ? frequency as to make the test result unusable. Other assessment procedures would have to be utilized in such instances. This may not always be a feasible alternative. Also the occurrence of self-selection would discourage researchers interested in the study of intact samples.

One might add that there is also the possibility of reducing negative reaction through improved administrative procedures. One of the advantages of the MMPI is its ease of administration. However, this advantage may have been pushed too far in settings where S is rushed into a room, handed a booklet and answer sheet, and instructed to fill it out, following which he is further "processed." Instead, one could introduce the test in a way which prepares S for its general content, and find ways of dealing directly with his predictable reaction after he has completed the inventory. It is of interest that the new MMPI instructions used by the Peace Corps clearly aim at enlisting the cooperation of the subject by informing and reassuring him about the use of the test results. Whether or not such procedures accomplish their aims is itself an empirical question.

One may wonder how repeated MMPI administrations might affect a person's attitude. Some of the Ss who had taken the MMPI before, initially commented, "Oh, no, not again."

The "invasion-of-privacy" issue and problems of professional ethics have not been considered here. Problems of face validity, apparent appropriateness, and "layman appeal" [cf. Cronbach, 1970, p. 142] have to some extent been considered in our discussion of item elimination and administrative procedures. The primary concern of this study, however, was to make an empirical inquiry into objections to MMPI items. It appears desirable to explore this area further and make an attempt to deal more systematically with the general problem of self-disclosure, considering situational factors, content domains, and individual differences. The exploratory work by Jourard [1964], Willerman [1962], and others is illustrative of possibilities in that direction.

The Effect of Eliminating Offensive Items on the Reliability and Validity of the MMPI

C. E. Walker

Over the years, objections to psychological testing have been expressed in a variety of ways and for a variety of reasons [Gross, 1962; Hoffman, 1961; Whyte, 1954]. The most recent encounter in this running battle has resulted in various hearings before Congressional committees and a full issue of the *American Psychologist* [Brayfield, 1965] devoted to this topic. Government agencies, school districts, and some employers have curtailed their use of various instruments, and laws are pending in Congress which would severely limit the use of psychological testing.

One study [Butcher and Tellegen, 1966; see IV, 3] has already appeared seeking to discover exactly what items are objected to and what the effect of eliminating such items has on the use of the instrument involved, in this case, the MMPI. Data were presented in this article relating to the number and types of items found offensive under normal and simulated job-seeking situations and inferences were drawn regarding the effect on the test of eliminating these items. In general, it was felt that elimination of such items would impair the validity of the instrument.

However, some agencies, for example the Peace Corps, appear to have adopted the attitude that instructions to the S indicating that he may omit items which he does not wish to answer will have no appreciable effect on the results. Thus, the MMPI booklet form used by the Peace Corps [Hathaway and McKinley, 1965] carries such instructions. This study investigated empirically the effect of instruc-

380

tions which indicate to the subject that he may omit items which he deems offensive.

Method

The MMPI booklet form was administered twice to 42 students enrolled in a general psychology course at Westmont College. The two testings were separated by a period of approximately four weeks. Half of the Ss took the test with the regular instructions. Half took the test on both occasions with the following additional instructions:

In addition to the instructions given on the front of the test booklet, you are also to observe the following:

If any question in the booklet strikes you as being *offensive* (that is, if you feel that the question is related to an area which you consider too private or personal to be asked of you in this type of inventory and it is therefore offensive to you to be asked to respond to it), circle the number of the question on the answer sheet with an O for "offensive."

Be sure to use the "O" category only for items which you consider personally offensive. If a statement simply does not apply to you or if it is something that you don't know about, make no mark on the answer sheet.

You may wish to comment on why some of the items are or are not offensive to you. If so, write the number of the item on the sheet provided and write your comments next to the number.

Results

Table 1 presents data regarding the frequency of items found offensive on testing 1 and testing 2 along with pertinent information regarding the item. Only 9 items were objected to by 3 or more Ss on either testing. Many items were objected to by 1 or 2 persons on one testing and none on the other.

An attempt was made to indicate the general content classification for each item considered objectionable. In each case, the item was assigned a classification only if the manifest content of the item clearly and unambiguously placed the item in a given category. In cases of doubt or question, the item was placed in the miscellaneous category.

Of the items considered offensive, 13 had manifest content dealing with sex, 9 dealt with religion, 7 with eliminative processes, 6

Table 1. Frequencies of Offensive Items

Testing 1		Testing 2	
Item No.	*f*	Item No.	*f*
14	5	14	5
18	3	18	4
37	2	37	0
63	6	63	8
133	1	133	2
302	2	302	1
462	5	462	7
474	5	474	6
476	1	476	2
486	5	486	6
519	2	519	3
533	1	533	3
542	6	542	7
11, 16, 20, 27, 35, 45, 53, 55, 58,73,101,128,167,199, 206,231,237,240,310,313, 314,315,324,332,369,373,413	1	20,53,58,98,179,206,387, 413,442,485,514,558,566	1

were personal evaluations or admissions, 5 were paranoid statements, 2 were somatic complaints, and 7 were miscellaneous.

An examination of the keys on which the items considered offensive appeared revealed that 15 of the 49 items were found on no regularly scored key. The keys and numbers of items appearing on each were as follows: F-7; Pd, Sc-6 each; Ma, Pa-5 each; Hs, D, Hy, Mf, Si-3 each; and L-1. Comparative studies were conducted between the number of *objections* to items (on the basis of offensiveness) and the number of *omissions* of items (presumably because they fell in "don't apply" or "don't know" categories) in these data. A distribution of item objections by Ss who received the special instructions on testing 1 and testing 2 was obtained as well as distributions for the number of omissions on testing 1 and testing 2 for both the regular and the special groups. Tests of significance were run between the special group objections on testing 1 and 2; the special group omissions between testing 1 and 2; the distribution of omissions for the regular group between testing 1 and 2; the distribution of omissions between the regular versus special group on testing 1; and, the distribution of omissions between the regular versus special group on testing 2. (In cases where the data were correlated, the Wilcoxon Matched Pairs Signed-Ranks test was used as a test of significance.

The Mann Whitney U test was used for the uncorrelated data.) Of these tests of significance, only 2 were found to be significant at or beyond the .05 level. Those found to be significant were the distribution for omissions for the regular group between testing 1 and 2 (fewer omissions on the second testing), and the distribution of omissions between the special group versus the regular group on testing number 2 (more omissions for the special group). There was a visible observable trend in most of the distributions for there to be fewer omissions and objections on the second testing.

In an effort to evaluate the reliability of the MMPI under the regular and special instructions, Pearson product-moment correlations were computed between the scores of the Ss on testing 1 and 2 for the regular-instruction and the special-instruction groups. These data are presented in Table 2. t tests were done to evaluate the magnitude of the differences between these reliability coefficients. The reliability coefficients for both the Hs and Mf scales were found to differ significantly at the .05 level. Several other comparisons showed a trend toward significance. Therefore, an overall sign test between the two distributions of reliability coefficients was accomplished. The reliability coefficients for the regular group were found to be significantly higher at the .05 level using a one-tail test.

Table 2. Means and Reliabilities of MMPI Scales for Regular and Special Instruction Groups

Scale	Regular Group			Special Group		
	Test 1	Test 2	r	Test 1	Test 2	r
L	3.71	3.71	.65	4.14	3.71	.63
F	4.42	3.90	.80	4.42	3.90	.76
K	16.52	18.76	.80	16.57	15.95	.81
Hs*	13.85	12.80	.66	13.85	11.95	.77
D	17.85	17.28	.79	17.00	18.09	.90
Hy	23.57	22.23	.76	21.90	20.85	.88
Pd*	22.42	21.42	.76	21.80	20.47	.82
Mf	34.09	33.76	.87	37.00	36.14	.97
Pa	9.85	9.71	.56	10.01	10.28	.77
Pt*	29.47	29.95	.60	29.85	29.57	.75
Sc*	27.61	28.66	.40	27.52	28.19	.78
Ma*	21.09	21.28	.39	19.85	20.14	.64
Si	21.76	21.61	.87	26.76	26.09	.82

*Values given are K-corrected.

In an effort to determine whether the validity of the tests was influenced by these special instructions, the means for the two groups on testing 1 and testing 2 were compared by means of t tests. No significant differences were found among any of the means for any of the scales. There did not appear to be any visual trend in the data and a Sign test accomplished for the two pairs of distributions indicated no significant differences.

Discussion

The content of the items and general frequency of items found offensive by our Ss agrees well with the Butcher and Tellegen data. In general, there were relatively few objections and very little unanimity as to which items were offensive. The content categories of items that seem to be most frequently objected to are sex, religion, and eliminative processes. Many Ss in both groups found none of the items objectionable or offensive on either testing. There was a tendency for fewer items to be seen as offensive on the second testing.

The data indicate that, if given instructions to omit items that are offensive, Ss will omit a sufficient number of items to impair the reliability of the instrument. This might be expected on two grounds. First, since fewer items will be responded to and the number of items scored in a given key are therefore fewer, the lower number of items per scale might automatically be expected to result in lower reliability. In addition, it is possible that a general test-taking set develops that leads to a different approach to the test and, as a result, lower reliability. The present data, however, do not yield sufficient information to choose between the two possibilities.

There is no direct evidence that this impairment of validity of the test occurred, at least to the extent that elevation of MMPI scales serves as an index of validity. However, the lower reliabilities demonstrated for the scales would suggest on theoretical grounds that validity might be impaired. Future studies should attempt to obtain more meaningful estimates of validity. Special attention should be paid to the effect of the special instructions on the shape of the profile of an individual in order to determine the effect on this type of validity and also to serve as a guideline for the interpretation of data gathered in situations where these instructions are mandatory.

An analysis of the reasons spontaneously given for finding items offensive revealed that most of the objections centered around general complaints of ambiguity or poor phrasing of the item, being forced to answer true or false without further comment or qualification, and similar traditional complaints about testing. A few of the comments dealt with the content of the items, and the idea was expressed that these matters (mostly eliminative processes) were private and probably irrelevant to the purpose of the test.

Summary

One group of 21 psychology students took the regular MMPI, and 21 others took the test with special instructions which permitted Ss to eliminate items which they found personally offensive. Analysis of the data indicated that few items were objected to and many Ss found no offensive items. A content classification revealed that items related to sex, religion, and eliminative processes were most offensive. Many of the offensive items were not on standard MMPI scales. Scales F, Pd, Sc, Pa, and Ma contained the largest number of offensive items. Comparison of test-retest reliabilities indicated that the special instructions tended to significantly reduce reliability. Examination of the means for the scales between the two groups showed no significant trend for either group to have lower means.

Altered Versions of the MMPI

W. G. Dahlstrom

Administration of the MMPI to most literate test subjects requires about an hour and a half. Some individuals sophisticated in taking tests may even complete the booklet form in less than fifty minutes, but very depressed or disorganized patients may work at the task only sporadically and extend the testing time to two or three days. In the latter cases, it is understandable that a psychologist may cast about for ways to shorten the task and ease the difficulties for the test subject. There are a few legitimate reasons to seek methods of shortening testing time, even for self-administered tests like the MMPI, but the increasing numbers and uses of short forms of the test cannot be readily justified in these terms. As Lachar [1979] points out, most instances of recourse to one or another of the MMPI short forms have been dictated by the personal preferences and activities of the psychologist rather than by the exigencies of the clinical or research situation. More compelling reasons can be advanced for extending the coverage in the MMPI and thus using an even longer testing time than for the current practice of abbreviated testing with reduced item coverage.

Shortened Administrations

In constructing the test, Hathaway and McKinley (see I, 1) envisioned a degree of flexibility and adaptability in the item pool of the MMPI that was unusual if not unique. Since each item in the orig-

386

inal form was on a separate card and the order of item presentation was randomly shuffled for each testing, it was assumed that the effects of the item context on the endorsements of any one item would average out. Thus, items could be added or deleted without any systematic contextual effect on those remaining. In actuality, of course, this feature was little used. On one occasion 55 new items were added to the inventory (related primarily to the evaluation of personality inversion); none was ever deleted. Soon after this augmentation, the first booklet form for group testing was developed, and in that form the MMPI became as fixed as any of the standardized personality tests.

On single occasions using any of the various versions of the card form, however, it was possible to shorten the time of administration of the MMPI quite easily; the 200 or more "non-working" items (those not scored on any of the clinical or validity scales) could simply be removed from the box and the remaining set of approximately 350 "working" items given to the subject for sorting. This was the original meaning of an MMPI "short form" [Olson, 1954]. All the answers needed to draw a standard profile were obtained; lost were answers to items being incorporated into new or revised scales, or items of special clinical interest (e.g., various critical items). It is important to note that in this method the scores on the basic scales were based on full item composition of each scale.

Booklet versions of the test do not possess this kind of flexibility; nevertheless various means have been tried to reduce administration time. In the first MMPI booklet, the organization of the items was dictated by the format of the only available answer sheet: the recording form for the card version with ten columns of 55 items each. The 300 working items making up the basic scales at that time (without K or Si) were scattered throughout the test booklet so that there was no easy way to guide the subject in answering only the items to be scored for the profile. When booklets were prepared early in the war for use by the United States Army [Morton, 1948], two versions were printed: TC-8a, the full 550 with 14 items duplicated for ease of machine scoring, giving a total of 564; and TC-8b, a short form of only 300 items. It was not long after the war that the list of non-working items began to shrink. When the familiar booklet version still in use was prepared for distribution by The Psychological Corporation, Hathaway arranged the order of items to have the working items included in the first 366 (with 16 items now duplicated in this booklet, again for scoring ease). By the time that Form R was designed, the item order was rearranged so that the scored items on the basic profile comprised the first 399 items. Eventually, the addition of new scales to the test resulted in every item appearing on some scale. The possibility thus evaporated of having a complete set of items covered at some arbitrary stopping-point on either version of the test. An examination of the scales given in Appendix I of Dahlstrom, Welsh, and Dahlstrom [1975] reveals the range of possibilities for use of the test.

Factor Scale Profiles

Since that time, there have been two major lines of research directed toward shortened versions of the MMPI: the first focused on the primary sources of variance in the standard scales with each factor represented by a new special scale; and the second involved efforts to estimate scale scores on the standard profile from an individual's answers to a very reduced set of items. The first approach was employed by Welsh [1954], for example, in the development of four research scales (A [anxiety], R [repression], C [control], and P [psychoticism]; see Appendix I in Dahlstrom, Welsh, and Dahlstrom, 1975) which he believed reflected the first four major factors that the basic scales of the MMPI have in common. Using such a set of four moderate-length scales (a total of 157 items), most of the common variance in the profile can be summarized. A very similar effort by Eichman [1962], using scales only half as long as Welsh's factor scales, also led to four scales with slightly different designations but with a similar rationale (I [anxiety], II [repression], III [somatization], and IV [acting out]; see Chapter 3 in Dahlstrom, Welsh, and Dahlstrom, 1972; also see Appendix I in Dahlstrom, Welsh, and Dahlstrom, 1975). Eichman's scales have somewhat different item composition for use with male or with female subjects; but for either sex a set of 80 items captures most of the common variance that can be estimated in the basic test profile.

The use of special factor scales like those of Eichman or Welsh may provide data on the common factor variance, but the information is obviously in an altered form and does not capture variances unique to one scale. Since the profile is not reproduced, none of the usual guides to test interpretation available on the MMPI can be used directly. Each of these authors has developed special interpretive material for use with these scales, but this line of research has not been carried very far in the MMPI literature. This limitation may not be important for personality research, but for clinical application each user would essentially have to develop local guides and pattern summaries for interpreting such factor profiles. This limitation does not seem to hold true for the alternative line of work on the MMPI: short forms in which there is a deliberate effort to reconstruct the standard profile from substantially fewer MMPI items. Unfortunately, as will be discussed below, the same caveat does apply to short-form estimations as well.

Mini-Mult

For his dissertation in 1967 at the University of Minnesota, James Kincannon attempted to adapt the MMPI to the format of a mental status examination and in so doing retain as many of the basic features of the test as possible. In this attempt he was following the lead not only of Jorgensen [1958] but also of Srole, Langner, Michael, Opler, and Rennie [1962] when they modified the form of MMPI statements into an interrogative form to be used as an interview in their field studies of the epidemiology of emotional disorders. Srole's work led to a door-to-door interview device, only 22 items long, that came to be called the Health Opinion Survey (HOS). (See Chapter 1 in Dahlstrom, Welsh, and Dahlstrom, 1975).

In his research, Kincannon [1968] finally selected 71 MMPI items for his screening instrument (plus a few additional new items covering problems with alcohol use). His mental status examination, called the Mini-Mult, had several features of importance to the present discussion. The change from the first-person declarative to the second-person interrogative in the item format, together with the brevity of the list of questions, made it feasible to give the test orally to many subjects unable to take the MMPI in its standard form (e.g., the very elderly, alcoholics in the early phases of detoxification, and mildly or even moderately mentally retarded subjects). The items chosen were by and large those that appeared on several of the basic scales, clinical and validity, so that information pertaining to as many scales as possible would be gained through a relatively short examination session. Kincannon felt that he had to abandon only the Mf (5) and Si (0) scales from the clinical set and the Cannot Say score from the validity set. By means of prediction formulas and conversion tables, he proposed estimating for the remaining scales the raw scores that a subject would have obtained if the entire MMPI had been administered in the usual format. If this estimation procedure can generate a dependable set of basic MMPI scores, then the K corrections can be added and the T-score conversions made, the profile drawn, allowing for a regular interpretation about the individual's personality and mental status, all from a brief mental-status interview. Although Kincannon's initial efforts to establish the degree of comparability of the behavioral samples obtained by means of the oral Mini-Mult and the MMPI seemed encouraging [Kincannon, 1968], subsequent studies did not support his initial optimism [Faschingbauer and Newmark, 1978; Newmark and Faschingbauer, 1978]. That is, group means and rough indexes of profile comparability were acceptably close on some subject populations, but many individual scale estimates and all variances were too low, even when the Kincannon-type scores and the standard MMPI scores were drawn, not from separate administrations of the MMPI and the Mini-Mult, but from the same set of answers to a *single* administration of the full MMPI. Clearly, the sample of 71 items with multiple-scale membership did not provide an adequate basis for estimating full MMPI profile patterns.

As was true for the factor-score profiles described above, it is quite feasible, of course, to start from scratch with an instrument like the Mini-Mult, or any of the other versions to be discussed below, and establish its empirical validities, develop new interpretive rules, and generate other guides to its use in research or clinical practice. The attraction of this particular approach to MMPI short forms, however, has been the possibility of obtaining virtually all of the personological validity of the test profile with a substantially smaller investment of time and effort. The subsequent research has generally been directed to the question of how many more items have to be added, rather than new validation of the short forms. The need for such direct validational research is particularly crucial for these brief procedures, however, since, as Lachar [1979] points out, one of the justifications for developing these versions is to use them on clients or patients for whom the regular MMPI is inappropriate. By necessity, then, the regular MMPI validities are unknown for these populations; it cannot be taken for granted that the profiles obtained by means of the brief procedures will automatically carry the same meaning as the regular MMPI profiles would were it possible to administer the full test to such subjects.

Recent Short Forms

Kincannon's effort did stimulate a large series of studies designed to improve upon the limitations of the Mini-Mult, preserving at least its virtues of brevity and multi-dimensionality if not its oral administrative format and special coverage of alcohol abuse. There followed in order of increasing numbers of items several special MMPI short forms: the Midi-Mult [Dean, 1972] with 86 items; Maxi-Mult₁ [McLachlan, 1974] with 94 items; Maxi-Mult₂ [Spera and Robertson, 1974] with 104 items; FAM [Faschingbauer, 1974] with 166 items; MMPI-168 [Overall and Gomez-Mont, 1974] with 168 items; and the Hugo Short-Form MMPI [Hugo, 1971] with 173 items. The Overall and Gomez-Mont MMPI-168 alone preserved the feature noted earlier in the discussion of shortened administrations of the regular MMPI booklet version; namely, the subject is asked to complete only the first 168 items in Form R, stopping at the bottom of page 7 in the step-down booklet. These procedures provide the examiner with a basis for estimating what the scores on the regular scales would have been if the subject had gone on to complete the remaining 231 items through item 399. (See Appendix K of Dahlstrom, Welsh, and Dahlstrom [1972] for a means of prorating full-scale scores from abortive administrations of the regular booklet form of the test.) All of the other short forms involve the test subject's skipping around in the test booklet to locate and answer the needed items for these shortened versions. The item composition, strategies of item selection, methods of estimation, and procedures for scoring these various forms have all been summarized in Faschingbauer and Newmark [1978].

Several different means have been employed to determine the relative success of these different abbreviated versions in estimating standard MMPI scores and configurations. Poythress [1978], among others, has concluded that the FAM and the MMPI-168 are the two most dependable short forms. Much of this confidence in these two versions comes from the study reported by Newmark, Ziff, Finch, and Kendall [1978]. It is particularly interesting in this regard to note the results of a recent empirical analysis of the comparability of the full MMPI with each of these versions made by Butcher, Kendall, and Hoffman [1979]. They have reanalyzed data from four published studies using these two short forms, including further analyses of the data from the Newmark et al. study. The ranges of differences that they found between the regular full scale scores and the estimated values using the items listed for either the MMPI-168 or the FAM versions of these scales were generally very large. Only in the Newmark et al. results are the estimated values close. The Butcher et al. study raises serious questions about short-form usage. That is, examination of the data in their tables reveals several distressing findings. In three of the four published studies [Clavelle and Butcher, 1977; Edinger, Kendall, Hooke, and Bogan, 1976; and Koss and

Butcher, 1973], the range of error in estimating full-scale values from short-form item subsets is discouragingly large. Sizable overestimations or underestimations in T-score values occur even when (as was the case in each of these latter three studies) the behavioral sample is a single administration of the MMPI. These full-scale values obviously are based to an appreciable extent upon the *same* item answers as the short-form scores. Even though part-whole correlations are involved in these estimations, the errors can be large; they often seriously alter the interpretive meaning of a scale elevation or a configuration in which the scale plays a part. Understandably, the range of errors is particularly large on those scales in which K corrections are made before T-score conversion, since there are two sources of error in such T-score estimations. That is, errors of estimation enter into the determination of the raw scores for both the basic scale itself and for the K-score value. As a result, the T scores based on either FAM or MMPI-168 are likely to be even further from the values that they should give to reproduce the full MMPI scores. As the values for scales 1, 4, 7, 8, and 9 in their study indicate, short-form values are further off target on these scales. For these same scales, identical scores between either FAM or MMPI-168 and the full MMPI are even rarer than they are on the noncorrected clinical scales.

Another startling result revealed in these findings, however, is the virtual absence of any of these difficulties in the data from the Newmark et al. study. That is, with the exception of a single subject in each sex group, the correspondence between short form and full MMPI is impressively close for both validity scales and clinical scales. The correspondence is as close or closer than would be achieved with successive administrations of the full MMPI [Rosen, 1953], yet these data come from *independent* administrations in a counterbalanced order of the MMPI and either one or the other of the short forms. Seldom does an error exceed a half standard deviation. The accuracy seems to be comparable for the two short-form procedures and for either sex. Most startling of all, perhaps, are the data of the Newmark et al. study on percentage of identical scores; for some scales the estimated value is precisely the full-scale T score in more than half of the cases.

As Butcher et al. conclude: "This necessitates that . . . (the Newmark et al.) study be replicated using a sample that is not extremely atypical." The general pattern of findings on short forms of the MMPI, with the exception of those of Newmark et al., do not support the use of any of these procedures as a substitute for the standard full MMPI. Since use of the objective inventories like those of the MMPI for research or clinical purposes requires very little professional time of the psychologist for administration or scoring, little is saved by using these abbreviated versions in direct cost to the practitioner or investigator, and a great deal may be lost to both the psychologist and the client.

References

References

Adams, C. R. A new measure of personality. *Journal of Applied Psychology,* 1941, 25, 141-51.

Adams, D. R., and J. L. Horn. Non-overlapping keys for the MMPI scales. *Journal of Consulting Psychology,* 1965, 29, 284.

Adorno, T. W., E. Frenkel-Brunswik, D. Levinson, and R. N. Sanford. *The authoritarian personality.* New York: Harper, 1950.

Ahana, E. A study on the reliability and internal consistency of a manifest anxiety scale. Master's thesis, Northwestern University, 1952.

Allport, G. W. A test for ascendance-submission. *Journal of Abnormal and Social Psychology,* 1928, 23, 118-36.

Allport, G. W. *Personality: a psychological interpretation.* New York: Holt, 1937.

Allport, G. W. *The use of personal documents in psychological science.* New York: Social Science Research Council Bulletin No. 49, 1942.

Altrocchi, J., O. A. Parsons, and H. Dickoff. Changes in self-ideal discrepancy in repressors and sensitizers. *Journal of Abnormal and Social Psychology,* 1960, 61, 67-72.

American Psychiatric Association. *Statistical Manual* (8th Edition). Washington, D.C.: American Psychiatric Association, 1934.

American Psychological Association. Technical recommendations for psychological tests and diagnostic techniques. *Psychological Bulletin Supplement,* 1954, No. 2, Pt. 2.

American Psychological Association. *Standards for educational and psychological tests.* Washington, D.C.: APA, 1974.

American Psychological Association. *Ethical standards of psychologists.* Washington, D.C., APA, 1977.

Arnold, D. A. The clinical validity of the Humm-Wadsworth temperament scale in psychiatric diagnosis. Doctoral dissertation, University of Minnesota, 1942.

Asch, S. Effects of group pressure upon the modification and distortion of judgments. Swarthmore College: Progress Report on Office of Naval Research Project, Task Order N7Onr-38003, 1950.

Ashton, S. G., and L. R. Goldberg. In response to Jackson's challenge: the comparative validity of personality scales constructed by the external (empirical) strategy and scales developed intuitively by experts, novices, and laymen. *Journal of Research in Personality*, 1973, 7, 1-20.

Atkinson, J. W., ed. *Motives in fantasy, action, and society*. Princeton: Van Nostrand, 1958.

Barnes, E. H. Factors, response bias, and the MMPI. *Journal of Consulting Psychology*, 1956, 20, 419-21.

Barron, F. Psychotherapy as a special case of personal interaction: prediction of its course. Doctoral dissertation, University of California (Berkeley), 1950.

Barron, F. An ego-strength scale which predicts response to psychotherapy. *Journal of Consulting Psychology*, 1953, 17, 327-33. (a)

Barron, F. Some test correlates of response to therapy. *Journal of Consulting Psychology*, 1953, 17, 235-41. (b)

Barron, F., and T. F. Leary. Changes in psychoneurotic patients with and without psychotherapy. *Journal of Consulting Psychology*, 1955, 19, 239-45.

Bass, B. M. Authoritarianism or acquiescence? *Journal of Abnormal and Social Psychology*, 1955, 51, 616-23.

Baughman, E. E., and W. G. Dahlstrom. *Negro and white children: a psychological study in the rural South*. New York: Academic Press, 1968.

Bechtoldt, H. P. Response defined anxiety and MMPI variables. *Proceedings of the Iowa Academy of Science*, 1953, 60, 495-99.

Beck, A. T. *Depression: clinical, experimental, and theoretical aspects*. New York: Harper & Row, 1967.

Bentler, P. M., D. N. Jackson, and S. J. Messick. Identification of content and style: a two-dimensional interpretation of acquiescence. *Psychological Bulletin*, 1971, 76, 186-204.

Benton, A. L. The interpretation of questionnaire items in a personality schedule. *Archives of Psychology*, 1935, 190, 1-38.

Berg, I. A. Response bias and personality: the deviation hypothesis. *Journal of Psychology*, 1955, 40, 61-72.

Berg, I. A. The unimportance of test item content. In B. M. Bass and I. A. Berg, eds. *Objective approaches to personality assessment*. Princeton: Van Nostrand, 1959.

Berg, I. A. Measuring deviant behavior by means of deviant response sets. In I. A. Berg and B. M. Bass, eds. *Conformity and deviation*. New York: Harper & Row, 1961.

Bernreuter, R. G. Theory and construction of the personality inventory. *Journal of Social Psychology*, 1933, 4, 387-405. (a)

Bernreuter, R. G. Validity of the personality inventory. *Personnel Journal*, 1933, 11, 383-86. (b)

Bernreuter, R. G. The present status of personality trait tests. *Educational Record Supplement*, 1940, 21, 160-71.

Bills, M. Selection of casualty and life insurance agents. *Journal of Applied Psychology*, 1941, 25, 6-10.

Black, J. D. The interpretation of MMPI profiles of college women. Doctoral dissertation, University of Minnesota, 1953. (*DA*, 1953, 13, 870-71)

Black, J. D. *Preliminary manual: the D-48 Test*. Palo Alto, CA: Consulting Psychologists Press, 1963.

Block, J. An experimental investigation of the construct of ego-control. Doctoral dissertation, Stanford University, 1950.

Block, J. A cluster-analysis of the IPAR Q-sort items. Berkeley, CA: Research Bulletin of the Institute of Personality Assessment and Research, 1954.

Block, J. On the number of significant findings to be expected from chance. *Psychometrika,* 1960, 25, 369-80.

Block, J. *The Q-sort method in personality assessment and psychiatric research.* Springfield, Ill.: Charles C Thomas, 1961.

Block, J. *The challenge of response sets.* New York: Appleton-Century-Crofts, 1965.

Block, J. On further conjectures regarding acquiescence. *Psychological Bulletin,* 1971, 76, 205-10.

Block, J., and D. E. Bailey. A cluster analysis of 82 inventory measures of personality, interest and intellect. IPAR Research Monograph, 1955. (a)

Block, J., and D. E. Bailey. Q-sort item analyses of a number of MMPI scales. Technical Memorandum, OERL TM-55-7, 1955. (b)

Block, J., and J. H. Block. An investigation of the relationship between intolerance of ambiguity and ethnocentrism. *Journal of Personality,* 1951, 19, 303-11.

Block, J., and H. Thomas. Is satisfaction with self a measure of adjustment? *Journal of Abnormal and Social Psychology,* 1955, 51, 254-59.

Block, J., and E. Turula. Identification, ego-control and adjustment. *Child Development,* 1963, 34, 945-53.

Block, J. H. An experimental study of a topological representation of ego-structure. Doctoral dissertation, Stanford University, 1951.

Block, J. H., and J. Block. An interpersonal experiment on reactions to authority. *Human Relations,* 1952, 5, 91-98.

Block, J. H., and B. Martin. Predicting the behavior of children under frustration. *Journal of Abnormal and Social Psychology,* 1955, 51, 281-85.

Boe, E., E. F. Gocka, and W. S. Kogan. A factor analysis of individual social desirability scale values. *Multivariate Behavioral Research,* 1966, 1, 287-92.

Boe, E., E. F. Gocka, and W. S. Kogan. Factor analysis of individual social desirability scale values: second order analysis. *Multivariate Behavioral Research,* 1967, 2, 239-40.

Bordin, E. S. A theory of vocational interests as dynamic phenomena. *Educational and Psychological Measurement,* 1943, 3, 49-65.

Braaten, D. Kooky personality test. *The Washington Star,* June 8, 1965.

Brayfield, A. H., ed. Special issue: testing and public policy. *American Psychologist,* 1965, 20, 857-1002.

Bruner, J. S., and L. Postman. Emotional selectivity in perception and reaction. *Journal of Personality,* 1947, 16, 69-77. (a)

Bruner, J. S., and L. Postman. Tension and tension-release as organizing factors in perception. *Journal of Personality,* 1947, 15, 300-8. (b)

Burkhart, B. R., W. L. Christian, and M. D. Gynther. Item subtlety and faking on the MMPI: a paradoxical relationship. *Journal of Personality Assessment,* 1978, 42, 76-80.

Buss, A. H. The effect of item style on social desirability and frequency of endorsement. *Journal of Consulting Psychology,* 1959, 23, 510-13.

Butcher, J. N., P. C. Kendall, and N. Hoffmann. MMPI short forms: CAUTION. *Journal of Consulting and Clinical Psychology,* in press.

Butcher, J. N., and A. Tellegen. Objections to MMPI items. *Journal of Consulting Psychology,* 1966, 30, 527-34.

Byrne, D., J. Barry, and D. Nelson. Relation of the revised repression sensitization scale to measures of self-description. *Psychological Reports,* 1963, 13, 323-34.

Byrne, D., and J. Holcomb. The reliability of response measure: differential recognition-threshold scores. *Psychological Bulletin,* 1962, 59, 70-73.

Cady, V. M. The estimation of juvenile incorrigibility. *Journal of Delinquency Monographs,* 1923, No. 2.

Cameron, N. *The psychology of behavior disorders: a bio-social interpretation.* Boston: Houghton Mifflin, 1947.

Capwell, D. F. Personality patterns of adolescent girls: I. Girls who show improvement in IQ. *Journal of Applied Psychology,* 1945, 29, 212-28. (a)

Capwell, D. F. Personality patterns of adolescent girls: II. Delinquents and non-delinquents. *Journal of Applied Psychology,* 1945, 29, 289-97. (b)

Carlson, V. R. Individual differences in the recall of word-association-test words. *Journal of Personality,* 1954, 23, 77-87.

Carpenter, B., M. Wiener, and J. T. Carpenter. Predictability of perceptual defense behavior. *Journal of Abnormal and Social Psychology,* 1956, 52, 380-83.

Carson, R. Issues in the teaching of clinical MMPI interpretation. In J. N. Butcher, ed. *MMPI research developments and clinical applications.* New York: McGraw-Hill, 1969.

Cattell, R. B. Theory of situational, instrument, second order, and refraction factors in personality structure research. *Psychological Bulletin,* 1961, 58, 160-74.

Cattell, R. B. *The scientific analysis of personality.* Chicago: Aldine, 1965.

Chapman, L. J., and R. D. Bock. Components of variance due to acquiescence and content in the F scale measure of authoritarianism. *Psychological Bulletin,* 1958, 55, 328-33.

Chodorkoff, B. Self-perception, perceptual defense, and adjustment. *Journal of Abnormal and Social Psychology,* 1954, 49, 508-12.

Christian, W. L., B. R. Burkhart, and M. D. Gynther. Subtle-obvious ratings of MMPI items: new interest in an old concept. *Journal of Consulting and Clinical Psychology,* 1978, 46, 1178-86.

Clavelle, P. R., and J. N. Butcher. An adaptive typological approach to psychiatric screening. *Journal of Consulting and Clinical Psychology,* 1977, 45, 851-59.

Clayton, M. B., and D. N. Jackson. Equivalence range, acquiescence, and overgeneralization. *Educational and Psychological Measurement,* 1961, 21, 371-82.

Cleckley, H. *The mask of sanity.* St. Louis: Mosby, 1941.

Cofer, C. N., J. Chance, and A. J. Judson. A study of malingering on the MMPI. *Journal of Psychology,* 1949, 27, 491-99.

Comrey, A. L. A factor analysis of items on the MMPI Hypochondriasis scale. *Educational and Psychological Measurement,* 1957, 17, 568-77. (a)

Comrey, A. L. A factor analysis of items on the MMPI Depression scale. *Educational and Psychological Measurement,* 1957, 17, 578-85. (b)

Comrey, A. L. A factor analysis of items on the MMPI Hysteria scale. *Educational and Psychological Measurement,* 1957, 17, 586-92. (c)

Comrey, A. L. A factor analysis of items on the MMPI Psychopathic Deviate scale. *Educational and Psychological Measurement,* 1958, 18, 91-98. (a)

Comrey, A. L. A factor analysis of items on the MMPI Paranoia scale. *Educational and Psychological Measurement,* 1958, 18, 99-107. (b)

Comrey, A. L. A factor analysis of items on the Psychasthenia scale. *Educational and Psychological Measurement,* 1958, 18, 293-300. (c)

Comrey, A. L. A factor analysis of items on the F scale of the MMPI. *Educational and Psychological Measurement,* 1958, 18, 621-32. (d)

Comrey, A. L. A factor analysis of items on the K scale of the MMPI. *Educational and Psychological Measurement,* 1958, 18, 633-39. (e)

Comrey, A. L., and W. M. Marggraff. A factor analysis of items on the MMPI schizophrenia scale. *Educational and Psychological Measurement,* 1958, 18, 301-11.

Cook, E. B., and R. J. Wherry. A factor analysis of MMPI and aptitude test data. *Journal of Applied Psychology,* 1950, 34, 260-66.

Cottle, W. C. A factorial study of the Multiphasic, Strong, Kuder, and Bell inventories using a population of adult males. Doctoral dissertation, Syracuse University, 1949. (Same title: *Psychometrika,* 1950, 15, 25-47)

Cottle, W. C. Card versus booklet forms of the MMPI. *Journal of Applied Psychology,* 1950, 34, 255-59.

Cottle, W. C. *The MMPI: a review.* Lawrence, Kansas: University of Kansas Press, 1953.

Couch, A., and K. Keniston. Yeasayers and naysayers: agreeing response set as a personality variable. *Journal of Abnormal and Social Psychology,* 1960, 60, 151-74.

Couch, A., and K. Keniston. Agreeing response set and social desirability. *Journal of Abnormal and Social Psychology,* 1961, 62, 175-79.

Cowen, E. L., S. H. Davol, G. Reimanis, and A. Stiller. The social desirability of trait descriptive terms: two geriatric samples. *Journal of Social Psychology,* 1962, 56, 217-25.

Cowen, E. L., M. G. Staiman, and D. L. Wolitzky. The social desirability of trait descriptive terms: applications to a schizophrenic sample. *Journal of Social Psychology,* 1961, 54, 37-45.

Cowen, E. L., and G. Stricker. The social desirability of trait descriptive terms: a sample of sexual offenders. *Journal of Social Psychology,* 1963, 59, 307-15.

Cowen, E. L., and P. Tongas. The social desirability of trait descriptive terms: applications to a self-concept inventory. *Journal of Consulting Psychology,* 1959, 23, 361-65.

Cronbach, L. J. Response sets and test validity. *Educational and Psychological Measurement,* 1946, 6, 475-94.

Cronbach, L. J. Further evidence on response sets and test design. *Educational and Psychological Measurement,* 1950, 10, 3-31.

Cronbach, L. J. Coefficient alpha and the internal structure of tests. *Psychometrika,* 1951, 16, 297-334.

Cronbach, L. J. *Essentials of psychological testing.* New York: Harper & Row, 1960. (3rd ed., 1970)

Cronbach, L. J., and G. C. Gleser. *Psychological tests and personnel decisions.* (2nd ed.) Urbana: University of Illinois Press, 1965.

Cronbach, L. J., and P. E. Meehl. Construct validity in psychological tests. *Psychological Bulletin,* 1955, 52, 281-302.

Crowne, D. P., and D. Marlowe. A new scale of social desirability independent of psychopathology. *Journal of Consulting Psychology,* 1960, 24, 349-54.

Crowne, D. P., and D. Marlowe. *The approval motive: studies in evaluative dependence.* New York: Wiley, 1964.

Cruse, D. B. Socially desirable responses in relation to grade level. *Child Development,* 1963, 34, 777-89.

Dahlstrom, W. G. Whither the MMPI? In J. N. Butcher, ed. *Objective personality assessment.* New York: Academic Press, 1972.

Dahlstrom, W. G., and G. S. Welsh. *An MMPI handbook.* Minneapolis: University of Minnesota Press, 1960.

Dahlstrom, W. G., G. S. Welsh, and L. E. Dahlstrom. *An MMPI handbook.* Vol. I: *Clinical interpretation.* Minneapolis: University of Minnesota Press, 1972.

Dahlstrom, W. G., G. S. Welsh, and L. E. Dahlstrom. *An MMPI handbook.* Vol. II: *Research applications.* Minneapolis: University of Minnesota Press, 1975.

Dean, E. F. A lengthened Mini: The Midi-Mult. *Journal of Clinical Psychology,* 1972, 28, 68-71.

Diamond, D. R. Enhancement of creativity: a study of approach and personality. Doctoral dissertation, University of North Carolina (Chapel Hill), 1971. (*DAI,* 1971, 32, 2998B)

Dicken, C. "Acquiescence" in the MMPI: a method variance artifact? *Psychological Reports,* 1967, 20, 927-33.

Drake, L. E. A social I.E. scale for the MMPI. *Journal of Applied Psychology,* 1946, 30, 51-54.

Drake, L. E. Differential sex responses to items of the MMPI. *Journal of Applied Psychology,* 1953, 37, 46.

DuBois, P. H. On relationships between numbers and behavior. *Psychometrika,* 1962, 27, 323-33.

Duff, F. L. Item subtlety in personality inventory scales. *Journal of Consulting Psychology,* 1965, 29, 565-70.

Edinger, J. D., P. C. Kendall, J. F. Hooke, and J. B. Bogan. The predictive efficacy of three MMPI short forms. *Journal of Personality Assessment,* 1976, 40, 259-65.

Edwards, A. L. The relationship between the judged desirability of a trait and the probability that the trait will be endorsed. *Journal of Applied Psychology,* 1953, 37, 90-93.

Edwards, A. L. *The social desirability variable in personality assessment and research.* New York: Dryden, 1957. (a)

Edwards, A. L. Social desirability and probability of endorsement of items in the Interpersonal Check List. *Journal of Abnormal and Social Psychology,* 1957, 55, 394-95. (b)

Edwards, A. L. Social desirability and the description of others. *Journal of Abnormal and Social Psychology,* 1959, 59, 434-36. (a)

Edwards, A. L. Social desirability and personality test construction. In B. M. Bass and I. A. Berg, eds. *Objective approaches to personality assessment.* Princeton: Van Nostrand, 1959. (b)

Edwards, A. L. Social desirability or acquiescence in the MMPI? A case study with the SD scale. *Journal of Abnormal and Social Psychology,* 1961, 63, 351-59.

Edwards, A. L. The objective assessment of human motives. In D. Levine, ed. *Nebraska symposium on motivation.* Lincoln: University of Nebraska Press, 1964.

Edwards, A. L., and C. J. Diers. Social desirability and the factorial interpretation of the MMPI. *Educational and Psychological Measurement,* 1962, 22, 501-9.

Edwards, A. L., and C. J. Diers. Neutral items as a measure of acquiescence. *Educational and Psychological Measurement,* 1963, 23, 687-98.

Edwards, A. L., C. J. Diers, and J. N. Walker. Response sets and factor loadings on sixty-one personality scales. *Journal of Applied Psychology,* 1962, 46, 220-25.

Edwards, A. L., and L. B. Heathers. The first factor of the MMPI: social desirability or ego strength? *Journal of Consulting Psychology,* 1962, 26, 99-100.

Edwards, A. L., and J. N. Walker. A note on the Couch and Keniston measure of agreement response set. *Journal of Abnormal and Social Psychology,* 1961, 62, 173-74.

Edwards, A. L., and J. A. Walsh. Relationships between various psychometric properties of personality items. *Educational and Psychological Measurement,* 1963, 23, 227-38.

Edwards, A. L., and J. A. Walsh. Response sets in standard and experimental personality scales. *American Educational Research Journal,* 1964, 1, 52-61.

Eichman, W. J. Replicated factors on the MMPI with female NP patients. *Journal of Consulting Psychology,* 1961, 25, 55-60.

Eichman, W. J. Factored scales for the MMPI. *Journal of Clinical Psychology,* 1962, 15 (Monogr. Suppl.), 363-95.

Eisenberg, P. Individual interpretation of psychoneurotic inventory items. *Journal of General Psychology,* 1941, 25, 19-40.

Eisenberg, P., and A. Wesman. Consistency in response and logical interpretation of psychoneurotic inventory items. *Journal of Educational Psychology*, 1941, 32, 321-38.

Elion, V. H., and E. I. Megargee. Validity of the MMPI Pd scale among black males. *Journal of Consulting and Clinical Psychology*, 1975, 43, 166-72.

Elliott, L. L. Effects of item construction and respondent aptitude on response acquiescence. *Educational and Psychological Measurement*, 1961, 21, 405-15.

Endicott, N. A., and J. Endicott. Objective measures of somatic preoccupation. *Journal of Nervous and Mental Disease*, 1963, 137, 427-37.

Endicott, N. A., and S. Jortner. Objective measures of depression. *Archives of General Psychiatry*, 1966, 15, 249-55.

Endicott, N. A., S. Jortner, and E. Abramoff. Objective measures of suspiciousness. *Journal of Abnormal Psychology*, 1969, 74, 26-32.

Eriksen, C. W. Some implications for TAT interpretation arising from need and perception experiments. *Journal of Personality*, 1951, 19, 282-88.

Eriksen, C. W. Defense against ego-threat in memory and perception. *Journal of Abnormal and Social Psychology*, 1952, 47, 230-35. (a)

Eriksen, C. W. Individual differences in defensive forgetting. *Journal of Experimental Psychology*, 1952, 44, 442-46. (b)

Eriksen, C. W. Psychological defenses and "ego-strength" in the recall of completed and incompleted tasks. *Journal of Abnormal and Social Psychology*, 1954, 49, 45-50. (a)

Eriksen, C. W. The case for perceptual defense. *Psychological Review*, 1954, 61, 175-82. (b)

Eriksen, C. W., and C. T. Browne. An experimental and theoretical analysis of perceptual defense. *Journal of Abnormal and Social Psychology*, 1956, 52, 224-30.

Eriksen, C. W., and A. Davids. The meaning and clinical validity of the Taylor anxiety scale and the hysteria-psychasthenia scales from the MMPI. *Journal of Abnormal and Social Psychology*, 1955, 50, 135-37.

Eriksen, C. W., and J. L. Kuethe. Avoidance conditioning of verbal behavior without awareness: a paradigm of repression. *Journal of Abnormal and Social Psychology*, 1956, 53, 203-9.

Eriksen, C. W., J. L. Kuethe, and D. F. Sullivan. Some personality correlates of learning without verbal awareness. *Journal of Personality*, 1958, 26, 216-28.

Eriksen, C. W., and R. S. Lazarus. Perceptual defense and projective tests. *Journal of Abnormal and Social Psychology*, 1952, 47, 302-8.

Evans, C., and T. R. McConnell. A new measure of introversion-extroversion. *Journal of Psychology*, 1941, 12, 111-24.

Eysenck, H. J. *The structure of human personality*. New York: Wiley, 1953.

Faschingbauer, T. R. A 166-item short form of the group MMPI: the FAM. *Journal of Consulting and Clinical Psychology*, 1974, 42, 645-55.

Faschingbauer, T. R., and D. A. Eglevsky. Relation of dogmatism to creativity: origence and intellectence. *Psychological Reports*, 1977, 40, 391-94.

Faschingbauer, T. R., C. D. Moore, and A. Stone. Cognitive style, dogmatism, and creativity: some implications regarding cognitive development. *Psychological Reports*, 1978, 42, 795-804.

Faschingbauer, T. R., and C. S. Newmark. *Short forms of the MMPI*. Lexington, Mass.: Lexington Books, 1978.

Fenichel, O. *Psychoanalytical theory of the neuroses*. New York: Norton, 1945.

Feshbach, S. The drive-reducing function of fantasy behavior. *Journal of Abnormal and Social Psychology*, 1955, 50, 3-11.

Fisher, J. Some MMPI dimensions of physical and psychological illness. *Journal of Clinical Psychology*, 1964, 20, 369-75.

Fiske, D. W., and P. H. Pearson. Theory and techniques of personality measurement. *Annual Review of Psychology*, 1970, 21, 49-86.

Ford, L. H., and M. Meisels. Social desirability and the semantic differential. *Educational and Psychological Measurement*, 1965, 25, 465-75.

Fordyce, W. E. Social desirability in the MMPI. *Journal of Consulting Psychology*, 1956, 20, 171-75.

French, J. W. *The description of personality measurements in terms of rotated factors.* Princeton: Educational Testing Service, 1953.

Frenkel-Brunswik, E. Mechanisms of self-deception. *Journal of Social Psychology*, 1939, 10, 409-20.

Fricke, B. G. Response set as a suppressor variable in the OAIS and MMPI. *Journal of Consulting Psychology*, 1956, 20, 161-69.

Fujita, B. Applicability of the Edwards Personal Preference Schedule to Nisei. *Psychological Reports*, 1957, 3, 518-19.

Gage, N. L., and B. B. Chatterjee. The psychological meaning of acquiescence set: further evidence. *Journal of Abnormal and Social Psychology*, 1960, 60, 280-83.

Gage, N. L., G. S. Leavitt, and G. C. Stone. The psychological meaning of acquiescence set for authoritarianism. *Journal of Abnormal and Social Psychology*, 1957, 55, 98-103.

Gilliland, A. R., and R. Colgin. Norms, reliability, and forms of the MMPI. *Journal of Consulting Psychology*, 1951, 15, 435-38.

Goldberg, L. R., and P. Slovic. Importance of test item content: an analysis of a corollary of the deviation hypothesis. *Journal of Counseling Psychology*, 1967, 14, 462-72.

Gordon, J. E. Interpersonal predictions of repressors and sensitizers. *Journal of Personality*, 1957, 25, 686-98.

Gordon, J. E. The stability of the assumed similarity response set in repressors and sensitizers. *Journal of Personality*, 1959, 27, 362-73.

Gordon, J. E. A communication: snooping and testing. *The New Republic*, Jan. 9, 1965, 28-30.

Gough, H. G. Simulated patterns on the MMPI. *Journal of Abnormal and Social Psychology*, 1947, 42, 215-25.

Gough, H. G. A new dimension of status: I. Development of a personality scale. *American Sociological Review*, 1948, 13, 401-9.

Gough, H. G. Studies of social intolerance: I. Psychological and sociological correlates of anti-Semitism. *Journal of Social Psychology*, 1951, 33, 237-46.

Gough, H. G. Predicting social participation. *Journal of Social Psychology*, 1952, 35, 227-33.

Gough, H. G. A nonintellectual intelligence test. *Journal of Consulting Psychology*, 1953, 17, 242-46.

Gough, H. G. An interpreter's syllabus for the California Psychological Inventory. In P. McReynolds, ed. *Advances in psychological assessment.* Vol. 1. Palo Alto, CA: Science and Behavior Books, 1968.

Gough, H. G., H. McClosky, and P. E. Meehl. A personality scale for dominance. *Journal of Abnormal and Social Psychology*, 1951, 46, 360-66.

Gough, H. G., H. McClosky, and P. E. Meehl. A personality scale for social responsibility. *Journal of Abnormal and Social Psychology*, 1952, 47, 73-80.

Gough, H. G., M. G. McKee, and R. J. Yandell. Adjective checklist analyses of a number of selected psychometric and assessment variables. Technical Memorandum, OERL TM-10, 1955.

Gough, H. G., and W. H. Pemberton. Personality characteristics related to success in practice teaching. *Journal of Applied Psychology*, 1952, 36, 307-9.

Graham, J. R. *The MMPI: a practical guide.* New York: Oxford University Press, 1977. (a)

Graham, J. R. Review of MMPI special scales. In P. McReynolds, ed. *Advances in psychological assessment.* Vol. 4. San Francisco: Jossey-Bass, 1977. (b)

Gredler, G. R., ed. Ethical and legal factors in the practice of school psychology. (Proceedings of the first annual conference in school psychology, Temple University, 1972) Harrisburg: Pennsylvania Department of Education, 1975.

Grigg, A. E., and J. S. Thorpe. Deviant responses in college adjustment clients: a test of Berg's deviation hypothesis. *Journal of Consulting Psychology,* 1960, 24, 92-94.

Gross, M. L. *Brain watchers.* New York: Random House, 1962.

Guilford, J. P. When not to factor analyze. *Psychological Bulletin,* 1952, 49, 26-37.

Guilford, J. P. *Personality.* New York: McGraw-Hill, 1959.

Guilford, J. P. *The nature of human intelligence.* New York: McGraw-Hill, 1967.

Guilford, J. P., and R. B. Guilford. Personality factors S, E, and M, and their measurement. *Journal of Psychology,* 1936, 2, 109-27.

Guilford, J. P., and R. B. Guilford. Personality factors D, R, T, and A. *Journal of Abnormal and Social Psychology,* 1939, 34, 21-36.

Gynther, M. D., B. R. Burkhart, and C. Hovanitz. Do face-valid items have more predictive validity than subtle items? The case of the MMPI Pd scale. *Journal of Consulting and Clinical Psychology,* 1979, 47, 295-300.

Gynther, M. D., and R. A. Gynther. Personality inventories. In I. B. Weiner, ed. *Clinical methods in psychology.* New York: Wiley-Interscience, 1976.

Hall, W. B., and D. W. MacKinnon. Personality inventory correlates of creativity among architects. *Journal of Applied Psychology,* 1969, 53, 322-26.

Hanley, C. Social desirability and responses to items from three MMPI scales: D, Sc, and K. *Journal of Applied Psychology,* 1956, 40, 324-28.

Hanley, C. Deriving a measure of test-taking defensiveness. *Journal of Consulting Psychology,* 1957, 21, 391-97.

Hanley, C. Responses to the wording of personality test items. *Journal of Consulting Psychology,* 1959, 23, 261-65.

Harman, H. *Modern factor analysis.* Chicago: University of Chicago Press, 1960.

Harris, R. E., and C. Christiansen. Prediction of response to brief psychotherapy. *Journal of Psychology,* 1946, 21, 269-84.

Harris, R. E., and J. C. Lingoes. Subscales for the MMPI: an aid to profile interpretation. Mimeographed materials, Department of Psychiatry, University of California (San Francisco), 1955. (Corrected version, 1968)

Hartshorne, H., and M. A. May. *Studies in deceit.* New York: Macmillan, 1928.

Hartshorne, H., M. A. May, and F. K. Shuttleworth. *Studies in the nature of character: III. Studies in the organization of character.* New York: Macmillan, 1930.

Hathaway, S. R. The personality inventory as an aid in the diagnosis of psychopathic inferiors. *Journal of Consulting Psychology,* 1939, 3, 112-17.

Hathaway, S. R. *Supplementary manual for the MMPI.* New York: The Psychological Corporation, 1946.

Hathaway, S. R. Scales 5 (masculinity-femininity), 6 (paranoia), and 8 (schizophrenia). In G. S. Welsh and W. G. Dahlstrom, eds. *Basic readings on the MMPI.* Minneapolis: University of Minnesota Press, 1956.

Hathaway, S. R. MMPI: professional use by professional people. *American Psychologist,* 1964, 19, 204-11.

Hathaway, S. R. Where have we gone wrong? The mystery of the missing progress. In J. N. Butcher, ed. *Objective personality assessment.* New York: Academic Press, 1972.

Hathaway, S. R. Through psychology my way. In T. S. Krawiec, ed. *The psychologists: autobiographies of distinguished living psychologists.* Vol. 3. Brandon, Vt.: Clinical Psychology Publishing Co., Inc., 1978.

Hathaway, S. R., and P. F. Briggs. Some normative data on new MMPI scales. *Journal of Clinical Psychology,* 1957, 13, 364-68.

Hathaway, S. R., and J. C. McKinley. A multiphasic personality schedule (Minnesota): I. Construction of the schedule. *Journal of Psychology,* 1940, 10, 249-54.

Hathaway, S. R., and J. C. McKinley. A multiphasic personality schedule (Minnesota): III. The measurement of symptomatic depression. *Journal of Psychology,* 1942, 14, 73-84.

Hathaway, S. R., and J. C. McKinley. *The Minnesota Multiphasic Personality Inventory.* (Rev. ed.) Minneapolis: University of Minnesota Press, 1943.

Hathaway, S. R., and J. C. McKinley. *The Minnesota Multiphasic Personality Inventory manual.* (Rev. ed.) New York: The Psychological Corporation, 1951.

Hathaway, S. R., and J. C. McKinley. *Minnesota Multiphasic Personality Inventory, Form S, Peace Corps Edition.* New York: The Psychological Corporation, 1965.

Hathaway, S. R., and J. C. McKinley. *Minnesota Multiphasic Personality Inventory manual.* (Rev. ed.) New York: The Psychological Corporation, 1967.

Hathaway, S. R., and P. E. Meehl. *An atlas for the clinical use of the MMPI.* Minneapolis: University of Minnesota Press, 1951.

Hathaway, S. R., and E. D. Monachesi, eds. *Analyzing and predicting juvenile delinquency with the MMPI.* Minneapolis: University of Minnesota Press, 1953.

Heineman, C. E. A forced-choice form of the Taylor Anxiety Scale. Doctoral dissertation, State University of Iowa, 1952. (*DA,* 1952, 12, 584) (Same title: *Journal of Consulting Psychology,* 1953, 17, 447-54)

Henderson, D. K. *Psychopathic states.* New York: Norton, 1939.

Hendrickson, G. Attitudes and interests of teachers and prospective teachers. Unpublished paper presented at Section Q, AAAS, Atlantic City, 1932.

Hoffman, B. The tyranny of multiple-choice tests. *Harper's Magazine,* 1961, 222, 37-44.

Holzberg, J. D., and S. Alessi. Reliability of the shortened MMPI. *Journal of Consulting Psychology,* 1949, 13, 288-92.

Holzman, P., and R. W. Gardner. Leveling and repression. *Journal of Abnormal and Social Psychology,* 1959, 59, 151-55.

Horst, P. *The prediction of personal adjustment.* New York: Social Science Research Council Bulletin No. 48, 1941.

Hovey, H. B. MMPI profiles and personality characteristics. *Journal of Consulting Psychology,* 1953, 17, 142-46.

Hugo, J. A. Abbreviation of the MMPI through multiple regression. Doctoral dissertation, University of Alabama, 1971. (*DAI,* 1971, 32, 1213B)

Humm, D. G., and K. A. Humm. Validity of the Humm-Wadsworth temperament scale: with consideration of the effects of subjects' response-bias. *Journal of Psychology,* 1944, 18, 55-64.

Humm, D. G., R. C. Storment, and M. E. Iorns, Combination scores for the Humm-Wadsworth temperament scale. *Journal of Psychology,* 1939, 7, 227-53.

Humm, D. G., and G. W. Wadsworth. The Humm-Wadsworth temperament scale. *American Journal of Psychiatry,* 1935, 92, 163-200.

Hutt, M. L. The use of projective methods of personality measurement in Army medical installations. *Journal of Clinical Psychology,* 1945, 1, 134-40.

Jackson, D. N. Acquiescence response styles: problems of identification and control. In I. A. Berg, ed. *Response set and personality assessment.* Chicago: Aldine, 1967.

Jackson, D. N. The dynamics of structured personality tests: 1971. *Psychological Review,* 1971, 78, 229-48.

Jackson, D. N. The relative validity of scales prepared by naive item writers and those based on empirical methods of personality scale construction. *Educational and Psychological Measurement,* 1975, 35, 361-70.

Jackson, D. N., and S. Messick. A note on "ethnocentrism" and acquiescent response sets. *Journal of Abnormal and Social Psychology,* 1957, 54, 132-34.

Jackson, D. N., and S. Messick. Content and style in personality assessment. *Psychological Bulletin,* 1958, 55, 243-52.

Jackson, D. N., and S. Messick. Acquiescence and desirability as response determinants on the MMPI. *Educational and Psychological Measurement,* 1961, 21, 771-90.

Jackson, D. N., and S. Messick. Response styles and the assessment of psychopathology. In S. Messick and J. Ross, eds. *Measurement in personality and cognition.* New York: Wiley, 1962. (a)

Jackson, D. N., and S. Messick. Response styles on the MMPI: comparison of clinical and normal samples. *Journal of Abnormal and Social Psychology,* 1962, 65, 285-99. (b)

Jorgensen, C. A short form of the MMPI. *Australian Journal of Psychology,* 1958, 10, 341-50.

Jourard, S. M. *The transparent self.* Princeton: Van Nostrand, 1964.

Kaiser, H. F. The varimax criterion for analytic rotation in factor analysis. *Psychometrika,* 1958, 23, 187-200.

Kassebaum, G. G., A. S. Couch, and P. E. Slater. The factorial dimensions of the MMPI. *Journal of Consulting Psychology,* 1959, 23, 226-36.

Kelly, E. L., C. C. Miles, and L. M. Terman. Ability to influence one's score on a typical pencil and paper test of personality. *Journal of Personality,* 1936, 4, 206-15.

Kenny, D. T. The influence of social desirability on discrepancy measures between real self and ideal self. *Journal of Consulting Psychology,* 1956, 20, 315-18.

Kincannon, J. C. An investigation of the feasibility of adapting a personality inventory for use in the mental status exam. Doctoral dissertation, University of Minnesota, 1967. (*DA,* 1967, 28, 2625B)

Kincannon, J. C. Prediction of the standard MMPI scale scores from 71 items: the Mini-Mult. *Journal of Consulting and Clinical Psychology,* 1968, 32, 319-25.

Kissin, B., H. Gottesfeld, and R. Dicks. Inhibition and tachistoscopic thresholds for sexually charged words. *Journal of Psychology,* 1957, 43, 333-39.

Klett, C. J. The social desirability stereotype in a hospital population. *Journal of Consulting Psychology,* 1957, 21, 419-21. (a)

Klett, C. J. The stability of the social desirability scale values in the Edwards Personal Preference Schedule. *Journal of Consulting Psychology,* 1957, 21, 183-85. (b)

Koss, M. P., and J. N. Butcher. A comparison of psychiatric patients' self-concept with other sources of clinical information. *Journal of Research in Personality,* 1973, 7, 225-36.

Koszalka, E. M. An exploration of the meaning of the personality dimensions of origence and intellectence among delinquent adolescents. Doctoral dissertation, University of North Carolina (Chapel Hill), 1976. (*DAI,* 1977, 38, 907B)

Kurland, S. H. The lack of generality in defense mechanisms as indicated in auditory perception. *Journal of Abnormal and Social Psychology,* 1954, 49, 173-77.

Lachar, D. How much of a good thing is enough?: a review of T. R. Faschingbauer and C. A. Newmark. *Short forms of the MMPI. Contemporary Psychology,* 1979, 24, 116-17.

Lachar, D., and R. S. Alexander. Veridicality of self-report: replicated correlates of the Wiggins MMPI content scales. *Journal of Consulting and Clinical Psychology,* 1978, 46, 1349-56.

Lachar, D., and T. A. Wrobel. Validating clinicians' hunches: construction of a new MMPI critical item set. *Journal of Consulting and Clinical Psychology,* 1979, 47, 277-84.

LaForge, R. Interpersonal domains or interpersonal levels? A validation of Leary's "MMPI Level 1 indices." Paper presented at the meetings of the Western Psychological Association, Santa Monica, California, 1963.

LaForge, R., T. F. Leary, H. Naboisek, H. S. Coffey, and M. B. Freedman. The interpersonal dimension of personality: II. An objective study of repression. *Journal of Personality,* 1954, 23, 129-53.

Laird, D. A. Detecting abnormal behavior. *Journal of Abnormal and Social Psychology,* 1925, 20, 128-41.

Landis, C., and S. E. Katz. The validity of certain questions which purport to measure neurotic tendencies. *Journal of Applied Psychology,* 1934, 18, 343-56.

Landis, C., J. Zubin, and S. E. Katz. Empirical evaluation of three personality adjustment inventories. *Journal of Educational Psychology,* 1935, 26, 321-30.

Lazarus, R. S. Is there a mechanism of perceptual defense? A reply to Postman, Bronson, and Gropper. *Journal of Abnormal and Social Psychology,* 1954, 49, 396-98.

Lazarus, R. S., C. W. Eriksen, and C. P. Fonda. Personality dynamics and auditory perceptual recognition. *Journal of Personality,* 1951, 19, 471-82.

Lazarus, R. S., and N. Longo. The consistency of psychological defense against threat. *Journal of Abnormal and Social Psychology,* 1953, 48, 495-99.

Leary, T. F. *Interpersonal diagnosis of personality.* New York: Ronald Press, 1957.

Lecky, P. *Self-consistency: a theory of personality.* New York: Island Press, 1945.

Leverenz, C. W. MMPI: an evaluation of its usefulness in the psychiatric service of a station hospital. *War Medicine,* 1943, 4, 618-29.

Levinson, M. H. Psychological ill-health in relation to potential fascism: a study of psychiatric clinic patients. In T. W. Adorno, E. Frenkel-Brunswik, D. Levinson, and R. N. Sanford. *The authoritarian personality.* New York: Harper, 1950.

Liberty, P. G., C. E. Lunneborg, and G. C. Atkinson. Perceptual defense, dissimulation and response styles. *Journal of Consulting Psychology,* 1964, 28, 529-37.

Lingoes, J. C. MMPI factors of the Harris and the Wiener subscales. *Journal of Consulting Psychology,* 1960, 24, 74-83.

Little, K. B., and J. Fisher. Two new experimental scales of the MMPI. *Journal of Consulting Psychology,* 1958, 22, 305-6.

Loevinger, J. Objective tests as instruments of psychological theory. *Psychological Reports,* 1957, 3, 635-94.

Loevinger, J. Measuring personality patterns of women. *Genetic Psychology Monographs,* 1962, 65, 35-136.

Loth, N. N. Correlations between the Guilford-Martin Inventory of Factors STDCR and the MMPI at the college level. Master's thesis, University of Minnesota, 1945.

Lucas, J. D. The interactive effects of anxiety, failure, and intraserial duplication. *American Journal of Psychology,* 1952, 65, 59-66.

McGee, R. K. Response style as a personality variable: by what criterion? *Psychological Bulletin,* 1962, 59, 284-95.

McKenna v. Fargo, 451 *F. Supp.* 1355 (1978).

McKinley, J. C., and S. R. Hathaway. A multiphasic personality schedule (Minnesota): II. A differential study of hypochondriasis. *Journal of Psychology,* 1940, 10, 255-68.

McKinley, J. C., and S. R. Hathaway. A multiphasic personality schedule (Minnesota): IV. Psychasthenia. *Journal of Applied Psychology,* 1942, 26, 614-24.

McKinley, J. C., and S. R. Hathaway. The MMPI: V. Hysteria, hypomania and psychopathic deviate. *Journal of Applied Psychology,* 1944, 28, 153-74.

McKinley, J. C., S. R. Hathaway, and P. E. Meehl. The MMPI: VI. The K scale. *Journal of Consulting Psychology*, 1948, 12, 20-31.

MacKinnon, D. W. Creativity in architects. In D. W. MacKinnon, ed. *The creative person.* Berkeley: University of California Extension, 1961.

McLachlan, J. F. C. Test-retest stability of long and short form MMPI scales over two years. *Journal of Clinical Psychology*, 1974, 30, 189-91.

McNair, D. M., M. Lorr, and L. F. Doppleman. *Manual for the Profile of Mood States.* San Diego: Educational and Industrial Testing Service, 1971.

McNemar, Q. The mode of operation of suppressant variables. *American Journal of Psychology*, 1945, 58, 544-55.

MacPhillamy, D. J., and P. M. Lewinsohn. Depression as a function of levels of desired and obtained pleasure. *Journal of Abnormal Psychology*, 1974, 83, 651-57.

Maller, J. B. The effect of signing one's name. *School and Society*, 1930, 31, 882-84.

Maller, J. B. *Character sketches.* New York: Bureau of Publications, Teachers College, Columbia University, 1932.

Marlowe, D., and D. P. Crowne. Social desirability and response to perceived situational demands. *Journal of Consulting Psychology*, 1961, 25, 109-15.

Mathews, A., and M. Wertheimer. A "pure" measure of perceptual defense uncontaminated by response suppression. *Journal of Abnormal and Social Psychology*, 1958, 57, 373-76.

Meehl, P. E. The dynamics of "structured" personality tests. *Journal of Clinical Psychology*, 1945, 1, 296-303. (a)

Meehl, P. E. An investigation of a general normality or control factor in personality testing. *Psychological Monographs*, 1945, 59, No. 4 (Whole No. 274). (b)

Meehl, P. E. A simple algebraic development of Horst's suppressor variables. *American Journal of Psychology*, 1945, 58, 550-54. (c)

Meehl, P. E. *Clinical versus statistical prediction: a theoretical analysis and a review of the evidence.* Minneapolis: University of Minnesota Press, 1954.

Meehl, P. E. Wanted—a good cookbook. *American Psychologist*, 1956, 11, 263-72.

Meehl, P. E. *Psychodiagnosis: selected papers.* Minneapolis: University of Minnesota Press, 1973.

Meehl, P. E., and S. R. Hathaway. The K factor as a suppressor variable in the MMPI. *Journal of Applied Psychology*, 1946, 30, 525-64.

Mees, H. L. Preliminary steps in the construction of factor scales for the MMPI. Doctoral dissertation, University of Washington, 1959. (*DA*, 1960, 20, 2905)

Messick, S. Response style and content measures from personality inventories. *Educational and Psychological Measurement*, 1962, 22, 41-56.

Messick, S. The psychology of acquiescence: an interpretation of the research evidence. In I. A. Berg, ed. *Response set and personality assessment.* Chicago: Aldine, 1967.

Messick, S., and D. N. Jackson. Acquiescence and the factorial interpretation of the MMPI. *Psychological Bulletin*, 1961, 58, 299-304. (a)

Messick, S., and D. N. Jackson. Desirability scale values and dispersions for MMPI items. *Psychological Reports*, 1961, 8, 409-14. (b)

Messick, S., and D. N. Jackson. Judgmental dimensions of psychopathology. *Journal of Consulting and Clinical Psychology*, 1972, 38, 418-27.

Metfessel, M. Personality factors in motion picture writing. *Journal of Abnormal and Social Psychology*, 1935, 30, 333-47.

Mischel, W. *Personality and assessment.* New York: Wiley, 1968.

Morf, M., and D. N. Jackson. An analysis of two response styles: true responding and item endorsement. *Educational and Psychological Measurement*, 1972, 32, 329-53.

Morton, M. A. The army adaptation of the MMPI. *American Psychologist*, 1948, 3, 271-72.

Mosier, C. I. A note on item analysis and the criterion of internal consistency. *Psychometrika*, 1936, 1, 275-82.

Mussen, P. H., and A. Scodel. The effects of sexual stimulation under varying conditions on TAT sexual responsiveness. *Journal of Consulting Psychology*, 1955, 19, 90.

Nelson, S. E. Psychosexual conflicts and defenses in visual perception. *Journal of Abnormal and Social Psychology*, 1955, 51, 427-33.

Newmark, C. S., and T. R. Faschingbauer. Bibliography of short forms of the MMPI. *Journal of Personality Assessment*, 1978, 42, 496-502.

Newmark, C. S., D. R. Ziff, A. J. Finch, and P. C. Kendall. Comparing the empirical validity of the standard form with two abbreviated MMPIs. *Journal of Consulting and Clinical Psychology*, 1978, 46, 53-61.

Norman, W. T. Relative importance of test item content. *Journal of Consulting Psychology*, 1963, 27, 166-74.

Norman, W. T. Psychometric considerations for a revision of the MMPI. In J. N. Butcher, ed. *Objective personality assessment.* New York: Academic Press, 1972.

Nunnally, J., and T. R. Husek. The phony language examination: an approach to the measurement of response bias. *Educational and Psychological Measurement*, 1958, 18, 275-82.

Nye, F. I. *Family relationships and delinquent behavior.* New York: Wiley, 1958.

Oettel, A. Leadership: a psychological study. Doctoral dissertation, University of California (Berkeley), 1953.

Olson, G. W. The Hastings short form of the group MMPI. *Journal of Clinical Psychology*, 1954, 10, 386-88.

Olson, W. C. The waiver of signature in personal reports. *Journal of Applied Psychology*, 1936, 20, 442-50.

Overall, J. E., and F. Gomez-Mont. The MMPI-168 for psychiatric screening. *Educational and Psychological Measurement*, 1974, 34, 315-19.

Page, H. A., and G. Markowitz. The relationship of defensiveness to rating scale bias. *Journal of Psychology*, 1955, 40, 431-35.

Page, J., C. Landis, and S. E. Katz. Schizophrenic traits in the functional psychoses and in normal individuals. *American Journal of Psychiatry*, 1934, 13, 1213-25.

Panton, J. H. Personality characteristics of aged inmates within a state prison population. *Offender Rehabilitation*, 1976, 1, 203-8.

Peck, R. The influence of anxiety upon effectiveness of counseling. Doctoral dissertation, State University of Iowa, 1950.

Perloe, S. I. Inhibition as a determinant of perceptual defense. *Perceptual and Motor Skills*, 1960, 11, 59-66.

Peterson, D. R. The scope, generality and meaning of verbally defined "personality" factors. *Psychological Review*, 1965, 72, 48-59.

Postman, L., J. S. Bruner, and E. McGinnies. Personal values as selective factors in perception. *Journal of Abnormal and Social Psychology*, 1948, 43, 142-54.

Poythress, N. G. Selecting a short form of the MMPI: addendum to Faschingbauer. *Journal of Consulting and Clinical Psychology*, 1978, 46, 331-34.

Rokeach, M. *The open and closed mind.* New York: Basic Books, 1960.

Rorer, L. G. The great response-style myth. *Psychological Bulletin*, 1965, 63, 129-56.

Rorer, L. G., and L. R. Goldberg. Acquiescence in the MMPI? *Educational and Psychological Measurement*, 1965, 25, 801-17.

Rosen, A. Test-retest stability of MMPI scales for a psychiatric population. *Journal of Consulting Psychology*, 1953, 17, 217-21.

Rosenzweig, S. A suggestion for making verbal personality tests more valid. *Psychological Review*, 1934, 41, 400-1.

Rosenzweig, S. A basis for the improvement of personality tests with special reference to the M-F battery. *Journal of Abnormal and Social Psychology*, 1938, 33, 476-88.

Ruch, F. L. A technique for detecting attempts to fake performance on a self-inventory type of personality test. In Q. McNemar and M. A. Merrill, eds. *Studies in personality.* New York: McGraw-Hill, 1942.

Saunders, D. R. A computer program to find the best-fitting orthogonal factors for a given hypothesis. *Psychometrika,* 1960, 25, 199-205.

Schaefer, E. S. A circumplex model for maternal behavior. *Journal of Abnormal and Social Psychology,* 1959, 59, 226-35.

Schofield, W. Clinical and counseling psychology: some perspectives. *American Psychologist,* 1966, 21, 122-31.

Sechrest, L. B., and D. N. Jackson. Deviant response tendencies: their measurement and interpretation. University Park, Pennsylvania: Pennsylvania State University Research Bulletin No. 19, 1961.

Seeman, W. "Subtlety" in structured personality tests. *Journal of Consulting Psychology,* 1952, 16, 278-83.

Seeman, W. Concept of "subtlety" in structured psychiatric and personality tests: an experimental approach. *Journal of Abnormal and Social Psychology,* 1953, 48, 239-47.

Shannon, D. T. The effects of ego-defensive reactions on reported perceptual recognition. Doctoral dissertation, Stanford University, 1955.

Shure, G. H., and M. S. Rogers. Note of caution on the factor analysis of the MMPI. *Psychological Bulletin,* 1965, 63, 14-18.

Spence, D. P. A new look at vigilance and defense. *Journal of Abnormal and Social Psychology,* 1957, 54, 103-8.

Spence, J. T. What can you say about a twenty-year old theory that won't die? *Journal of Motor Behavior,* 1971, 3, 193-203.

Spence, K. W., and J. Taylor. Anxiety and strength of the UCS as determiners of the amount of eyelid conditioning. *Journal of Experimental Psychology,* 1951, 42, 183-88.

Spence, K. W., and J. Taylor. The relation of conditioned response strength to anxiety in normal, neurotic and psychotic subjects. *Journal of Experimental Psychology,* 1953, 45, 265-72.

Spencer, D. Frankness of subjects on personality measures. *Journal of Educational Psychology,* 1938, 28, 26-35.

Spera, J., and M. Robertson. A 104-item MMPI: the Maxi-Mult. Paper presented at the APA, New Orleans, 1974.

Spielberger, C. D., R. E. Lushene, and W. G. McAdoo. Theory and measurement of anxiety states. In R. B. Cattell and R. M. Dreger, eds. *Handbook of modern personality theory.* Washington: Hemisphere Publishing, 1977.

Srole, L., T. S. Langner, S. T. Michael, M. K. Opler, and T. A. C. Rennie. *Mental health in the metropolis: the midtown study.* Vol. 1. New York: McGraw-Hill, 1962.

Stagner, R. The gullibility of personnel managers. *Personnel Psychology,* 1958, 11, 347-52.

Stein, K. B. Perceptual defense and perceptual sensitization under neutral and involved conditions. *Journal of Personality,* 1953, 21, 467-78.

Steinmetz, H. C. Measuring ability to fake occupational interest. *Journal of Applied Psychology,* 1932, 16, 123-30.

Stern, G. G., M. I. Stein, and B. S. Bloom. *Methods in personality assessment.* Glencoe: Free Press, 1956.

Stricker, L. Some item characteristics that evoke acquiescent and social desirability response sets on psychological scales. Princeton: Educational Testing Service Research Bulletin, 1962.

Strong, E. K. *Vocational interests of men and women.* Stanford: Stanford University Press, 1943.

Symonds, P. M. *Diagnosing personality and conduct.* New York: Appleton-Century, 1932.

Taylor, J. A. The relationship of anxiety to the conditioned eyelid response. *Journal of Experimental Psychology,* 1951, 41, 81-92.

Taylor, J. A., and K. W. Spence. The relationship of anxiety to performance in serial learning. *Journal of Experimental Psychology,* 1952, 44, 61-64.

Taylor, J. B. Social desirability and MMPI performance: the individual case. *Journal of Consulting Psychology,* 1959, 23, 514-17.

Taylor, J. B. A brief ranking method as an alternative to Thurstone scaling procedures. *Perceptual and Motor Skills,* 1968, 26, 533-34. (a)

Taylor, J. B. Rating scales as measures of clinical judgment: a method for increasing scale reliability and sensitivity. *Educational and Psychological Measurement,* 1968, 28, 747-66. (b)

Taylor, J. B. Item homogeneity, scale reliability, and the self-concept hypothesis. *Educational and Psychological Measurement,* 1977, 37, 349-61.

Taylor, J. B., L. Coyne, and M. Carithers. Empirical validity of two self-report methods. Topeka, Kansas: Document 73-05, Research Department, The Menninger Foundation, 1973.

Taylor, J. B., M. Ptacek, M. Carithers, C. Griffin, and L. Coyne. Rating scales as measures of clinical judgment. III: Judgments of the self on personality inventory scales and direct ratings. *Educational and Psychological Measurement,* 1972, 32, 543-57.

Terman, L. M. *Manual of the Concept Mastery Test.* New York: The Psychological Corporation, 1956.

Terman, L. M., and C. C. Miles. *Sex and personality.* New York: McGraw-Hill, 1936.

Thorndike, E. L., and I. Lorge. *Teacher's word book of 20,000 words.* New York: Teachers College, Columbia University, 1941.

Torrens, J. K. An investigation and evaluation of the Guilford Inventory of Factors STDCR with special reference to the MMPI. Unpublished paper, University of Minnesota, 1944.

Truax, C. B. The repression response to implied failure as a function of the hysteria-psychasthenia index. *Journal of Abnormal and Social Psychology,* 1957, 55, 188-93.

Tyler, F. T. A factorial analysis of fifteen MMPI scales. *Journal of Consulting Psychology,* 1951, 15, 451-56.

Ullmann, L. P. Productivity and the clinical use of TAT cards. *Journal of Projective Techniques,* 1957, 21, 399-403.

Ullmann, L. P. Clinical correlates of facilitation and inhibition of response to emotional stimuli. *Journal of Projective Techniques,* 1958, 22, 341-47.

Ullmann, L. P. An empirically derived MMPI scale that measures facilitation-inhibition of recognition of threatening stimuli. *Journal of Clinical Psychology,* 1962, 18, 127-32.

Vernon, P. E. The attitude of the subject in personality testing. *Journal of Applied Psychology,* 1934, 18, 165-77.

Wales, B., and W. Seeman. Instructional sets and MMPI items. *Journal of Personality Assessment,* 1972, 36, 282-86.

Washburne, A. C. Seven-year report from Neuropsychiatric Department, Student Health Service, University of Wisconsin. *Wisconsin Medical Journal,* 1946, 45, 195-204.

Washburne, J. N. A test of social adjustment. *Journal of Applied Psychology,* 1935, 19, 125-44.

Welsh, G. S. Factor dimensions of the MMPI. Mimeographed materials, University of North Carolina, 1954.

Welsh, G. S. Factor dimensions A and R. In G. S. Welsh and W. G. Dahlstrom, eds. *Basic readings on the MMPI*. Minneapolis: University of Minnesota Press, 1956.

Welsh, G. S. *Preliminary manual: the Welsh Figure Preference Test (research edition)*. Palo Alto: Consulting Psychologists Press, 1959.

Welsh, G. S. MMPI profiles and factor scales A and R. *Journal of Clinical Psychology*, 1965, 21, 43-47.

Welsh, G. S. Performance analysis of gifted adolescents on two intelligence tests. Office of Education Research Contract Report No. 7-C-009. Chapel Hill: University of North Carolina, 1968.

Welsh, G. S. *Gifted adolescents: a handbook of test results*. Greensboro, NC: Prediction Press, 1969. (Distributed by Consulting Psychologists Press)

Welsh, G. S. *Creativity and intelligence: a personality approach*. Chapel Hill: Institute for Research in Social Science, 1975.

Welsh, G. S. Personality correlates of intelligence and creativity in gifted adolescents. In J. C. Stanley, W. C. George, and C. H. Solano, eds. *The gifted and the creative: a fifty-year perspective*. Baltimore: Johns Hopkins Press, 1977.

Welsh, G. S. *Manual for the Welsh Figure Preference Test (revised edition)*. Palo Alto: Consulting Psychologists Press, 1979.

Welsh, G. S., and W. G. Dahlstrom, eds. *Basic readings on the MMPI in psychology and medicine*. Minneapolis: University of Minnesota Press, 1956.

Wenar, C. Reaction time as a function of manifest anxiety and stimulus intensity. Doctoral dissertation, State University of Iowa, 1950.

Wesley, E. Correlations between the Guilford-Martin Personality Factors O, Ag, Co, and the MMPI at the college level. Master's thesis, University of Minnesota, 1945.

Wesley, E. L. Perseverative behavior in a concept formation task. Doctoral dissertation, State University of Iowa, 1950.

Westin, A. F. *Privacy and freedom*. New York: Atheneum, 1967.

Wheeler, W. M., K. B. Little, and G. F. J. Lehner. The internal structure of the MMPI. *Journal of Consulting Psychology*, 1951, 15, 134-41.

Whyte, W. H. The fallacies of "personality" testing. *Fortune*, 1954, 50, 117-21.

Wiener, D. N. Subtle and obvious keys for the MMPI. *Journal of Consulting Psychology*, 1948, 12, 164-70. (Also abstracted in *American Psychologist*, 1947, 2, 296)

Wiener, D. N., and L. R. Harmon. Subtle and obvious keys for the MMPI: their development. Minneapolis: V. A. Advisement Bulletin No. 16, 1946.

Wiener, M., B. Carpenter, and J. T. Carpenter. Determination of defense mechanisms for conflict areas from verbal material. *Journal of Consulting Psychology*, 1956, 20, 215-19.

Wiggins, J. S. Interrelationships among MMPI measures of dissimulation under standard and social desirability instructions. *Journal of Consulting Psychology*, 1959, 23, 419-27.

Wiggins, J. S. Definitions of social desirability and acquiescence in personality inventories. In S. Messick and J. Ross, eds. *Measurement in personality and cognition*. New York: Wiley, 1962. (a)

Wiggins, J. S. Strategic, method, and stylistic variance in the MMPI. *Psychological Bulletin*, 1962, 59, 224-42. (b)

Wiggins, J. S. Substantive dimensions of self-report in the MMPI item pool. *Psychological Monographs*, 1966, 80, No. 22 (Whole No. 630).

Wiggins, J. S. Personality structure. *Annual Review of Psychology*, 1968, 19, 293-350.

Wiggins, J. S., and L. R. Goldberg. Interrelationships among MMPI item characteristics. *Educational and Psychological Measurement*, 1965, 25, 381-97.

Wiggins, J. S., L. R. Goldberg, and M. Appelbaum. MMPI content scales: interpretative norms and correlations with other scales. *Journal of Consulting and Clinical Psychology*, 1971, 37, 403-10.

Wiggins, J. S., and V. R. Lovell. Communality and favorability as sources of method variance in the MMPI. *Educational and Psychological Measurement,* 1965, 25, 399-412.

Wiggins, J. S., and C. Rumrill. Social desirability in the MMPI and Welsh's factor scales A and R. *Journal of Consulting Psychology,* 1959, 23, 100-6.

Wiggins, J. S., and J. Vollmar. The content of the MMPI. *Journal of Clinical Psychology,* 1959, 15, 45-47.

Willerman, B. The concealment of self: method of study and some cross-cultural comparisons. Paper presented at the APA, St. Louis, 1962.

Willoughby, R. R. The concept of reliability. *Psychological Review,* 1935, 42, 153-65.

Willoughby, R. R., and M. E. Morse. Spontaneous reactions to a personality inventory. *American Journal of Orthopsychiatry,* 1936, 6, 562-75.

Witkin, H. A., H. B. Lewis, M. Hertzman, K. Machover, P. B. Meissner, and S. Wapner. *Personality through perception.* New York: Harper, 1954.

Worchel, P. Adaptability screening of flying personnel: development of a self-concept inventory for predicting maladjustment. USAF (Randolph AFB, Texas), Report No. 56-62, 1957.

Wrigley, C., and J. O. Neuhaus. The matching of two sets of factors. Urbana, Illinois: Contract Memorandum Report A-32, University of Illinois, 1955.

Zax, M., E. L. Cowen, W. Budin, and C. F. Biggs, The social desirability of trait descriptive terms: applications to an alcoholic sample. *Journal of Social Psychology,* 1962, 56, 21-27.

Zax, M., E. L. Cowen, and M. Peter. A comparative study of novice nuns and college females using the response set approach. *Journal of Abnormal and Social Psychology,* 1963, 66, 369-75.

Zubin, J. The method of internal consistency for selecting test items. *Journal of Educational Psychology,* 1934, 25, 345-56.

Index

Index